The Uskoks of Senj

The dress of an uskok leader, reproduced from Cesare Vecellio's *Habiti antichi et moderni* (Venice, 1590). The accompanying text gives details of uskok life and dress as they appeared in Venetian eyes toward the end of the sixteenth century. (By permission of the British Library.)

THE USKOKS OF SENJ

PIRACY, BANDITRY,
AND HOLY WAR IN THE
SIXTEENTH-CENTURY ADRIATIC

Catherine Wendy Bracewell

Cornell University Press

ITHACA AND LONDON

First published 1992 by Cornell University Press.

International Standard Book Number 0-8014-2674-X
Library of Congress Catalog Card Number 91-55548
Printed in the United States of America
*Librarians: Library of Congress cataloging information
appears on the last page of the book.*

♾ The paper in this book meets the minimum requirements
of the American National Standard for Information Sciences—
Permanence of Paper for Printed Library Materials, ANSI Z39.48-1984.

For Ron and Helen Bracewell

Contents

Illustrations and Maps

Figures

Maps

Table

Acknowledgments

Anyone who spends a long time doing research in many places must expect to incur a heavy load of scholarly debts. Part of my pleasure in completing this book comes from the chance to thank those who have helped me so generously—it is a pleasure clouded only by the knowledge that I cannot mention them all personally. I am grateful for the assistance I have received from the staffs of the archives where I have worked, especially those in Venice, Dubrovnik, Zagreb, and Zadar. I particularly thank Ivan Pederin, archivist of the Venetian period at the Zadar Historical Archive, for his invaluable aid. Archival research is largely a solitary quest after the past, but many friends in Yugoslavia did their best to ensure that my pleasant hours among the papers were followed by equally pleasant (and equally enlightening) hours in the real world. I must single out the Šikić family of Dubrovnik for special thanks for the conversations in the kitchen after the archives had closed and for the long rambles through the very places I had been reading about in the documents, to which I owe much of my sense of the cultural and physical landscape of Dalmatia. In England, I have benefited from the resources and good will of the British Library and, in particular, the library of the School of Slavonic and East European Studies, University of London, where the tolerant librarians satisfied my innumerable requests and allowed me to rummage happily through the rare book collection.

My arguments and conclusions have been sharpened by suggestions and criticism I received in response to papers delivered at the American Historical Association annual convention; the Institute of Historical Research, University of London; King's College, University of London; the University of Manchester; and the Zagrebački književni razgovori and the Institut za istraživanje folklora, Zagreb. The organizer of the last-named seminar, the late Lydia Sklevicky, had the gift of evoking inspiration far beyond her own field—I only wish she could still receive my thanks. Many others have patiently listened to my arguments and have commented helpfully on my work, in particular my colleagues and students at S.S.E.E.S.

My work on this book began at Stanford University. The project has changed greatly since, and if it is in any measure improved, some of the credit rests with Judith Brown and Nancy Kollman, both of whom gave me invaluable advice. I owe Wayne Vucinich an even greater debt of gratitude, not only for his unflagging interest and encouragement but also for enticing me into the study of history in general, and the history of the South Slavs in particular. I am also deeply indebted to Ivo Banac of Yale University. In his efforts on my behalf he has been not only inventive in suggestion, diligent in criticism, and merciless in the exposure of error and illogic, but also steadfast in friendship.

Anything I can say here will be inadequate recompense for the support I have had from Bob Shoemaker, friend, husband, and fellow historian. He has kept me going with a judicious mixture of interest and impatience, and I have learned more from him than he realizes. This book is dedicated to my parents, Helen and Ron Bracewell, my first and best teachers. From the beginning they encouraged me to ask questions and showed me the pleasure of searching for answers. Much of what I am as a historian is due to them.

While I was reading the proofs of this book, Dubrovnik, Zadar, and other cities in Croatia were being shelled in a bitter and destructive war. Whether the archives I used will survive is still unclear. Documents—like the human lives they record—are fragile things. Many of the subjects discussed here, however, seem to be more enduring. Conflicts born out of religious, ethnic, and political divisions; an idea of honor that glorifies violence; the logic of betrayal, revenge, and reprisal: all these play as deadly a role today as they did in the sixteenth century. I hope that this book can contribute, in a small way, to a better understanding of these long-lived values and patterns of behavior. Is it too much to hope that such an understanding might some day help to end them?

C. W. B.

Sheffield, England

Conventions and Abbreviations

The confusing welter of peoples and tongues that characterizes the Balkan frontier presents the scholar with a problem in achieving the standardization of terminology and consistency of usage so highly valued by the authors of style manuals. The following notes are intended to explain the solutions I have adopted here.

According to W. H. Fowler in his *Modern English Usage*, the use of capitals, apart from certain elementary rules, is largely governed by personal taste. As one Venetian observer pointed out in the seventeenth century, "The term uskok denotes not a nation but a profession,"[1] and so I have chosen to use it here in lowercase, treating it in the same way as the term "cossack." It is perhaps worth pointing out that I invariably capitalize both "Vlach" and "Morlach"—unlike those authors who distinguish between an ethnic and a social meaning—because that distinction cannot always be sharply drawn and because I believe that these terms still had a residual ethnic meaning in this period.

In current English usage the term "Turk" has acquired an ethnic meaning, entirely inappropriate to this area, where so-called Turks were often recently converted Slavs. In the sixteenth century "Turk" was used much more broadly, to refer to the Ottoman state, to Muslims, or even to Christian subjects of the Ottoman Empire. I have used the term "Ottoman" when the emphasis is on state administration and "Muslim" when the emphasis is on religion, but I have also sometimes used the term "Turk" (without any ethnic connotation) more generally, following the conventions of the time.

Anyone writing on this area faces insoluble orthographic problems.

[1]Cited by Philip Longworth, "The Senj Uskoks Reconsidered," *Slavonic and East European Review* (London), 57, no. 3 (1979): 353.

Although in this period a single town might be known as Zengg, Segna, and Senj (with different possible spellings of each variant), I have usually employed the version currently in use in the country in question. (For those not familiar with Serbo-Croatian, Senj is pronounced Señ— *not* to rhyme with Stonehenge.) I have substituted the English equivalent only if it is widely known (thus Vienna, not Wien). In quotations I have given the form used in the original, followed by the modern form, if different, in square brackets.

A similar problem arises with personal names. The name of the uskok vojvoda called Ivo Senjanin in the oral epics is given in many different forms in various languages. Even his own signature exists in three forms: Iuan Vlatkho, Gioanne Novakovich alias Vlatcovich, and Givan Wlatcovich. As a rule I have used modern orthography for names in the text, so that he appears here as Ivan Vlatković. Only where it is not clear what the modern equivalent might be, and in quotations, have I preserved the original orthography.

Unless otherwise noted, all translations are my own.

Abbreviations and Archival References

A.H.	Arhiv Hrvatske (Zagreb)
A.S.	Arhiv Slovenije (Ljubljana)
A.S.F.	Archivio di Stato, Florence
A.S.V.	Archivio di Stato, Venice
H.A.D.	Historijski Arhiv, Dubrovnik
H.A.R.	Historijski Arhiv, Rijeka
H.A.Z.	Historijski Arhiv, Zadar
I.Ö.H.K.R.	Innerösterreichischer Hofkriegsrat (Croatica)
S.S.E.E.S.	School of Slavonic and East European Studies

I have cited archival documents by giving the archive, the collection, the number of the file or volume, and, where the document is paginated, the page number, with verso indicated by an apostrophe (e.g., H.A.D., Lettere di Ponente 15: 122′). Where the document is not consistently paginated, has several varying page numbers, or is loosely bundled in a file, I have identified it by a date (e.g., A.S.V., Provveditori da Terra e da Mar 1318: 6 June 1596) or by a document number (e.g., H.A.Z., Fond Šime Ljubića, 2/33). The Venetian calendar began the new year on 1 March. In the text I have given dates in the modern convention, but I have followed the original form in the notes, adding m.v. (*modo veneziano*) where necessary.

C. W. B.

The Uskoks of Senj

Ove pisme svakomu drage neće biti, jer medju njima malo ima razlikosti, nahodeći se u svim iste riči, kakonoti ove: junak, vitez, delija, leventa, zmija, zmaj, vuk; lav, soko, ora, gnizdo sokolovo i mač, sablje, kopje, Kraljević, Kobilić, Zdrinović, kolajne, medalje, dukale, odsičaše, robje dovodjaše, itd. Kad bi moguće bilo, imala bi jedna od druge biti posve različita, ali budući svi vitezovi imenovani od iste kriposti, s istim ričima služiti se bî potribito za ukazati njihova junaštva. Kome su ugodne, neka ih piva: kome nisu, neka idje spavati.

(These songs will not be to everyone's taste, for there is little variation among them, all of them containing the same words, such as: hero, knight, horseman, galley slave, serpent, dragon, wolf, lion, falcon, eagle, falcon's nest and sword, sabers, lances, Kraljević, Kobilić, Zdrinović, necklets, medallions, decrees, heads chopped off, slaves carried away, etc. Were it possible, each would be completely different from the others, but as all the knights here named possess the same virtues, the same words must be used to describe their exploits. May those who find them pleasing sing them; may those who do not go off to sleep.)

—Andrija Kačić-Miošić,
Razgovor ugodni naroda slovinskoga (Venice, 1756)

CHAPTER ONE

Introduction

The uskoks of Senj are the heroes of one of the cycles of South Slav folk epics, but they are not simply the stuff of legend. The archives and the histories of nearly all the cities and states that rimmed the Adriatic in the sixteenth century are filled with references to these sea and land raiders who served as irregulars in the Habsburg border garrison in Senj for almost a century. The uskoks aroused strong and contradictory emotions among their contemporaries. The Habsburg archdukes and the Emperor, with papal support, hailed the uskoks for their role as a bulwark of Christendom, crediting them with preserving Europe from the onslaught of the Turk. Fra Paolo Sarpi, the contemporary Venetian theologian and historian, denounced them as pirates and brigands, echoing the opinions of the Venetian officers responsible for the security of the Adriatic and the anxious merchants who saw their ships off with the phrase "God preserve you from the hands of the uskoks of Senj." Although the rural populations along the borders—Ottoman, Venetian, and Habsburg—left little of their own testimony, clearly the uskoks received their most consistent support from these people, in spite of all prohibitions and in spite of the fact that in the long term they probably suffered the most from the uskoks' raids. Long afterward the peasants and pastoralists of the border preserved vivid memories of the uskoks in epic songs about their bravery, their often bloody deeds, and their rigorous code of honor, glorifying them as heroes and symbols of freedom from all authority.

The uskoks have continued to draw the attention of historians, whose assessments have been no less contradictory than were those of contemporaries. But despite this constant interest, surprisingly little attention has focused on the uskoks themselves and their own perceptions of their role. Who were these men, and why did they provoke such violently contrasting opinions? This book attempts to answer these questions.

The Uskoks of Senj between Three Empires

The uskoks developed as a military community where the borders of three empires met on the shores and hinterland of the Adriatic. In the eyes of the Republic of Venice, the Adriatic of the sixteenth century was a Venetian sea—its "gulf." The Republic's possessions edged much of the eastern shore, from Istria south to the Bay of Kotor, each city commune surrounded by its small circle of protective territory, while the Adriatic islands as far as Korčula stood like a stationary fleet off the Dalmatian coast. But by the early sixteenth century the Serenissima's Dalmatian hinterland had fallen to the Ottomans. As far north as Lika, the hinterland was held in the firm grasp of the Turk—in many places Ottoman territory was within eyeshot of city walls—and Venice's possessions were open to any Ottoman attack. The Ottoman advance had stopped short of the Kvarner Gulf (Quarnero). After 1526 the stretch of territory south of Rijeka and north of the Zrmanja, a part of the *reliquiae reliquiarum* of once-powerful Croatia, was held by the House of Austria, inheritor of the crowns of Croatia and Hungary. This Croatian Littoral and its hinterland formed the nucleus of the Habsburg Military Frontier system against the Turk, the *maritima confinia*. Here, at various fortress towns defended by military captaincies, the Habsburgs stationed troops of regular and irregular soldiers. (See Maps 1 and 2.)

One of these, on the barren karst coast at the foot of the Velebit mountains, and situated beneath a mountain pass that channels the *bora*, the furious northeast wind, was Senj. In the sixteenth century it was a small town, surrounded to the distance of a mile or two by a dense forest that, together with the high mountains at its back, cut off any attack from the land. It lacked a protected harbor, so that as a contemporary noted, the barks and small craft had to be "drawn onto land before the gate of the city, and tied and anchored as though they were at sea, otherwise the *bora* that comes up suddenly there would carry them away."[1] For almost a century this was the principal resort of the uskoks.

The Ottoman invasions of the Balkan Peninsula with their plundering raids and destructive skirmishes set large portions of the population in motion. Many crossed the frontier to take refuge in the territories of neighboring states. Some formed units for defense or retaliation against

[1]*Commissiones et relationes venetæ*, vols. 1–3, Monumenta spectantia historiam Slavorum meridionalium, 6, 8, and 11, ed. Šime Ljubić (Zagreb, 1876–80), vol. 3, p. 63.

1. Croatian Military Frontier, c. 1579.

the Ottoman enemy, often clustering around the border fortresses. These refugees were known by various names: *prebjezi*, Vlachs, uskoks. Although at first used generally as a term for refugees (the word itself derives from the Croatian verb *uskočiti:* to jump in), in time the term "uskok" came to be applied especially to those who settled in Senj as border irregulars, and was eventually extended to all citizens of Senj (although they themselves rarely used the word). The uskoks, most of whom received no pay, were largely dependent on plunder for their livelihood (and the fact that they so supported themselves without further draining the empty coffers of the Frontier authorities, and indeed paid a portion of their booty to their military commanders and to the Habsburgs themselves, made them particularly attractive as border troops).

Uskok raids across Ottoman territory took two main forms: directly south into the Lika area, which bordered on the territory of the Habsburg captaincy centered in Senj; and into the Ottoman hinterland of Dalmatia, which could be reached only by sea, and by crossing the territory of Venice or the Republic of Dubrovnik (Ragusa). In conventional military maneuvers, carried out under the leadership of border officers, the uskoks could number as many as two thousand. More often, however, they set out in smaller bands, some ten to thirty in a company, under the command of one of their own leaders. During raids lasting weeks or months, the uskoks lived off the land or what they could capture, ambushing merchant caravans or Ottoman border troops, plundering cattle and taking prisoners for ransom.

Very early, the uskoks extended their raids to the shipping of the Adriatic, plundering Ottoman merchants and their goods. These goods were increasingly carried on Christian vessels and formed an important part of the Adriatic trade. They were often carried on Venetian ships, but other merchant fleets, such as those of Dubrovnik and Ancona, also carried Ottoman goods. Claiming the right and the duty to plunder the goods of the infidel, uskok bands in their small light barks ambushed shipping in Dalmatia's ports and coastal waters and ransacked cargoes for merchandise belonging to Turks and Jews. Christian merchants, too, inevitably suffered losses in these raids. With their limited numbers and small primitive craft it is hard to believe that the uskoks could have posed the threat to shipping that they did, yet fear of them was a factor that led Venice to send its great galleys to guard the merchantmen that sailed north from Split, carrying the trade that had arrived overland from the Levant.

Uskok raids came to be a serious irritant to Venice, for they disturbed relations with its Ottoman neighbors, relations Venice was anxious to keep peaceful. While the Republic was at war with the Porte (1537–39 and 1570–73), the Signoria encouraged uskok actions against the Turk and engaged uskoks in the Venetian forces. In peacetime, however, Ottoman authorities seized on uskok actions as an opportunity to complain to Venice over the alleged complicity of Venetian citizens in these attacks and threatened to send in their own fleet if Venice could not secure the waters of the Adriatic, as guaranteed in the Ottoman-Venetian treaties of 1540 and 1573. Similar considerations troubled the uskoks' relations with Dubrovnik, which found itself, as a Christian city under Ottoman protection, in an awkward position between the Porte and the uskoks.

The Signoria's repeated response was both to oppose the uskoks directly with orders forbidding cooperation between uskoks and Venetian subjects in Dalmatia and limiting their operations in the Adriatic, and to attempt through diplomacy to force their Habsburg masters to rein them in or remove them from Senj entirely. Attempts to halt cooperation between the uskoks and the people of Venetian Dalmatia were fruitless, although Venice renewed its decrees regularly, adding ever more horrible punishments. Venetian approaches to the Habsburgs were also ineffective. At the court of the Archduke of Styria in Graz, the spectacle of Venice embroiled with the Porte was not unwelcome. Furthermore, the Habsburgs countered any complaint about the uskoks with a demand for free navigation, fueled by their resentment of the Republic's pretensions to Adriatic supremacy. The Signoria's complaints usually had a more sympathetic hearing in the Emperor's court in Vienna, especially because the Ottomans threatened reprisals against the Habsburg borders for uskok attacks, but any serious move to replace the Senj garrison was hindered by the Archduke's plea of lack of means. The frequent Habsburg commissions to Senj did little more than return a fraction of the most recent plunder and once again prohibit unauthorized raiding across Venetian territory, to small effect.

The escalation of Venetian attacks on the uskoks and blockades of the trading ports of the Croatian Littoral from the 1590s eventually forced the Habsburgs to make some concessions to the Republic by restricting the liberties of the uskoks. With the end of the Habsburg-Ottoman Long Turkish War in 1606, the Habsburgs, the Ottoman Empire, and Venice were all formally at peace. Raiding and acts of war were forbidden to all sides. The Habsburgs now increasingly viewed uskok actions as a liability, and strictly prohibited unauthorized raiding, but they did not provide subsidies to the Senj garrison to make up for the loss of booty.

Inevitably, uskok raids continued. Still irritated by both the raids and Ottoman complaints, the Signoria took advantage of its strong alliances and the Archduke's domestic difficulties to act decisively against Senj and its protectors. The Venetian fleet blockaded the Littoral against shipping and uskok expeditions, and eventually declared war against the Habsburgs in November 1615—"the Uskok War." With the Venetian troops unable to consolidate their early victories, and with the Archduke distracted by the prospect of inheriting the responsibilities of the Empire, a peace was negotiated in Madrid in 1617, by which the Habsburgs agreed to remove the uskoks from Senj and burn their ships. The uskoks of course protested, but by the end of 1618 many of them had been moved to the interior of the Croatian Military Frontier. Small independent uskok operations continued through the 1620s, from both Senj and the surrounding areas, but with the Venetian-Ottoman wars of the seventeenth and eighteenth centuries the focus of new uskok activity shifted to the Venetian military border in Dalmatia.

The uskoks of Senj were not forgotten, however. In the vocabulary of the Venetians, 'uskok' remained so firmly linked to the corsairs of Senj that they avoided using the term for the refugees who made up their own Dalmatian militia in the Candian and Morean wars of the seventeenth and eighteenth centuries, though their Ottoman adversaries had no doubt that they were being raided by uskoks. Nor did the border population forget the uskoks, spreading their fame far beyond the Adriatic hinterland through the epic songs that preserved the memory of their exploits. The great popularity of these songs only a little more than a century after the expulsion of the uskoks from Senj can be seen from the large number included in the first substantial collection of these oral epics, the Erlangen manuscript, written down in the early eighteenth century.[2] Tales of the uskoks continued to compel the imagination into the twentieth century, not only in oral literature but also in plays, novels, and scholarly monographs.

Approaches to the Uskoks

One explanation of the contradictory assessments of the uskoks lies in the varying purposes for which they have been used. Most considerations of the uskoks, beginning with contemporary observations and continuing to the present day, have concentrated on the three great empires that met in the Adriatic and have seen the uskoks' significance in the context of the interactions between these powers. The conflicts over the uskoks provide an admirable device through which to focus on the shifting relationships of Venice, the Habsburg monarchy, and the Ottoman Empire in the sixteenth and early seventeenth centuries.[3] Such studies have usually concentrated on great power relations, treating the uskoks only inasmuch as they were the occasion of conflict. Indeed, most have centered on Venice's economic and territorial interests in the Adriatic, and the threat, both direct and indirect, posed to these interests by the uskoks (and behind them the Habsburgs and the papacy). Too often interpretations of the uskoks' motives in such studies have been based on the consequences of their actions for the Republic: because their raids, though ostensibly directed against the infidel, also harmed Christian interests, the uskoks must necessarily have been hyp-

[handwritten marginal note: historiography]

---

[2]G. Gesemann, ed., *Erlangenski rukopis starih srpskohrvatskih narodnih pesama*, Zbornik za istoriju, jezik i književnost, section 1, vol. 12 (Belgrade, 1925). Many others have since been collected and published, most recently in A. Mijatović, ed., *Senjski uskoci u narodnoj pjesmi i povijesti* (Zagreb, 1983).

[3]For examples see Paolo Sarpi, *La Repubblica di Venezia, la Casa d'Austria, e gli uscocchi*, ed. Gaetano Cozzi and Luisa Cozzi (Bari, 1965); M. Kravjànszky, "Il processo degli uscocchi," *Archivio veneto* (Venice), 5 (1929): 234–66; Silvino Gigante, "Venezia e gli uscocchi, 1570–1620," *Fiume: Semestrale della Società di studi fiumani* (Rijeka), 9 (1931): 3–87; A. Grünfelder, "Studien zur Geschichte der Uskoken" (Ph.D. diss., Universität in Innsbruck, 1974).

ocrites, concealing their lust for booty behind a facade of religion. Much of the reality of uskok life has found no place in these interpretations because it casts little light on the Venetian-Habsburg rivalry.

A second approach to the uskoks treats their story as one of resistance to oppression by alien powers, a struggle against Venice and the Turk. Much of this writing is rooted in the nineteenth-century romantic rediscovery of the national past of the South Slavs.[4] Here too the conflicts between Venice, the Habsburgs, and the Ottoman Empire provide the frame of reference, and the uskoks' significance is derived from their relations with these powers. This historiography has paid more attention to the uskoks' motives (usually defined as national and religious), though the projection of contemporary political concerns onto the past sometimes mars its value. Such studies have increased our knowledge of uskok actions by sifting through the sources to build up a narrative of battles and raids, usually focusing on uskok military prowess against Venetian forces and, in less detail, against the Ottomans.[5] This concentration on the objects of uskok attack, however, has been at the expense of an understanding of the internal development of the uskok phenomenon.[6]

Neither of these approaches is completely satisfactory in helping us to understand the uskoks and their place in the sixteenth-century Adriatic borderlands. The economic, political, and religious competition between the three empires that met in the Adriatic was the fundamental condition for the existence of the uskoks: it created the niche they exploited so successfully for nearly a century. Yet the relations between these powers are not in themselves sufficient to explain all aspects of the uskoks' history. Nor is it possible to see the uskoks simply as the expression of resistance to foreign power, whether religious or national. These approaches have offered us only one-dimensional, cardboard images of the uskoks, primarily in speculating on their motives: as in the sixteenth century, on the one hand they have presented the uskoks as common criminals, driven by greed for booty, while on the other they have depicted them as fighters for national or religious liberation, justice, and

[4]Bare Poparić took this national perspective to extremes in *Povijest senjskih uskoka* (Zagreb, 1936), but it is also apparent in the work of Jovan Tomić, "Crtice iz istorije senjskih uskoka," *Letopis Matice srpske* (Novi Sad), 205–10 (1901): 18–53, and "Iz istorije senjskih uskoka, 1604–1607," *Letopis Matice srpske* (Novi Sad), nos. 237–41 (1906–7); and Gligor Stanojević, *Senjski uskoci* (Belgrade, 1973). August Šenoa's novel *Čuvaj se senjske ruke* (Zagreb, 1962, [1875]) was the first (and is still the best crafted) example of this approach.

[5]Bogumil Hrabak's studies are particularly noteworthy examples of this perspective, presenting much detailed material on uskok actions while avoiding the tendentious arguments of nationalist historiography.

[6]A more detailed analysis of uskok historiography can be found in C. W. Bracewell, "The Uskoks of Senj: Banditry and Piracy in the Sixteenth-Century Adriatic" (Ph.D. diss., Stanford University, 1985).

revenge. Both these judgments, however, have been made in the context of other arguments, without much attention to the views of the uskoks themselves. Traditional historiography has so far failed to address directly the social, economic, and cultural context of the uskok story. But without a sensitive examination of their society and the world in which they moved, we cannot evaluate the assessments of the historians or, more important, can we hope to understand the roles the uskoks played in their own time.

Let us begin with definitions. As noted above, some of their contemporaries, particularly the Venetians and Turks, labeled the uskoks pirates and brigands. To the Habsburgs they were a part of the Military Frontier, referred to as soldiers and servicemen, while those who were not officially part of the paid garrison were singled out as soldiers of fortune (*venturini*). The uskoks simply referred to themselves as heroes. Each of these terms implies a very different perspective on the uskoks.

In legal terms the uskoks were not pirates, even when they were plundering Ottoman cargoes from Christian ships. There was a clear distinction in the sixteenth century between pirates and corsairs, and between irregular soldiers and brigands. What distinguished the corsair was a commission from the ruler to make war on an enemy of the state. Thus the corsair or privateer could claim a legitimacy that the pirate, who raided without distinction, lacked; and similarly, the irregular border soldier operated within the law that the brigand flouted. The reliance on irregulars both on land and sea was a response to the financial constraints of warfare on the early modern state, obviating the necessity to maintain a full-time fleet or a standing army. The actual mechanics of raiding came to much the same thing, but in irregular warfare private gain was harnessed to the purposes of the state, for both the corsair and the border soldier were rewarded with their own plunder. Thus it was not personal profit that distinguished between the pirate and the corsair—both were motivated by the hope of booty—but the legitimacy conferred by a recognized authority.

As soldiers of the Military Frontier, the uskoks of Senj operated within a recognized framework of war between the Habsburgs and the Ottoman Empire—or perhaps more precisely between the two warring civilizations of Christendom and Islam, for this conflict was not restricted to those periods of formally declared war but continued constantly even during the times of official truce between the two states. It was this conflict that justified and legitimated the uskoks' raids in their own eyes and the eyes of their patrons. Their victims' views, however, could be quite another matter. As Fernand Braudel pointed out, the term 'pirate' became common in Mediterranean usage only in the seventeenth century, evidence of an emotional reaction to a change in raiding that arose from rivalry among Christian states as much as from the older, more readily accepted division between Islam and Christendom.[7] Much earlier than this, however, Venice and others had already damned the uskoks as pirates, brigands, and evildoers, resenting the effects (direct or indirect) of uskok warfare and stigmatizing it as simple robbery. How the uskoks were defined depended very much on who was speaking.

Such categories also affect the way in which the uskoks' history can be written. The disparaging labels used by those who were threatened—pirate, bandit, brigand—imply that the uskoks were nothing more than violent and irrational offenders against public order. These terms have the effect of belittling the actors' ideas and self-perceptions and denying them any coherent values. To accept the simple definition of soldiers, on the other hand, is to assimilate the uskoks to the goals and policies of the Habsburg state and Military Frontier, once again denying them, to a certain extent, autonomy. Without adopting the uskoks' own self-image as heroes, this book examines the labels pinned on the uskoks but also goes beyond them to focus on the actions and perceptions of the uskoks themselves.

This problem of definition and of labeling is one of the issues dealt with by those who have written about banditry since Eric Hobsbawm opened up the subject twenty years ago, identifying a type of outlaw regarded as a criminal by the state but as a hero by the peasantry.[8] Though the label 'brigand' or 'bandit' and, from a different perspective, 'social bandit' might not be wholly appropriate to the uskoks, many of the problems and approaches formulated in this literature are highly pertinent to a study such as this.

The debate that emerged from Hobsbawm's work focused on the political dimension of banditry. Some critics (notably Anton Blok) believe that the bandit's usual political role was not so much as a voice of peasant protest as an instrument of local elites.[9] When power was unequally distributed in a society, bandits had to look for support where they were most likely to find it. According to this view, bandits were forced to negotiate with the elites to survive, and so were inevitably placed in opposition to the peasants. Thus these critics dispute whether bandits could ever represent the interests of the poor. To a degree the uskoks followed this pattern. They found a patron in the state itself, or rather its representative, the administration of the Habsburg Military Frontier, and this patronage helped to minimize the class character of the uskok

[7]Fernand Braudel, *The Mediterranean and the Mediterranean World in the Age of Philip II*, trans. by Siân Reynolds, 2 vols. (New York, 1972–73), vol. 2, pp. 866–67.

[8]Eric Hobsbawm, *Primitive Rebels* (Manchester, 1959), and *Bandits* (London, 1969).

[9]Anton Blok, "The Peasant and the Brigand: Social Banditry Reconsidered," *Comparative Studies in Society and History* (Cambridge), 14 (1972): 498–500.

uskoks' place / in power / structure

phenomenon. The military administration channeled the energies of its uskok recruits into raids against its Ottoman enemies. In practice, these raids affected not only purely military targets but also the peasant population of these territories. But at the same time the uskoks (like many bandits) were never sufficiently secure in their official support to ignore the reactions of the rural population, and they strove to retain the peasants' cooperation as best they could. In a sense, both Hobsbawm and Blok emphasize only one aspect of the social network the bandit must operate within at the expense of others. In asking where the uskoks' interests and their loyalties lay, we must consider their place within the power structure in its entirety, and their relations with both the weak (but not powerless) and the powerful (but not omnipotent).

The relationship between the attitudes of the rural poor and the acts of the bandits, another issue raised in the discussion of banditry, is also relevant to the uskok problem. While Hobsbawm saw peasant glorification of some bandits as evidence of bandit solidarity with the poor (and of a common expression of protest), others have denied that bandits ever spared the peasant in real life and have attributed the popular image of the noble robber to peasant idealization, a dream of "what ought to be."[10] Analyses of bandit myths, legends, and songs have stressed the psychological needs they met (affirming the peasant's hope for justice and fascination with violence) and their role as a vehicle for the discussion of social values, regardless of the realities of bandit actions.[11] Where real-life contacts between bandits and the peasants are examined, on the other hand, what these bandits actually did seems to be more important in shaping their relations. It seems likely that some bandits did indeed serve peasant interests on occasion, even if inadvertently—at least to the extent of protecting them from other, more ruthless plunderers. Such acts could be vital in gaining peasant approval and support, even if colored by fear. Moreover, where the official authorities evoked only fear, a bandit who conformed to traditional ideals could expect both fear and admiration from the rural population.[12] Like many bandits, the uskoks had an ambiguous relationship with the rural population, for although they took from the peasant and the shepherd, they also received aid from them. Understanding to what extent the uskoks enjoyed popular

[10]Hobsbawm, *Bandits*, chap. 9, and "Social Bandits: Reply," *Comparative Studies in Society and History* (Cambridge), 14 (1972): 505: "It seems simplest to assume that there is some relation between a bandit's real behavior and his subsequent myth." For criticism of this stance, see especially Blok, "The Peasant and the Brigand," pp. 500–501.

[11]See, for example, John S. Koliopoulos, *Brigands with a Cause* (Oxford, 1987), p. 279; S. Wilson, *Feuding, Conflict, and Banditry in Nineteenth-Century Corsica* (Cambridge, 1988), pp. 355–56.

[12]For a useful discussion of this point, see Phil Billingsley, *Bandits in Republican China* (Stanford, 1988), pp. 179–91.

legitimacy requires close attention to the character of uskok actions and the meanings these had for various social groups.

The uskoks have often been equated with hajduks, outlaws operating within the Ottoman Empire in the Balkans. Hobsbawm singled out the hajduks as a special category of bandit, distinguished by their semi-institutionalized character and by their political role as rebels against the Turk.[13] This interpretation echoed a long-established nationalist and Marxist historiography, which relied largely on popular sources to present the hajduks as heroes of national, religious, and social struggle, fighting both the Ottomans and Ottoman feudalism.[14] As in the more general debate over relations between bandits and the rural population, recent contributions to the study of the hajduks have emphasized that much of the burden of hajduk raiding fell on the shoulders of their co-nationals under Ottoman rule, citing examples that demonstrate hajduk indifference to national, religious, or social distinctions among their victims.[15] This questioning of the hajduks' religious and national consciousness raises the issue of what might be called hajduk ideology. To understand hajduk plundering (and perhaps also hajduk legitimacy), we need to understand not only their economic motives but also their values and norms, whether these affected their actions, and how far these were shared. Little so far has been achieved along these lines, though the suggestion that the hajduks originated primarily among military irregulars of pastoral origins whose privileges were being curtailed by the Ottoman state opens up an interesting avenue for further research.[16]

For the most part, hajduk attitudes and values can be inferred only from their acts. Because of the circumstances of their existence and the sorts of sources left by the Ottoman authorities who pursued them, little of their own testimony has survived, particularly for the earlier periods. Furthermore, from the evidence that does survive, it is unclear how explicitly their ideas—whether hatred of an alien Muslim conqueror or resentment of an oppressive socioeconomic system—were formulated, or indeed how general they may have been. It is here that the differences

[13]Hobsbawm, *Bandits*, pp. 73–74.

[14]See, for example, Dušan Popović, *O hajducima*, 2 vols. (Belgrade, 1930–31); R. Samardžić, *Hajdučke borbe protiv Turaka* (Belgrade, 1952). B. Tsvetkova, in *Khaĭdutstvoto v bŭlgarskite zemi prez 15–18 vek* (Sofia, 1971), and "The Bulgarian Haiduk Movement in the Fifteenth to Eighteenth Centuries," in *East Central European Society and War in the Pre-Revolutionary Eighteenth Century*, ed. G. Rothenberg et al. (Boulder, Colo., 1982), pp. 301–38, uses a greater variety of (primarily) Ottoman sources, but follows the same interpretation.

[15]Fikret Adanir, "Heidukentum und osmanische Herrschaft," *Südost-Forschungen* (Vienna), 41 (1982): 43–116; Slavko Gavrilović, *Hajdučija u Sremu u XVIII i početkom XIX veka* (Belgrade, 1986).

[16]Adanir, "Heidukentum und osmanische Herrschaft." Koliopoulos, *Brigands with a Cause*, also discusses links between the Greek klephts and shepherds and attempts to throw light on the actions and values of postindependence klephts by examining their social origins.

hajduks
uskoks
uskoks

between the hajduks and the uskoks are crucial. While the hajduks operated within the confines of the Ottoman Empire, in short-lived bands with little formal organization or support (even from their own ecclesiastical hierarchy), the uskoks were caught up in a broader conflict between empires. This position had the effect not only of sustaining uskok activity well beyond the normal span of a hajduk band but of generating and preserving many sources dealing with their actions and attitudes, including some of their own testimony. In further contrast to the hajduks, the uskoks explained and justified their actions through a very explicit set of ideas, in particular adapting to their own uses an ideology of the defense of Christendom originally formulated by the Habsburgs and the Catholic Church. As a result, the historian is able to examine both uskok actions and uskok ideology in some detail, as well as the ways they influence each other in practice.

The uskoks were by no means unique in the sixteenth and seventeenth centuries. They were but one of a variety of free military frontier communities that lived from—and prolonged—the conflict on the long border between Islam and Christianity which divided the Mediterranean and ran through Danubian Europe to the Crimea and the Caucasus. Similar organizations, reacting to similar circumstances, were to be found on the Islamic side of this frontier in North Africa, among the Barbary corsairs of Algiers, Tunis, and Tripoli who sailed with the patronage of the Ottoman Sultan under the banner of *jihad*; or in the Ukraine and the Crimea, where cossack bands raided independently or on behalf of the Christian princes of Poland-Lithuania or Muscovy.[17] Comparisons with such groups can help to isolate the underlying structural factors that shaped the development of the uskok community. On both sides of this frontier, states relied on independent irregulars to man their borders. These communities were shaped by the divisions of the frontiers, in particular that between faiths, which provided both sides with an ideology of holy war: Muslim jihad or Christian crusade. At the same time, however, local inhabitants facing each other on either side of a border often had interests enough in common to achieve at least some mutual understanding with their putative enemies, regardless of the interests of their respective central authorities in distant capitals. The idea of perpetual holy war did not always correspond to the realities of

---

[17]William H. McNeill, *Europe's Steppe Frontier, 1500–1800* (Chicago, 1964), analyzes one part of this frontier; Andrew Hess, *The Forgotten Frontier: A History of the Sixteenth-Century Ibero-African Frontier* (Chicago, 1978), looks at another. S. Bono, *I corsari barbareschi* (Turin, 1964), is a good introduction to the North African corsairs; Peter Earle, *The Corsairs of Malta and Barbary* (London, 1970), compares them with the corsairs raiding under the protection of the Order of St. John; Linda Gordon considers the cossacks as a type of social bandit in *Cossack Rebellions* (Albany, N.Y., 1983).

frontier life. As a result, the warfare that developed along these borders is sometimes described as anarchic, a *bellum omnium contra omnes*, in which frontiersmen raided indiscriminately, constrained by little but their own immediate interests.[18] Nonetheless, these frontiers did operate according to their own laws, though not necessarily those of the states that claimed to rule them. In the frontier no-man's land where the authority of the state did not reach, the inhabitants worked out their own codes of behavior. They also developed new forms of community and identity. Part of the task of this book is to understand how such principles operated on the frontier of the Adriatic hinterland and how they are reflected in uskok actions and uskok attitudes.

By the late sixteenth century the Islamic-Christian frontier was undergoing two great changes, the first affecting both sides equally, the second perhaps more important for the states of the West. The first of these was the disengagement from the religious conflicts that had created this frontier in the first place. Braudel points out the way in which, toward the end of the sixteenth century, the age of external wars between the two hostile civilizations of Islam and Christendom was succeeded by an age of internal wars, intestinal conflicts that pitted Catholic against Protestant, Sunni against Shiite.[19] After the Battle of Lepanto in 1571, the Christian commitment to crusade began to wane as the Catholic princes turned to face their rivals in the Protestant north. At the same time the direction of Ottoman military activity shifted east, away from Europe and the Mediterranean. There was a resurgence of crusading enthusiasm at the turn of the century, coinciding with the Long Turkish War of 1593–1606 (and extinguished well before the Protestant revolt broke out in 1618 in Bohemia), but in general considerations of holy war were giving way to political and economic rivalries within Europe.[20] Nevertheless, although the vision of crusade may have lost its power in the courts and capitals where policy was made, and may have necessitated a reassessment of the role of the military frontiers, the idea was a long time dying in the popular mind. The world of the uskoks was affected by both the official withdrawal from this conflict and the lingering popular legitimacy conferred by the ideal of holy war and the defense of Christendom.

The changing vision of the frontier was also affected by a second process in the border societies of the West—the slowly growing claims to

[18]Longworth describes uskok border warfare in these terms: "Only inertia, the balance of terror and the relative prospects of pay and plunder determined the allegiances of the unfortunate people of the region. The Uskoks' raiding activities were essentially devoid of ideological objectives" ("The Senj Uskoks Reconsidered," p. 365).

[19]Braudel, *The Mediterranean*, vol. 2, pp. 842–44.

[20]This is also the theme of Alberto Tenenti's *Piracy and the Decline of Venice, 1580–1615,* trans. Janet Pullan and Brian Pullan (Berkeley, Calif., 1967), which examines the process through the actions of corsairs in the Mediterranean.

a monopoly of military authority by the centralizing monarchies. The consolidation of state control over the means of violent coercion meant that the free military communities were gradually absorbed into the new armies and subordinated to a centralized bureaucracy. This process, punctuated by frequent rebellions, can be traced among the cossacks; at first the Poles attempted to register them and organize disciplined regiments under Polish command, and in the mid-seventeenth century the Russians integrated a cossack officer corps into their military system. (A rather different process can be observed in the Ottoman Empire, as central imperial control began to decay after the sixteenth century and the North African corsairs gradually shook off any effective control from Istanbul.) In the Habsburg case, military administration was one of the first areas of governmental centralization. Ferdinand I first appointed a colonel to command the Frontier under the authority of the Emperor and the archdukes; in 1556 the imperial Hofkriegsrat (Court War Council) was established in Vienna; and when this was reorganized in 1578, control of the Frontier passed to the newly created Hofkriegsrat in Graz. The Graz Hofkriegsrat was not a very efficient tool of monarchical absolutism, for the Archduke shared his authority over it with the Inner Austrian Estates.[21] Nevertheless, it was through the Hofkriegsrat, the General of the Frontier, and the Military Frontier commissions that central control was gradually extended over the border irregulars, particularly as the Habsburgs needed to keep peace on the Ottoman border in order to concentrate on internal conflicts. Through the uskoks it is possible to follow the effect of this centralization on the free military community as the leaders were gradually coopted and the rank-and-file tamed—though not without resistance.

This book begins by placing the uskoks in the context of the border world, examining the processes that shaped it and the military communities that grew from it. Contemporary interpretations of the uskoks turned on who they were and how they lived: here several chapters look at the origins of uskoks and the economic and military constraints within which they operated. These are followed by an analysis of their mental world, their ideas, values, and beliefs—both those they proclaimed as their own special raison d'être and those they shared with the rest of the border—and how these ideas affected uskok organization. To study how their circumstances and their beliefs interacted in practice, a chapter examines uskok relations with the world outside Senj. All these threads are then drawn together in a chapter that concentrates on the turn of the

---

[21]Gunther Rothenberg, *The Austrian Military Border in Croatia 1522–1747*, (Urbana, Ill., 1960), pp. 34, 48–49. See also V. Thiel, "Die innerösterreichische Zentralverwaltung, 1564–1749," *Archiv für österreichische Geschichte* (Vienna), 105 (1917): 1–210. In the text, "Hofkriegsrat" refers to the War Council in Graz, unless otherwise specified.

sixteenth century in order to examine the ways in which the uskok world was changing and the uskoks' reactions to these changes. Throughout, the emphasis is on the social, economic, and political realities that produced the uskoks and on the ways in which these people responded to the problems that confronted them. This approach concentrates on the uskoks themselves, asking not only what they did, but why they did it; asking not just what were their relations with their allies, their victims, and each other, but also how they perceived and justified these relations.

Sources

A problem that has left its mark on most studies of the uskoks (indeed, on most studies of corsairs, brigands, and frontiersmen) is that of evidence. In trying to understand the uskoks, the historian can examine their economic conditions, social organization, and political circumstances. But in addition to such factors, the uskoks acted in the context of a set of cultural values—ideas of what was right and wrong, honorable and dishonorable—and much of what they did can be understood only in terms of the tension between these ideals and the social, political, and economic circumstances of the border. Only occasionally can we hear these beliefs and values stated by the voices of the uskoks themselves. More often we must examine them through the eyes of outsiders, who were moved by different purposes and governed by other assumptions. Nonetheless, in the conviction that the uskoks' world cannot be comprehended completely without an attempt to recover these attitudes, we must pay careful attention not only to individual incidents and the patterns that emerge from raiding as a whole, but also to their other actions, their rituals, and above all to the language that expresses their values.

The diplomatic conflict between Venice, the Habsburgs, and the Porte over their activities generated a seemingly inexhaustible volume of material about the uskoks. But how much can these sources tell us about the uskoks themselves, and how reliable are they in this respect? In answering these questions we must differentiate among the various types of documentation. The purely diplomatic sources (letters between heads of state, reports of ambassadors) are the least useful for our purposes. They were written, for the most part, by men at a remove from the uskoks themselves and were rarely directly related to their actions, being more concerned with questions of negotiation, tactics, and diplomacy. Because of their political purposes they cannot always be considered completely reliable in what information on the uskoks they do contain.

The reports of those more closely concerned with the uskoks are of greater interest, but they pose different problems. These include the administrative reports of Venetian civil and military representatives, reports by officials of the Military Frontier, intelligence dossiers from informers and spies, complaints from Ottoman border officials, ecclesiastical visitation records and reports, and descriptions from various independent observers—not all hostile to the uskoks. These are usually fairly reliable in detail, though what is selected for report depends very much on the interests of the observer, and allowances must be made for distortion caused by second- or thirdhand reporting or by bias. This type of document makes up the bulk of evidence on uskok actions. Three of these deserve special mention: a long essay in dialogue form by an anonymous Italian supporter of the uskoks, usually known by the name of one of the interlocutors, the merchant Giovanni of Fermo;[22] another long report on Senj by Vettor Barbaro, the Provveditore Generale's secretary in Senj during the negotiations over the uskoks in 1601;[23] and the reports of Marc'Antonio de Dominis, the Bishop of Senj at the end of the sixteenth century.[24] All these men had personal experience of the uskoks and give many details of life in Senj, while reaching very different conclusions on the uskoks' motives and their role in the warfare of the Adriatic.

Yet another type of material is provided by judicial documents: complaints or testimony before Venetian courts and officials in Dalmatia, interrogations of captured uskoks or of those suspected of aiding the uskoks, the testimony of witnesses before Miltary Frontier commissions. These too require caution and careful attention to the position and interests of the witness. When the penalty for cooperation with the uskoks of Senj was death, one must question the candor of a Dalmatian fisherman reporting an encounter with uskoks to the local Venetian authorities. On the other hand, these records often preserve the responses of uskoks themselves, or of those who had much in common with them, and can yield valuable insights into their attitudes.

[22]Discovered in the Medici Archives in Florence and published by Franjo Rački, "Prilog za poviest hrvatskih uskoka," *Starine* (Zagreb), 9 (1877): 172–256.

[23]This has not been published, though Provveditore Generale Pasqualigo incorporated parts in his report to the Senate in 1602 (*Commissiones et relationes venetæ*, vols. 4–7, Monumenta spectantia historiam Slavorum meridionalium, 47, 48, 49, and 50, ed. G. Novak [Zagreb, 1964–72], vol. 6, pp. 93–116). I have used a ms. copy in H.A.Z., Fond Šime Ljubića, 2/33.

[24]De Dominis' accounts of Senj are published in K. Horvat, ed., *Monumenta historiam uscocchorum illustrantia*, vol. 1, Monumenta spectantia historiam Slavorum meridionalium, 32 and 34 (Zagreb, 1910–13), and Šime Ljubić, "Prilozi za životopis Markantunu Dominisu," *Starine* (Zagreb), 2 (1870):1–260. These also print an anonymous account of Joseph Rabatta's commission to reform Senj in 1601, probably by de Dominis (Horvat, *Monumenta uscocchorum*, vol. 1, pp. 395–422; Ljubić, "Prilozi," pp. 45–59). These reports were apparently used by Archbishop Minuccio Minucci in writing his *Storia degli uscocchi*, in Paolo Sarpi, *Opere*, vol. 4 (Helmstadt [Verona], 1763), pp. 217–62.

A surprising number of letters or reports survive from the uskoks themselves. Not all of them were illiterate; many uskoks, both leaders and rank-and-file, signed their names to petitions and official letters. The uskoks left no autobiographies such as have been used in studies of banditry in more modern times (the nearest approximation is perhaps the petition from the uskok vojvoda Ivan Vlatković, appealing his death sentence and rehearsing his sacrifices to the House of Austria). The letters addressed to those in positions of power on the Military Frontier or in Venetian Dalmatia, however, provide valuable evidence of the uskoks' own perceptions of their role (or of how they wanted to be perceived). And, finally, insurance documents, notarial records, baptismal registers, pay documents, military censuses, and other similar administrative records preserve evidence of uskok activity which is slightly less problematical, at least as far as deliberate distortion or bias is concerned.

As I have indicated, the nature of these sources exposes the researcher to the dangers of bias and lack of balance. However, while material dealing—for example—with the bands of brigands in the early modern period is nearly always derived from those responsible for pursuing and punishing them, the material on the uskoks comes from a much wider variety of sources, with widely varying attitudes. We can thus balance one bias against another, building up a more nuanced picture of the uskoks. Venetian materials provide the best evidence of uskok actions in Dalmatia and across the Venetian border into the Ottoman hinterland, but they are selective in what they report. Military Frontier sources can provide a counterweight, but they are not so detailed or numerous, especially in regard to individual raids or bands. They are much more helpful on the internal organization and financing of the uskoks and, as one would expect, on their relationship with the representatives of the Habsburg state. Both of these sources are balanced by Ottoman material, for the most part border officials' correspondence preserved in the Venetian, Ragusan, and Habsburg archives. Papal sources give yet another perspective on the uskoks. I have tried to avoid uncritically reproducing the prejudices of my sources by collecting a variety of evidence on any particular subject whenever possible and by concentrating as much as I could on local sources, for these seem to offer the most knowledgeable information on the uskoks, if not perhaps the least biased. These materials include many that previous writers have passed over, either because of ignorance of their existence or because they did not suit an author's approach to the subject (especially where this was primarily concerned with the relations between states). Many of these have come from the archives of the Dalmatian communes, with their records of petty civil and criminal proceedings, financial transactions, and notarial documents; the archives of Rijeka, which record both mutual interests and economic rivalries with Senj; the archives of the Carniolan Estates in Ljubljana; and the archives of Dubrovnik, a republic that shared many of the pressures and prejudices in regard to the uskoks felt by its great rival Venice but responded to them slightly differently.

CHAPTER TWO

The Borders and
Border Military Systems

In the sixteenth century the Croatian lands felt the full magnitude of the Ottoman invasions. The force of the onslaught was deflected only by the barriers of geography—the forbidding mountains, the sea. No wonder the Ottoman armies were seen by those in their path as some natural disaster, a conflagration blasting and destroying the land, after which only "black stones remain, and leafless pines."[1] The results of the invasions were political collapse, economic disarray, and social dislocation on the borders. As new frontiers took shape, a pattern of attack and defense, raid and counterraid developed in the borderlands between the empires, each side mirroring the other in organization and way of life.

The Ottoman invasions and conquests of the fifteenth and sixteenth centuries, the advance of the armies of Islam, and the defenses thrown up by the West were the factors that created this borderland, and the opposition between Christianity and Islam, between the Western powers and the Ottoman Porte, was the source of much of the conflict in this area. Other tensions and conflicts also existed: political and economic rivalry between the Habsburgs and Venice; the competing economic interests of various social groups (stockherders and farmers; nobles, citizens, and peasants; frontier soldiers and magnates); ethnic and confessional antagonisms. But the context of the struggle between the warring empires of East and West influenced all these other antagonisms and polarized relations on the border, so that the conflicts that constantly troubled this region were expressed largely in terms of the opposition between Islam and Christianity. Yet though this struggle orga-

---

[1]"Ostane crn kami, i brez listja bori." Marko Marulić in his poem "Molitva suprotiva Turkom," in *Pjesme Marka Marulića,* Stari pisci hrvatski, 1, ed. I. Kukuljević-Sakcinski (Zagreb, 1869), p. 245.

19

nized and directed other tensions, it did not entirely subsume them. The problems of the uskoks illustrate this point—though their struggles are a part of the conflict between the West and the Ottoman Empire, and though these combatants exploited them in their rivalry, to view the uskoks solely from this standpoint obscures the real nature of their dilemmas and makes many of their actions incomprehensible.

The Impact of Ottoman Invasion

Those who describe the steady advance of the Ottoman forces through the Balkans deep into Europe and the retreat of the divided, impotent Western powers, customarily call the roll of Christian defeats and enumerate the Ottoman conquests of fortresses, regions, and states. One by one the Balkan defenses raised by the Serbian and Bosnian states, the Croatian and Hungarian nobility, the Habsburgs and the Venetian Republic fell. With the final conquests of Bosnia (1463) and Hercegovina (1482), the Dalmatian coast and the lands of the Croatian-Hungarian kingdom lay open to the Turks. The defeat of the flower of the Croatian nobility at Krbava Field in 1493 left a large part of Croatia defenseless. The Venetian territories, too, as far as Friuli, were under constant attack during the 1499–1503 war with the Ottomans. The resumption of the Ottoman offensive against Europe and the seizure of Belgrade in 1521 were followed by assaults on the Croatian borders and the fall of the Croatian towns of Skradin and Knin (1522), Ostrovica (1523), and Sinj (1524) and crowned by the total defeat of the Hungarian army, which had been reinforced by Croatian and Serbian detachments, at Mohács (1526). The tally of fallen fortresses continues: in 1527 Obrovac and Udbina, in 1528 Jajce and Banja Luka. One town after another was captured. In 1537, with the conquest of Klis, the last Croatian stronghold south of the Velebit mountain range, the Ottomans consolidated their hold on the Dalmatian hinterland from the Zrmanja to the Neretva rivers, leaving only the Croatian Littoral, the Dalmatian communes, and the territory of Dubrovnik beyond their grip. (See Map 2.)

A list of battles and defeats does little more than hint at the massive dislocation of life the invasions caused. The Ottoman conquest of the Balkan Peninsula did not simply substitute one authority for another. Although the conquerors assimilated many of the patterns of life and retained them with only slight changes, the disruption caused by the invasions themselves and the changes introduced by the Ottomans altered the path of development in these areas. And the effects of the invasions in the Balkans did not stop at the borders of the conquered

2. Ottoman conquests in the sixteenth and seventeenth centuries.

territories: they produced profound social and economic changes in the lands that faced them.

An Ottoman offensive consisted of three stages: raiding and pillaging forays by irregulars; siege and conquest of the major fortresses by the regular army, which then used these as bases to gain control of the countryside; and the consolidation of power by a military government and garrisons.[2] The preliminary raids were the most devastating, de-

[2]Halil Inalcık, "Ottoman Methods of Conquest," *Studia Islamica*, 2 (1954): 103–29.

signed to establish favorable conditions for an easy conquest by terrifying the population, weakening manpower and resources, and breaking the will of the people to resist. With the fall of Bosnia, bands of lightly armed, highly mobile Ottoman irregulars began to strike into southern Hungary, through Croatia as far as Carniola, Carinthia, and Styria, into Istria and Friuli. These forays were generally of short duration, for the bands avoided confrontation with the defending armies and skirted fortifications, preferring plundering to combat. A single area often suffered a number of such raids in the course of a year—sudden descents by armed horsemen who plundered livestock and belongings, burned fields and dwellings, and carried off captives to be sold as slaves. These tactics could reduce the countryside to a wasteland. The description of his native Split given by Marko Marulić in a letter of 1522 to Pope Hadrian VI gives a vivid picture of a region devastated by Turkish raids:

> We are troubled by daily attacks of the infidel Turks; they harass us incessantly, killing some and leading others into slavery; our goods are pillaged, our cattle are led off, our villages and settlements are burned; the fields from which we drew our livelihood are in part laid waste and in part deserted, for those who once worked them have been carried off; and instead of fruit they bear brambles. We defend our safety with our walls alone, and we are content that our Dalmatian cities are not yet besieged or attacked, due to some, I know not what, alleged peace treaty. But only the cities are spared, and all else lies open to pillage and rapine.[3]

Booty was a major goal of the Ottoman pillaging forays—livestock, goods, and files of shackled prisoners to be sold as slaves. A member of a Western embassy to the Turks, Benedikt Kuripešić, in 1530 reported seeing Christian prisoners in Bosnia being driven like cattle back from the market because they had not all been purchased.[4] This was by no means a petty trade. Although many raids might net only a few captives, whole villages were sometimes carried off. Even small raids, repeated again and again, could drain the population resources of a region. The Venetian reports from Dalmatia in Marino Sanuto's diary give the details of raid after raid, particularly between 1499 and 1503, when Venice and the Turks were in open war. A 1501 report by Jacomo da Molin, Captain of Zadar, notes that more than 10,000 people and 80,000 animals, taken by the Turks in three raids or killed by the plague, had vanished from the Zadar territory.[5] Sanuto preserved reports of raids on the Croatian Lit-

---

[3]Quoted in Daniel Farlati, *Illyricum sacrum*, 9 vols. (Venice, 1751–1819), vol. 3, p. 433.
[4]Benedikt Kuripešić, *Putopis kroz Bosnu, Srbiju, Bugarsku i Rumeliju 1530* (Sarajevo, 1950), p. 20.
[5]In Marino Sanuto, *I diarii di Marino Sanuto*, 58 vols. (Venice 1879–1903), vol. 3, p. 1618.

toral as well, recording the frequent descent of Ottoman troops on the area around Senj in the 1520s and 1530s.

Perhaps the single most significant aspect of these Ottoman invasions can be seen in the numbers of people they set in motion. The Ottoman conquest brought about great demographic changes on the Balkan Peninsula—changes that altered forever the ethnic and confessional patterns of both the conquered territories and the areas abutting them. Those areas which offered the most resistance to Ottoman invasion, which were most exposed to Ottoman attack and the disruption of war, naturally sustained the heaviest losses of population.

Those not carried off into captivity, killed during battle, or dead of the plague or of famine saved themselves in flight, leaving the uncertainty of life in a land under siege, abandoning their lands and homes. Individuals and families fled, panic-stricken, just beyond the range of fighting, moving as the border followed them. Others fled farther abroad. By the end of the 1520s Senj, its hinterland so often attacked by the Ottomans, had suffered a collapse of its trade due in part to emigration. "Only a few inhabitants remain," wrote the citizens to Ferdinand I in 1529, "of whom the larger part have recently been captured by the Turks, and the others, not wishing to fall into captivity, have been forced to travel the world seeking another haven where they can live with their families."[6]

What could the inhabitants of the borders do, too weak to resist effectively, but await destruction or flee the battleground? Petar Zoranić discusses this dilemma in his romance *Planine*, written in the 1530s. One of his shepherds, not an Arcadian swain but a recognizable mountain stockherder, speaks of those who have fled to foreign realms, "u tuja vladanja pobigli," while "mi eto, kako ovca drugu zaklanu gledajući, svoj kolj čekamo. I mi bismo od ovud pobigli, dali nas slatkost baščine ne uzdrži." ("We, like sheep watching others butchered, await our own slaughter. We too would flee from here, did not the sweetness of our birthright hold us back.")[7] Even the lands of the invader could seem a safe haven. The Rector of Zadar reported to the Venetian Senate in 1528 that "all the poor subjects have been forced to abandon their homes and possessions, and have left, and continue to go to live in foreign lands, part in the places of the land of the Porte, in order not to be made slaves in perpetuity with their families."[8] Emigration from the Croatian border

---

[6]In Emilij Laszowski, ed., *Monumenta habsburgica regni Croatiæ, Dalmatiæ, Slavoniæ*, 3 vols., Monumenta spectantia historiam Slavorum meridionalium, 35, 38, and 40 (Zagreb, 1914–17), vol. 1, pp. 171–73.

[7]Petar Zoranić, *Planine*, Pet stoljeća hrvatske književnosti, 8 (Zagreb, 1964), verse 16, line 134.

[8]*Commissiones et relationes venetæ*, vol. 2, pp. 41–42.

areas continued throughout the sixteenth century, stronger in the first half of the century than the second, but always increasing with renewed war or with the outbreak of plague or famine. Even whispers of war could set off panicky flight: in 1594 there were reports from Dalmatia that many subjects of the Ottomans, with all their possessions, had left the Empire to live in Venetian Dalmatia, "a certain rumor passing among them that the Ottoman Empire was about to end."[9] These flights left large areas desolate. Entire villages ceased to exist, even their names forgotten, though the stone walls of ruined houses might mark where they had stood. When Ottoman administration was imposed on Lika in 1527, the few settled areas were outnumbered by abandoned fortresses and empty villages.[10] On the rest of the Croatian border the pattern was much the same.

In time the wastelands created by war were resettled. Under quieter conditions some emigrants returned to their native homes, including some who had fled from the Zadar area to Apulia and Abruzzi. They began to return when circumstances improved, reassured by the security provided by new fortifications, or because they were not happy in their new homes. A Venetian observer noted, "They cannot accommodate themselves either to the language or to the customs . . . and they would rather be at the mercy of the Turks and return to their homeland, than stay in a place they find tiresome and insupportable."[11] More often the empty lands were given to new settlers. As the old inhabitants withdrew to the north and northwest they were replaced by currents of migration from the south and east. Many of these new colonists were stockherders, Vlachs from the Dinaric mountain areas, encouraged by the colonizing policies of the Ottoman Empire but also following the natural path of migration from the barren mountains to the more fertile plains.[12] There had been Catholic Vlach communities, some Romanic,

[9]H.A.Z., Ispisi tajnog vatikanskog arhiva Fra Dane Zeca, C. Urbin. 1062: 141.

[10]Stjepan Pavičić, "Seobe i naselja u Lici," *Zbornik za narodni život i običaje južnih slavena* (Zagreb), 41 (1962): 119–20.

[11]*Commissiones et relationes venetæ*, vol. 1, p. 172.

[12]Between the fourteenth and the seventeenth centuries the word 'Vlach' covers a variety of meanings—designating national affiliation, occupation or social status, or denoting otherness of almost any variety. The different uses of the term are not easily separated, and it is often difficult to discover the precise significance of the word in a given instance. Originally used as a national designation for the Romanic or Romanized population of the Balkan Peninsula, in the middle ages the term became a social designation as well, denoting nomadic or transhumant stockherders, distinguished from ordinary peasants and shepherds by their legal status and by the services they performed as soldiers, professional stockherders, and couriers and porters (see Milenko Filipović, "Struktura i organizacija srednjovekovnog katuna," *Simpozijum o srednjevekovnom katunu* [Sarajevo, 1963], pp. 42–112, for a discussion of Vlachs in the medieval Balkans). This second meaning of 'Vlach' can extend to Slavs as well as people of Romanic extraction. In the medieval Croatian and Serbian states the Vlach stockherders lived under their own leaders in semiautonomous groups

some partly Slavicized, in medieval Croatia. These new colonists, how-ever, were primarily Orthodox Vlachs from deep within the Ottoman territories. Throughout the sixteenth and seventeenth centuries migra-tional currents of stockherding military colonists flowed down from the mountains of the Balkan hinterland, moving with their flocks across the high plains, settling in the foothills and the valleys, passing by areas still held by the old Catholic or Islamized population for the regions closest to the border, taking over the abandoned villages and using the bramble-choked fields for pastures.

While the constant warfare of the border was inimical to peasant cul-tivators, it attracted the stockherders. So-called Vlach privileges depended to a great degree on the military service they rendered in exchange for their autonomy and tax concessions. Away from the borderlands, the services performed by Vlach groups (as couriers, professional stock-herds, guards of roads and passes) did not safeguard them from increas-ing taxation and other encroachments on their privileges in the course of the sixteenth century. On the border, however, their taxes were lowered and their internal autonomy was less circumscribed in direct proportion to the increased value of their military role to their rulers. This flow of humanity did not stop at the Ottoman border but in time crossed to settle the deserted territories of Venetian Dalmatia and the Croatian borderlands.

Conflict and Community on the Borders

When the old population patterns were shuffled and new ones began to emerge in the course of the migrations of the sixteenth century, new tensions and conflicts emerged as well. Tracing these fractures not only gives us a map of conflict but also helps to bring into relief the ways in which people on the border joined in communities of common interest and identity. Political identity, ethnicity, confessional, cultural, and eco-

---

throughout the mountainous no-man's-lands of the Balkans. Not subject to the same laws and customs that bound the villages, they were administered under special arrangements. Nor were they tied to the land. They lived a transhumant life with their flocks, pasturing in the mountains in the summer, descending to the valleys in the winter. In most areas they were freed of all feudal obligations except a set tax in cash by household (or hearth) rather than by head, but in return they served as soldiers and transported goods and messages. The Ottomans preserved the Vlach system much as they found it, using this seminomadic, militarized section of the rural population as a source of colonists and as irregular troops to augment the border forces. As they had under earlier rulers, such colonists performed a military function under the Ottomans in return for privileges and autonomy. In the six-teenth century the term 'Vlach' often refers to this social role, whether or not it has any additional ethnic meaning.

nomic patterns all help to illustrate the ways in which groups on the border were divided or brought together.

The awareness of belonging to a national community, of membership in a nation—though not nationalism in the modern sense—is very clear in the anti-Ottoman Croatian literature of the sixteenth century. It is most apparent in the works of Dalmatian writers, who were cut off from the remnants of the Croatian state. This heightened awareness is less an abstract idea of Croat or Slavic unity or reciprocity than a practical reaction to threats to the existence of the nation: primarily the advancing Turk, but also the political threat of Venice and (among some writers) the cultural hegemony of the Italian world. Dinko Zavorović, around 1602, summed up the whole history of fifteenth and sixteenth-century Croatia by quoting a Latin couplet by a contemporary, Daniel Divnić: "Turha heu! rapuit rura et gens extera iura. / Praestat sola fides, caetera rapta vides." ("The Turks, alas, have pillaged the countryside and a foreign race [Venice] the law. Only faith remains, the rest you see plundered.") The *orationes pro Croatia*, the speeches and epistles that bear witness to the magnitude of the Ottoman threat and beg or demand Western aid, express a fear not only for Christendom but for the nation. In spite of the epistles of men such as Frane Trankvil Andreis, Marko Marulić, and Simun Kozičić Benja, pleading for their *infaelix patria*, little response came from the West.[13] Unity in the face of a common foe was ever more necessary. To renounce this community, to forget one's language and nation, was to weaken the defenses against the foe. The elegies lamenting the devastated and dismembered homeland and the reproaches to those who are ashamed of their native tongue are filled with an awareness of the Croat nation as a historical entity. Although not all these writers were patricians, this is nonetheless the literature of the elite, the city dwellers, the educated, the clergy—an intellectual vision of identity. But to what degree did the common people share the concerns of these writers over the dismemberment of Croatia and the belief in the role of the nation as a unifying force in the face of attack from outside?

Perhaps a desire for political unity with the rest of Croatia and independence from Venetian rule can be seen in the popular traditions of

[13]Divnić translated from Marin Franičević, *Povijest hrvatske renesansne književnosti* (Zagreb: Školska knjiga, 1983), p. 680. Even in the fifteenth century the Croatian humanist Janus Pannonius had seen little hope of aid against the Turk from the divided West: "France sleeps, Spain cares not for Christ, England declines due to rebellions of the magnates, neighboring Germany convenes useless assemblies, Italy trades. . . ." ("Gallia dormitat, nec curat Iberia Christum, / Anglia gentili seditione ruit; / Proxima conventus Germania cogit inanes, / Permutat merces Itala terra suas") (Veljko Gortan and Vladimir Vratković, eds., *Hrvatski latinisti*, 2 vols., Pet stoljeća hrvatske književnosti, bk. 2 [Zagreb, 1969], vol. 1, pp. 169-70). V. Gligo has collected a number of these pleas for help against the Turk in *Govori protiv Turaka* (Split, 1983).

allegiance to the Croatian-Hungarian crown in Dalmatia and the hinterland. Venetian reports throughout the sixteenth century note this inclination first to the King of Croatia and Hungary, then to the Habsburgs, bearers of the Croatian crown.[14] In 1515 Sanuto entered reports of agitation in Dalmatia in support of the King of Hungary.[15] Such reports continued throughout the century: "I believe that Your Serenity [Venice] is patron of this city [Šibenik], not to say of the entire province, to the extent that the Crown of Hungary lies distant; for there are many of these subjects who bear that Kingdom in their hearts as their natural Ruler, and they feel the rule of Your Serenity to be a thing which they have chosen through election only."[16]

Venice saw this inclination as a nostalgia of the patriciate for the more rigidly feudal society of the Croatian-Hungarian kingdom, in which they would hold more power, "because when they were under the protection of the King of Hungary they lived freely, and the government of the city was in their hands."[17] The citizens and people of the communes were better disposed to Venetian rule, which supported them in their struggles for political power with the patriciate. Nonetheless the citizens too preserved a fondness for the Croatian-Hungarian kingdom, a memory of more prosperous days under its crown. An echo of this tradition of political identity can be seen in the readiness of communities on the Ottoman border to pledge their fealty to the Habsburg Emperor, "desiring to submit themselves and take shelter beneath the wings of the most serene House of Austria and under the yoke of Christianity" according to the leaders of Lika, the onetime "principality of Gio. Carlovich [Ivan Karlović]," Croatian Ban and lord of Krbava, who had lost this region to the Turks.[18] Claims to membership in this political community could be one way of asserting an independent identity.

Most of Dalmatia was united in resistance to the Ottoman invader and in the "desire to recover the borders, their patrimony, which they constantly bewail, and aspire to all the day long," according to a Venetian official.[19] Discontent with Venetian rule sprang in part from impatience

[14]Since 1102 the Kingdom of Croatia had been joined with that of Hungary in a personal union under the suzerainty of the Hungarian dynasty. In 1527 a Habsburg, Ferdinand I, was elected to the throne of Croatia. Under the Hungarian kings, the islands and the coast, with the ancient Croatian capital of Biograd, had been an integral part of Croatia. By 1420, however, Venice had gained control of most of this region, and as Venetian Dalmatia it began to be considered separately from Croatia, the territory of which was further reduced by the Ottoman conquests.

[15]Sanuto,*I diarii*, vol. 19, p. 455.

[16]*Commissiones et relationes venetæ*, vol. 5, p. 223 (Vettor Dolfin, Rector of Šibenik, 1597).

[17]Ibid., vol. 3, pp. 3–4 (Giovanni Battista Giustiniano, syndic of Dalmatia, 1550s).

[18]A. Theiner, *Vetera monumenta Slavorum meridionalium historiam illustrantia*, 2 vols. (Rome, 1863–75; reprint, Osnabrück, 1968), vol. 2, p. 103.

[19]H.A.Z., Fond Šime Ljubića, 2/21: 4.

with Venice's careful relations with the Ottomans. In 1574, in the aftermath of the war of Cyprus, a hard time for the people of Dalmatia, the Rector of Split reported that

> the people are not as they were before, but the wicked have led them into a bestial rage. . . . For some time there has been a *piesma* [Cr.: song] on everyone's lips; no one knows who wrote it, but it may be by Francesco Boctuli, a poet and a writer, and it says in this song that the Turk is running water that erodes, and that the Doge is a sandbank which has been carried away little by little by the river. And other things are said, also a little acerbic, and the people sing it under the palace windows, when it is dusk.

The Venetian Rector pretended not to hear.[20] But when the Habsburgs began an offensive against the Ottoman Empire in the Long Turkish War (1593–1606), Venice could not ignore the fact that its Dalmatian subjects, despite the government's prohibitions, supported the Habsburg cause, both in spirit and in deed. Nobles as well as commoners joined in the attempt to retake the fortress of Klis from the Ottomans, and even after the failure of the Klis operation they continued to "favor marvellously in secret the uskoks [troops of the Emperor], and they rejoice when they hear of some success of theirs, and on the other hand they sorrow over damages done to them," according to the Rector of Trogir in 1598.[21] Joining operations organized by the Habsburgs against the Ottomans was certainly also an outlet for political protest and a manifestation of anti-Venetian sentiment, and perhaps a way of expressing community with the rest of Croatia. In the sixteenth century Croatia was territorially fragmented—only the remnants of the remnants still preserving Croatian statehood—and a large part of its population had fled into diaspora in other lands. Nevertheless, a sense of political unity embracing the Croat nation could still be detected in many strata of society.

Such a sense of a collective identity is more difficult to find among the stockherder-colonists who settled in the border areas under Ottoman ægis, either in their own self-images or in the descriptions of others. The precise significance of the various appellations contemporaries used for these groups constitutes something of a problem for the historian trying to analyze their sense of identity. Although border authorities might refer to them as immigrants (uskok, *pribeg, transfugus*) or as former Ottoman subjects (*herübergefallne Turgkhen*), most often they are identified by some variant of the term 'Vlach' or 'Morlach.' In the sixteenth century on the Ottoman border and the Habsburg Military Frontier, the term 'Vlach' *usually* denoted a specific social role, that of a stockherder-

---

[20]In V. Solitro, ed., *Documenti storici sull'Istria e la Dalmazia* (Venice, 1844), p. 212.
[21]In *Commissiones et relationes venetæ*, vol. 5, p. 263.

colonist with military obligations executed in exchange for tax concessions. More broadly, the Venetian term 'Morlach' in the sixteenth century *usually* referred to the whole subject population of the Ottoman
hinterland (as distinct from Venetian subjects), regardless of their ethnic
identity and whether or not they were military colonists, stockherders,
or peasants. There are glimpses of a common social identity among some
of these "Vlach sons," as they called themselves, an identity based on
the military privileges they enjoyed under the Ottomans. These distinguished them from the ordinary subjects, and the Vlachs were determined to preserve these privileges when they emigrated to Christian
territory. But how much did the stockherder-settlers who are identified
as Vlachs retain a separate, Romanic ethnic character that differentiated
them from the Slavs on the border? Sometimes the two ethnic groups
were clearly seen to be separate, as is the case in a Habsburg reference
from 1538 which distinguishes between one group of refugees from the
village of Srb on the upper Una (*Sirfen*, or Serbs) and another group,
Romanic Vlachs from Obrovac: "Vlachs, whom we call old Romans"
("Walächen welche bei uns allt Römer genennt sein").[22] In other places,
the Vlach groups seem to have been completely Slavonicized (though
even in such cases a consciousness of separate origins may have persisted).[23] To tease out the ways in which these Vlachs presented their
own identities, we must examine each group separately.

Although a few historians have identified all these Vlach colonists as
Serbs and although nearly all the colonists identified as Serbs came from
a section of the Ottoman population which enjoyed Vlach privileges and
performed certain concomitant obligations, not all Vlach colonists can
be called Serbs. Some of these colonists quite clearly retained a separate
Romanic identity, as noted above, and some were also Catholic, particularly those Vlach groups who had lived on the border since medieval
times.[24] Before the end of the sixteenth century the national appellation

[22]In Laszowski, *Monumenta habsburgica*, vol. 2, pp. 409-10. The distinction was preserved by Ferdinand I, who referred to these same groups as "Rasciani sive Serviani atque
Valachi, quos vulgo Zytschy vocant" ("Rascians or Serbs, and Vlachs, who are popularly
called Ćići"; ibid.). These Vlachs had retained their Romanic language, which led to their
name of Ćići (from *ce*: what). Other Romanic Vlachs in the Cetina region and elsewhere
were also identified with this group of Ćići in the sixteenth century. Romanic origins can be
detected in the names of some other Vlachs on the Christian borders: Drakula and Manoilo,
for example, in one group in the Una region in 1596 (Aleska Ivić, ed., "Neue cyrillische
Urkunden aus den Wiener Archiven," *Archiv für slavische Philologie* [Berlin], 30 [1909]: 212).
[23]See for example the Catholic Vlachs settled in Prilišće and Rosopojnik by 1544, in R. Lopašić, ed., *Urbaria lingua croatica conscripta*, 1, Monumenta historico-juridica Slavorum
meridionalium, 5 (Zagreb, 1894), pp. 381-82. On this problem see also Ivan Božić in *Istorija
Crne Gore*, ed. M. Đurović (Titograd, 1970), vol. 2, pt. 2, p. 349.
[24]*Commissiones et relationes venetæ*, vol. 2, pp. 253-54; vol. 4, p. 443; K. Horvat, ed.,
"Glagoljaši u Dalmaciji početkom 17. vijeka," *Starine* (Zagreb), 33 (1911): 548.

'Serb' is used only occasionally for the settlers on the borders themselves. Their Orthodoxy, however, is often identified as Serbian (*fede
serviana, Rassiane fidei*). Particularly after the reestablishment of the Serbian Church in 1557, the Patriarchate, with its system of metropolitans
and bishops extending among all Orthodox settlements, served to reinforce the identification of Orthodoxy with Serbdom among the South
Slavs. Yet in the early years after the Ottoman conquest, the Orthodox
ecclesiastical organization was slow in consolidating and making itself
felt. With the wave of Orthodox immigration from within the Ottoman
Empire to the Habsburg border in the 1590s, the Vlach colonists are
identified more and more often with Serbs, but it was not until the early
seventeenth century, with the migration of compact groups of colonists
from Serbian lands into the Habsburg borders, especially in Slavonia,
that an Orthodox church organization was established which could
serve as a cultural, political, and national focus for the Orthodox colonists on Habsburg territory. At the same time, the rights of the Vlach
military communities were formally codified and extended to the Military Frontier as a whole. Not until then did Vlach frontiersmen began to
act as a corporate body on the basis of their common rights and their
common religion.[25] Earlier than this, however, there is little evidence
that these settlers perceived themselves as members of a wider ethnic or
national community.

These new settlers differed greatly in their way of life from the older
peasantry. Cultural differences and economic competition between the
Vlach stockherders and the sedentary agricultural population were
enough to cause friction, and the scarce resources of the mountain pastures encouraged competition among these pastoralists, expressed in
threats or the use of force against both rivals and their flocks. Animal
theft and raiding were common; so were feuds. Stalking from one pasture to the next, draped in their shaggy woolen cloaks, and placing a
high value on heroism, vengeance, and autonomy, the Vlachs could
seem wild and lawless to the settled villagers of the coastal plains with
their more urbanized civilization. In 1553 a Venetian official had given a
vivid picture of one group of Vlachs living on the northern bank of the
Velebit Channel (the *montagne della Morlacca* of the Venetians): "The inhabitants are all called Morlachs and have an appearance more feral than
human. They live near the roads and rob and kill travelers and despoil
them, and they think it praiseworthy indeed to live by robbery. They live
on milk and cheese, because livestock is all that they possess, and they

[25]See for example Nada Klaić, *Društvena previranja i bune u Hrvatskoj u XVI i XVII stoljeću*
(Belgrade, 1976), on seventeenth-century frontier uprisings, and Branko Sučević, "Razvitak
'vlaških prava' u Varaždinskom generalatu," *Historijski zbornik* (Zagreb), 6 (1953): 33–70, on
Vlach rights.

are people of the Serbian and heretical faith [*di fede serviana et eretica*] and are subjects of the Turk. They are coarse and dirty and live together with their animals constantly."[26] The lowlanders mocked the customs and speech of these mountain stockherds when they came down to sell cheese or to take seasonal work. The island girl of the comedy *Hvarkinja* by Marin Benetovic (†1607) rejects with scorn the idea that she might favor the attentions of a visiting Vlach from the mainland marches: "I'd rather marry a Turk than have to go around in black and wear a kerchief" like a Vlach woman ("Pri bîh za Turčina, nut da bi mi u modrinu hodit i heveljicu nosit").[27]

Where the new settlers from the hinterland came into contact with the older population, particularly on the borders, contrasts between the groups were emphasized and stimulated this awareness of difference. Tension sometimes exploded into conflict. In the winter the flocks of the stockherders poured down from the high mountains into the fields of the lowland peasants—a phenomenon that had been controlled and regulated in those places where the two cultures had been in contact for centuries. Where they now met for the first time, without traditional controls, crops were trampled, grazing lands disputed. The peasants were not always safe from the plundering that supplemented the livelihood of the Vlach military irregulars, whose extensive privileges already stirred envy in their peasant neighbors. 'Shepherd' and 'Vlach' could become terms of abuse. In 1530 some military colonists on the estate of Juraj Frankopan of Slunj in northern Croatia complained to a Habsburg Frontier official. They had come from Ottoman territory to settle. They had been allowed to settle on Frankopan's estate, but they were not allowed to mingle with the other subjects, who would not sell them food or let them into their homes. They were resentful that booty they regarded as legitimate had been taken away from them—but even angrier that it had been remarked that they were "shepherds and not good men" when they were good enough to be faithful servants ("ut sumus pastores et non sumus boni homines").[28]

The Orthodoxy of most of these new Vlach settlers from the hinterland also differentiated them from the Catholic peasantry. The rift between the Eastern and Western churches could strain difficult relations on the border still further. Within the Ottoman Empire the Orthodox Church was recognized as one of the millets (a legal-administrative unit) that made up the Ottoman state apparatus. Catholic priests, however, were under the control of Rome and were thus regarded as a fifth

---

[26]*Commissiones et relationes venetæ,* vol. 2, pp. 253–54.
[27]Benetović, *Djela,* p. 181.
[28]In Laszowski, *Monumenta habsburgica,* vol. 1, p. 463.

column within the Ottoman Empire. Although the Catholic population and the Franciscans were recognized in Bosnia, they lacked the state support given the Orthodox Church. Conflict between the two communities arose when the Orthodox clergy tried to exploit their advantage, particularly in the matter of the collection of ecclesiastical tithes from Catholics, an action that provoked strong resistance from Catholic communities in Bosnia.[29] On the other side of the frontier, the Orthodox settlers in Venetian Dalmatia and the Croatian territories were regarded as schismatics by the Catholic ecclesiastical hierarchy, which maintained sanctions against them. (After 1604 Catholicism would be the only officially recognized confession in Croatia.) Religious rivalries and antagonisms went beyond ecclesiastical competition and combined with other conflicts to shape the relations between individuals on the border. Were the Catholic uskoks in the service of the Habsburg Military Frontier who plundered the Orthodox subjects of the Porte urged on by an awareness of religious and cultural rivalry with their victims as well as by the need for a livelihood in the precarious circumstances of the border?

Difference of confession alone, however, was not an insurmountable barrier to relations between the inhabitants of the border, particularly in regions where the population was scattered and priests were few. Indeed, areas lacking ecclesiastics of the usual denomination sometimes switched from one rite to the other. Catholic observers of the sixteenth and seventeenth centuries report over and over that the lack of priests and the ignorance of the people resulted in conversions to Orthodoxy.[30] These conversions were especially frequent in Bosnia, where religious offices for the Catholic population were performed by Franciscans, who could operate from only a small number of monasteries. We can trace the same changes among Orthodox believers, as reported by the Venetian Provveditore Generale Giacomo Foscarini in 1572, writing about the Orthodox inhabitants of the Klis sancak, or district: "They are of the Serbian faith, but because they practice their religion but little, and receive little instruction in it, and because of the lack of priests, their faith is rapidly weakening."[31] A transition between confessions was made easier by the similarities between the rites, for each possessed a Slavic liturgy. Where differences in confession reinforced other social or economic divisions, they could exacerbate resentment and conflict, yet

---

[29]B. Đurđev et al., eds., *Historija naroda Jugoslavije*, 2 vols. (Zagreb, 1953–59), vol. 2, pp. 105–8. Documents in Josip Matasović (ed.), "Fojnička regesta," *Spomenik Srpske kraljevske akademije* (Belgrade), 67 (1930): 61–431; K. Jurišić, *Katolička crkva na biokovsko-neretvanskom području u doba turske vladavine* (Zagreb, 1972), pp. 227–30.

[30]Krunoslav Draganović, ed., *Massenübertritte von Katholiken zur "Orthodoxie" im kroatischen Sprachgebiet zur Zeit der Türkenherrschaft* (Rome, 1937).

[31]In *Commissiones et relationes venetæ*, vol. 4, p. 44.

antagonism to the other church or its members was by no means inevitable.

Perhaps, by leaving a consideration of the relations between Muslim and Christian until last, this discussion has inverted the normal expectations of the border. The commonest image of conflict on this border is, above all, that of the Ottoman raiders descending on an unprotected village to plunder and destroy. The importance of the struggle between Islam and Christianity as the framework for ideas of community and conflict in the sixteenth century cannot be discounted. Certainly the fear of attack from the hated infidel was ever-present. The Turk was the standard against which the Christian population of the borderlands measured wickedness—"worse even than a Turk." In Dalmatia both men and women insulted their enemies with imputations of illicit relations with Turks ("puttana delli turchi": "your mother is a whore and solicits Turks publicly in Ragusa [Dubrovnik]"), and the insulted parties in response filed criminal complaints against the slanderers.[32] Bloody combat between Christian and Muslim was a constant part of life and has come to be taken for granted by the historian much as it was by the sixteenth-century observer.

As this discussion has emphasized, however, this conflict between Christian and Muslim was not the only element that shaped border life. In spite of the picture of constant warfare that contemporary accounts evoke, the two groups did not meet only in battle. More peaceful activities brought the two worlds together, particularly as the frontiers stabilized toward the middle of the century. Christians took wheat to be ground in Ottoman border mills, Ottoman subjects worked Christian land, merchants from the Ottoman hinterland bought and sold goods in Dalmatian towns, frequenting the taverns and guest houses to such an extent that the Zadar Synod forbade tavernkeepers and private persons to procure Christian women for Muslim merchants, "even if they are public prostitutes."[33] Where there was daily contact, acquaintance and friendship could follow, despite the watchful eyes of church and civil authorities. The Zadar Synod of 1579 found it necessary to forbid priests to attend ceremonies of blood brotherhood, singling out in particular (in addition to those ceremonies between men and women and those between Catholics and "Greek schismatics") those between Christians and Turks, "which familiarity presents an occasion for many sins."[34] One of the sins bred by familiarity was marriage across religious lines,

[32]H.A.Z., Arhiv Omiša, 36/1.

[33]"Etiam si publicae meretrices essent" (in A. Marani, ed., *Atti pastorali di Minuccio Minucci, Arcivescovo di Zara (1596–1604)*, Thesaurus ecclesiarum Italiæ, ser. 3 (veneto), bk. 2 [Rome, 1970], p. 83).

[34]Farlati, *Illyricum sacrum*, vol. 5, p. 134.

again forbidden by the church. Although such unions were the occasion of scandal in sixteenth-century Dalmatia, they were certainly not unknown.[35]

It should not be forgotten that many Muslims on the frontier were also Slavs. These converts may have experienced a certain alienation from family and culture because of the legal and economic advantages conferred by conversion to Islam, the stigma of apostasy, or the desire to assimilate into a superior social class.[36] Yet in the border areas of the sixteenth century, converts did not necessarily completely reject a former way of life; they retained many of their original systems of beliefs and customs, assimilating such un-Muslim features as saints, icons, and baptism into Balkan folk-Islam. The preservation of such cultural patterns can be seen in the practices among Bosnian Muslim converts reported by the traveler Paul Rycaut in the 1660s—they read the Gospels, circumcised their children, believed that Mohammed was the Holy Ghost, and drank wine even in Ramadan (though to cause less of a scandal they did not put spices in it). These Muslims kept ties with their Christian neighbors and protected them from the excesses of other Turks.[37] In addition to a common cultural heritage, expressed in shared beliefs and practices, many Muslim Slavs retained an awareness of their origins. Bishop Antun Vrančić, writing in 1559 to Hasan-bey, an Ottoman provincial administrator and military commander, found it worthwhile to play on their common nationality: "The letter from Your Lordship was the gesture of a good neighbor, and it gave us much pleasure, most of all because of the kinship that exists between us owing to the fact that we both belong to the Croatian nation, from which both Your Lordship and myself pride ourselves to have descended. . . . For the sake of our common Croatian origin . . ."[38]

Nor were family ties easily dissolved by conversion, particularly in the border areas of the sixteenth century where many of the Muslims were only a generation or two removed from conversion. State archives are most likely to record such links between important people, who could grant favors,[39] but humble examples of ties of family or common origin

[35]See T. Matić, "Hrvatski književnici mletačke Dalmacije i život njihova doba," *Rad JAZU* (Zagreb), 231 (1925): 237–38; and Solitro, *Documenti storici sull'Istria e la Dalmazia*, pp. 217–20.

[36]S. Vryonis, "Religious Changes and Patterns in the Balkans, Fourteenth–Eighteenth Centuries," in *Aspects of the Balkans: Continuity and Change: Contributions to the International Balkan Conference Held at UCLA, October 23–28, 1969*, ed. H. Birnbaum and S. Vryonis (The Hague, 1972).

[37]P. Rycaut, *The Present State of the Ottoman Empire, 1668* (London, 1668; reprint, New York, 1971), p. 131.

[38]Gortan and Vratković, *Hrvatski latinisti*, pp. 636–39.

[39]Sanuto records the relations in the first decades of the sixteenth century between Murat-bey Tardić, a convert from a Šibenik family who had risen to the position of military

are not lacking. One of the reasons, Venetian commanders complained to the Ottoman authorities, that the uskoks could not be restrained was that "every one of them has friends and relatives in [Ottoman] territory, not only among the Morlachs, but also among the Turks themselves, who support them, favor them, and share their booty."[40] Was it such ties of family and friendship that brought renegade Muslims (Turco Marco, Martin Poturica, Sule Bosotina, previously known as Suleiman) to Senj to join the uskoks and to raid their former companions?

Maps divide these areas into neat regions, their dashed lines separating Venetian Dalmatia from the Ottoman Empire and the Ottoman Empire from the Habsburg territories. The boundaries these lines represent fluctuated throughout the sixteenth century, carefully surveyed after each peace, mapped by international commissions and confirmed by treaty, village by village. These lines often conformed to divisions imposed by geography: the course of a river, the crest of a mountain range. Yet in many ways these political borders did not coincide with social or economic boundaries and divisions and were in some cases almost irrelevant to the people they ostensibly divided. We have seen how migration served to blur ethnic and confessional boundaries as large groups of people moved from one area to another. Migration spread both Catholic and Orthodox, Croat and Serb communities throughout the frontier region. The entire way of life of the stockherding Vlachs ignored borders—their flocks followed other rules, moving down to the seaside or the river valleys in the cold winter months and up to the mountains in summer, regardless of the political boundaries they transgressed. Although legal boundaries defined the official limits of political authority, other forces—tradition, loyalty, national allegiances—perpetuated the influence of outside political entities on populations beyond their own borders. Neither populations, economic networks, nor social tensions and conflicts were limited by the borders that divided the Ottoman Empire from the Republic of Venice and from the Habsburg monarchy.

These state boundaries and political divisions, however, serve to define a larger area, the borderlands where the two worlds of Christianity and Islam meet. Here the Ottoman *jihad*, the holy war to extend the domain of Islam, was opposed by the *antemurale Christianitatis* in Croatia, the front line of defense against the Muslim conqueror. This border was the scene of incessant bloody skirmishes and raids, first during the Ottoman invasions and continuing even after the borders had

---

commander of the Bosnian sancak, and his brother Juraj, a priest in his native city, who repeatedly interceded with his Muslim brother on behalf of Venice. See in particular Sanuto, *I diarii*, vols. 54, 55, 56, and 57.

[40] A.S.V., Archivio dei Baili Veneti a Constantinopoli, 305: 2 Dec. 1590.

stablilized. Petty warfare was independent of official peace treaties. Formal truce between the states did not deter the inhabitants of the borderlands from plundering raids—nor did such raids affect the treaties.
As noted in an anonymous report on Senj from 1601: "In these parts it is
understood that neither a peace nor a truce is broken unless artillery is
brought up to assault the cities or fortresses with the aim of occupying
them."[41] Here raiding and plunder became the daily way of life for
martial groups loosely associated with the military systems of all the
border states: the Ottoman border raiders or martoloses and the uskoks
of the Christian states.

Border Military Systems

In the sixteenth century both sides of the Ottoman-Christian border
supported a permanent, institutionalized system of raiding. The refugees set in flight by the Ottoman advances and the new settlers recruited
by the border authorities formed the nucleus of plundering bands on
both sides. With the exception of the Republic of Dubrovnik (where
political circumstances precluded any overt support of raiding bands),
each border state found it profitable to assimilate such groups, incorporating them into their military systems under a variety of names.
'Uskok' was one such term. The political divisions of the region organized the development of these raiding bands. Relations among the
states determined whether their activities would be encouraged, to what
extent they would be assimilated, and where their raids would be directed. But just as the powers exploited these bands for their great rivalries, so too the uskoks took advantage of the institutional niche they
found on the border and acted independently of their official patrons,
responding to pressures other than the interests of the states that supported them.

The Ottomans had assimilated plundering bands into their frontier
military system with their first conquests. Chief among these were the
martoloses (from the Greek *armatolos*: guard, soldier): a military organization similar to that of Vlachs from the interior who, before the
Ottoman invasions, had served in similar capacities in their homelands,
guarding roads and providing transportation and military services in
return for certain tax privileges, relative autonomy, and freedom of
movement.[42] The Ottomans adopted this system with little change,

---

[41]In Horvat, *Monumenta uscocchorum*, vol. 1, p. 398.

[42]Milan Vasić, *Martolosi u jugoslovenskim zemljama pod turskom vladavinom*, Akademija
nauka i umjetnosti Bosne i Hercegovine, Djela 29, Historical-philological section, 17 (Sara-

incorporating these Vlach rights into their system of military organization. Many of the martoloses and other Christian irregulars were indeed drawn from the ranks of the Vlach stockherder-colonists who were settled on the Ottoman borders, but others could also acquire Vlach privileges by military service. Refugees who fled into Ottoman lands, for whatever reason, could also find posts among the Christian irregulars in Ottoman service, as well as opportunities for plunder and material enrichment. That this choice was not uncommon even in the early days of the border can be seen from the 1440 statute of Poljica forbidding any subject of Poljica to join the Turks or martoloses on pain of death and confiscation of property.[43]

Christian groups in Ottoman military service performed functions ranging from policing the interior of the state to defending garrisons on the borders. It was for their raids of neighboring Christian territory, however, that the martoloses were most feared by the frontier population of the Christian states. Martolos raids were carried out either independently or in cooperation with other branches of the Ottoman army, and they played an important part in Ottoman military tactics, disrupting enemy defenses and preparing an area for conquest. Their booty was by no means a negligible factor in inspiring the raiders, and it was divided between the participants and the border authorities.[44] These Ottoman Christian raiders were little different in their organization and technique from raiders on the other side of the border. The similarities did not escape contemporary observers, who sometimes refer to them as Turkish uskoks.[45] Minuccio Minucci, Archbishop of Zadar, whose contemporary history of the uskoks condemned their irregular warfare as little better than banditry, described the martoloses at the beginning of the seventeenth century as "a wicked and barbarous militia, of the same order as the uskoks themselves."[46] And indeed, former martoloses were soon found in the ranks of the uskoks on Christian territory.

The first reliably dated use of the term 'uskok' for the armed bands of refugees that appeared with the establishment of the border between

jevo, 1967), and B. Đurđev, "O vojnucima sa osvrtom na razvoj turskog feudalizma i na pitanje bosanskog agaluka," *Glasnik Zemaljskog muzeja,* new series, Social Sciences (Sarajevo), 2 (1947): 75–138.

[43]Zvonimir Junković, ed., "Izvorni tekst i prijevod Poljičkoga statuta," *Poljički zbornik* (Zagreb), 1 (1968): 36–37.

[44]In 1476–77 the fifth part of booty owed by the Smederevo martoloses to the Sancak-bey, the governor of the province, was the enormous sum of 30,000 akçe—equivalent to the annual income of three good-sized fiefs (Vasić, *Martolosi,* pp. 46–47, 76–77).

[45]H.A.D., Lettere di Levante, 22: 202; Rački, "Prilog za poviest hrvatskih uskoka," p. 200.

[46]Minucci, *Storia degli uscocchi,* p. 223. The term 'martolos' was adopted by both Venetian and Habsburg authorities for frontier irregulars used against the Turk. Vasić, *Martolosi,* pp. 194–200; Lopašić, "Prilozi za poviest Hrvatske XVI i XVII vieka," pp. 161–62, 171, 173, 174, 178.

Christendom and Islam in Croatia is found only in the 1530s. Nevertheless, groups of fugitives were probably joining together to raid their former homelands, now in Ottoman possession, as early as the 1460s, after the fall of Bosnia. Certainly by the 1480s, with the Ottoman conquest of Hercegovina and the ensuing wave of refugees to Venetian and Ragusan territory on the central coast, refugees were raiding Ottoman territory, bringing back booty in cattle and captives. In this early period, from the 1480s to the 1530s, fugitives and emigrants set in flight by the turmoil and uncertainty of the invaded lands provided the nucleus of uskok bands. Wherever refugees settled, there raiding bands formed. Even from such distant havens as Apulia, groups of refugees returned to plunder. In 1498 the Ragusan Senate reported that Vlachs from Rudine and Donji Vlasi, having fled the Turks to southern Italy, were returning to harass the subjects of the Porte and of Dubrovnik ("de Apulia venerunt ad hec loca et faciebant damnum subditis nostris et subditis Turchorum").[47] Sanuto's diaries mention numerous groups of these refugee uskoks in the early years of the sixteenth century. For the most part these stayed closer to their old homes, leading a precarious existence in the no-man's-lands on the borders between the states. As far as can be seen from his brief summaries, these were short-lived groups, banding together to provide for themselves and their families in the uncertain frontier world and at the same time revenging themselves on the invader. A typical note describes the actions of a group of uskoks in the Šibenik area around 1504 who had "left the Turkish borders toward Bosnia and settled on our territory" and molested the Turks, "in their persons and in their property."[48] Such uskoks would continue to settle on Venetian territory and raid from there in spite of Venetian peacetime prohibitions, regularly being enlisted in Venetian border forces when open war with the Ottomans broke out.

So long as such bands did not trouble local citizens, subjects of Venice or of the Habsburgs, and so long as they did not provoke too much retaliation from the Ottoman authorities, they were left alone by their new rulers. When these rulers were at war with the Ottomans, government and military leaders tried to incorporate these bands into their own forces, attracting more refugees and eventually drawing other recruits,

---

[47]H.A.D., Acta Consilium Rogatorum, 28: 109'. These Italian refugee settlements continued to foster uskoks: in 1536 cattle belonging to Ottoman subjects was stolen near Trogir "by some Apulian refugees," formerly subjects of the Habsburg Emperor, together with some people of Senj (Laszowski, *Monumenta habsburgica*, vol. 2, p. 264). Even ten years later, in 1546, as the peak of migration to Apulia was tailing off, the Venetian Senate found it necessary to order naval commanders to prohibit the passage "which those uskoks who live in Apulia make to Dalmatia and the islands" (quoted in Vuk Vinaver, "Senjski uskoci i Venecija do Ciparskog rata," *Istorijski glasnik* (Belgrade), 3–4 (1953): 50.

[48]Sanuto, *I diarii*, vol. 6, p. 82.

not necessarily refugees or immigrants, into these now official or semi-official uskok bands.

Under the Croatian-Hungarian kingdom and later under the Habsburg monarchy (both states almost constantly at war with the Ottomans), uskok raiding was very early placed on a permanent footing and given official status. Both the border authorities and private landlords welcomed settlers and refugees for their military potential and as replacements for the war-weakened peasantry. The existence of a defensive border against the Ottomans, organized on both a private and a state basis, encouraged the institutionalization of the raiding activities of the new settlers. Their military role was formalized and defined in agreements, either with private landholders or with the military authorities, which regulated the terms of their land tenure and military service. In turn, the border fortresses and garrisons provided convenient centers around which uskok bands could form. The social organization of the new settlers and the institutionalization of their military activities was carried out on the basis of preexisting patterns: local military institutions and, more generally, traditions of military privileges and Vlach rights, both those that had already existed in Croatia and those imported by the new settlers.

From the earliest incursions of the Ottomans into Croatia the burden of raising a defense force had rested on the noble landholders. Although it was their particular responsibility to organize defenses on their own estates, few could afford to arm fortresses effectively. The deserted border estates provided neither income nor manpower.[49] New settlers who took on military duties on these estates, under agreements specifying their obligations and privileges, improved the ability of the noble families to deal with defense, but these usually did not replace all of the former population or their functions.[50] Feudal incomes were lessened, for the new settlers were excused from most monetary dues. Most of these settlers were stockherders and only slowly shifted to agriculture—as a result the landlord's fields were unworked. The upkeep of fortifications and the supply of garrisons on desolated holdings became a burden to many border landholders, who began to importune their king to take over the responsibility for defense. Some offered their holdings to their ruler in exchange for more secure properties farther from the

[49] A recent survey of urbaria and censuses has shown that after the Ottoman attacks of the 1470s only 40–50 percent of peasant holdings in Croatia and Slavonia remained settled. Josip Adamček, *Agrarni odnosi u Hrvatskoj od sredine XV do kraja XVII stoljeća* (Zagreb, 1980), p. 69.

[50] For a discussion of this phenomenon see Adamček, *Agrarni odnosi*, pp. 424, 700–706; Klaić, " 'Ostaci ostataka' Hrvatske i Slavonije u XVI stoljeću (od mohačke bitke do seljačke bune 1573. g.)," *Arhivski vjesnik* (Zagreb), 16 (1973): 289.

border, others sold them to the state, others asked that their ruler provide the garrisons. In this way much of the border territory came into the hands of the Habsburgs, forming a state-controlled Military Frontier (*Militärgrenze*). It was on the territory of the Military Frontier that uskoks were most numerous and most active in the sixteenth century.

The formal organization of the Military Frontier in Croatia dates from 1522, but its antecedents lie in the frontier defense system Matthias Corvinus organized in the middle of the fifteenth century.[51] Corvinus had backed up the feudal cavalry and the peasant insurrections—forces that could not stop Ottoman raids but only assemble with their passing and hope to confront them on their return—with a series of frontier defense units formed from the Bosnian and Serbian refugees that had fled into Croatia and Hungary. In 1469 a captaincy was founded in Senj to oversee military organization on the Croatian border. In the chaos that attended the dissolution of state authority in Croatia and Hungary after Corvinus' death this border system was allowed to collapse, and the defense of the border was once more primarily in the hands of individual nobles with holdings on the frontier. With the renewed Ottoman offensive of the 1510s, however, it became clear that this unorganized defense could not stay the onslaught, even had the impoverished border landlords been able to bear the expense. The Estates of Inner Austria (Styria, Carinthia, and Carniola) proposed the creation of a defensive zone in Croatia. In 1522, in Nuremberg, the Imperial Diet agreed that the Habsburg Archduke Ferdinand should be ceded the Croatian border fortresses Senj, Krupa, Knin, Skradin, Klis, and Ostrovica. At his election as king of Croatia five years later Ferdinand promised to maintain troops in Croatia to defend the Frontier.[52] He also took over direct control of the two border captaincies—Senj and Bihać. Financial support by the Inner Austrian Estates and Ferdinand's military obligations laid the foundations of the Military Frontier.

This administrative unit was separate from the civil government of Croatia, but not separate in territory. In its early period the Frontier consisted of large and small fortifications organized into captaincies. The number of fortifications for which Ferdinand was responsible grew rapidly. By the 1530s frontier defense was organized in three areas: the Croatian Frontier, the Slavonian Frontier, and the Maritime Frontier, which was centered on the Senj captaincy, the original core of the Frontier. In 1553 the Frontier was united under a single military command

[51]For general histories of the Military Frontier see Rothenberg, *Austrian Military Border in Croatia*; J. Amstadt, *Die k.k. Militärgrenze, 1522–1881* (Würzburg, 1969); D. Pavličević, ed., *Vojna krajina: povijesni pregled, historiografija, rasprave* (Zagreb, 1984).

[52]Ferdo Šišić, ed., *Acta comitalia*, 5 vols., Monumenta spectantia historiam Slavorum meridionalium, vols. 36, 38, 39, 41, and 43 (Zagreb, 1915–18), vol. 1, pp. 54–55.

headed by Colonel Hans Ungnad. In 1578 the supreme command of the Frontier was passed by Emperor Rudolf to Archduke Charles of Inner Austria (Styria, Carinthia, Carniola, Rijeka, and Trieste), who held a broad authority over the Frontier from the Adriatic to the Sava, administered through the Hofkriegsrat in Graz. Even the civil governor of Croatia, the Ban, was subordinate to the General of the Frontier in military matters. Thus the Military Frontier was like an administrative overlay on Croatian territory. Its military leaders commanded the military colonists, the regular troops, and the fortresses. In theory the Frontier authorities had no control over the internal affairs of Croatia except in military matters.

The entire edifice rested on the military colonists, who provided most of the manpower and who brought with them the social organization and the forms of warfare that were to shape the character of frontier life. In principle the Military Frontier fortifications were to be garrisoned by a standing force of mercenaries; however, in spite of Ferdinand's promise to the Croatian Sabor (Diet) to furnish troops to the border, and even with the subsidies from the Inner Austrian Estates, the Frontier was in perpetually straitened circumstances. Even the most strategically placed fortifications were chronically short of supplies. Because of the difficulty of raising subsidies for supplies and men, the number of experienced (and expensive) mercenaries in the garrisons was always small. From 1537 to 1556 the muster rolls show little increase in their number, in spite of the overall growth of the border: an average of five hundred German mercenaries formed the core of the defense system in this period,[53] clearly an insufficient force to preserve the whole length of the border from Ottoman raids, let alone to withstand a major attack. Instead, the authorities relied for the bulk of their forces on refugees from the Ottoman areas, who were settling in substantial numbers on the Military Frontier from the 1520s on, crossing the border in organized groups and negotiating detailed agreements on the conditions of their service with the Habsburg Frontier officials.

In the 1530s an important new element was added to the refugees who fled to Christendom from the Ottoman border regions. The immigration to the Military Frontier began to include a large number of men who had hitherto been a part of the Ottoman military system—martoloses, Vlach military colonists, and other irregulars—for the most part Christian, on occasion a reneging convert to Islam. After the Battle of Mohács (1526), with the relative stabilization of the Bosnian border, the Ottoman authorities had begun to limit the privileges of the Christian irregulars, imposing

---

[53]Lopašić, *Acta historiam confinii*, vol. 3, pp. 390–91; Rothenberg, *Austrian Military Border in Croatia*, p. 31.

upon them the same tax obligations owed by the peasantry.[54] Any allegiance felt by these forces to the Ottoman state was not strong enough to outweigh their loss of status and income. Dissatisfied groups of such border auxiliaries, with their families, began to cross into Habsburg territory. Here they entered the Habsburg Military Frontier system, promising to fight against the Turks in the same way that they had earlier fought against Christians, "acting and proceeding against the enemy in all things as they forced us to do previously," provided their privileges were guaranteed.[55] Recommending that they be taken into the Habsburg military system, the Ban wrote, "These are eminent and dangerous soldiers among the Vlachs, and they did much damage to this kingdom [Croatia] and to Carinthia while they were among the Turks, but now they have returned to the Christian faith." If they were provided for, he continued, all the other Ottoman Vlachs would follow them, allowing Croatia to protect its border.[56] Throughout the sixteenth century many Ottoman irregulars crossed the frontier to take up service on the Croatian border, individually or in groups.

This migration influenced the development of the Habsburg Military Frontier. The martoloses and Vlach irregulars who crossed to Habsburg territory brought with them expectations and habits developed under the Ottoman system, and they were anxious to retain their previous privileges. With the settlement of large numbers of these military colonists the institutional organization of the Military Frontier took on the shape that would characterize it, a shape that in many ways mirrored the military border on the Ottoman side.

Typically, the military colonists in the Habsburg lands held crown land in return for military service and were subject solely to the Frontier authorities. In general the privileges they enjoyed corresponded to those claimed by irregulars on the Ottoman side of the border: a simple hearth tax, no obligations other than military service, and rights to a proportion of the booty.[57] On both sides of the border this arrangement corre-

---

[54]See, for example, B. Đurđev, ed., "Požeška kanun-nama iz 1545 godine," *Glasnik Zemaljskog muzeja* (Sarajevo), n.s. 1 (1946); Kuripešić, *Putopis kroz Bosnu, Srbiju, Bugarsku i Rumeliju*, p. 22. See also Halil Inalcik, "Military and Fiscal Transformation in the Ottoman Empire," *Archivium ottomanicum*, 6 (1980): 283–337.

[55]In Aleksa Ivić, ed., "Dolazak uskoka u Žumberak," *Vjesnik Kraljevskog hrvatsko-slavonsko-dalmatinskog zemaljskog arhiva* (Zagreb), 9 (1907): 128–29.

[56]In Laszowski, *Monumenta habsburgica*, vol. 1, pp. 415–16.

[57]The Žumberak uskoks offer a good example of the process. In the 1530s some 3000 uskoks, refugees from Bosnia, were settled by the Habsburg military authorities in Žumberak. They rejected the privileges offered them at first by the Habsburgs which would have placed them, in essence, in the position of serfs (Ivić, "O prvoj srpskoj seobi u Žumberak," *Vjesnik Kraljevskog hrvatsko-slavonsko-dalmatinskog zemaljskog arhiva* [Zagreb], 20 [1918]: 252–60). Eventually they were granted crown lands on the border, which they held as hereditary fiefs in return for military service. They were subject solely to the Military Fron-

sponded to the system of Vlach rights. This is not to say that all the military colonists or uskoks were Vlachs. But a strong part of the immigration to the Habsburg Military Frontier was made up of Vlach-based groups. These were particularly noticeable in the 1530s and 1540s, when the organization of the border was being formalized.[58]

The Habsburg authorities did not resist the assimilation of these privileges into the military system. The uskoks answered the needs of the border—a large supply of forces with a minimum of cash outlay. Resistance was all the less because these privileges were not a new and alien social phenomenon. Similar patterns had existed here earlier—the Catholic Vlachs of the fifteenth century and other "free" groups who had fulfilled their obligations to their landlords by providing military service rather than by paying taxes and other forms of rent.

The military colonists on the Habsburg Frontier also retained a certain internal autonomy within the military structure of the Frontier. They chose their own immediate leaders, both civil and military, themselves. The Military Frontier recognized these leaders by negotiating with them over conditions of settlement, granting them salaries and commands, and providing them with large land grants (measures that would eventually increase social stratification and tie their leaders to the Frontier commanders). The Habsburg authorities appointed the highest military commands and allowed the local leaders to take care of organization on lower levels. Formal military exercises were planned and led by officers of the Military Frontier, but the daily life of raid and counterraid was in

---

tier authorities and were exempt from feudal taxes and obligations for twenty years, after which they were to pay one Hungarian *forint* per hearth (a tax equivalent to the *filurija* paid by the Vlachs in Ottoman territory). Although at this point the Habsburg court anticipated that they would later be subject to agricultural obligations, these were never imposed. Three years later the privileges for the Žumberak uskoks provided for a constant annual salary for their military leaders and pay for the rank-and-file uskoks during those months when they were officially mobilized, and regulated the division of booty: two-thirds of everything taken in battle was to belong to the soldiers themselves. The remainder was to go to the King, to be used for special awards and to redeem those in Ottoman captivity. Those without pay (and without official rank in the Frontier) kept all their booty (Lopašić, *Acta historiam confinii*, vol. 1, pp. 5–6).

[58]Vasić has stressed (in *Martolosi*, pp. 41–44, 199) that the martoloses of the Ottoman borders, and also the corresponding forces on the other side, were assimilated into the frontier systems as strata that had earlier been privileged (primarily as Vlach stockherders) and that they were by no means ordinary serfs. Particularly in regard to the Habsburg Military Frontier in the sixteenth century this is too extreme a view. The social organization of the Frontier was based on the privileges of these groups, but membership was not limited to them. The border organizations also attracted peasants and absorbed them, allowing them to rise to a higher status and free themselves of feudal obligations. Certainly the peasants around the Military Frontier envied the privileges of the uskoks and strove to attain them. The achievement of the Military Frontier uskok rights was one of the dreams of private Vlachs and peasant rebels in the peasant rebellion of 1572–73. See Nada Klaić, " 'Ostaci ostataka,' " p. 291.

the hands of the uskoks themselves, so that most operations were organized on the local level and social and military hierarchies and methods of warfare retained their traditional patterns.

It should be emphasized that the rank-and-file colonists were paid only when they were mobilized, as was the custom with mercenaries. Nor were all the settlers guaranteed a position with pay. Ordinary irregulars could not depend on a military stipend as their primary source of support, nor was the land granted them always enough to guarantee them a livelihood, although it was intended to provide an income adequate to equip the frontiersman for service.[59] Some uskoks traded in livestock or produce, or in the goods given them as part of their wages, as can be seen from their exemptions from various taxes and tariffs.[60] But, like many pastoralists, they supplemented their income with raids. Booty and plunder were an important part of income on the frontier, particularly for those with no official position and thus no stipend. Ivan Lenković, Commander of the Frontier in 1551, described these men as stockherders and plunderers who moved with their flocks from one wild mountain to another, pillaging Turks and Christians. "This is the source of their livelihood," he wrote, "and not the plow or hoes."[61] The agreements negotiated with the new settlers reflected the expectation that booty would be an important source of their livelihood. Those who fought without pay and position were to retain all their booty, and booty was the source of the only material levy demanded of paid irregulars. The organizational structure that developed on the basis of these agreements perpetuated the emphasis on plunder as the source of income.

The political divisions of the border organized and directed the uskok phenomenon, and the border military systems provided the uskoks with an institutional structure. The conflict between the three great empires that met on the Croatian borders provided an environment in which such raiding bands could flourish. But the uskok groups that found a niche in the military systems of the borders did not raid only when their great protectors were at war. Often their raiding caused considerable strain to their protectors, who were unable to control the actions of their uskok recruits. The clashes between these states, though they provided the framework for uskok action, were not the sole causes of it, and the factors that moved the states were not always identical with the motives behind uskok raids.

The perpetual warfare of the frontier; the lack of effective control by the central governments; the irrelevance of political boundaries to the

---

[59]Lopašić, *Acta historiam confinii*, vol. 3, p. 432.
[60]Ibid.
[61]In Laszowski, *Monumenta habsburgica*, vol. 3, p. 521.

social, ethnic, and religious divisions in the border population and the resulting difficulty in identifying differences between raider and victim (or the difficulty of reconciling these with current concepts of these divisions) have caused historians to regard the warfare of the border as essentially chaotic and anarchic. Yet this was not a war of destruction and annihilation. Military operations for the purpose of destroying the enemy and conquering territory were far less a part of border warfare than were plundering raids, usually involving a minimum of confrontation and battle. Cattle, captives, goods: these were the objects of border attacks. Warfare here is a constant and complex interchange and reinvestment of goods and men.[62]

Nevertheless, it would be incorrect to assume that subsistence was the only motive for such raids. Economic demands shaped the form of uskok life in the same way as the political and military demands of the states did, but none of these was the sole determining factor. The uskok phenomenon derived from the complex reality of border life, acted on by social, religious, national, economic, political, and military forces, each modifying the others, and each with a different strength in differing circumstances. Disentangling this web of possibilities is a daunting task—hopeless in the case of the many bands that operated for a short time on the frontier, leaving only a brief record in the register of some government official. In the case of the uskoks of Senj, however, who found a place in the Habsburg Military Frontier that sheltered them for almost a century, the documentation is more ample.

Klis and Senj in the Military Frontier

The Croatian border cities whose defense had been ceded to Archduke Ferdinand by the Imperial Diet in 1522 would have formed a defensive cordon against the Turk running down from Senj through Knin and Skradin south of Velebit to the fortress of Klis, perched in the mountains above the Venetian town of Split. Knin and Skradin fell almost immediately in a vigorous Ottoman offensive that would continue through the 1530s. Other border garrisons shared the same fate. In 1527, with the surrender of the Obrovac garrison, Klis, the southernmost outpost of the Croatian frontier, was isolated from the rest of the Maritime Frontier by

[62]For perceptive remarks on the social and economic organization of the frontiers, see Sugar, *Southeastern Europe under Ottoman Rule, 1354–1804* (Seattle, 1977), pp. 106-7, and Peter Sugar, "The Ottoman 'Professional Prisoner' on the Western Borders of the Empire in the Sixteenth and Seventeenth Centuries," *Etudes balkaniques* (Sofia), 7 (1971): 89-91.

Ottoman troops on land and by the Venetian fleet at sea. Far to the north lay Senj, the center of the captaincy.

It was in the 1520s and 1530s that Klis and Senj became centers of uskok activity, as military enclaves in the path of Ottoman expansion. These fortresses offered a measure of security to refugees fleeing the devastation of the hinterland and provided posts in the garrison for those who could bear arms. The commanders were not reluctant to take on these uskok troops. Although important outposts against the Ottoman advances, Klis and Senj, like most of the Habsburg garrisons, were kept in straitened circumstances by rulers who could not always find the funds to support them. The mercenaries and regular troops, their pay sent late or not at all, joined these uskok recruits in plundering raids against the Ottomans. As early as the 1520s and 1530s nearly all the elements that would characterize the uskok phenomenon can be seen in Klis and Senj: the cooperation between regular garrison troops and refugees; raids to supplement low or nonexistent pay; the choice of the "Turks" as their direct victims, without excessive scruples over the interests of Venetian subjects; the importance of aid from supporters on Venetian and Ottoman territory. The pattern of Habsburg policy toward the uskoks too was already set: anxious to avail themselves of an inexpensive source of recruits, they accepted their services and paid them as little as possible, encouraging their resistance to the Ottomans with the image of an uskok *antemurale Christianitatis*—though attempting nonetheless to restrict the raiding when it conflicted with Habsburg diplomatic interests.

Reinforcements for the Klis garrison came from the hinterland, from areas hard pressed by the Ottomans. As early as 1504 Georgius Milithich (Militić) and his brother, refugees from Bistrica on the plain of Livno, had come to Klis with thirty-two horsemen, prepared to serve against the Turk for 320 gold florins annually.[63] Militić and his brother, with cavalrymen and horses at their disposal, were probably Croatian nobles dispossessed by the Ottomans. Such refugees were accompanied by many less wealthy and distinguished recruits also fleeing the Turks. With the increased Ottoman attacks in the region between the Cetina and the Zrmanja rivers in the 1520s, uskoks became more numerous in Klis. Troops from the nearby border fortresses of Knin, Skradin, and Ostrovica probably found refuge in Klis as, one by one, they fell to the Turk. References to uskoks, *forestieri*, and *transfugae* "who were accustomed to do damage to the Turks"[64] in the Klis garrison become commonplace in the early 1530s. In 1535 Captain Antun Tadiolović of Senj reported that under Captain Kružić of Klis there were two Vice Captains, one an

63Vjekoslav Klaić, *Povijest Hrvata*, 5 vols. (reprint, Zagreb, 1973), vol. 5, p. 30.
64In Sanuto, *I diarii*, vol. 56, p. 478.

uskok, Toma Gvozdenić, the other a native. Examined on the state of the troops in Klis he responded: "They are very poor, and live by nothing other than theft and robbery, for they have no other jurisdiction, and there are more than 200 among the paid soldiers . . . if they were not forced to live by plunder as they do, one hundred persons would be enough to guard the walls, with supplies and munitions, and it could not be taken in one hundred years, being an impregnable fortress."[65]

Klis was never to be well enough supplied to achieve this state. Throughout his tenure of Klis and Senj, Captain Petar Kružić directed a constant stream of pleas to King Ferdinand, begging for back pay for the garrison, for supplies, and for munitions and warning against the possibility of the fall of the fortresses, particularly Klis. In 1525 two worried Venetian syndics, looking beyond their jurisdiction to Croatian territory, reported that although Klis and its port of Solin were "places of the greatest importance, and highly valued as being on the pass into Turkish territory, and the gates to Trogir and Split," Klis was nevertheless "in the very worst condition, in men, supplies and everything else, so that it is in the most manifest danger."[66] In response to Kružić's pleas, the court often urged him to hold out until supplies could be found and meanwhile to encourage the garrison "however best you can."[67] Ferdinand himself stressed "the Republic of Christ, your own glory, and our cause" in a letter urging the garrison to persevere against "the oppression of these most monstrous Turks."[68] But the troops could not be fed on glory and Kružić despaired of holding the fortress with soldiers who often went months without pay.[69]

Nevertheless, the troops in Klis held their own, repulsing Ottoman sieges and on occasion sallying out to attack Ottoman bases.[70] More often, however, the Klis soldiers carried out raids whose primary goal was plunder to supplement their meager rations, as Captain Tadiolović of Senj noted in 1535. Both regular troops and uskoks took part in these raids, plundering the lands of the infidel whether or not their masters

[65]In Laszowski, *Monumenta habsburgica,* vol. 2, pp. 233–34.

[66]In *Commissiones et relationes venetæ* , vol. 2, p. 16.

[67]In Laszowski, *Monumenta habsburgica,* vol. 2, pp. 149, 306.

[68]In ibid., vol. 2, p. 333.

[69]In 1528 the fifty soldiers in the regular salaried Klis garrison had received no pay for nine months (Laszowski, *Monumenta habsburgica,* vol. 1, p. 128). In 1531 Kružić renounced all responsibility for Klis because of the lack of pay and provisions and a few days later refused to return to the fortress because he feared for his life from his own troops, rebellious because of lack of pay (in ibid., vol.1, pp. 326–27; vol. 2, p. 33). In 1536, just before the final Ottoman siege of Klis, he begged Ferdinand to entrust the fortress to someone else (in ibid., vol. 2, p. 147).

[70]Notably in 1532, when the Klis garrison, with the aid of troops from Senj and Rijeka, destroyed the new Ottoman fortifications in Solin, a little port that had supplied Klis (ibid., vol. 2, pp. 137, 174, 180; Sanuto, *I diarii,* vol. 56, pp. 984–85, 1025).

were officially at war. During one truce with the Ottomans, Ferdinand reproached Kružić, saying, "You offer not only favor, but aid and assistance to many uskoks who have come from Turkish parts, and permit them, together with your subordinates, to carry out many incursions and depredations, of people as well as animals in the said Turkish places, and to do other damage, taking booty and captives in Venetian territory."[71] These raiders claimed "Turks" as their victims, whether on Ottoman or Venetian territory, not hesitating to take Ottoman caravans as they left Šibenik, provoking the Venetians, as Ferdinand went on to complain.[72] Another raid netted the Klis uskoks 1000 oxen, 100 horses, and 5000 sheep from some Vlachs called Popovići (who had apparently brought their flocks down to the village of Zbičje, in the district of Trogir, to winter). In reference to this raid Kružić made it clear that he considered the frontier garrisons the defenders of Christianity against the Turks and that in his eyes "all who live beyond the mountain," that is, all the subjects of the Porte, were "Turks"—and thus legitimate victims.[73]

The Signoria's careful attitude toward the Ottomans, who were affronted by the Klis assaults on Ottoman trade with Venice and Dubrovnik, and a certain suspicion that Kružić was trying to implicate the Republic in actions directed against the Ottomans,[74] ensured that the Venetians extended little help to the fortress when the Ottomans besieged it in 1536. In fact, the Venetian Senate explicitly ordered Split not to give aid of any kind to Klis.[75] When Petar Kružić was killed in battle, the garrison yielded the fortress to the Ottoman conquerors. Although Ferdinand complained that the fortress had contained a quantity of supplies, rumors persisted that poor provisioning had been the cause of the Ottoman victory.[76]

With the fall of Klis in 1537 the tale of the uskoks in Senj traditionally begins. When Klis surrendered, the garrison and citizens were permitted to leave before the Ottoman troops occupied the fortress. It was this group of uskoks and soldiers who were supposed by later chroniclers to have fled to Senj and reestablished the nucleus of an uskok organization

[71]In Laszowski, *Monumenta habsburgica*, vol. 2, p. 252.

[72]In ibid., pp. 253–54.

[73]In ibid., vol. 1, pp. 456. (The document is misdated 1530; it should instead be 1535—cf. ibid., vol. 2, p. 258.)

[74]"The said Kružić thinks of nothing but how to damage the subjects and towns of Your Serenity and how to find ways to induce the Turk to harm this city [Split] and its surroundings, and in addition wants to prove to the Turks that we share in the damage which they [the Klišani] do to them with their armed barks" (Rector of Split, 11 June, 1536, in ibid., vol. 2, p. 278).

[75]In H.A.Z., Arhiv Splita, 78/1: 8.

[76]Ferdinand's views in Vjekoslav Klaić, *Povijest Hrvata*, vol. 5, p. 149; the Venetian Papal nuncio's report on Klis, 9 May, 1537, in *Nunziature di Venezia*, vols. 1, 2, 5, 6, 8, 9, and 11, Fonti per la Storia d'Italia, 32, 45, 85, 86, 65, 117, and 118 (Rome, 1958–67), vol. 2, p. 113.

there.[77] There had been many ties between the two garrisons. For at least six years (1523–29) Klis and Senj had been joined under Kružić's captaincy, and the two garrisons had frequently operated together. When Klis fell to the Ottomans, Senj was the nearest Habsburg garrison—though as war between the Porte and the Venetian Republic broke out in that same year many of the displaced uskoks may have found positions in nearby Split.[78]

The beginnings of uskok activity in Senj, however, dated from well before the fall of Klis. In the 1520s and 1530s the term 'uskok' was not used as freely in connection with Senj as with Klis and Žumberak on the border of northern Croatia—except for an isolated mention of a Gjuro Uschok in the Senj garrison in 1530.[79] Perhaps Klis, more directly in the path of Ottoman advances in the 1520s and 1530s, was an earlier center. Yet Senj too reports similar experiences in this period. In the late 1520s, as the Ottoman threat became more immediate and as immigration in the face of Ottoman advances began to affect Senj, there are reports of raiding activity emanating from Senj. Venetian representatives along the coast, concerned in the 1520s and 1530s for peace with the Porte, carefully monitored the actions of the Senjani. From about 1524 the raiders from Senj began to plunder Ottoman territory and to seize Ottoman merchants and their goods at sea—"and this should certainly be called piracy," Sanuto noted.[80] The Senj garrison carried out military actions against the Ottomans in these years under its Captains, in particular attacking Obrovac, which the Ottomans had taken in 1527, and firing its port in 1530 in a successful attempt to hinder the Ottomans from establishing a naval base there.[81] But other raids had plunder and booty as their more immediate goal. One typical raid in the spring of 1533 was led by Matija Busanić, an uskok originally from the garrison of Ostrovica. His band of Senj uskoks plundered an Ottoman village, killing eight "Turks" and seizing some horses. When an Ottoman border official demanded of the Venetians that the booty be recovered, the Provveditore Generale in Dalmatia sent troops to various places to intercept the uskoks, "but these thieves had fled by a different route."[82]

---

[77]Minucci, *Storia degli uscocchi*, p. 220; *Commissiones et relationes venetæ*, vol. 2, p. 211. Later historians, too, connected the flight of the Klis uskoks to the beginning of uskok activity in Senj (e.g. Horvat, *Monumenta uscocchorum*, vol. 1, p. vii).

[78]The muster roll of the Split Militia does show a number of Klis recruits for 1537–38 (H.A.Z., Arhiv Splita, 161: "Ruolo e registro Contabile delle Compagnie della Militia Veneta, 1535–46"). In addition, the Split registers begin to note restrictions aimed at harnessing the actions of the uskoks in Venetian service (H.A.Z., Arhiv Splita, 78/1: 23', 35).

[79]In Laszowski, *Monumenta habsburgica*, vol. 1, p. 439.

[80]Sanuto, *I diarii*, vol. 36, p. 450.

[81]Ibid., vol. 53, pp. 164, 217, 238, 257, 294, 332.

[82]Ibid., vol. 58, p. 73.

Although well before 1537 there had been uskoks in Senj's garrison from Ottoman territory, raiding in the same way as the Klis uskoks, the fall of Klis did increase Senj's importance both to the uskoks and to the Military Frontier. The Ottoman border with Croatia was now consolidated to the north as far as the limits of the Senj captaincy. In 1540 Venice, after a short period of encouraging military colonists during the war of the Holy League, stopped recruiting uskoks when it renewed peace with the Porte, and Senj became a magnet for uskoks who had nowhere else to flee.

CHAPTER THREE

Origins and Motives of the Uskoks

Because the name uskok implies a refugee from across a
border, usually assumed to be that with the Ottomans, the uskoks that
filled Senj throughout the sixteenth century are most often identified
with former Ottoman subjects. Yet some uskoks were natives of Senj,
and many were recruits from Habsburg lands threatened but not yet
captured by the Ottomans. Others were Croats from Venetian Dalmatia
and Dubrovnik, Albanians from the Venetian territories to the south,
and even Italians from the western shore of the Adriatic. These uskoks
came to Senj throughout the sixteenth century and into the first years of
the seventeenth, and their pattern of immigration changed perceptibly
over the century in consonance with the changing pressures that sent
recruits to the uskoks. This chapter considers that pattern: the rise and
fall of immigration, the uskoks' places of origin, their social and national
backgrounds, and the reasons behind their journeys to Senj. An understanding of these matters may not provide a sufficient explanation of the
uskoks' behavior, as some contemporary observers implied, but the
uskoks' background and experiences shaped their attitudes and actions
in ways that any appraisal of the uskok phenomenon must take into
account.

Origins and Numbers

It is not an easy task to map the changing character of the uskok
community in Senj. The national or ethnic composition of the uskoks is
particularly difficult to specify on the basis of random contemporary
observations. Occasionally an individual is noted as belonging to an
unusual nationality, as were several uskoks from the western shore of

the Adriatic and the Krmpote Vlachs (Krmpoćani) from the Obrovac region, who apparently retained a separate national character into the seventeenth century. In the late sixteenth century the Venetians explained the distressingly cordial relations between the uskoks and the militia in Dalmatia in terms of national identity: "Your Serenity will never be well served against the uskoks by Croats, since both the one and the other are of the same nation."[1] The same national categories are used to explain the heated conflict between the uskoks and the Venetian Albanian troops. Habsburg sources also occasionally identify the uskoks in Senj as Croats—usually in opposition to so-called Germans (subjects of Inner Austria), who were entitled to a certain number of places in the garrison.[2] Yet nationality was only occasionally an aspect that observers found relevant to their interpretations of uskok behavior. More often, contemporary sources dwell on state jurisdiction or citizenship, repeating some variation of the formula used by a Rector of Šibenik in the late sixteenth century: the uskoks of Senj "are of three nations or jurisdictions: first, Imperial [Habsburg] natives of that area; second, Turkish subjects; third, subjects of Your Serenity."[3]

Such comments do not betray an ignorance of the cultural or emotional aspects of nationality in this ethnically mixed border zone; rather, they reflect the diplomatic preoccupations of their authors. Even while recognizing jurisdictional divisions, most observers recognized that citizenship and national identity were not the same, implying that although uskoks were subjects of different states, they shared a common background. As Provveditore Generale Almorò Tiepolo wrote in 1593: "Uskoks are three sorts of men [Habsburg, Venetian, and Ottoman subjects] of the same nation and language, mixed together in these depredations."[4] But contemporary characterizations of the uskoks' national identity do not entirely satisfy twentieth-century definitions of the concept and should not be accepted uncritically. The first problem is that the criteria shaping these characterizations are rarely specified. Such terms as 'Croat' vary in meaning, and, even when it is possible to determine a precise meaning from the context, the perceptions of these outside observers are

[1]In *Commissiones et relationes venetæ*, vol. 5, p. 255. 'Croat' in this context seems to be a broadly national attribution and not limited to the idea of Croatian state jurisdiction, for both Habsburg subjects and Venice's Dalmatian subjects are included in the Croat militia in Dalmatia. Other Venetian reports frequently make the same point about relations between the uskoks and the Dalmatian militia. See *Commissiones et relationes venetæ*, vol. 5, p. 58, and (a slightly different version) A.S.V., Senato, Secreta, reg. 66: 26', "Crouati della medesima natione che gli uscocchi"; *Commissiones et relationes venetæ*, vol. 5, p. 213.

[2]Lopašić, *Acta historiam confinii*, vol. 1, p. 136. See also ibid., p. 280. This opposition between Croat and German could involve criteria based on state jurisdiction (inhabitant of the state of Croatia) as well as national identity (e.g., Croatian-speaking).

[3]In H.A.Z., Fond Šime Ljubića, 8/18.

[4]In *Commissiones et relationes venetæ*, vol. 5, pp. 50–51.

not evidence of the sense of identity felt by the uskoks themselves. And again, this subjective sense of identity is not made entirely plain by the national terms the uskoks used—infrequently—to describe themselves. What did the Senj leader Ivan Vlatković mean in 1612 when he called himself "a poor imprisoned Croatian soldier"?[5] The phrase is less a clue than a part of the larger puzzle—how the uskoks viewed themselves and their relations with the wider world—and must be placed in the context of the uskok phenomenon as a whole to yield its full significance. For now it is enough to note that both observers and the uskoks themselves used the vocabulary of national or ethnic identity as one way of describing uskok origins, using the term 'Croat,' 'Slav,' or sometimes 'Morlach' (in Venetian sources) to emphasize uskok ties with the indigenous population of the islands, coasts, and hinterland and, more rarely, commenting on the presence of other nationalities (Vlachs, Italians, Albanians, "Turks," Germans) in the uskok ranks.

Citing place of origin provides a slightly different way of analyzing the composition of the uskoks in Senj, and at the same time avoids some of the problems posed by the scanty and problematic evidence. Although this approach brings us little closer to the uskoks' own views of their identity, it does make it possible to follow changes in the character of the uskok community, while avoiding anachronistic interpretations of the meaning of these changes. Observers have left general remarks, like those quoted above, on the composition of the garrison. Isolated comments on the origins of this or that individual provide more specific evidence by which we can check the general picture that emerges. There is still a danger, however, that such information is weighted by a bias of the source. References to uskok origins in diplomatic exchanges may be shaped by a desire to attach or avoid blame for raiding activities. Most evidence on individual backgrounds refers to uskok leaders or especially notorious uskoks and may not accurately describe the rank-and-file. Furthermore, Venetian (and Ragusan) observers were most likely to report on those uskoks with whom they were most familiar or whose activities threatened them most directly: those from Venetian territories or areas directly on the border.

One broader and more general source of information on the origins of the uskoks does exist: their names.[6] In view of the widespread popula-

[5]In Lopašić, *Acta historiam confinii*, vol. 2, p. 38.

[6]Given names are often advanced as a source for distinguishing religion or even nationality (see Vasić, *Martolosi*, pp. 144–59), but this method is of doubtful reliability in the absence of other strong supporting evidence. Some given names have a strong regional or confessional coloration (Mihovil is a particularly characteristic Croat name, for example, and Abdulah [slave of God] is a common given name for a convert to Islam). Yet these are not hard and fast rules. Moreover, given names were usually translated into the language of

tion movements of these years, as well as the transformations worked on Slavic names by German or Italian orthography (not to mention by the obvious distress of secretaries faced with long and unfamiliar foreign names), attributions based on surnames must necessarily be approached cautiously. Nevertheless, names do provide one of the few ways of deciphering the origins of the uskoks. The use of surnames was normal in Dalmatia by the sixteenth century and was also common in the hinterland of Croatia and Bosnia. Many such surnames give up little information of themselves (those based on given names, for example, like the relatively common Petrović), but others reveal their origins in a number of ways. Some are tied to specific places, particularly those based on clan names. The Paštrovići, of whom there were several among the Senj uskoks, came from the Bay of Kotor area associated with that clan. This name also provides a confessional attribution, as the Paštrovići were Orthodox. Other uskok surnames (or perhaps more accurately nicknames) are derived from place names: Plavgnanin (Plavljanin: from Plavno near Knin), Waschacz (Bažac: from Bag), Vragnanin (Vranjanin: from Vrana). Similarly, some uskoks had no true surname but were identified by place of origin: Ivan von Topulskh (Topusko), Rade da Cosovo (Kosovo), and so on. Out of some 838 uskok families specifically mentioned in the Senj captaincy between 1530 and 1620, 261 (or approximately 31 percent) can be connected with a place of origin, either on the basis of the name itself or because the place is specifically identified in the documents. This percentage, though not very large, does make it possible to trace directly the areas from which the uskoks came and to see how these changed over time. (This material is presented in graphic form in Maps 3–7.)

Two detailed muster registers for the Senj garrison have survived, one from 1540, the other from 1551. These provide a basis for an analysis of the origins of the uskoks who held an official post in the garrison and received a stipend in the first half of the sixteenth century. The register for 1540 gives the names (and wages for a three-month period) of the officers and soldiers in Senj and in the outlying settlements of Otočac, Starigrad, Brlog, and Prozor.[7] The list contains the names of 236 soldiers, 161 stationed in Senj itself. The members of the garrison who can be identified as being from Inner Austria and those with markedly German names were probably part of the Teutsche Knechte, 15 to 20 career soldiers from Inner Austria who formed the German guard for the citadel. Of the 54 names on the pay list which can be connected with a specific

---

a particular document. Ivan Vlatković might appear as Zuane or Hans, but the deduction that he was Venetian or German would not be justified.

[7] In Lopašić, *Acta historiam confinii*, vol. 3, pp. 392–95.

place, the largest number came from Senj itself. These old Senj families provided almost a quarter of the Senj officer corps. There were natives of Senj among the officers in Otočac as well. Habsburg subjects from outside Senj formed the second largest identifiable group in the garrison. Apart from a few from the nearby settlements of Brinje and Ledenice, these came from two general areas: from the Croatian Littoral and Habsburg Istria and from the hinterland east of the Senj captaincy, an area subject to frequent Ottoman attacks. At least five more members of the garrison came from Venetian Dalmatia and one came from Dubrovnik. Only three can be associated with areas actually under Ottoman occupation.[8] (For a schematic representation of uskok distribution by origin, 1530–50, see Map 3.)

The 1540 pay list thus shows the garrison of Senj, apart from the German guard, made up largely of recruits from nearby—for the most part from Habsburg territories exposed to Ottoman attack but not yet conquered. The command of the garrison was heavily weighted in favor of the noble Senj families. A great proportion of the able-bodied men in Senj, refugees or not, must have served in the garrison, for two years previously the entire population of the city—men, women, and children—had been estimated at only 1000 people.[9] Even clergymen and artisans (cobblers, a smith, a furrier) received pay in the service of the border.

These statistics do not necessarily give an accurate picture of the entire military population of Senj in 1540. Many recent arrivals to the garrison most certainly concealed their origins under names that do not betray their backgrounds. Many recruits must have been added to the garrison after 1528, when the original garrison of 150 men under Erasmo Sauer was described as seriously weakened by death and capture and by the fact that no replacements could be found.[10] There were certainly also other recent arrivals in Senj who received no stipend and were therefore not recorded on the pay list. They may have swelled the number from Ottoman territory considerably. On the basis of the pay list no large influx of uskoks from Klis can be identified, though some of these did eventually end up in Senj. Very likely, recruits from Ottoman territory

[8]Nineteen families, with 24 members in the garrison, were long-time inhabitants of Senj. They provided 11 out of the 47 officers (those paid ten gulden or more for this three-month period). The 23 members of the garrison identifiable as Habsburg subjects from outside Senj had surnames associated with Brinje, Ledenice, Bag, Bribir, Rijeka, Kastav, Sandt Serf, Ogulin, Modrus, Plaški Slunj, Dubovac, Dreznik, Belaj, Bihać, and Blagaj. The five from Venetian Dalmatia were associated with Baška on Krk, Zadar, Novigrad, and Brač. The three areas under Ottoman occupation were Banjedvor, Požega, and Jajce. See also Stjepan Pavičić, "Senj u svom naselnom i društvenom razvitku," pp. 341–55.

[9]Laszowski, *Monumenta habsburgica*, vol. 2, p. 407.

[10]In ibid., vol. 1, pp. 129–30.

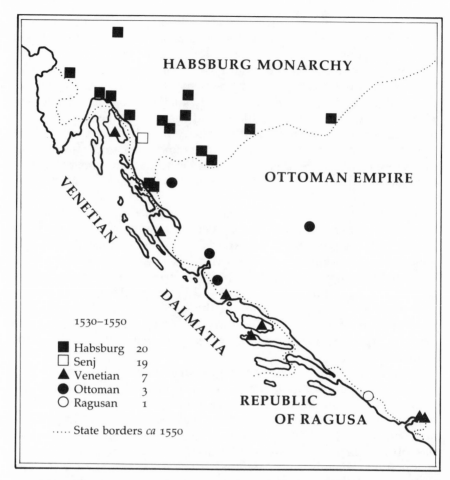

HABSBURG MONARCHY

OTTOMAN EMPIRE

VENETIAN

DALMATIA

1530–1550

■ Habsburg 20
□ Senj   19
▲ Venetian   7
● Ottoman   3
○ Ragusan   1

····· State borders *ca* 1550

REPUBLIC
OF RAGUSA

3. Uskoks in Senj: distribution by origin, 1530–50. Each symbol on the map represents the place of origin of an uskok family in Senj between 1530 and 1550. (Where
there are more than can conveniently be represented by individual symbols, a
number has been inserted, as in the case of Senj.) The total number of families listed
in the table on the map is greater than that shown on the map, both because the map
shows only the Croatian border (and not, for example, Inner Austria), and because
some individuals are identified only by citizenship and not place of origin (e.g., "a
subject of the Turk"). Most of the material presented here comes from the 1540 Senj
pay list (Lopašić, *Acta historiam confinii*, vol. 3, pp. 392–95).

also increased markedly after 1541, when Venice expelled from Dalmatia those who had crossed over to fight against the Turk in the course of the recent war.

The pay list of 1551 confirms a large influx of new recruits, still primarily Habsburg subjects, into Senj over the preceding decade.[11] The numbers of paid soldiers in the Senj garrison had risen sharply in the 1540s in the face of Ottoman advances, though after the conclusion of a five-year truce in 1547 the Habsburgs had somewhat reduced the size of the expensive garrison.[12] Of the 276 men in the garrison in Senj, only 46 remained from the pay list of eleven years earlier. Service in the border wars was no sinecure. Of the paid garrison, more than four-fifths were new recruits. In 1551 the officers' posts were still largely in the hands of professional soldiers from the Austrian lands and members of old Senj families. Senj families were also well represented among the ranks. As in 1540, the paid garrison drew heavily on Habsburg subjects, including only a few members from Venetian Dalmatia and the Ottoman territories. This same year Ivan Lenković, Captain of Senj, seemed to confirm the impression the pay list gives of the small number of Ottoman subjects in the Senj garrison, noting that of the several hundred paid soldiers in the area only 15 to 20 were uskoks in the sense of having fled from Ottoman territory (although he had some 2500 of these under his command elsewhere on the border). This is probably a deliberate underestimation, however, given in response to Venetian complaints.[13]

The Military Frontier muster registers and troop lists for the 1540s and 1550s do not yet mention uskoks under that name in Senj (nor of course do they include the unpaid venturini). Very few Habsburg Military Frontier documents relating to the uskoks in Senj survive from this period. In 1546 Anton Granvelle, Ferdinand's adviser on foreign affairs, disclaimed all knowledge of the uskoks the Venetians complained about.[14] If Habsburg officialdom was less concerned with the uskoks who were providing troops in Senj than with the advances of the Ottomans in central Croatia and Hungary, the Signoria took the matter of uskok raiding very seriously, having suffered from a series of conflicts with

[11]Lopašić, *Acta historiam confinii*, vol. 3, pp. 392–95.

[12]Ibid., vol. 3, pp. 406–11. Members of twenty families from Senj were employed in the garrison in all, both among officers and in the ranks. Habsburg subjects from elsewhere on the border were heavily represented in the captaincy (24 new recruits in all): some four new recruits were from the Croatian Littoral, and the rest were from the hinterland, particularly from the border areas (Cetin, Cazin, Slunj, Topusko, Kladuša, Ogulin, Novigrad na Uni). At least eight new recruits came from Venetian Dalmatia (Rab, Zadar, Novigrad, Šibenik, Kotor). The nine or so recruits that can be identified as having come from Ottoman-occupied territories came from areas close to the coast (Makarska, Obrovac) or from Lika.

[13]Ibid., vol. 3, p. 395.

[14]In G. Turba, ed., *Venetianische Depeschen vom Kaiserhofe*, vol. 1, pp. 472–73.

Ottoman officials who accused the Republic of negligence, at the least, in patrolling the seas. By 1542 a Venetian official was reporting that "there are in Senj two hundred paid uskoks, retained in the name of the King of the Romans [Ferdinand], men most prompt and quick to any robbery or murder, and besides these they are joined in great numbers by others from Croatia and Slavonia who are content to live in Senj with no stipend whatever and accompany the others on expeditions to take booty."[15] Although the muster registers of 1540 and 1551 show no great influx of Ottoman Vlachs into Senj, it is apparent that in Senj, as well as elsewhere in Habsburg territory, border defenses were being organized on a similar pattern to those in the Ottoman Empire, using irregulars, largely recent colonists, living from their plunder, to reinforce the regular garrisons.

A greater number of Ottoman and Venetian subjects joined the uskoks in Senj in the late 1550s and 1560s. (See Map 4.) Giovanni Antonio Novello, who had been entrusted with a Venetian mission to Senj in 1559, reported back to the Senate, stressing the presence of Ottoman subjects among the uskoks: "In Senj and Bakar at present there are about 250 uskoks including those who were at one time *carazzari* [subject people][16] of the Porte and who have fled to the lands of his [Habsburg] Majesty; Senjani; and subjects of Your Serenity, banished by the Rectors of Dalmatia: all three sorts of men pass under this name of uskok." Of the ten leaders of the uskoks he lists, four were Habsburg subjects, three Venetian, and three Ottoman.[17] It was about at this time that the word 'uskok' began to be used as a general term for raiders, rather than specifically for refugees.

The continuous Ottoman raids on the Croatian border between the Kupa and the Una rivers, hardly abating even during the short periods of truce, required that the numbers in the Senj garrison be kept high in the 1560s and 1570s, absorbing new recruits from the borders. (See Map 4.) In 1568 a Venetian emissary to Archduke Charles wrote that the uskoks were more numerous than ever before thanks to Senj's increased reputation. Senj was no longer a magnet only to refugees from the Habsburg frontier, "for not only subjects of the Turk who have escaped

---

[15]In *Commissiones et relationes venetæ*, vol. 2, p. 164. In spite of this observer's emphasis on the contribution to the uskok forces from Habsburg territory (Croatia and Slavonia), he mentions the aid the uskoks receive from friends and relatives in "all the lands of Dalmatia as far as Kotor."

[16]From Turkish *haraç*, land-use tax (though here probably the *cizye*, a poll tax paid by non-Muslims, is meant).

[17]In A.S.V., Provveditore Sopraintendente alla Camera dei Confini, 244: 14 Apr. 1559. This probably refers to the numbers of stipendiati, as an Austrian source records 257 paid soldiers in Senj in 1557. Loserth, *Innerösterreich*, p. 206.

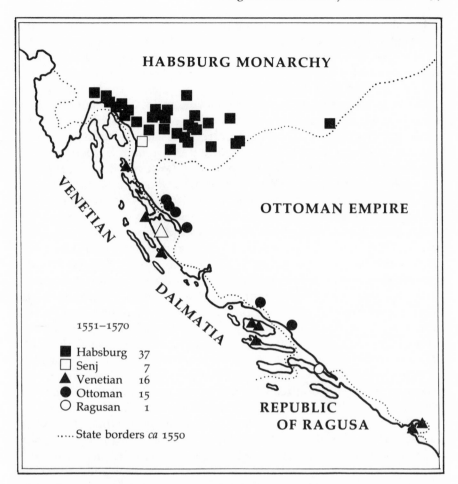

4. Uskoks in Senj: distribution by origin, 1551–70. This map shows the origins of uskok families mentioned for the first time as residing in Senj between 1551 and 1570. Most of the material presented here comes from the 1551 Senj pay list (Lopašić, *Acta historiam confinii*, vol. 3, pp. 406–11.) The Croatian border between the Una and the Kupa was exposed to heavy Ottoman raiding in the 1540s and 1560, and a large number of recruits fled to Senj from here.

from their places and have gone to live there are given refuge under the name of uskoks, but also many who have been banished from Ancona, Urbino, and Apulia, and also exiles from all the islands and nearby towns of Your Serenity, and deserters from the galleys, who act as guides and leaders for these wicked men."[18]

[18]In Horvat, *Monumenta uscocchorum*, vol. 1, p. 5. For numbers in the garrison, see Ivić, *Migracije Srba u Hrvatsku*, p. 124; Loserth, *Innerösterreich*, p. 206.

Uskok immigration to Senj continued in the 1570s and 1580s, but the main catchment area for new recruits began to change. Although Ottoman troops continued to plunder from Bosnia into Croatia between the Kupa and the Una, fewer new recruits in Senj were explicitly connected with these Habsburg hinterland territories. The reorganization of the Military Frontier in 1578 and the establishment of other captaincies (in Bihać, Ogulin, Karlovac) provided a chain of fortifications and border settlements which could absorb such recruits—it was no longer necessary to make the jouney to Senj. Now the Ottoman border provided most of the new immigration to Senj—not, however, Bosnia proper or the recently occupied area between the Una and the Kupa, but rather the Dalmatian hinterland, in particular the Ottoman-occupied territories belonging to Zadar, Trogir, and Šibenik. (See Map 5.) These areas had been ravaged in the Venetian-Ottoman war of 1570–73, and many Ottoman subjects from the hinterland had entered Venetian service. When these were demobilized many, unable to accustom themselves to the peaceful life Venetian relations with the Ottoman Empire demanded, sooner or later ended up in Senj. (These would later be claimed by the Republic as Venetian subjects on the basis of their previous service under the Lion of St. Mark). Others went directly from Ottoman territory to Senj, as in the case of those involved in the abortive attempt to take Klis in the 1580s. References to Ottoman uskoks increased markedly in this period, and by 1588 it was estimated that nine-tenths of the uskoks in Senj were originally from Ottoman territory.[19] Dalmatians too continued to make up a large part of uskok recruits. The Capitano contra uscocchi wrote that same year that "the largest part [of the Senj uskoks] are Morlachs, Turkish subjects, and a part are subjects of Your Serenity, from the province of Dalmatia, who have been banished for their faults by the judiciary, or who go to Senj and become uskoks wishing to lead an evil life, and some are deserters from the fleet, and some are from the places of the Emperor and the Archduke."[20]

In the 1590s Senj received a new wave of immigration from the Ottoman territories and Dalmatia. (See Map 6.) The decade had begun with a widespread famine in Dalmatia and the Bosnian hinterland, so extreme that the Ottomans had forbidden the export of grain, one of the mainstays of the Dalmatian towns. Open war between the Habsburgs and the Porte once again broke out in 1593, to last until 1606 (the Long Turkish War), disturbing life not only on the Habsburg frontier but also on the border between Venice and the Ottomans, in spite of the fact that Venice and the Porte renewed their peace treaty in 1595. Redoubled

[19]Horvat, *Monumenta uscocchorum*, vol. 1, p. 57.
[20]In *Commissiones et relationes venetæ*, vol. 6, p. 18.

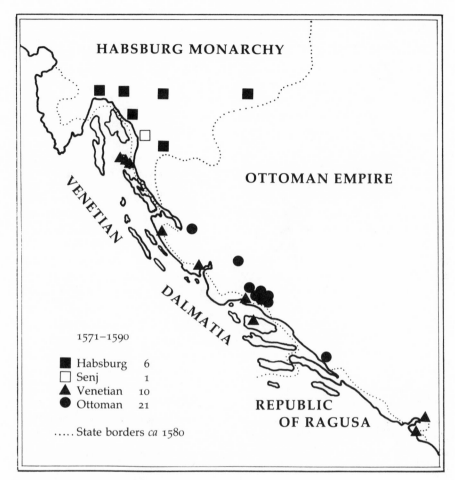

HABSBURG MONARCHY

OTTOMAN EMPIRE

VENETIAN

DALMATIA

1571–1590

■ Habsburg 6
□ Senj 1
▲ Venetian 10
● Ottoman 21

..... State borders *ca* 1580

REPUBLIC
OF RAGUSA

5. Uskoks in Senj: distribution by origin, 1571–90. In comparison to Maps 3 and 4, the smaller number of uskok families represented here implies that immigration to Senj dropped sharply between 1571 and 1590, but this small number is the result of a smaller pool of data: no pay lists or similar sources are available for this period. The large cluster of recruits from the Ottoman hinterland of Split reflects the rebellion and eventual emigration associated with attempts to take the fortress of Klis.

uskok attacks on Ottoman territory in these years were accompanied by Habsburg and papal propaganda among the Ottoman Christians, urging them to rise and throw off the yoke of the Turks, "the eternal evil enemy of the name and faith of Christ."[21] Many recruits from the Ottoman hinterland and Dalmatia came to Senj in this period, particu-

[21]See Rudolf's proclamation of 1595, in Lopašić, *Acta historiam confinii*, vol. 1, pp. 195–96.

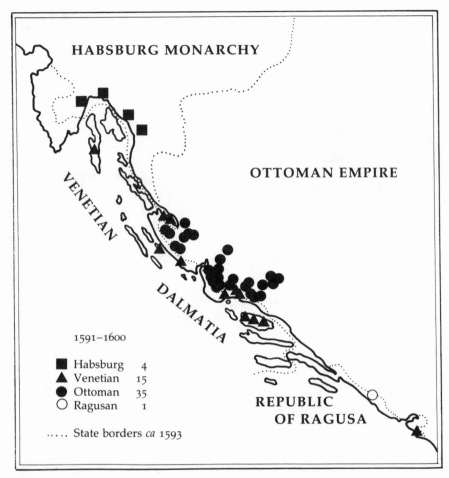

6. Uskoks in Senj: distribution by origin, 1591–1600. The contrast between the number of families first mentioned in Senj represented here, and those in Maps 3 and 4, shows very clearly the shift in the primary field of uskok recruitment from the Kupa-Una region to the Dalmation hinterland. These large Vlach migrations from the Bosnian hinterland to the Habsburg border during the Long Turkish War seem to have settled east of Senj for the most part. The Vlach migration most directly affecting Senj was that of the Krmpoćani, Vlachs from the Obrovac area, who settled around Senj and in Vinodol from the late 1580s. This map, like Map 5, reflects events around Klis, particularly in 1596.

larly after the unsuccessful attempt to take Klis in 1596, when people from the territories of Zadar and Klis who had joined the conspiracy fled afterward to Senj fearing Ottoman or Venetian reprisals. One thousand uskoks or more are reported in Senj in these years.[22] It would be well to heed a warning from an observer familiar with the uskoks' manipulation of their myth at the end of this period: "Although sometimes when they have gone out to raid it has been said that there were seven or eight hundred of them, or even one thousand—but this is characteristic of the country, that they willingly add to the renown of these people, and the uskoks themselves happily put these rumors about."[23] Even so, the last decade of the sixteenth century saw many new recruits arriving in Senj.

The population growth due to immigration to Senj in the 1590s was somewhat offset not only by natural attrition and by the inevitable loss of life that affected a group that lived by raiding and warfare, but also by emigration. Some refugees had always passed through Senj without settling there, preferring a grant of land farther north on the Zrinski and Frankopan estates, balancing comparative security against restricted liberty as private military colonists. But now crowded conditions, irregular pay, and lack of provisions made the uskok life in Senj less attractive than it had been. In 1593, following several years of dearth in Dalmatia and Istria, General Juraj Lenković reported to the Frontier officials that some uskoks were selling their belongings and leaving Senj because they could not find food.[24]

It was in the 1590s, too, that Venice dramatically escalated its measures against uskok raiding. The Venetian forces blockaded Senj and the Croatian Littoral and ambushed and executed uskoks, bringing scarcity to the city and an added uncertainty to an already dangerous existence, and the number of new recruits to Senj diminished. At the height of a Venetian blockade in 1599 Archbishop Minuccio Minucci reported from Zadar that the number of uskoks in Senj "is not rising as it used to, for no one goes to shut themselves up willingly where there is nothing to eat nor to drink. In the last few days a few of the leaders have been killed or hanged, and others have come voluntarily to take a stipend from these *signori* [Venice]."[25] Under conditions of scarcity and want, with little

---

[22]There were 650 in 1591 (A.S.V., Senato, Secreta, Materie miste notabili, 27: 11 June 1591); 1000 in Senj, 3500 in the area in 1593 (Leva, *Legazione di Roma di Paulo Paruta*, pp. 140–41); 1000 in Senj, and 700 in raiding parties in 1598 (*Commissiones et relationes venetæ*, vol. 5, p. 243, and Tomić, "Crtice," p. 36).

[23]In *Commissiones et relationes venetæ*, vol. 5, p. 280.

[24]In Lopašić, "Prilozi za poviest Hrvatske," p. 62.

[25]In Horvat, *Monumenta uscocchorum*, vol. 1, p. 256. Provveditore Generale Pasqualigo accepted several uskok bands into Venetian service, including one headed by Luka Milošević, one of those who had conspired to take Klis in 1596 (A.S.V., Provveditori da Terra e da Mar, 923: 1 Mar. 1600).

opportunity for plunder, some uskoks began to negotiate terms of service elsewhere—particularly those who had come to Senj from the Venetian fleet. In 1592, at the height of his campaign against Senj, Almorò Tiepolo, the Provveditore Generale appointed to deal with the uskoks, told of uskoks who wished to return once more to Venetian service, saying that if he would "reduce their exiles and take them on again either as marines on the galleys or in the armed barks as soldiers, so that they would have a way of making a living, they would be content to return to the devotion of Your Serenity and to live loyally under your shadow until death."[26] Such offers were again recorded in 1598 and 1599, when the Croatian Littoral was again strictly blockaded.[27] Under such conditions many of those who would have gone to Senj to make their fortunes were discouraged. By 1601 it was reported that the number of uskoks had dropped by half because of these energetic Venetian measures and the stringent Habsburg reforms aimed at the uskoks under Commissioner Joseph Rabatta. A Venetian observer reported, "Last Christmas they had nothing to eat but oil left over from an earlier raid, and a little pork, without bread and without wine, as a result of which no one (or few people) have been going to turn uskok, the reputation and opinion of the liberty and comfort which they had been accustomed to find there having waned."[28]

The Frontier authorities continued to encourage immigration from Ottoman territory to the Senj area until the Long Turkish War ended. In 1600 it was reported that 100 such refugees had been conducted to Senj and another 200 to the hinterland, and in 1605 some 700 Krmpote Vlachs emigrated to the Senj hinterland.[29] But few of these immigrants settled permanently in Senj as uskoks, for the early seventeenth century found Senj less attractive to new immigrants: the continued Venetian blockades, the end of the Long Turkish War in 1606 and quieter relations on the Habsburg-Ottoman border, the Military Frontier's reluctance to accept further immigration, and more resolute attempts by the Military Frontier officials to prevent uskok raiding both in Venetian and Ottoman territory and to remove the now troublesome uskoks to the hinterland— all these events made life in Senj unattractive. When raiding was forbidden, many of the unpaid venturini left Senj to raid independently or to take service elsewhere.[30] Immigration to Senj from the Ottoman hinterland and Venetian Dalmatia did not cease entirely even with the 1617 Treaty of Madrid, which ended the war between the Habsburgs and

---

[26]In A.S.V., Provveditori da Terra e da Mar, 1261: 23 May 1592.

[27]In ibid., 922: N. Donà's dispatches of Nov. 1598, June–July, Sept. 1599.

[28]Vettor Barbaro, in H.A.Z., Fond Šime Ljubića, 2/33: 282.

[29]A.S.V., Provveditori da Terra e da Mar, 923: 31 Oct. 1600 (interrogation of Vicenza Salinovich of Senj); Lopašić, *Acta historiam confinii*, vol. 1, p. 340.

[30]I.Ö. H.K.R., Croatica, fasc. 12, 1606, Oct. No. 27 (3 Oct. 1606).

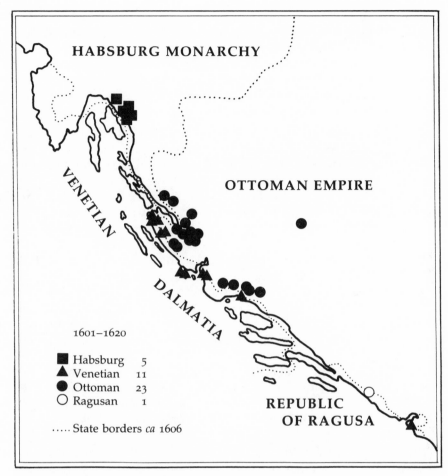

7. Uskoks in Senj: distribution by origin, 1601–20. In spite of the reduced number of new settlers, Map 7 still confirms the primacy of Dalmatia and its Ottoman hinterland as a recruiting ground for Senj. Some of the uskok families represented here are mentioned on the list of those removed to the inland fortresses of the captaincy according to the Treaty of Madrid.

Venice; the treaty required that the uskoks be completely removed from Senj. (See Map 7.) As late as 1620 new uskoks were still arriving in Senj—though the number of uskoks in Senj had dropped to about one hundred.[31] Over the century the character of the city's population had

[31]*Commissiones et relationes venetæ*, vol. 6, p. 293. Some former uskoks also returned to Senj, including some who had taken service with the Grand Duke of Tuscany when banished during the reforms of the previous years (A.H., Spisi Like i Krbave, 1/3 [19 Oct. 1623]).

changed drastically. In 1618 an Austrian commissioner in Senj found that "everyone here is either a Turkish renegade or a Vlach, and there are only five houses of true Senjani, and these are not soldiers."[32]

Why Become an Uskok?

The origins of the uskoks and the reasons that took them to Senj were at the foundation of contemporary explanations of the motives and behavior of the uskok. Friends of the uskoks of Senj presented them as Ottoman subjects, the victims of Turkish tyranny who fled to Senj, avenging themselves by raiding Ottoman subjects. Their enemies responded that the uskoks who attacked only Turks may have been such people but that more of the uskoks were common criminals who went to Senj in flight from justice or in search of easy booty, like as not Venetian subjects from Dalmatia. Inasmuch as they had not fled from Turkish tyranny, they had no ideological basis for their raids and—allegedly—no compunction about the victims they chose.[33] The preceding pages have shown that uskoks came not only from Ottoman territory but also from Habsburg and Venetian soil and included a sprinkling of recruits from other areas as well. The relative importance of each of these catchment areas changed over the period of uskok activity, with old Senj families and Habsburg recruits gradually being outnumbered by Ottoman and Venetian refugees. How different were the experiences and the motives that drove these different groups to Senj, and what were the effects of changes in recruitment patterns on the attitudes of the uskoks?

Senjani. Although many Senj citizens had fled in the face of the Ottoman invasions, other old families remained in the city, and there were legal and social distinctions between the old Senjani and the immigrants. Under the provisions of the city statute, immigrants were *incolæ*, permanent residents of the town with no special rights, with none of the obligations and privileges of the native inhabitants. Even though the number of old Senj families became quite small, the consciousness of a social difference between old Senjani and uskok newcomers was maintained for a very long time. In 1615, after nearly eighty years of uskok immigration to Senj, the new bishop noted in his initial report: "Residents [*incolæ*] are called by the common name of uskoks. However, in their language this should be reserved for those who were born outside

---

[32]In I.Ö. H.K.R., Croatica, fasc. 14, 1618, Apr. No. 4 (30 Apr. 1618).
[33]This reasoning has been repeated by Longworth, "The Senj Uskoks Reconsidered," p. 365, and Adanir, "Heidukentum und osmanische Herrschaft," pp. 82–88.

Senj and set up house there afterward, the number of whom for a long time has been greater than that of the Senjani, who scarcely make up ten families. All the others are Morlachs who fled from the hands of the Turks, and Venetian exiles. Nevertheless, they are all called by this term—a painful and irritating name to those few whose families have ancient origins in Senj."[34] Nevertheless, interlacing relationships eventually did much to blur the distinctions between native Senjanin and immigrant uskok, linking families in a community of interest, regardless of their origins. Intermarriage between Senj families and the newly arrived uskoks helped to weave these ties.[35] So did their common interest in raiding as the basis of the town's economy (though this activity began to break down in the seventeenth century with the growth of restrictions on raiding).

The pay lists of 1540 and 1551 have shown us the importance of the long-established Senj families in the paid garrison during the earliest decades of uskok activity in Senj. As time went on, other Senjani took an active role in uskok warfare, both as officers in the garrison and as unpaid raiders. These included not only representatives of the noble families of Senj, who had long followed military careers, but also more humble citizens. In 1558 the two hundred raiders in Senj included "the servants of the Captain, and of the gentlemen of the area, and others from the town, such as cobblers, tailors, and other artisans."[36] Another characteristic statement from this dossier notes that "when five or six

---

[34]In Marko Jačov, ed., *Spisi tajnog vatikanskog arhiva XVI–XVIII veka*, Zbornik za istoriju, jezik i književnost srpskog naroda, Section 2, vol. 22 (Belgrade, 1983), p. 30.

[35]This melding was nothing new. Senj had been incorporating foreigners into its society since well before the uskok period. Some of its prominent noble families had originated as merchants from Italy: the Milanezi, Veronezi, Furlanići (from Friuli). These had married in Senj and had become completely Croatianized by the sixteenth century. Many uskok newcomers became domesticated in the same way. The Daničićes, one of the most famous families of uskoks, originally probably from Bosnia, settled and brought up several generations of uskoks in Senj, becoming prominent members of Senj society as well as noted uskoks. According to an eighteenth-century genealogy of the Daničić family, Juraj Daničić, the second uskok vojvoda of this name, married a daughter of the old Senj nobility, Helena Veronez, in the 1580s, while his brother Matija Daničić married Katerina Mikulanić, daughter of an uskok who had been accepted as a citizen of Senj and whose family would eventually be ennobled under Emperor Rudolf II. The third generation of Daničić children, in turn, also married into old Senj families (the Blagajići) as well as into newer uskok lines (the Hreljanovići). Juraj Daničić was granted land in Žrnovnica in 1583 by Rudolf II, and he and his three brothers were granted noble status in 1587. (Neither their connections nor their military prowess provided an immediate open-sesame to full participation in Senj society, however, for the patent of nobility by which the Daničić family was accepted into the Senj nobility is dated 1751.) See Mile Magdić, ed., "Prilozi za poviest starih plemićkih obitelji senjskih," *Starine* (Zagreb), 12 (1880): 224–29, and "Prilozi za poviest starih plemićkih porodica senjskih," *Starine* (Zagreb), 17 (1885): 51. (The Mikluanić family background is discussed in I.Ö. H.K.R., Croatica, fasc. 12, 1607, Nov. No. 25 [29 Sept. 1607].)

[36]In A.S.V., Provveditore Sopraintendente alla Camera dei Confini 244, Processus Vegliæ: 3 May 1558 (testimony of Gasparo da Fano).

barks go out pirating, the servants of the gentlemen of the place go also, and those who have no servants go themselves."[37] The sons and grandsons of these families would continue to raid together with the more recent uskoks, both as leaders and as members of the rank-and-file, into the seventeenth century.

Senj's military tradition and connection with the frontier organization, dating from the establishment of a captaincy in the town in 1469, perhaps gave the Senjani an initial advantage in achieving high rank in the garrison (reflected in the number of officers from Senj recorded in the early pay lists). Nevertheless, the experiences of the two categories of uskoks, indigenous and immigrant, were not significantly different. Although Senj served as a place of refuge, it was not itself invulnerable to Ottoman attack. By the beginning of the sixteenth century the town itself had been under threat more than once, and it was increasingly cut off from its hinterland by martolos raids. It was true that the Senjani among the uskoks had not been uprooted from their native homes, but on the other hand they were only the remnants of the original inhabitants of Senj, many of whom had fled in the face of Ottoman attack.

Refugees from War. It was incessant warfare with the Ottoman forces that made soldiers of the families of Senj, and it was also war that sent many refugees into the ranks of the uskoks. The distribution and volume of uskok recruits match the ebb and flow of war on the border—the immediate effect of open war along the Ottoman border was to increase the number of displaced people who then became uskoks in Senj. As raids continued in peacetime, even though on a smaller scale, so too refugees from the "little war" continued to arrive in Senj. Some of the Habsburg subjects in the garrison were career soldiers from Inner Austria, among these the fifteen to twenty German soldiers stationed in Senj as a guard for the Nehaj fortress. However, many more of the Habsburg subjects among the uskoks were men of the borders, who came to Senj from frontier areas exposed to heavy Ottoman martolos raiding, defended by weak frontier fortifications, with few closer military installations where they could seek refuge and employment. They, like other refugees from Venice and the Ottoman territories, rather than go abroad in search of military employment, had been caught up willy-nilly by Turkish wars on their doorstep.

Not only the raids of the Ottoman troops and their auxiliaries swelled the ranks of the uskoks: the raids of the uskoks themselves contributed to the devastation that drove the people off their land. In 1597 the Venetian Papal nuncio reported that the uskoks "have consumed the whole

---

[37]In ibid., 4 May 1558 (testimony of Hieronimo Venesich of Baška).

life of the province [Dalmatia and Istria], so that many peasants, compelled by necessity, have joined them, and from being plundered have become plunderers."[38] Even a prisoner in Senj, taken captive for ransom, might become an uskok himself.[39] The descriptions of some uskok raids suggest that they were deliberately intended to compel the victims to flee to Senj. One uskok leader in Senj, Andrija Frletić, led an expedition against the flocks of his own father, a "Turk," "wishing in this way to force his father to leave Turkey, become an uskok, and come to live in Senj."[40] Presumably this would be most easily accomplished by ruining him. Uskok raids in Lika had the same goal on a larger scale, like raids elsewhere on the Military Frontier which served to depopulate the Ottoman border and strengthen the Habsburg side. Such campaigns of uskok harassment and devastation often culminated in the emigration of entire villages, led by uskok guides, and their resettlement on Habsburg territory. The degree of coercion involved in such defections from Ottoman rule is difficult to divine. In any case, resentment of the uskoks' part in such forced migrations does not seem to have precluded such émigrés from joining uskok ranks to raid their earlier homes.[41]

The Tyrannies of the Turk. Whoever may have been directly responsible for the catastrophes of war which sent the inhabitants of the borders fleeing to the uskoks in Senj, it was the "tyrannies of the Turk" that contemporaries saw as being primarily responsible. This was the interpretation given by Minucci (and many others) of the origins of the uskoks:

[38]In Horvat, *Monumenta uscocchorum*, vol. 1, p. 156. As early as 1533 raids from Senj had provoked Ottoman subjects to beg their rulers to protect them from the constant plundering "for if not they will be forced to abandon their homes and come to dwell on the territory of the [Venetian] Republic" (Sanuto, *I diarii*, vol. 57, pp. 507–8). In spite of the fact that the raids may have been the immediate reason for their flight, even these refugees in Venetian Dalmatia soon saw the benefits of joining the uskoks.

[39]The interrogation of an uskok in the 1611 Senj court records deals with the plunder of some silk on an uskok raid: "It is true that I was Vojvoda Miho Vlatković's captive, and I went with the heroes when the silk was taken, and I redeemed myself with it from said Vojvoda Miho and went free of him, and I have married here in Senj" (in Lopašić, *Acta historiam confinii*, vol. 2, p. 14).

[40]In A.S.V., Provveditori da Terra e da Mar, 425: 29 Jan. 1612.

[41]The Krmpote Vlachs settled around Obrovac provide a good example of this pattern. They were regularly raided by the uskoks from the 1580s. In the early 1600s several large groups were persuaded to emigrate to Habsburg territory and settle near Senj, notably a band of more than seven hundred in 1605. Some Krmpoćani joined the uskoks as individuals, and on occasion larger numbers joined the Senj troops as reinforcements for special undertakings. In 1612 the Senj uskoks and the Krmpoćani were planning a large raid on their earlier homes. See Lopašić, *Acta historiam confinii*, vol. 1, p. 340; Tomić, "Iz istorije senjskih uskoka, 1604–1607," p. 53; Stanojević, "Prilozi za istoriju senjskih uskoka," p. 137; A.S.V., Provveditori da Terra e da Mar, 425: 14 Jan. 1612, 22 Jan. 1612, 4 Feb. 1612.

This name, without however any odor of infamy, began to acquire renown
. . . less than 100 years ago when the Turkish armies . . . were troubling the
borders of Croatia and Dalmatia; so that at that time many valorous men,
unable to live under the tyrannies of the Turk, recalling that they were born
in the faith of the Evangelist, leaving the territories already conquered by
the enemy, retired to some stronghold of Christianity and there, urged on
by sorrow for that which they had lost, and for their subjugated fatherland
. . . raided daily, and did the Turks much harm.[42]

Even after uskok raids had begun to do serious damage to Venetian
interests and tolerance for their raids on Ottoman lands had turned to
dismay and active opposition, Venetian observers still identified Ottoman
tyranny as the main motive for Ottoman subjects to join the uskoks.[43]

What precisely did this Turkish tyranny entail? Apart from the violence of the process of conquest, religious oppression was most often
emphasized. It was because the uskoks "recalled that they were born in
the faith of the Evangelist" that they fled the Muslim conqueror, and it
was to avenge this faith that they raided in retaliation. But religious
persecution was not a marked feature of Ottoman administration in the
sixteenth century. Non-Muslims were subject to higher taxes and special
obligations, but within the Empire religions other than Islam were tolerated and protected, and the administration of non-Muslims was carried
out largely through their own ecclesiastical hierarchies. Although forced
conversions were not attempted in sixteenth-century Bosnia, the occupation of Christian lands by Muslim armies, the conversion of churches
into mosques, the introduction of the child-levy or *devşirme*, and the
conscription of Christians into the Ottoman militia to fight against
Christian states were all probably experienced as facets of religious
oppression. Apart from the approach of conquering armies, however,
few of these changes seem to have aroused men from their lands to join
the uskoks. Instead of provoking rebellion, the introduction of a new
and privileged religion led to widespread voluntary conversion in Bosnia.

[42]Minucci, *Storia degli uscocchi*, pp. 218–19. A century and a half later Giacomo Diedo's
history of Venice could still find sympathy for the original uskoks "who drew their origins,
far from shameful, from certain valorous men impatient of living under the yoke of the
Ottomans; for when those Provinces were occupied, they were forced to save their lives
and their liberty on that coast of cliffs and crags" (*Storia della Repubblica di Venezia*, vol. 2,
pp. 315–16).
[43]See for example *Commissiones et relationes venetæ*, vol. 4, pp. 317–18 (1558); H.A.Z., Fond
Šime Ljubića, 8/21: "The uskoks for the most part are Morlachs, former subjects of the Turk,
who have fled to Senj, unable to bear the tyrannies of the Turkish ministers" (early 1580s);
and *Commissiones et relationes venetæ*, vol. 5, p. 212: "The Turkish subjects, not being able to
tolerate their barbarities, their tyrannies, and their cruelty, fled and united with these
[uskoks]" (1596). This, of course, was always the Habsburg and papal interpretation of the
uskoks' motivation.

But just as the threat of Ottoman victory could be interpreted as a religious threat, so too economic and administrative abuses could be seen as religious oppression in the context of an Islamic state where the Muslim population enjoyed significant advantages (even though the elite was not limited solely to Muslims).

Economic and administrative abuses were far more widespread than religious persecution on the sixteenth-century Ottoman border, and far more likely to provoke the population into rebellion and flight. These began to appear in the Ottoman Balkans from the mid-sixteenth century.[44] The Ottomans needed increased revenues for their expanded administration and for the maintenance of an army that relied more and more on mercenaries. They raised taxes and introduced and then institutionalized special levies. The Ottoman feudal system began to change: land that had been granted to *sipahis* (cavalrymen) as a reward for military service at the pleasure of the central government was converted to hereditary property. The central administration had less and less control over the local military elites and often could not prevent them from making higher demands of the peasants on their estates or from extracting these increased dues by illegal and violent methods. At the same time many of the privileges of the Christian population were curtailed.

The general malaise of the late sixteenth-century Ottoman Empire was perceived on the local level as economic oppression and social injustice. Increased demands meant more pressure on the peasant producers of wealth. The obligations, taxes, and strict rules of conduct of the Ottoman state might be resented but were bearable. But a sudden increase in taxes, the arrival of a new, self-willed administrator, the collapse of the system of justice, the replacement of routine by unpredictable chaos or the gradual worsening of conditions to an unendurable point could push the peasantry to rebellion or into the ranks of the uskoks. One example from an Ottoman source, a 1590 *arz* (statement) issued by the *kadi* (magistrate) of Gabela on the Neretva River, illustrates the type of problem which arose. The people of the Neretva delta, a favorite approach of the uskoks to the shipping from this point, had been free of all taxes and obligations except for a tribute of 100 *aspers* and 20 *aspers* for extraordinary expenses, a sum used to maintain guards. Recently the area had received a new tax contractor, who demanded higher taxes and additional levies: "Where the poor subjects had paid 120 *aspers* in all as tribute, the said Mehmet-aga, contrary to the order of the Sultan, takes 300 *aspers* from each as tribute, and against orders rides through the areas six and seven times a year with 30 people at a time, doing the greatest wrongs and injustices to the aforementioned subjects." As a

[44]Inalcık, "The Ottoman Decline and Its Effects upon the *Reaya*," pp. 338–54.

result most of the population fled to the Venetian islands.[45] Reports from the Venetian border areas do not ignore the place of economic pressures among the "Turkish tyrannies" inflicted on the Ottoman subjects, "who are fleeing from the many outrages, extortions, and taxes to which the sancak-beys and their ministers subject them." These burdens made it impossible for them to live under the Ottomans. In this particular case, the Venetian officials were reluctant to accept this immigration, but "it is a lesser evil that they flee to us, than if they were to go to Senj."[46] Other sources make it clear, however, that when such Ottoman emigrants became discontented with their circumstances in Dalmatia, they quite often did go on to Senj.

People living close to the edge, those with few privileges and little economic power, in this case primarily the poorer Christian peasants with little land, were the first to be ruined by any general worsening of conditions and the first to see the road to a recovery of sorts lying through Senj. Not only the peasantry was affected. The positions of various privileged Christians, in particular the Christian military auxiliaries, were steadily eroded over the century. These formerly privileged groups either retained their privileges by converting to Islam or rebelled against the Ottoman system. Any chance explosion of rebellion against local conditions could lead these Christian Ottoman subjects to raise themselves "from the Turkish lands, in order to live faithfully among Christians and to be able to die in Christendom."[47]

This was the statement of a large group of Krmpote Vlachs who had been guards of the Lika Sancak-bey, but whose resultant privileges were being curtailed by the Ottomans. After years of individual migration to Senj, in the early 1600s they fled as a group from Ottoman territory near Obrovac to Lič, in the Habsburg hinterland of Vinodol. Their interpretation of their motives is revealing. Although they had been in the service of the Ottoman military system and were rebelling against their loss of economic and social privileges within this system, they presented their choices in terms of the religious divisions of the border and their flight as divinely guided. (While still in Lika they had been "illuminated in our hearts by the Holy Spirit, and called into the desert of Lič by St. John the Baptist in a night-dream.")[48] Perhaps they framed this explanation pri-

---

[45]Arz issued by Mehmet, kadi (judge) of Gabela on the Neretva river, 1590, obtained in Istanbul by the Venetian bailo (in A.S.V., Archivio dei Baili Veneti a Constantinopli, 305: 1590).

[46]Anonymous report of the early 1580s from Dalmatia, which gives the details of taxes sent to Istanbul from Zemunik: 500 and more thalers every quarter, all taken from the Christian Morlachs (in H.A.Z., Fond Šime Ljubića, 8/21).

[47]In Laszowski, "Urbar vinodolskih imanja knezova Zrinskih," pp. 106–7 (and Lopašić, Acta historiam confinii, vol. 1, pp. 343–44).

[48]In Á. Karolyi, " 'Vlachen'-Auswanderung aus der Gegend von Bihać zu Ende des 16.

marily to appeal to the Habsburg authorities, yet it is easy to see how increased taxes and the loss of privilege could be experienced as religious oppression in the circumstances of the border. In the minds of Christian subjects, the opposition between Christianity and Islam combined with other, more material grievances to give their resentment against Muslim rulers and lords an ideological basis. Whatever the individual motives for flight to Senj, the uskoks would phrase their resentments against the Turk in the vocabulary of crusade.

Muslim borderers also found Senj a magnet, for economic and administrative abuses in the Ottoman Empire affected Muslim subjects as well as Christians. The discontent of the Muslim peasantry in Bosnia at their increasing obligations is usually discussed only from the later seventeenth century, when several rebellions call attention to its existence, but evidence of dissatisfaction can be seen much earlier in the sixteenth century in the emigration of Muslims to the Christian borders.[49] Some Muslims joined with Christian subjects of the Porte in protest and rebellion. In 1604, for example, the leaders of the population of Popovo and Zažablje, Ottoman territories in the Hercegovinian hinterland of Dubrovnik, joined together to abjure their Ottoman rulers and to offer their loyalty to the Habsburg crown. In addition to Orthodox and Catholic leaders, there was a Muslim representative, Husein Pašić, and it was specifically noted that all three faiths were in agreement on this matter. (Their proclamation began: "At the meeting and assembly of all Popovo and Zažablje, all together, before Turks, Catholics and Orthodox, with one will, desire and heart. . . .")[50]

The names and nicknames of a number of uskoks suggest Muslim connections: Muradt, Turco Marco, Turco Ivan, Guli-baba, Poturicza. Venetian informants give tantalizing glimpses of renegade Muslims in Senj: "Churem Hajduk, formerly a Turk from Velim"; "Vuksan Vulatcovich from Žegar, Turkish territory, formerly a Turk, turned Christian";

Jahrhunderts," *Wissenschaftliche Mitteilungen aus Bosnien und der Herzegovina* (Vienna), 2 (1894): 266. Many other such letters and petitions use the same religious vocabulary. See, for example, the letter of the leaders of Lika in 1609, asking for aid for a rebellion against their Ottoman overlords "for the glory of God, and the exaltation of the holy mother church, and for our salvation" (in Theiner, *Vetera monumenta Slavorum meridionalium historiam illustrantia*, vol. 2, pp. 101–3).

[49]See A. Sućeska, "Bune seljaka muslimana u XVII i XVIII stoljeću," *Zbornik radova Istorijskog instituta*, 1 (Belgrade, 1976). As early as the 1590s the Archbishop of Zadar, Minuccio Minucci, proposed a special fund to provide for the many Muslim immigrants who had fled to Zadar and converted (Marani, *Atti pastorali*, pp. 50, 52–53, 59–60).

[50]"Na zboru i skupštini svega Popova i Zažablja inokupno pred Turci, karstijani i hristjani, ednom volom i hteniem i srciem . . ." (in Ć. Truhelka, ed., "Nekoliko mladjih pisama hercegovačke gospode pisanih bosančicom iz dubrovačke arhive," *Glasnik Zemaljskog muzeja* (Sarajevo), 26 (1914): 478). *Kršćani* and *hristjani* in opposition generally refer to Catholic and Orthodox respectively, though both words mean, literally, 'Christian.'

"Zorzi Vragnanin from Vrana, a Turkish fortification in the district of Zadar, formerly a Turk, turned Christian, familiar with Lika."[51] There is so little information about these renegades in Senj that it is difficult to speculate on their motives. Certainly the increases in taxes and the other economic pressures that can be traced from the mid-sixteenth century affected the Muslim peasants, though these were fewer in number and slightly less burdened with taxes than Christians of comparable status. It seems safe to assume that the Muslim recruits to Senj came primarily from their ranks.

Given the crusading self-image and attitudes of the Christian border, there can be little doubt that a Muslim recruit, whatever his motives for going to Senj, would soon be baptized a Christian. It would be interesting to know how such former Muslims among the uskoks responded to the air of religious zeal which characterized the resentment of the Christian refugees from the Ottoman Empire, but there is very little evidence. In 1599 one Muslim, taken prisoner on a raid, turned uskok and was immediately baptized in Senj—apparently less from conviction than from convention. A Venetian emissary in Senj reported the case: "He is Albanian and speaks a little Croatian. When I asked him to make the sign of the Cross he laughed and said he didn't know how." Nor did he know the Pater Noster or any other prayers. The Venetian despaired of his fate ("What can he learn of Christianity here, where they live from plunder!") and reported himself convinced that this Ali had become an uskok only to save his life and to enrich himself. Perhaps this was so. Because of the way the context of border warfare was framed, however, flight from Ottoman territory and participation in the uskok opposition to the Ottomans, whatever the original motive, had to be expressed in religious terms. No other category existed.

Muslim origins or connections were certainly no hindrance to acceptance and advancement among the uskoks. Ali, the Albanian Muslim recruit, was accepted among the uskoks and betrothed to a Senj girl immediately after his baptism, though she was still too young to wed. One Sule Bosotina from Zemunik, "formerly a Turk called Suleiman," at twenty-six "became a Christian in Senj, having become an uskok." He was the leader of a band of uskoks, with a wife, sons, and two brothers in Senj. (His ten-year career as an uskok ended when, dissatisfied with his rarely paid wages and his plundering operations curtailed by the strict Venetian blockade of 1599, he arranged to desert to the Venetians on the promise of a regular salary.)[52]

Occasionally, discontent with the Ottomans erupted in large-scale

[51]In A.S.V., Provveditori da Terra e da Mar, 922: 12 Mar. 1599.
[52]In ibid.: 12 Mar. 1599; 23 July 1599; 21 Sept. 1599; 923, 1 Mar. 1600.

rebellion, and the subsequent flight from retribution and resettlement of the population on Habsburg territory would bring many new recruits to Senj at once. Emigration from the Klis sancak provides an example of the ways in which Ottoman subjects became uskok recruits. In the wake of the Ottoman capture of Klis in 1537, a number of soldiers of the Klis garrison eventually took service in Senj, a link that was mythologized by the uskoks and their observers as the origin of Senj's role as a defender of the border of Christendom. In the decades that followed, the Ottoman authorities, finding it difficult to ensure order and security in the exposed border district of Klis, imposed economic and administrative pressures on the population; these were compounded by raids from across the border. A steady trickle of individuals left the district to join the uskoks in Senj, the events that provoked their flights illustrating their discontents: a crop failed, a new tax imposed, privileges rescinded, an official murdered. By 1572 the Klis sancak was in a state of unrest, as a Venetian observer noted:

> The Christians pay a tribute or *haraç* to the Turks, and they are oppressed, vexed, and tyrannized by the Turks beyond all measure, their goods are plundered by force, and many times their sons are taken too, and are made apostate, later to be seen in a state and a religion foreign to them. They are never the patrons of what they own, or sure of enjoying what they possess. They desire nothing else, as has often been heard from them, than to see a strong Christian banner unfurled in war, on which they could lean. They would take up arms and revenge themselves for the many violences used against them.[53]

The belief that the Christians under Ottoman rule would eagerly take up arms encouraged a series of plots to retake Klis with the aid of uskoks—each accompanied by a rebellion in the sancak. An unsuccessful attempt by Venetian forces in 1572, in the course of Venetian-Ottoman hostilities, relied on uskoks in Venetian service, many of whom had fled from the sancak in the course of the war.[54] A decade later resentment against the Ottomans once again encouraged a conspiracy to deliver Klis into the hands of the uskoks with the aid of the local population. Among the conspirators was the leader of the Klis martoloses, Dimitar Rupčić, who would become a noted uskok harambaša in the years following the failure of the attempt and the subsequent flight to Senj of many of those involved.[55] The example of the Klis conspirators

---

[53]In *Commissiones et relationes venetæ*, vol. 4, pp. 46–47.

[54]A.S.V., Capi del Consiglio dei Dieci, Lettere dei Rettori, 301: 4 Nov. 1572. This volume also contains many other reports on attempts to take Klis in 1572 and 1582.

[55]Ibid., 26 Aug. 1582. Rupčić was described in 1599 as being originally from Poljica, by then a long-time inhabitant of Senj, with a stipend of 12 florins a month (A.S.V., Provveditori da Terra e da Mar, 922: 12 Mar. 1599).

inspired other uprisings in the sancak. One area near the borders of the Trogir district found that it was "no longer able to bear the insolences, violences against their women, and the other dishonest things" the local officials committed against them. The villagers made common cause with the uskoks and "through their spies gave up these Turks to the uskoks," joining them in killing some thirty of the Muslim officials, "and so executed their vendettas against them." Immediately afterward, fearing retribution from the sancak-bey, the entire village (about three hundred people) fled, guided by the uskoks, to the Croatian border, where many joined the uskoks in Senj.[56] The next attempt to take Klis, in 1596, in which the greater part of the province of Poljica joined other inhabitants of the sancak in rebellion against Ottoman administration, also ended in a large-scale flight to Senj, where the refugees rejoined their compatriots, emigrants from earlier years.[57] Uprisings of this sort, however, happened only seldom in comparison to individual acts of rebellion and flights from retribution, which were less dramatic but in their cumulative effect on the character of the uskoks just as important. It would be wrong to interpret this effect as solely a matter of the numbers of Ottoman subjects joining the uskoks—the fact of their flight "from the Turkish lands, in order to live faithfully among Christians," as the Krmpote Vlachs put it, and their reception by Senj and by Western observers as rebels against the infidel, also had an important effect on subsequent perceptions of their place as border soldiers.

Flight from Venetian Territory. Of course, heroic rebellion against Ottoman tyranny and flight to the uskoks to take vengeance, viewed from another perspective, could be seen as insolent crime against the authority of the state and flight from well-merited justice. In the eyes of many Venetian administrators, the same acts that when committed by Ottoman subjects were acts of rebellion against Turkish tyranny, when committed by Venetian subjects were heinous and arrogant crimes. The difference in Venetian attitude according to the origins of the uskoks can be seen in Provveditore Generale Zuane Bembo's remarks of 1598: "[The uskoks] are of two sorts of persons, either Turkish subjects or subjects of Your Serenity. The former flee from their country because of the extortions and tyrannies to which the Turks subject them; the latter leave the

---

[56] A.S.V., Archivio dei Baili Veneti a Constantinopoli, 305: 14 Apr. 1583. See also Horvat, *Monumenta uscocchorum*, vol. 1, pp. 34–35; *Commissiones et relationes venetæ*, vol. 6, p. 19. L. Jelić, ed., "Isprave o prvoj uroti za oslobodjenje Klisa i kopnene Dalmacije od Turaka g. 1580–1586," *Vjesnik Kraljevskog hrvatsko-slavonsko-dalmatinskog zemaljskog arhiva* (Zagreb), 6 (1904): 97–113, gives other descriptions of Klis discontent.

[57] *Commissiones et relationes venetæ*, vol. 6, p. 54. See also Chapter 7 for the 1596 attempt to take Klis.

islands and other places, and also the galleys of Your Serenity, and for the most part are people who, having committed some excess or crime, rather than fall into the hands of justice, flee and go to Senj."[58]

In spite of the Venetian distinction, the line between the motives of Ottoman and Venetian uskoks is not so clear. The commission of some prosaic domestic crime sent many a fugitive, both Venetian and Ottoman, to Senj. Petty crime was not limited by citizenship, nor was rebellion against state authority a prerogative only of Ottoman subjects. Many Venetian Dalmatians were also affected by socioeconomic changes and administrative abuses. Like many uskoks from Ottoman territory, Dalmatian uskoks came primarily from the poor and those whose privileges were suddenly threatened. Like Ottoman uskoks too, Dalmatian subjects could often place their motives for flight to Senj in the context of struggle against the Turk.

The Ottoman invasions and Venice's disastrous Turkish wars caused a general decline of Dalmatia's economy throughout the sixteenth century. There was some revitalization of trade on islands less exposed to the Ottoman onslaught, but elsewhere, particularly on the mainland, war and emigration led to a sharp drop in the population and a fall in production of all types. Even after the establishment of official peace after the 1570–73 war the results remained. Venice's renewed trade with the Ottoman Empire did little for the revitalization of the local economy. The profits went to foreign companies—in particular those based in Venice. Even the success of Split was as a transit port, for local production received little impetus from its growth, and in addition its success led to the decline of several other smaller ports. Much Dalmatian territory was lost to the Ottomans in the 1570–73 war, so that the communes were deprived of their agricultural hinterlands. Famine and plague appeared again and again, and even in years of good harvest grain had to be imported from Italy. The narrow lands that remained to the towns were crowded with recently arrived refugees, who had to accept whatever conditions they were offered on the landlords' fields or else work Ottoman land, far from the protection of Venetian troops. Venetian administrators constantly referred to the poverty of all classes in Dalmatia, though as one rector remarked of the Šibenik area, "They are all, without distinction, poor, but the peasantry of the district more so than the rest."[59] Another rector of the same district, again discussing its poverty, remarked that "this is the reason that there are so many criminals and that they hazard every sort of larceny."[60] Recently arrived refugees

[58]In ibid., vol. 6, p. 243.
[59]Ibid., vol. 6, p. 140.
[60]Ibid., vol. 6, p. 122.

huddled in ramshackle suburbs at the gates of the cities. Outside the walls of Šibenik there were 275 people living in some fifty-seven huts built of sod *"alla rustica."* Impoverished, with no secure source of support, free of the discipline of the city gates and at liberty day and night to come and go as they chose, these refugees in particular did not hesitate to take up with the uskoks.[61] This picture of the Šibenik district in the mid to late sixteenth century would have been equally applicable to most of Dalmatia, where impoverished and resentful Venetian subjects and recent immigrants raided across the border, either independently or in company with the uskoks.

Venice strictly prohibited any plundering of Ottoman territory or citizens because it posed danger to Venetian-Ottoman relations. Raiders were severely punished if they could be caught, not always an easy task, for the local peasantry united to protect those whose actions they approved—and the official policy of conciliation of the border Ottomans was not universally popular. Some independent raiding went on almost constantly, as Ottoman complaints to the local authorities attest. In the context of one raid from the Zadar district in 1557 the Venetian rector reported back to the Signoria: "To tell Your Serenity the truth, the Turks are more molested by those of the district than those of the district are molested by the Turks, for the greater part of them are indomitable thieves, and men of the borders, worse than which cannot be said."[62] In speaking of the cooperation of Venetian subjects with the uskoks in their depredations, the Rector of Hvar noted in 1577, "I cannot take any remedy. . . . What can I do? This sort of man hides in the mountains and the forests, and little cares if I issue a proclamation or banishment against him." He had tried this solution, but "they come and go where they like, in contempt of the regiment, as I understand various other outlaws in this jurisdiction do, and they have such charity among themselves, if that is the right word, that one never denounces another."[63]

In spite of its limited effectiveness, the punishment for raiding or for helping the uskoks, particularly if the perpetrator could not be apprehended (as was often the case), was most often banishment—exile from the local district or, in more serious cases, from all possessions of the Republic, under pain of a fine or death. Where else should an exiled man take refuge but in Senj? Exiles from Dalmatia and the islands were noted in Senj by the 1560s.[64] Toward the end of the sixteenth century the authorities had so often resorted to banishment in Venetian Dalmatia that in the 1590s they questioned the indiscriminate use of this punish-

---

[61]Ibid., vol. 6, p. 133.
[62]Ibid., vol. 3, p. 102.
[63]In A.S.V., Archivio dei Baili Veneti a Constantinopoli, 305: 16 Mar. 1577.
[64]Horvat, *Monumenta uscocchorum*, vol. 1, p. 5.

ment for an increasing variety of offenses, for banishment was "a source of damage, and notable mischief, for when men are banished they go with the uskoks and become our enemies."[65]

Perhaps partly as a result of Dalmatian participation in the conspiracies to deliver Klis to the uskoks and the obvious opposition of some Dalmatians to Venetian relations with the Ottomans, many rectors seem to have felt a need for severe measures and tight controls over their subjects. By 1613 Filippo Pasqualigo, Provveditore Generale in Dalmatia, was reporting to the Senate that Venice's subjects were "lacerated not only by the uskoks and by the troubled borders but also (it can be said because it is the truth) by many of those who are sent to govern them." Istria in particular was "more than ever like a moribund body, almost deprived of spirit, languishing, so to speak, beneath the eyes of its ruler." The rectors had raised the punishments in civil and criminal cases and had introduced many high fines and new restrictions, so that the people cannot "go in and out of their lands, their barks, even their own houses, sell or buy even an apple or any other little thing; nor even, one could say, open their mouths or draw a breath" without breaking some rule and finding themselves fined or banished.[66]

In 1573 the Rector of Šibenik faced a population that lived under such a system and that was "by nature opposed to enduring commands, even if light and pleasant," particularly in the rebellious atmosphere that followed the attempt on Klis the previous year, and he decided to detain offenders immediately, for otherwise they fled to the countryside, "where they remain, and live in security, with no fear or suspicion that they will be molested . . . and if it becomes necessary to proceed against someone to punish him for some crime, he immediately goes with the uskoks as his only refuge . . . but this takes place for the most part among the lower sort [*la gente bassa*], workers in the fields and similar types." Either at large in the fields or with the uskoks, he continued, such a fugitive was secure from attack by his fellow citizens.[67]

The Rector did not specifically mention the crimes these uskok fugitives had committed. Certainly some fugitives were murderers or thieves. The oft-stressed sympathy and support these criminals could count on suggests, however, that many of their acts were crimes only in terms of Venetian law. They did not conflict with the shared values of the community, particularly of the rural population, which was most often accused

[65]In *Commissiones et relationes venetæ*, vol. 5, p. 233. See also ibid. vol. 5, pp. 210, 212; vol. 6, p. 171.

[66]This was even less supportable as these people "border closely on the lands of another ruler [the Habsburgs], where the people enjoy many liberties and are in truth better treated" (in *Commissiones et relationes venetæ*, vol. 6, pp. 197–98).

[67]In ibid., vol. 5, p. 223.

of supporting these fugitives. Little popular sympathy was shown for crimes that transgressed these values, such as theft between neighbors, murder, or sexual crimes, all punishable not only by Venetian law but also by the customary law of the community. But it was primarily the interests of the state that were harmed by such acts as the theft and contraband sale of salt (a state monopoly since Venice's acquisition of the Dalmatian communes in the fifteenth century). This was a practice the Venetian rectors often reported. One complained about theft from the salt pans: "I do not know what shift to make, for I fear that the people are almost all of an accord, so that to increase the guard would mean, perhaps, to increase the number of thieves."[68] Raiding the "Turk," in spite of the danger of bringing retaliation on the area, was also approved by much of the population, though not by Venetian administrators. The support extended to uskok fugitives by their fellows in the teeth of Venetian displeasure hints that becoming an uskok in some circles had the same flavor of reaction to perceived injustice among Dalmatians as it had among Ottoman subjects, for much the same reasons.

Resumption of Military Service. Demobilized soldiers and marines were also to be found among uskok recruits. Some of these military men had served under the Ottomans, as had Dimitar Rupčić, leader of the Christian martoloses of Klis, and the Krmpote Vlachs, who had acted as Ottoman irregulars, fleeing to Habsburg territory when their privileges and posts were curtailed. Others were local peasants and refugees from the borders, recruited into Venetian service during the Ottoman wars, whom peace suddenly made redundant. In 1539 and 1573 Venetian commanders disbanded the troops they had so recently drummed up, turned away the Ottoman subjects anxious to enlist, and ordered that all raiding, encouraged until so recently, cease. Some of the troops found permanent places in the city garrisons or on the galleys. Many more, however, had to be settled with some other source of income. Land was not so abundant that this was easy—except in Istria and on some of the islands—and many of the former soldiers were not willing to move so far. Nor were some anxious to return to the back-breaking labor and precarious existence of the peasant's life. In military service the soldier and the salaried oarsman had experienced a new life, free of the indignity of the personal obligations of the peasant. Demobilized, the former soldier was doubly at liberty, freed both of army discipline and of obligations to a master. Outside the social hierarchy and reluctant to return to its bonds such men—not only demobilized troops, but also many deserters from the galleys—found the freedoms of uskok life attractive. Filippo Pas-

---

[68]Ibid., vol. 6, p. 122.

qualigo, Provveditore Generale of Dalmatia, had this picture in mind when he recommended that the Signoria not recruit Croats into military service. "When they are dismissed, not wishing to return to the sweat of the hoe, accustomed to another way of life, they turn instead to plunder, for the most part with the uskoks."[69]

Many of these military men had originally come to Venetian Dalmatia from the Ottoman hinterland and had signed up with the Signoria to fight the Turks. When it became a crime to continue these battles in peacetime, they found a market for their services in Senj. Sometimes a lingering bitterness and a sense of betrayal can be detected on both sides. Something of the sort colored the careers of Martin Posedarski and Marko Margitić. Both had been commanders under the Venetians but had deserted to Senj sometime in the early 1590s. Margitić apparently brought with him his entire unit of mercenaries.[70] In Senj they became popular uskok leaders, participating in the 1596 attempt on Klis, and were involved in numerous raids on Venetian territory. Posedarski is supposed to have helped raise the imperial standard over Venetian Plomin in 1599 in an attack prompted by the Venetian blockade of Senj,[71] and in 1600 he reported to the Military Frontier that "these Venetians are in a great rage against Marko and me because we left them and came to serve the house of Austria, and they constantly threaten to pay this debt off for us."[72] Both were hanged by Habsburg Commissioner Rabatta under pressure from Provveditore Generale Pasqualigo.[73]

Juraj Maslarda, originally from Ottoman territory, was another such deserter. He had originally served the Republic of Dubrovnik and then went to Senj to become an uskok leader with a large following. His subsequent raids on Dubrovnik's territory seem to have enraged the Ragusan senators beyond usual bounds, for in 1596 they commissioned an agent in Rijeka to see that a death sentence passed by Archduke Ferdinand against Maslarda was carried out. Foreseeing that the Captain of Senj would be reluctant to act, they proposed that he either be persuaded by a gift of up to 500 thalers ("as little as you can manage to spend") or that the agent arrange to have Maslarda secretly assassinated. "Whatever appears best to you, so long as this execution be put into effect however possible, particularly in Maslarda's case, as he is a rebel against us and our particular enemy."[74]

---

[69]Ibid., vol. 6, p. 190.

[70]Lopašic, *Acta historiam confinii*, vol. 1, p. 302.

[71]A.S.V., Senato, Secreta, reg. 92: 22 Jan. 1599; Provveditori da Terra e da Mar, 922: 12 Mar. 1599.

[72]In Lopašic, *Acta historiam confinii*, vol. 1, p. 273.

[73]Horvat, *Monumenta uscocchorum*, vol. 1, pp. 339, 405.

[74]In H.A.D., Lettere di Ponente, 7: 211–11'. The attempt failed—Maslarda continued to raid Ragusan territory until Commissioner Rabatta had him killed in 1601. See Chapter 8.

Dalmatia had other malcontents, who traced the troubles of the province to two sources: the Turks, whose wars ate away the territories that had fed the towns and whose presence on the borders was a constant threat; and the Republic of Venice, who had failed to defend Dalmatia and whose deferential attitude toward the Ottomans did not help to regain Dalmatia's lost lands. (Much the same could be said about Ragusan rebels, except that they added to this list the Senate of Dubrovnik.)[75] Individual misfortune, as well as collective disaster, could find relief in complaint against Venice, a tendency the rectors saw plainly and were quick to forestall when they could with carefully chosen distributions of favor.[76] But the official persecution of the uskoks—although many in Dalmatia credited them with keeping the province safe from the Turks, especially in 1596, when Venetian officials opposed the Christian attack against Ottoman Klis—encouraged a mistrust of Venetian policy in Dalmatia and reinforced popular sympathy for the uskoks. Those who fled to evade Venetian retaliation for some misdeed—especially a misdeed directed against the Turk—often brought with them to Senj a grudge against the Signoria and its policies in Dalmatia.

Adventurers. Not only those whom circumstances had conspired to ruin—through the misfortunes of war, a too-heavy tax, the threat of Venetian punishment, or some other unforeseen twist of fate—joined the uskoks. Once Senj had gained a reputation as a haven for raiders, particularly once the Ottoman trade in the Adriatic became an uskok target, the uskoks attracted adventurers who wanted to get rich quickly and were not too fastidious about the source of their profits, for, as a Venetian noted in 1596, "the sweetness of this life draws many to it, and the nature of evil men inclines always to the worse."[77] Toward the end of the sixteenth century official complaints were heard from Dalmatia that such men, after "they had robbed enough to last a short while" were able to return home, even if they had been banished in the meantime.[78] To obtain a pardon one had only to appear before a naval commander, who, desperate for crewmen, would commute the sentence in return for ser-

---

[75]See for example Marin Držić's seditious proposals to Cosimo I, Grand Duke of Tuscany, in *Djela Marina Držića*, Stari pisci hrvatski, 7, ed. M. Rešetar (Zagreb, 1930), pp. cxxxi–cxlvii.

[76]One letter to the Signoria from Split, dealing with the ceremonious distribution of food in the face of famine and imminent rebellion in 1574, remarked that the point was "to keep the people in a good temper, which covers a multitude of evils." (Solitro, *Documenti storici*, vol. 1, p. 245).

[77]In *Commissiones et relationes venetæ*, vol. 5, p. 212.

[78]In ibid., vol. 6, p. 55. See also *Commissiones et relationes venetæ*, vol. 5, p. 243. The relatively light punishments handed down to those involved with the uskoks after the Klis affair in 1596 (see Chapter 7) confirm this view (H.A.Z., Arhiv Splita, 140/9: 3385'–89, 392–92', 404').

vice for a year or two at half pay, or even at full pay. Indeed, the returned uskok did not have to serve the term himself if he could provide a substitute. "Many are induced to do the same after their example, seeing that these, taken from the hoe and the plough, badly dressed and barefoot, have become fat and prosperous in a short time."[79] By the early seventeenth century this abuse was widespread. The Captain of the Gulf summed up the official view of the situation in 1608:

> [The uskoks] are infinitely increased for the most part by subjects of Your Serenity, either freemen or soldiers on warships who desert over enduring the slightest inconvenience or out of fear of justice when they have committed even the smallest of crimes. After committing their fill of robberies and murders, if by chance they no longer like such a life, they contrive to return and reenter the service of Your Serenity. They can do this easily enough—particularly those who have immortalized themselves, as they say, with the name of assassins—receiving a reward for their criminal operations rather than punishment. . . . From which it results that many good men, after the example of the wicked ones, resolve to do the same to alter their fortunes, finding the road to return again to grace so level and easy.[80]

Adventurers of this type there certainly were in Senj, coming from all the areas of the border, but they would have had reason to stay only while the uskoks' raids were successful. Such uskoks did not stay in Senj when Venetian blockades bottled up the uskok barks in the Velebit Channel, so that they were unable to raid or to bring in shipments of supplies and grain from the Croatian Littoral and prospects of rich booty were very slender. In the 1590s and early 1600s, when Venetian pressures on Military Frontier officials to restrain uskok action were at their height, many uskoks entered Venetian service, and others left Senj to raid as renegades, recognizing no external authority.[81]

Such pirates did not need to go to Senj at all. By the end of the sixteenth century alarmed Venetian commanders, concerned for the security of the Adriatic, were reporting the appearance of bands of pirates who plundered "under the name of uskoks" but who had no connection with Senj.[82] These were "some other evildoers, usurpers of that name, small friends of the true uskoks" who borrowed the notoriety of the Senj name.[83] It was nothing new that others should masquerade as

---

[79]In *Commissiones et relationes venetæ*, vol. 5, p. 243.

[80]In ibid., vol. 6, p. 148.

[81]A.S.V., Provveditori da Terra e da Mar, 1261: reports by Provveditore Generale Tiepolo, 1592; and ibid., 425: reports by Provveditore Generale Venier, 1611–12, contain numbers of accounts of both types of defection from Senj.

[82]See, for example, *Commissiones et relationes venetæ*, vol. 5, pp. 48, 211–12.

[83]In H.A.Z., Ispisi tajnog vatikanskog arhiva Fra Dane Zeca: C. Urbin,. no. 1068.

Senj uskoks to disguise their acts. In 1546 the Senate noted that "it is quite true that under this guise and this name of uskok there are many wicked men who take to the road and do much damage." The Dizdar (or commander) of Obrovac himself had been forced to admit that "around 80 Turks left Obrovac dressed as uskoks, and sailed in three barks toward Pag, Rab, and Krk, where they made a great plunder of captives, animals, and barks laden with goods."[84] But the Venetians were just as ready to hide behind the uskok reputation: "In Dalmatia the ministers of Your Serenity constantly inflict the greatest damages on the Turks, and when they are found out, or a complaint is lodged with Your Serenity, the response is always that they were uskoks. At the same time the armed ships of Your Serenity constantly plunder the Turkish ships and their subjects at sea, and the excuse is given that they were uskoks."[85] In one specific incident, the Ottoman administrator of Makarska accused the men of Omiš of dressing as uskoks and plundering a caravan above Makarska to frighten trade away from the port, complaining that "if there was previously one Senj, there are now two Senjs, the second one being Omiš."[86]

The uskok imitators who began to appear in the late 1500s and early 1600s, however, were for the most part independent plundering bands made up primarily of Venetian subjects, sometimes former uskoks, but more often having no connection with Senj.[87] As in the case of Dalmatian recruits among the uskoks, it was often said that these pirates were indiscriminate in their choice of victims, pillaging not only the subjects of the Turk but also other Venetian subjects. Raiding style was sometimes used as the touchstone for identifying the bands, as in the case of twenty men who had plundered some barks in the Kvarner Gulf, "taking in addition their foodstuffs and their own garments, and also treating them badly, and for this reason it is clear that these are not uskoks, but Albanians, deserters from the [Venetian] armed barks and the galleys and others, whose number is growing in Istria . . . under the shadow of uskoks."[88] Christoforo Valier, Provveditore Generale in Dalmatia, explicitly pointed to both their origins and their actions in differentiating between the uskoks of Senj, "natives of Senj, Croatians, and Morlachs from Turkish parts," who "take nothing from the subjects of Your Serenity except what they need for their own use and for food," and "ban-

---

[84]In A.S.V., Senato, Secreta, reg. 65: 23–23' (23 June 1546).

[85]In Gustav Turba, ed., *Venetianische Depeschen vom Kaiserhofe*, 3 vols. (Vienna, 1889–95), vol. 3, p. 510 (quoted by G. Soranzo and G. Michieli, 16 Nov., 1570).

[86]In H.A.Z., Arhiv Omiša, 171/3, no. 113: no date, but with late sixteenth-century papers.

[87]"They are more often thieves from the neighboring areas and subjects of Your Serenity, under the name of Senjani, rather than these other people of ill repute" (in A.S.V., Provveditori da Terra e da Mar, 1313: 6 June 1612).

[88]In A.S.V., Provveditori da Terra e da Mar, 1265: 15 Apr. 1606.

ished Dalmatians, deserting galiots, and subjects dissatisfied with Your Serenity," who "hold these poor people in perpetual affliction and oppression, stealing their animals, taking their revenues, pillaging their houses, plundering and killing without respect or distinction."[89] Giovanni of Fermo, in his defense of the Senj uskoks, protested that these pirates gave Senj a bad name, though he admitted that they were joined by an occasional uskok of Senj: "Under the name uskok there are many islanders from Krk, Pag and Rab, which lie across from Senj, and also from the other islands of Dalmatia belonging to Zadar, Šibenik, Trogir, Split, and Hvar, who devote themselves to plundering the barks that come from *sotto vento*, that is from Apulia and the Marches, with merchants who come to sell goods in Dalmatia. The blame is then put on those of Senj; though some rogue or another from among their number, banished from the city and from the lands of the Archduke may join them as well, after being notified by smoke signals from the island that there is booty a little way off."[90]

Making clear distinctions between these independent Dalmatian pirates and the uskoks is difficult, however. Adventurers moved in and out of the ranks of the uskoks in Senj according to the opportunities and constraints of the moment. In spite of Valier's opinion, neither place of origin nor membership in the uskok ranks guaranteed that a raider would operate according to a particular set of attitudes and rules (which might be described in other terms as distinguishing between social bandits and common criminals). Both Dalmatian pirates and Senj uskoks could mix hatred of the Turk, a resentment against Venice, and the need for booty in equal proportions. Those for whom booty was paramount, however, usually sought their fortunes outside Senj, free of the watchful Venetian patrols of the Velebit Channel, and free too of the regulations of the Military Frontier and, perhaps most important, the uskok code of behavior, which, as examined in Chapter 6, was a demanding one.

Regardless of the new constraints an uskok life imposed, flight to Senj could appear as social liberation as well as economic opportunity. Uskok freedoms appealed to men who were "tired of rural life, and discontented, invited to live from plunder, with license and with little labor."[91] The chafing bonds of an old life—the demands of landlord, family, and the land itself—could be shaken off in flight to Senj. Uskok life was essentially that of a mercenary soldier—it was freely chosen and freely left. Its opportunities were not circumscribed by birth or status—they could be won by individual skill and bravery. Some certainly saw becom-

---

[89]In *Commissiones et relationes venetæ*, vol. 5, pp. 211–12.
[90]In Rački, "Prilog za poviest hrvatskih uskoka," p. 180.
[91]In *Commissiones et relationes venetæ*, vol. 5, p. 243.

ing an uskok as a means of social mobility and could point to the example of Juriša Hajduk, who, it was said, "was of lowly birth, but borne along by time and by fortune, had become leader of the uskoks."[92] It was primarily men from these less privileged parts of society who chose this road, "the lower sort," to repeat a Venetian evaluation, "such as workers in the fields, and other similar types."[93] Even so, the opportunities Senj offered were not scorned even by nobles whose status could no longer assure them a living. Perhaps the most illustrious example was Martin Posedarski, a count of Posedarje who claimed descent from Torquatus of Rome, who became an uskok leader in Senj when the Turk swallowed up his estates near Zadar.

The pattern of immigration to Senj changed substantially over the sixteenth century. The uskoks came first from nearby Habsburg territories threatened by the Ottomans and then, with changes in the border wars and with the growth of Senj's reputation, from the whole Croatian-Ottoman border area, particularly from the long Venetian frontier with the Turk. As the preceding analysis has shown, the experiences that drove these immigrants to Senj, whether from Ottoman, Venetian, or Habsburg territory, were similar in many ways. It is difficult to assign any particular set of experiences or motives solely to a single category of uskok recruits. Many Venetian Dalmatians, like Christian subjects of the Porte, could blame their discontents on the Turk and justify their uskok raids as vengeance against oppression and persecution. Similarly, Senj offered the same opportunities to the Ottoman adventurer as to the Dalmatian pirate. In spite of the distinctions that contemporary observers made between the different groups of uskoks, origins offer no sure guide to their subsequent attitudes and actions.

Nevertheless, the shifts in the pattern of immigration reflected in the changing composition of the uskok ranks did affect the character of the uskok phenomenon. Changing patterns of recruitment influenced uskok operations by broadening Senj's ties with different parts of the border. Each area that sent recruits to Senj became a base for future uskok actions, as each new arrival added his own network of friends and family (and enemies) to the complex relationships Senj maintained with the world. The rise in the number of uskoks who went to Senj by way of Venetian Dalmatia did not necessarily increase the number of simple adventurers among the uskoks, but it did add to Senj's store of local

---

[92]In Rački, "Prilog za poviest hrvatskih uskoka," p. 205. Minucci remarks that Juriša "from a tiller of the soil (*zappatore*) had become a great robber, made famous by the vigor of his body and the ferocity of his spirit" (Minucci, *Storia degli uscocchi*, p. 257).

[93]In *Commissiones et relationes venetæ*, vol. 5, p. 223.

knowledge and experience of Venetian Dalmatia—a prerequisite for sending raids to any area. Some Venetian observers blamed this connection for the rise in the number of raids at sea and across the territory of the Republic. "These [Venetian] subjects have been the cause of all the problems, because with their knowledge of the area and of navigation they guide the others in their piracy, and infest places where they would never had gone, had they not come from there themselves."[94] But not only Venetian subjects returned to Dalmatia as uskoks. Ottoman refugees too could pose a danger, as some Venetian officials quickly recognized, recommending that these be settled in Istria or in other less vulnerable areas. These Ottoman subjects

> after having committed some crime in the lands of the Grand Turk, retire to the cities, fortresses, and villages of Your Serenity in Dalmatia, with no other end than to flee Turkish punishment, where they remain as long as they like, and become familiar with the lay of the land; and after forming close friendships with our subjects they leave for Senj, and then come murdering by land and sea, now here, now there, without exception. . . . Your Serenity may believe me, that of 100 Morlachs who come to Dalmatia, several remain here less than a year before going to Senj and returning to do ill with the uskoks.[95]

Other, less easily weighed effects of uskok attitudes and behavior derived from individual uskok origins and motives. For almost a century Senj served as a magnet for all sorts of displaced people: uprooted by war and disaster, fleeing from persecution or from justice, without positions, banished, footloose and adventurous, or simply unwilling to fit into their expected roles. Perhaps not all, but many of these people (whether Ottoman, Venetian, or Habsburg subjects) left their homes and became uskoks in reaction to a change for the worse, real or threatened, in their socioeconomic status. These suffered an encroachment on what they saw as their just rights—rights to life and liberty, to land, to established rents and taxes, to traditional privileges, to antagonism to an enemy. Such wrongs must have left them with a sense of legitimate grievance. For Christian subjects of the Porte, socioeconomic grievances were magnified and transformed by religious and cultural differences with their rulers. Venetian subjects too cast the Ottomans as the primary villains, the enemy whose wars had led to Dalmatia's sixteenth-century predicament. The national and cultural gulf between rulers and ruled in Dalmatia was not so extreme as in the Ottoman Empire, but opposition to Venice's conciliatory relations with the Turks lends a certain political

[94]In H.A.Z., Fond Šime Ljubića, 2/33: 282'.
[95]In *Commissiones et relationes venetæ*, vol. 5, p. 226.

air to the grievances of some Dalmatian subjects, particularly as the Habsburgs, the most active crusaders against the Porte in the Balkans and the successors to the Croatian-Hungarian crown of Dalmatia's good old days of the fourteenth century, were willing rivals to Venetian rule.

As the most important Frontier fortification in a large area, particularly after the fall of Klis in 1537, Senj offered such recruits a new life, the chance of a military position, and the possibility of growing rich on Ottoman plunder. The Senj uskoks provided a permanent focus for discontent. Whatever the reason for leaving home behind, Senj was always there, a recognized alternative for the rebel, the adventurer, and the refugee. After the collapse of an insurrection against Ottoman authority or as a result of a transgression against Venetian authority, Senj was the natural refuge. But the channel for discontent the uskoks provided also acted as a safety valve. Energies that might otherwise have resulted in rebellion were redirected in flight to Senj. There the grievances of the uskoks were channeled into border warfare. The changing forms this warfare took depended not only on the aims of the Military Frontier authorities but also on the changing focus of resentment, reflecting changes in the experiences and motives of those who came to Senj.

CHAPTER FOUR

The Raiding Economy

In 1590 the Captain appointed to Senj by the Military Frontier emphasized that "the Senjani have no other way to live than by going to plunder the lands of the enemy by way of the land and by sea." To forbid this was to take the bread from their mouths.[1] How did this need for booty shape the uskoks' actions?

Military Frontier Subsidies

An anonymous report from 1601 (probably by Bishop de Dominis) described the circumstances of the uskoks thus:

> It is well known that it is the custom for the militia on the borders to make raids on enemy territory and, with the the ransom of slaves and the plunder of the enemy's goods, to provide for themselves and make up for their lack of wages; as the Princes never pay their soldiers sufficiently or promptly enough to maintain the soldier and his family in comfort and well-being. Nor does the border offer any aid in vines, farms, pastures, trade or commerce, so of necessity it follows that in the border garrisons the one and only exercise, that best understood and most practiced, is that of plundering; and the longer the war, the more this is refined. . . . Senj has surpassed all the other places of the border in this refinement of raiding and pillaging.[2]

The uskoks in Senj had to provide for themselves. Elsewhere on the Military Frontier military colonists had been settled on the abandoned border with land grants and tax exemptions on the goods, livestock, and

---

[1]In Lopašić, *Acta historiam confinii*, vol. 1, p. 157.
[2]In Horvat, *Monumenta uscocchorum*, vol. 1, p. 396.

crops they produced and traded for their own upkeep. Only a proportion of these were taken into the garrisons as standing troops and they received wages only when they were in active service. During wartime these border colonists could not work their land efficiently and so they lived largely on their plunder, but when they were forbidden to raid they could turn to their fields and livestock to support themselves.[3] The uskoks who settled around the small fortresses in the hinterland of the Senj captaincy—Brinje, Otočac, Brlog, Prozor—followed this pattern, for the terrain permitted agriculture and stockherding. These joined with the uskoks of Senj only on the largest expeditions.[4]

But the uskoks who settled in Senj itself had no such lands. Senj, on the barren karst coast at the foot of the Velebit mountains, was not surrounded by the fertile fields of the hinterland marches. The few vineyards beneath the city walls did not even provide enough wine for the uses of the town and could hardly support several hundred uskok immigrants and their families. The townspeople of Senj did control some vineyards on Krk, the large Venetian island directly opposite the city.[5] Often these were rented out to locals for cultivation. Such land was private property acquired by purchase, not distributed by the Military Frontier authorities. Some of these possessions did in time come into the hands of uskoks, but they were a limited and uncertain source of income, because they were small and because the vineyards and their products were so easily confiscated by Venetians.[6]

[3]See the controversy between F. Čulinović, "Mogu li se pokreti krajišnika uvrstiti u seljačke bune?" and B. Sučević, "Šta su bili krajišnici?" *Historijski zbornik* (Zagreb), 5 (1952): 427–52.

[4]A Venetian spy in 1591 noted that "other individual fortresses around Senj can produce about 1000 men, but those of Senj are prompt to action, while these others are not so prompt" (in A.S.V., Senato, Secreta, Materie miste notabili, 27: 11 June 1591 [Andrea Gugliemi]). Because of the income from their fields, the garrisons of these fortresses were less dependent on uskok raids for their sustenance and took a smaller part in raiding. The Hofkriegsrat occasionally supplied the hinterland fortresses with agricultural necessities, such as the 1000 *star* of summer wheat needed in Otočac for sowing in 1593 (Grünfelder, "Studien zur Geschichte der Uskoken," p. 35), while Senj received only grain for consumption. (The *star* was a measure used for grain, differing in size according to local standards. A Rijeka *star* was equivalent to 38 liters. See Zlatko Herkov, *Mjere Hrvatskog primorja*, Historijski arhiv u Rijeci i Pazinu, posebnja izdanja, 4 [Rijeka, 1971], pp. 48, 53.)

[5]Venetian authorities differed on the wisdom of allowing Senjani to hold property on Krk. In 1527 the Rector forbade further such sales of land (*Commissiones et relationes venetæ*, vol. 2, p. 38). In 1571, however, the current Rector reported that Senjani still held many vineyards in Baščanska draga. He approved, because land ownership prevented the uskoks from plundering the area and the possibility of confiscation of this property provided a means of retaliating against the uskoks ("Relatione di A. Bondumieri," in *Atti e memorie della Società istriana di archeologia et storia patria* [Parenzo], 2 [1886]: 110).

[6]In 1543, the Provveditore of Krk was ordered to sequester and sell goods owned by Miloš Pariževič, vojvoda of the uskoks, and by his associates, to cover uskok damages to Venetian subjects, although it was at least two years before this order was carried out (A.S.V., Senato Mar, reg. 27: 45'; 59–59'[1543]; reg. 28: 82 [1545]). For another example of a Venetian confisca-

Perhaps because the Hofkriegsrat could not provide the uskoks in Senj with land, the paid garrison was supposed to receive slightly more than was customary in other parts of the border. The stipendiati, uskoks enrolled in military service, were to receive subsidies the year around, not just when they were mobilized. The Military Frontier system was supposed to use part of the money allocated to the uskoks to purchase and deliver grain for the paid garrison, instead of distributing this money as individual salaries. Only seldom, however, did this system function smoothly. In 1601 Vettor Barbaro, the Venetian secretary sent to observe the reforms in Senj, identified the weaknesses in Senj's system of maintenance, informing his superior that "this place is maintained more by reputation and appearance than by good and real provisions, for the soldiers almost never have their pay, and are usually owed from forty to fifty months' wages, on account of which they have a little grain from week to week, from a storehouse [*fondaco*] kept in Fiume [Rijeka] based on the income of the countryside of Pisino [Pazin], which is not enough for a supplement to their bread, and they never have more than eight to ten days' provisions there, though their aid and succor could easily be cut off either by land or by sea."[7]

Both the rank-and-file and the Military Frontier officers in Senj found this state of affairs unsatisfactory, but there were few improvements to the haphazard and hand-to-mouth way in which Senj was financed over the uskok period.[8] An endless stream of letters flowed from Senj to the Military Frontier authorities, to the Archdukes, and to the Emperor (in his role as King of Croatia), complaining about problems with pay and provisions and warning of the consequences. A small sample of these letters shows little change throughout the century in the nature of the complaints. The Captain of Klis warned in 1530 that the soldiers were threatening to leave because they had not been paid, and a few years later, in 1536, the stipendiati of Senj and Otočac wrote to King Ferdinand that "already many years have passed since we were last paid." In

---

tion of Senj property on Krk, in 1558–59, see *Commissiones et relationes venetæ*, vol. 3, p. 138, and Turba, *Venetianische Depeschen vom Kaiserhofe*, vol. 3, pp. 30, 86, 167, for a report on the Habsburg reaction. At this time Senj's goods on Krk were worth 3516 ducats.

[7]In H.A.Z., Fond Šime Ljubića, 2/33: 280'.

[8]The list of references to Military Frontier payments for Senj for 1579–1600 and 1604–16 compiled by Grünfelder from documents in the Kriegsarchiv do not document Senj's finances in their entirety (records of appropriations approved by the Estates, for example, often bear little relation to the sums actually received in Senj). Nevertheless, the picture that emerges from these references confirms the more impressionistic evidence in the Captains' reports, the uskoks' complaints, and foreign observers' accounts, of irregular appropriations, delays in the disbursement of funds, great variations in the quantities of supplies purchased for the garrison (from 200 to 1800 *star* of grain annually), and infrequent and partial payment of uskok wages (Grünfelder, "Studien zur Geschichte der uskoken," pp. 29–48).

November 1579 Captain Kaspar Raab reported that there was no grain at all in the city and that "the longer this disorder continues in arrears, the more danger is to be feared." Some of the unpaid uskoks had already sailed out to seek supplies in an illicit raid. By the following March only one month's pay of the three months' pay authorized had been issued, and the uskoks had become openly rebellious. In 1607 it was reported that the uskoks had been waiting for their wages for some fifty months and that unless supplies were sent they would break the Ottoman truce with plundering raids, for "the soldiers cannot live on air." (On this occasion a shipment of wheat was approved, though it had still not arrived in Senj six months later.)[9]

Part of the problem in provisioning Senj lay in the difficulty of raising the subsidies. After 1522 the Estates of Inner Austria promised regular contributions for the upkeep of the Military Frontier, and in 1578 the Estates of Carniola and Carinthia accepted the responsibility of supporting the Croatian Frontier, but in practice these monies were often paid late, only in part, or not at all.[10] The Estates sometimes refused to approve appropriations or, even after approving them, postponed payment (as happened in 1610, when the Carniolan and Carinthian Estates delayed payment of the wages approved for Senj from month to month, well into the following year).[11]

Even after the Estates had disbursed their subsidies, the uskoks' wages were subject to speculation by the Military Frontier authorities responsible for the distribution of pay and provisions to the border. By the mid-sixteenth century it was customary for the soldiers of the Senj captaincy to receive their pay, when it arrived, only partly in cash, with the rest issued in goods or in grain. Giovanni of Fermo, himself a sharp merchant, explained the profit the paymasters made by this system:

> His Imperial Majesty often keeps [the uskoks] short of their pay; and I have several times happened to be in Fiume [Rijeka] or Senj when the commissioners came to pay them the 20, 30, or 40 consecutive [monthly] wages they were owed. They pay off these, and give them 20 or more in advance, in the following way: one-third in cash, one-third in worked silver in various forms, and one-third in kerseys [woollen cloths] of various colors, or other cloths; so that if they wish to have ready money, they are forced to sell back

[9]Horvat, *Monumenta uscocchorum*, vol. 1, p. 466 (1530); vol. 2, p. 75 (1607); Laszowski, *Monumenta habsburgica*, vol. 2, p. 266 (1536); I.Ö. H.K.R., Croatica, fasc. 3, 1580, Jan. No. 46 (20 Nov. 1579 [Raab] and Mar. 1580); A.S., Deželni stanovi za Kranjsko, 292e: 2480–81 (5 July 1607); I.Ö. H.K.R., Croatica, fasc. 12, 1607, Nov. No. 27 (4 Dec. 1607).

[10]Rothenberg, *The Austrian Military Border*, pp. 53–54; Vasko Simoniti, "Doprinos Kranjske financiranju protuturske obrane u 16. stoljeću," in *Vojna Krajina: Povijesni pregled, historiografija, rasprave*, ed. D. Pavličević (Zagreb, 1984), pp. 205–13.

[11]Grünfelder, "Studien zur Geschichte der Uskoken," p. 43.

these cloths at a low price. I believe this to be done only by the commissioners and not by the rulers, because they take advantage of the pay money
and take these goods on credit for a long period, and they make up to three
percent or more on this speculation for themselves.[12]

The garrison and the Captain objected to payment in goods, requesting cash instead.[13] Cash payments too, however, were subject to speculation, for money earmarked for the garrison could be exchanged by
the paymasters for gold at a favorable rate and then distributed to the
uskoks at a much higher rate of exchange, the profits going into the
pockets of the military entrepreneurs of the Frontier. Abuses of this sort
had been common since at least 1530, when the garrisons in Senj and
Brinje had complained of irregularities in their pay,[14] but other refine-
ments were introduced over the century, such as the practice of issuing
scrip redeemable at a later date for the pay due, which was then bought
up from the uskoks by the military commissioners for cash, but at a
discount, to be redeemed later at the full value.[15] As a result the money
meant for Senj "passes through many hands: those of the secretaries of
that country, those of the commissioners and of the paymasters; and all
of them speculate with it, so that little money is sent to Senj, and it
arrives only with great delays."[16]

Some of this money, intended to provision the garrison in Senj with
grain, was funneled through a storehouse in Rijeka, administered by a
quartermaster responsible for purchasing, shipping, and distributing
the grain. For more than thirty years this post was filled by Jeremias
Hoff, a merchant of Rijeka (himself accused more than once of speculation with Senj funds).[17] In 1591 he estimated that each man in the garrison required one-half a *star* (about one bushel) of grain each month. To
maintain the garrison of four hundred paid men for an entire year, he
needed to purchase 2,400 *star* of grain.[18] Only very rarely, however, could
the Senj quartermaster be sure of having that much grain at his disposal.

[12]In Rački, "Prilog za poviest hrvatskih uskoka," p. 192.

[13]In 1602 the rumor that the uskoks would be paid in cloth prompted them to request that
they be given cash (A.S.V., Provveditori da Terra e da Mar 1321: 5 Dec. 1602 [interrogation of
a man of Senj]); and in 1611 the uskoks requested cash payment after they had been issued a
derisory amount in hides (Grünfelder, "Studien zur Geschichte der Uskoken," p. 45).

[14]Laszowski, *Monumenta habsburgica*, vol. 1, p. 254.

[15]F. Moačanin, "Društveni razvoj u Vojnoj Krajini," in *Vojna Krajina: Povijesni pregled,
historiografija, rasprave*, ed. D. Pavličević (Zagreb, 1984), p. 91.

[16]In A.S.V., Provveditori da Terra e da Mar, 313: 3 Jan. 1603.

[17]Lopašić, *Acta historiam confinii*, vol. 1, p. 133; vol. 2, pp. 17, 34, 36; H.A.R., Zapisnici
sjednica općinskog vijeća u Rijeci, 1593–1607: 251' (3 Apr. 1606); Gestrin, *Mitninske knjige*,
pp. 319, 374; I.Ö. H.K.R., Croatica, fasc. 4, 1585, Jan. No. 12: 1–1' (10 Jan. 1585); fasc. 9, 1597
Dec. No. 45 (Dec. 1597).

[18]Grünfelder, "Studien zur Geschichte der Uskoken," p. 32.

Occasionally it was possible to fill the Senj storehouse with a cargo of grain that the uskoks had captured or that Rijeka officials had confiscated as contraband. Far more often it had to be purchased from Ancona and the Marches, Ljubljana or Istria (particularly from the Pazin area, which the Hofkriegsrat designated as a supply center for Senj in the 1590s). When Military Frontier funds were not forthcoming on time or in sufficient quantity to make the necessary purchases, merchants had to be persuaded to make deliveries on account. Even when some funds (rarely as much as had been requested) were sent promptly, other disasters hindered the quartermaster's task: grain might be scarce and prohibitively expensive if harvests had been poor; shipwreck and unfriendly Venetian naval officers threatened the safe arrival of seaborne cargoes; officials in Rijeka or Karlovac might divert supplies intended for Senj to other purposes; or the Rijeka city council might obstruct the collection of the grain by the Senj soldiers.

Even when the commissioners finally came to Senj to distribute the pay arrears, the salaried uskoks often received very little cash. The grain rations, of course, represented a portion of the uskoks' pay, and the costs of purchase and transportation were deducted from their wages. Similar deductions were also made for allocations of cloth issued from the Military Frontier warehouses and even, on occasion, for the munitions issued for use on raids. The commissioners might also hold back money to cover the costs of restoring plunder if it had been necessary to placate the victims of uskok raids, as was the case in 1581, when the pay commissioners "recovered all the goods still in existence from the vessel taken at Premuda, and held back as much of [the uskoks'] wages as was found lacking."[19] As the years passed, even the full amount bought less and less, for while prices increased throughout the century, the uskoks' wages remained at much the same level. According to the pay list of 1551, uskoks in the ranks were paid between three and five florins a month. Their wages had not risen by 1579 (when the average monthly wage for an ordinary uskok was four florins), and even by 1601 the uskoks in the outlying fortresses of the Senj captaincy were still being paid only four florins a month, though in Senj the sum had risen to five or six florins.[20] Toward the end of the century, inflation had whittled away much of the earlier value of the uskoks' pay.[21]

---

[19]Report from Nicolò Spalatin of Rab, in A.S.V., Archivio dei Baili Veneti a Constantinopoli, 305: 16 Mar. 1581.

[20]I.Ö. H.K.R., Croatica, fasc. 3, 1579, Feb. No. 40: 3–5; H.A.Z., Fond Šime Ljubića, 2/33: 283. See also I.Ö. H.K.R., Croatica, fasc. 12, 1606, Nov. No. 6 ("Extract aus dem Musterregister"); fasc. 13, 1609, June No. 13 (5 July 1609).

[21]Between 1551 and 1600, the price of wheat in Ljubljana (one of the sources for the uskoks' provisions) rose 200 percent (F. Gestrin, "Gospodarstvo in družba na Slovenskem

With no land to work and only a part of the garrison paid, and that irregularly, the uskoks of Senj supported themselves primarily by the fruits of plunder. The Habsburgs and the Military Frontier authorities had an ambiguous attitude to this solution to the uskoks' economic quandary. The Hofkriegsrat usually saw the uskoks' ability to find their own supplies in raids as a virtue. But, particularly in peacetime, the raids of the uskoks were a political embarassment and often provoked Ottoman or Venetian antagonists to acts that imperiled the Habsburg state. Whenever uskok plundering threatened Habsburg relations at a vulnerable point, stronger and more effective controls in Senj were proposed. More effective controls in Senj depended, however, on finding some means of maintaining the garrison in Senj—and that required money. As the Captains of Senj constantly reminded the Hofkriegsrat and the Archduke in Graz, the uskoks could not be prevented from raiding if they were not paid.

This realization led to attempts to find a source of income for the uskoks which would not tax the Military Frontier coffers. One plan was to seek contributions from others who had an interest in the actions of the uskoks. Chief among these was the Pope, who, as the titular head of Christendom, could be expected to support the uskoks' raids against the infidel and who also had a material interest in protecting the Papal States' shipping trade in the Adriatic from raids. These two motives had been entwined in the 1520s and 1530s, when the Pope had accompanied an annual contribution to the defense of Klis with requests that the Captains of Senj desist from plundering grain shipments from the Papal States.[22] By the 1570s uskok raids on ships sailing from Ancona, in search of merchandise belonging to Ottoman subjects and Jews, were causing the Holy See much anxiety about the security of its shipping.[23] A solution was negotiated in 1579, when a group of uskoks went to Rome and won the promise of an annual subsidy in recognition of their importance

---

v 16. stoletju," *Zgodovinski časopis* [Ljubljana], 16 [1962]: 20.) Grain prices on the Croatian Littoral followed a similar pattern: wheat sold for 20 to 50 *soldi* a *star* in 1530 in Rijeka (Z. Herkov, ed., *Statut grada Rijeke*, pp. 114, 308); and for 10 *lire* (200 *soldi*) a *star* in 1593 in Vinodol (Lujo Margetić, ed., *Iz vinodolske prošlosti* [Rijeka, 1980], pp. 171–73).

[22]In 1525 the German Papal nuncio noted that the border officials tried to have it both ways: "When they rob grain from the Holy See they are the Captains of Senj; when they want a subsidy from the Holy See they are the Captains of Klis" (in H.A.Z., Ispisi tajnog vatikanskog arhiva Fra Dane Zeca II: Vat. sign. Nunz. Germ. No. 55, p. 128; also pp. 114, 169′). There is much information on the papal subsidy to Klis in the 1530s in Petar Kružić's correspondence (in Laszowski, *Monumenta habsburgica*, vol. 2, pp. 29, 125, 127, 149, 220–22, 246, 334). Appeals for papal aid to the border were also made in the 1540s and 1550s (ibid., vol. 3, pp. 4, 388).

[23]In 1571 the Papal nuncio to Venice reported worries about the security of goods sent to Ancona (*Nunziature di Venezia*, vol. 9, p. 451); in 1575 and 1576 the Pope had to intercede with the Emperor for the return of goods taken by the uskoks from Levantine Jews on an Ancona ship (Horvat, *Monumenta uscocchorum*, vol. 1, pp. 14, 15–16).

as a bulwark against the Turk, on the condition that they not harm the subjects of the Holy See or molest ships going to and from the papal ports.[24]

Perhaps inspired by this success in finding monetary support abroad, the uskok vojvodas, or military leaders, tried to secure a stipend from the Republic of Venice in the 1580s, again on the promise that they would not attack subjects of Venice and would confine their raids to Ottoman territory. In spite of negotiations with Nicolò Surian, the Provveditore dell'Armata, which even laid down the level of stipend the uskoks expected (thirty ducats a month for Vojvoda Daničić, eleven ducats for the rank and file), these plans were not carried out, though the discussions seem to have improved relations between the Venetian naval commanders and the uskoks briefly.[25] Many other, more elaborate plans to provide for the uskoks, such as Bishop de Dominis's scheme to use the income from the sale of the local forests to the Venetian Arsenal, never got beyond the paper stage.

The inevitable collapse of these schemes was not always a cause for despair among the Habsburg authorities. Diplomatic circumstances had

[24]The agreement was negotiated with the help of Germanico Malaspina, Papal nuncio at the court of Archduke Charles in Graz; Johann Kobenzel, an adviser to Archduke Charles; and Benedetto Rottondo, Archdeacon of Trogir. Malaspina was particularly concerned that the Senj border should be strengthened to protect Friuli against Ottoman attacks. For details of the negotiations see Horvat, *Monumenta uscocchorum*, vol. 1, pp. 22–25, Lopašić, *Acta confinarii*, vol. 1, pp. 84–85; 89; Theiner, *Vetera monumenta Slavorum meridionalium historiam illustrantia*, vol. 2, pp. 70, 76; Rainer, *Nuntiatur des Germanico Malaspina*, p. 8. At first 2000 florins were sent to Senj in cash and distributed among the uskoks, though there seems to have been some disagreement in Senj about how the money should be divided. Subsequently the subsidy took the form of shipments of grain for the Senj *fondaco*, rather than for uskok stipends, though even this did not forestall all complaints. The payments seem to have been discontinued after 1586, though it is not clear whether the change was caused by continued raiding by dissatisfied uskoks, the changed policies of the new pope, Sixtus V, or for some other reason. Sarpi suggests that "because [the subsidy] was not divided to everyone's satisfaction, those who were dissatisfied did not abstain from their vexations [of papal ships]" (in *La Repubblica di Venezia*, p. 410). But for Sixtus V's efforts to reduce papal spending see Rački, "Prilog za poviest hrvatskih uskoka," p. 183, and Ludwig von Pastor, *Geschichte der Päpste in Zeitalter der katolischen Reformation und Restauration*, vol. 10 (Freiburg im Breisgau, 1926), p. 87. In 1597 an archducal commission suggested that the Pope could collect a subsidy for the uskoks from all the Italian principalities "to insure their trade," each paying in proportion to their traffic on the Adriatic, but there seems to have been little enthusiasm for this revival of an uskok protection racket (I.Ö. H.K.R., Croatica, fasc. 9, 1597, Oct. No. 25: 21–23').

[25]The documents detailing Vojvoda Daničić's negotiations with Nicolò Surian are in A.S.V., Provveditore Sopraintendente alla Camera dei Confini, 243: 1 Feb. & 18 Feb. 1580 (N. Surian); 24 May 1580 (Alvise Balbi); 24 May 1580 (Zorzi Danicich). The affair was summarized by Surian in his report to the Senate (H.A.Z., Fond Šime Ljubića, 7/121: 1583; Gigante, "Venezia e gli uscocchi," pp. 26–28). Captain Raab later accused Daničić of secret negotiations with the Venetians, and judging by the testimony of the uskoks he certainly seemed to have agreed on a truce, but it is unclear whether this involved the payment of stipends or indeed whether Raab had approved it (I.Ö. H.K.R. Croatica, fasc. 4, 1584, Apr. No. 2: 61 [Sestriz]; 114 [Khaizot]).

only to change, and the same officials who had recently spoken of stronger controls and the need for uskok subsidies would be granting the uskoks license to plunder and urging that they compensate for their lack of provisions with Ottoman booty. Similarly, each proposal that the uskoks be removed from Senj and replaced by more disciplined troops would in the end be resolved in favor of the uskoks, no matter how disruptive their actions may have appeared. Until 1618 the Habsburg's attitude would always echo the answer that Ferdinand I made to the Venetian ambassador's complaints in 1553: "Only these people seem suited to guard the borders, being courageous and willing to suffer; which neither Germans, nor men of any other nation could do, but only these, who are able to fight for many days with only a single loaf of bread per man."[26] That single loaf of bread cost the Habsburgs far less than the regular wages necessary to maintain a garrison of more disciplined German troops in Senj.

Venetian critics often suggested that Habsburg tolerance of the uskoks was less a matter of official penny-pinching than of ministerial greed. Variations on the tale of a costly pearl necklace seen adorning the neck of the Archduke's wife by the very same Jewish merchant who had lost it to the uskoks were repeated endlessly as evidence of the lucrative bribes the very highest authorities received from the uskoks.[27] Uskok plunder did indeed contribute to Military Frontier finances, for the commanders claimed a certain proportion of all booty (the *regalia*), to be surrendered before the spoils were divided among the participants. This arrangement was carefully regulated and was in line with the obligations of soldiers elsewhere on the border.[28] Over and above such obligations, however, the uskoks were accustomed to make a selection during the division of booty of "the best things and the most precious, taken out to give to the Ministers of the Princes, who profit from them greatly."[29] Although these gifts may have purchased protection for the uskoks, they

[26]In Kravjànszky, "Il processo degli Uscocchi," p. 242.

[27]*Commissiones et relationes venetæ*, vol. 6, p. 14 (possibly the origin of the tale); Minucci, *Storia degli uscocchi*, p. 225; Rački, "Prilog za poviest hrvatskih uskoka," p. 241; *Ragioni della Republica Venetiana contra Uscochi* (Dalmazagho, 1617), n.p. (a more general version).

[28]For the division of booty in Senj and elsewhere on the frontier, see Lopašić, *Acta historiam confinii*, vol. 1, p. 65; Ivan Kukuljević-Sakcinski, ed., *Acta Croatica*, Monumenta historica Slavorum meridionalium, 1 (Zagreb, 1863), p. 280; Ivić, "Prilozi za povijest Hrvatske i Slavonije u 16. i 17. veku," pp. 302–3. In Žumberak the uskoks surrendered one-third of the booty to their superiors (Lopašić, *Acta historiam confinii*, vol. 1, pp. 5–6). See also Vojin Dabić, "Prilog proučavanju ratne privrede u hrvatskoj, slavonskoj i banskoj krajini od polovine XVI do kraja XVII veka," *Istorijski časopis* (Belgrade), 22 (1975): 91–95. This sort of arrangement was normal military usage throughout Europe in this period (Fritz Redlich, *De praeda militari: Looting and Booty, 1500–1815*, Vierteljahrschrift für Sozial- und Wirtschaftsgeschichte, 39 [Wiesbaden, 1956], pp. 13–14, 41–44).

[29]In H.A.Z., Fond Šime Ljubića, 2/33: 281.

did little to secure the uskoks' day-to-day needs. Indeed, Minucci suggested that the need to produce such bribes stimulated yet more raiding, "for having contributed so much to satiate the greed of their Captain and various others who commanded the Captain, and to maintain themselves in favor with the ministers of the Imperial Court, and the ministers of the Archducal Court in Graz . . . only a tiny part remained for themselves."[30]

The Economics of Raiding

Livestock. Undoubtedly, much uskok raiding was directly linked to dearth in Senj. The complaint runs as a leitmotif through all attempts to restrict uskok actions, voiced by anxious Venetian commanders who braced themselves for uskok expeditions as supplies in the city ran low; by the Captains of Senj, granting permission for forays ("as giving them a way of getting some booty for themselves, for without it they cannot live, particularly as . . . they are owed twenty-one months' wages");[31] and by the uskoks themselves ("the soldiers say that they cannot live on air").[32] In some cases it is possible to correlate the intensity of raiding with specific pressures on resources, such as delays in official supplies, or scarcity caused by Venetian blockades. To a great degree, the uskoks' raids had as their aim not the physical destruction of the enemy but the acquisition of plunder. Uskoks were certainly known to fire Ottoman towns and to ambush Ottoman troops, particularly under the military leadership of their Captain, but much more often their ambushes were laid for caravans of goods and their raids were timed to correspond to the movement of flocks or the rhythms of shipping.

Raids into Lika and the Ottoman hinterland yielded booty primarily in cattle, needed to augment the unreliable grain shipments provided by the Hofkriegsrat. In 1598 Captain Paradeiser described the seasonal pattern of raids: "In winter when, in the snow and intense cold, the enemy drives their cattle to the seaside, and keeps them there, and there is no danger to worry about" the uskoks usually "sally out for meat and other things they are not able to buy to supply their bare wants. . . . In the summer they cannot maintain themselves with such commodity and good opportunity, because of hardship and the fear of the enemy, who are then abroad and causing them worry, so that they must remain in the

---

[30]Minucci, *Storia degli uscocchi*, p. 225.

[31]Report of an anonymous spy in Senj, quoting the Captain, in A.S.V., Provveditori da Terra e da Mar, 420: 18 July 1606.

[32]In A.S., Deželni stanovi za Kranjsko, 292e: 2480–81 (5 July 1607).

fortress to ensure its defense and security."[33] The two great festivals of winter and spring, Christmas and Easter, were regularly the occasion for uskok raids against the Vlach flocks then grazing on the sheltered shores of the Adriatic, where the cattle could easily be seized and transported back to provide for celebrations in a season when supplies were often exhausted. Cattle seized on the coast might be driven back up the island of Pag and then ferried across to the mainland. When there was no immediate threat of pursuit, the animals were slaughtered immediately and the meat packed into barks to be shipped back to Senj. If circumstances were threatening, the uskoks might ransom the cattle back to the owners. Captured cattle brought into Senj were usually distributed and consumed quickly. (Some uskoks made sure that they ate their fill by coming ashore some miles below Senj and gorging themselves on hastily roasted meat before returning with the rest of their booty.) A part of the meat might be preserved for later consumption, but salt for treating a large cargo of meat was often not available. The salt trade in the Adriatic was strictly controlled by Venice, and the Provveditore Generale had been known to interrupt the importation of salt from Istria deliberately in order to hinder Senj's efforts to stretch out its meat supplies.[34] Consequently, the uskoks raided frequently to ensure a supply of meat.

Reports of constant small livestock raids form the bulk of Ottoman complaints against the Venetian commanders responsible for the security of the border, each new letter much like those preceding it, lamenting the capture of a few head of cattle or one or two captives in conventional phrases. These letters tell us very little about the circumstances of the uskoks' raids, but their numbers testify to the scale of this petty cattle rustling. Most of the animals came from Ottoman territory, but as it became more difficult to take booty in Lika toward the end of the sixteenth century, the uskoks began to requisition provisions from Venetian subjects on the islands or the coast. Here they often paid for the animals they seized, though they might also extract a petty tribute in roast mutton by a combination of threats and boasts, and it was not unknown that they should use brute force to satisfy their hunger. The Venetian practice of compiling dossiers of uskok actions for diplomatic use gives us a detailed picture of these small raids. Here too the cumulative effect of their requisitions could be remarkable. A dossier of uskok actions in northern Dalmatia, primarily between February and April 1606, shows the predominance of animal theft—some sixty-two separate raids carrying off from one to sixty head of livestock, totaling 495 head of various types of livestock. Interspersed among these incidents were less

---

[33]In I.Ö. H.K.R., Croatica, fasc. 9, 1598, Mar. No. 56 (31 Mar. 1598).
[34]A.S.V., Provveditori da Terra e da Mar, 922: 2 July 1600.

frequent demands for wine, bread, clothes, and similar necessities. Not all their requisitions were stolen—many of the complainants reported that the uskoks had paid (or promised to pay) for their supplies, and given Venetian strictures against consorting with uskoks, many payments may have been tacitly passed over in the reports.[35]

Why did the uskoks engage so heavily in stealing animals rather than other food supplies? Part of the answer lies in the economy of the border, which had shifted decisively from agriculture to stockherding. In the unstable conditions caused first by the Ottoman incursions and then by prolonged border warfare, much fertile agricultural land had been converted to pasturage. This was the case in the Zadar district for, as a Venetian syndic noted, it was easier to save cattle than produce before the onslaughts of the Turk.[36] Elsewhere abandoned land had been taken over by stockherder settlers, who brought their flocks with them and only slowly turned to farming. (Perhaps, too, a widespread Balkan shift to livestock raising in the sixteenth century was a response to changing European trade patterns.)[37] Not only was livestock portable and immediately useful for uskok needs, it was also the most available product of the rural economy. Furthermore, the uskoks were not the only ones engaged in cattle raiding; it was commonplace among the pastoral peoples of the border, for whom cattle theft had both an economic function (the redistribution of resources) and a cultural one (competition over honor and power).[38]

Captives. were the second most important objects of the uskoks' Ottoman raids, and many Ottoman subjects, both Muslim and Christian, were taken prisoner. The trade in captives (either for ransom or for sale as slaves) was, like cattle raiding, a long-established practice in the Mediterranean borderlands. Although the Dalmatian communes had legislated against the slave trade in the late middle ages, the practice was given a new impetus from the end of the fifteenth century, as thousands of captives were carried off to Anatolian slave markets by the invading Turks. In subsequent centuries the seizure, ransom, and sale of pris-

---

[35]A.S.V., Provveditori da Terra e da Mar, 420: May 1606.

[36]In *Commissiones et relationes venetæ*, vol. 3, pp. 18–19.

[37]Fikret Adanir, "Tradition and Rural Change in Southeastern Europe during Ottoman Rule," in *The Origins of Backwardness in Eastern Europe: Economics and Politics from the Middle Ages until the Early Twentieth Century,* ed. Daniel Chirot (Berkeley, 1989), pp. 144–46; see also B. McGowan, *Economic Life in Ottoman Europe: Taxation, Trade, and the Struggle for Land, 1660–1800* (Cambridge, 1981), p. 39.

[38]Compare the studies of contemporary animal theft in Greece in J. C. Campbell, *Honour, Family and Patronage: A Study of Institutions and Moral Values in a Greek Mountain Community* (Oxford, 1964), and Michael Herzfeld, *The Poetics of Manhood: Contest and Identity in a Cretan Mountain Village* (Princeton, 1985).

oners became a commonplace of warfare on both the Muslim and Christian sides of the frontiers. Subjects of the Porte served as domestics in Dalmatian and Italian households, rowed as galley slaves for the maritime powers of the West, and labored on the feudal estates of Carniolan landowners. In Senj, however, captives were of little use as a work force (indeed, their presence in Senj was often a nuisance, for they had to be fed from their captors' scanty provisions, and arrangements for their detention were not escape-proof). For the uskoks, captives were of value solely as articles of commerce, whether for ransom, sale, or exchange.

Ransom was the most common method of turning a captive into capital. Arrangements would often be agreed upon immediately after the prisoner was taken, either with the prisoner himself, with relatives, or with a ransom broker. The ransom itself might consist of a sum of money or, more often, a payment in kind. Such ransoms were important as a source of provisions for the city. In times of scarcity, uskoks might refuse to accept money, demanding instead grain and meat—more valuable commodities in their straitened circumstances.[39] Because such sources of supply were so important to the city, the negotiation and delivery of these ransoms were not always left to the vagaries of the individual captor and debtor. These could be an official matter, arranged at the highest level. In 1588 the Captain of Senj, Furio Molza, organized an uskok expedition down the coast to collect a large ransom in grain, "which was offered to me by the Turks, who asked that their ransoms be collected in those parts." On this occasion the uskoks succeeded in bringing the badly needed grain to Senj, with the loss only of a Turkish captive demanded *in dono* by Pisani, the Venetian Capitano contra uscocchi. They were not always so lucky, however, if Pisani's claims to have confiscated a number of grain barks sent to Senj as ransom were true.[40]

With Venetian officials diligently suppressing such avenues of supply, ransoms could be more discreetly discharged in cash, either sent to Senj itself or collected elsewhere by agreement—even, to divert Venetian suspicions, by the women of Senj, who went "under the guise of their feminine sex and in the name of familial ties to the places of the Venetian Republic where they made their contracts, receiving their debts in cash or in merchandise from the subjects of the Turk in payment of their

[39]This was the case in 1600, when the uskoks were reported to be ransoming their prisoners immediately for grain and meat, "not wanting to take ransoms in cash or in any other kind of goods" because of the famine in Senj (in A.S.V., Provveditori da Terra e da Mar, 923: 2 July 1600 [Pasqualigo]). An earlier attempt by Venetian commanders to prevent the transport of Turkish ransoms in wheat and corn to Senj had caused an outcry from the entire Senj community at the "injury and ruin" they would suffer (in A.S.V., Provveditore Sopraintendente della Camera dei Confini, 243: 8 Dec. 1579).

[40]A.S.V., Provveditore Sopraintendente della Camera dei Confini, 303: 18 Feb. 1588 (Furio Molza, Senj); *Commissiones et relationes venetæ*, vol. 6, p. 12.

ransoms."[41] Ottoman officials seem to have interfered with this trade only rarely, more often attempting to forbid the practice of paying ransom as a whole rather than obstructing individual payments.

If a ransom could not be arranged conveniently or if a more attractive market was available, the rights to uskok captives might be sold. Usually this trade simply meant that the purchaser, often from Dalmatia, would set and collect the ransom from the prisoner. Muslim captives might also be sold as slaves, usually to Italian merchants who came from Naples or Genoa, seeking galley slaves for the ships of the papal navy or the fleet of the Grand Duke of Tuscany. Such merchants might also purchase women and girls, sought as domestics in wealthy households on the other shore of the Adriatic. Senj and Rijeka were well-known sources of supply for such merchandise, and on occasion large numbers of uskok prisoners were sold into Western slavery through these ports.[42] The slave traders were particularly welcome in Senj when other markets for captives had dried up. In 1589 the Pope's attempts to buy Turkish slaves for the galleys of Naples "brought the greatest joy to the Senjani and their leaders for, because of the prohibition issued by the Paşa or sancak [Ottoman administrators] of these borders, they have not had any benefit from the captives they had taken (all ransoms having been forbidden), and now they have found this way to sell them off."[43]

But slave sales were only an intermittent source of income for Senj, and the uskoks always ransomed more captives than they sold. The demand for Turkish slaves in the West was in decline from the end of the fifteenth century (the needs of the galleys could usually be supplied more cheaply by domestic convicts) and the uskoks could not always be

[41]In A.S.V., Senato, Secreta, Materie miste notabili, 27: 12 Mar. 1591 (Contarini).

[42]June 1583: Military Frontier order that captives taken in Lika by Senj raiders to be sold "beyond the sea" (later rescinded) (Ivić, *Migracije Srba u Hrvatsku*, p. 47); 10 Dec. 1587: report of the General of Military Frontier to Archduke Charles on the sale of "a good number" of captured Vlahs and Turks to an Italian merchant (Lopašić, *Acta historiam confinii*, vol. 1, pp. 154–55); 1587–90: various documents on the trade in slaves carried out by Giovanni Ambrosio Benedetti, merchant of Genoa, and others, including 1587: list of expenses for the purchase and shipment of fourteen slaves bought in Senj (Pompeo Molmenti, *Venice: Its Individual Growth from the Earliest Beginnings to the Fall of the Republic*, trans. Horatio F. Brown, 6 vols. (Cambridge, Mass., 1905–6), vol. 2, pt. 2, pp. 306–8); 5 Feb. 1589: agreement between Benedetti and others for the purchase of slaves ("of the Turkish nation and no other sort") in Senj (Tenenti, "Gli schiavi di Venezia alla fine del cinquecento," pp. 62–63); same date: note of Benedetti's expenses and assets in Senj (A.S.V., Miscellanea di Atti Diversi Manoscritti, 134/6: 5 Feb. 1589); 1590: contract made in Ravenna to buy Turkish slaves in Senj (ibid.: 3 June 1590); 1589: report on the extent of trade in slaves captured by uskoks by the Chancellor of Rijeka ("No ship leaves Fiume [Rijeka] for Apulia without a Turkish slave—male or female—on board") (in A.S.V., Provveditori da Terra e da Mar, 416: 8 May 1589).

[43]Report to Austrian commissioners in Senj from Chancellor of Rijeka, in A.S.V., Provveditori da Terra e da Mar, 416: 8 May 1589; I.Ö. H.K.R., Croatica, fasc. 5, 1589, Feb. No. 2: 9 Feb. 1589.

sure of finding a buyer for their captives. Even when there was a sudden urgent need for oarsmen, the prices offered for slaves were significantly lower than those the uskoks could usually hope to receive as ransoms. Throughout the sixteenth century, contracts for the purchase of galley slaves from the Croatian Littoral specified a maximum final price of 35 to 60 ducats.[44] In contrast, the ransom of an Ottoman subject could be anything from 80 to 150 ducats, with ransoms of more than 200 ducats not uncommon for wealthy or important Muslims.[45] Captives served yet another purpose: to redeem fellow uskoks in captivity on the other side. The women of Senj were particularly active in this trade, buying up the rights to captives with the intention of using them to ransom their husbands and sons from the Turks. One of the uskoks' complaints against Commissioner Joseph Rabatta in 1602 was that he had allowed twenty Turkish prisoners to escape through his negligence, thus ruining the women who had purchased them to redeem husbands in Ottoman captivity.[46]

Trade Routes. Finally, trade routes (either those followed by the hinterland caravans or the coastal shipping lanes) were also a profitable target, though of secondary importance when compared to the cattle raids into the Ottoman hinterland. The uskoks had plundered Ottoman trade on the Adriatic at least since the 1520s, when Sanuto noted the plunder of Ottoman merchandise by some men of Senj near Zadar, and since this date Venetian representatives had protested against uskok piracy, their protests growing more strident as the Republic claimed ever

[44]9 April 1549: Galley slaves for the Grand Duke of Tuscany, not to cost more than 35 gold *scudi* (A.S.F., Mediceo del Principato, 2077: 34–35; see also R. Livi, *La schiavitù domestica nei tempi di mezzo e nei moderni* [Padova, 1928], p. 331); 1589: prices of 30 sequins for a Morlach captive, 40 for a Turk for the galleys of Naples agreed with the Captain of Senj and the uskok leaders (A.S.V., Provveditori da Terra e da Mar, 416: 8 May 1589); 1590: contract for the purchase of Morlach galley slaves for the Grand Duke of Tuscany, to cost 40 *scudi* each (A.S.F., Mediceo del Principato, 2077: 633; see also Livi, *La schiavitù domestica*, p. 334). A *scudo* and a ducat were roughly equivalent; one gold sequin (*zecchino*) was worth ten *lire* (or about one and a half ducats) in 1593.

[45]A series of depositions from Trogir compiled in 1558 (as part of a Venetian dossier to be used against the uskoks in negotiations with Habsburg emissaries) gives ransoms set on Morlach subjects of the Turk ranging from 75 ducats for a woman to an upper limit of 225 ducats for a man (A.S.V., Provveditori Sopraintendenti alla Camera dei Contini, 244: Processus Tragurii, 1558). These amounts may have been slightly inflated, given the purpose of the document, but the ransoms asked by uskoks in the 1570s and 1580s are more or less the same and are about equal to those asked by citizens of Trogir of their prisoners of war in 1573 (10 to 80 ducats for a child or a woman, 80 to 150 ducats for a man, with high ransoms of 300 ducats or more for wealthy individuals). (The list of Trogir ransoms, giving name of owner, name, original price paid, ransom, current location and religion [Christian or Muslim] of captive, is in H.A.Z., Arhiv Trogira, 28: "Proclama. circa descriptionem sclavorum.")

[46]Lopašić, *Acta historiam confinii*, vol. 1, pp. 300–305.

greater responsibility for the security of the Adriatic.[47] Attacks on shipping were usually concentrated on the coastal trade: the barks that plied
between the islands or from town to town up and down the shore,
always keeping the land in sight, carrying mixed cargoes of local produce—cheeses and hides bought from the mountain Vlachs, some salted
sardines, a few barrels of wine or jars of oil. This trade had been the
natural prey of sea robbers, lurking in inlets along the rocky coast, since
antiquity. But the uskoks also took on larger targets. The *marciliane* and
brigantines that carried Ottoman goods to Dubrovnik and Ancona could
be ambushed in the maze of shallow channels that led through the
Neretva delta, and even the galleys sailing from the Albanian coast or
Dubrovnik to Venice were vulnerable when at anchor or crippled by bad
weather. (See Figure 1.)

Tribute. The uskoks acquired some of their plunder by *refraining* from
raiding. From about 1576 tributary villages on Ottoman territory paid the
uskoks a tax (usually called a *haraç*, after the Ottoman tax) to be freed from
pillaging. These tribute relations appear to have begun as unofficial arrangements between the uskok vojvodas and the villages.[48] By 1579, however, attempts had been made to put these agreements on a formal footing. In 1579 the Archdeacon of Trogir proposed to Archduke Charles that
the Ottoman villages in the Trogir hinterland return beneath the Habsburg
crown as former subjects of the Kingdom of Croatia and Hungary. They
would pay a tribute of two florins a house annually, and in return asked
for privileges protecting them from the uskoks.[49] By 1588 it was reported
that the uskoks were collecting tribute "from the mouth of the Neretva as
far as the borders of Zadar, to the amount of one sequin a house, for two or
three days' journey inland, and from the [Ottoman] Captain of Obrovac
himself, which sum must, in my opinion, amount to at least 2000 sequins."[50] By 1599 it was estimated that approximately four thousand households on Ottoman territory paid tribute in this way to the Habsburgs.[51]

[47]Sanuto, *I diarii*, vol. 36, p. 450; H.A.Z., Ispisi tajnog vatikanskog arhiva Fra Dane Zeca
II, Nunz. Germ., 55: 26'.
[48]See Chapter 7 for further details on the development of the tribute system.
[49]Lopašić, *Acta historiam confinii*, vol. 1, pp. 81–88.
[50]In *Commissiones et relationes venetæ*, vol. 6, p. 15. In a letter to the Beylerbey of Bosnia
written in 1591, the Sultan noted that "a good 10,000 households of Ottoman subjects [in the
hinterlands of Zadar, Šibenik, Split, and Trogir] are forced to pay tribute to the Christians as
well." This is mentioned in the context of uskok raids on the area, but probably also
includes the villages in areas disputed between Venice and the Porte (In *I libri commemoriali*,
vol. 25, pp. 60–61). Similar tribute arrangements were also made elsewhere on the Ottoman
borders toward the Military Frontier in exchange for protection from raiding. See Dabić,
"Prilog proučavanju ratne privrede," pp. 100–101.
[51]*Commissiones et relationes venetæ*, vol. 5, p. 281. They paid three thalers a household,
amounting to 12,000 thalers annually.

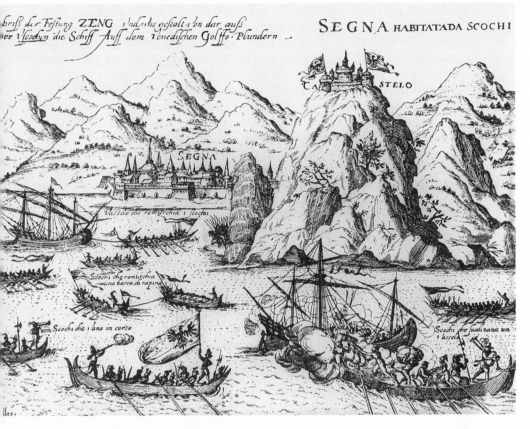

1. "Abriss der Festung Zeng" (Sketch of the Senj Fortress) (1617). A fanciful view of Senj and the Nehaj fortress by Georg Keller. In the foreground, uskoks plunder bales of merchandise from a trading vessel. (Reproduced from *Senj*, Hrvatski kulturni spomenici, vol. 1, ed. Artur Schneider [Zagreb: JAZU, 1940].)

The Habsburg authorities disagreed on the wisdom of granting official protection to Ottoman subjects at all, lest the privileges given to tributaries should protect enemies of the Frontier, such as martoloses or Ottoman spies. In addition, the Captains of Senj doubted that the uskoks would be able to take sufficient plunder if they could not pillage the subjects of the Porte. If, however, such privileges were to be granted, the commanders were determined that the resulting income should be used toward the needs of the Military Frontier and not diverted by the Crown in private grants.[52] This was indeed the way matters were eventually

[52]Lopašić, *Acta historiam confinii*, vol. 1, pp. 89–90, 93, 157–60; *Commissiones et relationes*

resolved, probably because the border troops, including the uskoks, were so actively involved in collecting the tribute payments.

Yet, it is difficult to tell how much of this tribute money the uskoks actually received. Even under the unofficial arrangements negotiated between the uskoks and their tributaries in the 1570s, the Frontier officials had received a share of the proceeds.[53] With the institutionalization of the tribute arrangements, the military commanders took more control over the distribution of the money the uskoks collected. Although the authorities had battled to retain this income for Military Frontier uses, it did not necessarily go directly to the uskoks themselves. By the early 1600s a great part of the tribute was claimed as a perquisite of office by the Captain of Senj or by the General of the Frontier. When they were forbidden to raid after the 1606 peace with the Porte, the uskoks asked that these monies be used to pay the garrison in Senj, rather than be sent to their Military Frontier superiors, emphasizing that it was due to the uskoks ("for fear of our valor") that these Ottoman subjects paid the tribute. Rudolf II confirmed Senj's rights to this income, castigating the General of the Frontier for usurping it. "There are not a few of you, and especially you, Veith Khisel, who care not for these liberties and privileges, and fear not to infringe and violate them. Furthermore you dare to snatch from their hands and sell for yourselves the tribute or contributions from the many Turkish villages and properties that our soldiers of Senj compelled to submit to this payment many years ago, by their heroism and their arms, and by the spilling of their blood, hazarding their own lives." The Hofkriegsrat in Graz appears to have been reluctant to enforce this decision because the General would lose substantial income.[54] Whether or not they received a larger share of the money, the uskoks continued to collect tribute from Ottoman villages, occasionally organizing raids when the payments were not prompt.[55]

---

venetæ, vol. 6, p. 15. When Rudolf II tried to grant his chancellor Faust Vrančić rights over the Ottoman population of Knin, who paid a tax for protection from the uskoks, there was a great outcry from Senj that these tribute monies should be so diverted (Lopašić, *Acta historiam confinii*, vol. 1, pp. 145–46, 157–60).

[53]I.Ö. H.K.R., Croatica, fasc. 2, 1579, May No. 11: 12–14'. In 1582 witnesses testified that Vojvoda Daničić had sent on to the General of the Border the splendid gifts of a horse and carpet given to him by his tributaries (I.Ö. H.K.R., Croatica, fasc. 4, 1584, Apr. No. 2: 54–54' [Stipanovitsch]; 81 [Bratkhovitsch]). Another witness reported that Ottoman tributaries had sent the General a fine steed and Captain Raab a nag (*ain klepper*) (ibid.: 89', [Jurovitsch]).

[54]In Lopašić, *Acta historiam confinii*, vol. 1, pp. 351–53; vol. 3, pp. 437–38; Sarpi, *La Repubblica di Venezia*, pp. 24–25. In 1607 the General of the Frontier countered these claims by collecting testimony from a number of Senjani to the effect that the tribute money had always been reserved for the use of the General himself (I.Ö. H.K.R., Croatica, fasc. 12, 1607, Nov. No. 25: 6–20', 29 Sept. 1607).

[55]A.S.V., Provveditori da Terra e da Mar, 1321: 28 Dec. 1602; H.A.D., Lettere di Levante, 41: 52'–53 (15 July 1605); A.S.V., Provveditori da Terra e da Mar, 424: 18 March 1610; Horvat, *Monumenta uscocchorum*, vol. 2, p. 95.

The Raiding Areas. The uskoks of Senj had three main fields of operation: Ottoman Lika, the territory east of the Velebit mountain range; the Hercegovinian hinterland farther south, particularly the areas beyond the territory of Dubrovnik; and the waters of the Adriatic. From the earliest mention of uskoks in Senj all these territories had been subject to attack, but the importance of each area as a source of plunder changed over the century. These changes were reflected in the character and goals of uskok raids. Lika was the area closest to hand and the easiest to reach from Senj by land. This was the site of much of the uskoks' early raiding, but as Ottoman and uskok raids despoiled the province, it offered less in the way of booty. When Lika was resettled and fortified by the Ottomans in the 1580s, raids there also became more hazardous. The uskoks continued to send expeditions there, but with the exception of the occasional successful cattle raid, these took on a more conventional military flavor, as uskok units burned towns and destroyed Ottoman fortifications. Uskok expeditions farther afield became commonplace, as the uskoks sailed south and struck across Venetian or Ragusan territory into the Bosnian and Hercegovinian hinterland. This new reliance on sea routes to reach their targets may have contributed to the simultaneous increase in plunder at sea, as they ventured into waters they had seldom visited formerly. In 1588 the Venetian Collegio della Militia da Mar stated that over the previous two years the uskoks had "not only risen in number but are also strengthened in quality" because of the rich booty they were taking at sea, "there being no doubt that the raids they make by way of land are of very little moment, consisting ordinarily of plundering animals or capturing some soul or other, for the most part either impotent old men, or women."[56] Perhaps the Collegio dismissed hinterland raiding too easily in its concern over maritime losses to the uskoks. The uskoks were never solely, or even primarily, sea raiders. Their piracy was largely a matter of ransacking vessels they found in port, often while on an expedition to raid inland. Unlike the corsairs of North Africa or Malta, they usually did not take the ships as prizes, to be refitted as corsairs, but instead reloaded their merchandise into their own small, fleet barks. With these they could easily surprise a ship at anchor, disembark unnoticed for a swift descent on an inland village, or flee hastily among the islands or if necessary abandon the bark on shore in the face of unexpected pursuit. Not until the very end of the uskok period, when Andrija Frletić and others took service with the Viceroy of Naples, did uskoks become deep-sea corsairs.

Possibly the quantity of booty the uskoks were able to take toward the end of the century contributed to Senj's reputation and the rise in the

[56]In A.S.V., Senato, Secreta, Materie miste notabili, 27: 10 May 1588.

number of the uskoks. Their growing numbers made it all the more difficult for them to sustain themselves when Venetian blockades and tighter Military Frontier controls on raiding in the 1590s and early 1600s kept them bottled up in the Velebit Channel. Under these circumstances they were forced back on the resources of Lika, Krbava, and the Ottoman hinterland of Zadar, where, a Venetian reported, "without acquiring that enormous booty they were accustomed to find at sea, but only animals and the occasional captive, plunder of little importance, they often suffer vigorous encounters with the Ottoman cavalry, resulting in the imprisonment and death of their own, and often a greater loss than a gain, so that they live in great desperation."[57] This desperation more than once found relief in booty plundered from Venetian subjects, either on the nearby islands or in Istria. Even Commissioner Rabatta, no friend of the uskoks and delegated to control them, protested that Venetian intransigence meant that the uskoks, cut off from their normal fields of operation by blockades, were forced to take booty where they could find it, and this meant on Venetian territory or at sea (which in the eyes of the Signoria amounted to the same thing):

> The Senjani, before they were besieged by the Venetians and prevented from going freely into the lands of the Turk to take the tribute and ransom from which the maintenance of their incomes depends, had never performed those actions (except for the most trifling) which displease the Venetians; but since the siege has deprived them of this liberty, these operations have become more a necessity, if they do not wish to die of hunger, than a wish to do ill; and they have gone out to plunder [Venetian subjects], the resulting damages being greater or lesser according to the harassment or blockade they have been subject to from the Venetians and their fleet.[58]

Trade as a Function of Plunder

Before the incursions of the Ottoman armies and the coming of the uskoks, Senj had been a transit port with a thriving trade fair. A late fifteenth-century merchant's handbook put Senj in the same category as Dubrovnik and Zadar and indicated a developed trade between Senj and Venice in iron, copper, lead, and tin from the mines in the city's hinterland; in grain and flour; in cloth of linen, silk, wool, and fustian; and

---

[57]In *Commissiones et relationes venetæ*, vol. 6, p. 100. And see Provveditore Generale Donà, 1599, on the difficulties faced by the uskoks in sustaining the current level of plunder (under conditions of blockade) "the booty they can make by land alone not sufficing for these most greedy people" (*Commissiones et relationes venetæ*, vol. 5, p. 282).

[58]In Lopašić, *Acta historiam confinii*, vol. 1, p. 285.

in wood and wood products.[59] This trade flagged in the face of the Ottoman conquest of the hinterland to the south and the continuing threat to the more northerly routes from maurauding raiders. Already by 1529 the citizens of Senj were complaining that if the roads closed by the Ottoman raiders were not freed, "there will be no reason for us to live here . . . if they close off access by the sea no one will be able to come to us by land even if they wanted to . . . and the merchants in this way will have no one with whom to trade."[60] They were right. With the cutting of the trade routes to the interior, Senj's importance as a transit port was virtually destroyed.

The town itself produced very little, apart from wood and charcoal from the nearby Velebit forests. Their most important product at the beginning of the century had been oars and masts for the Venetian Arsenal.[61] The danger posed by Ottoman raiding parties soon made wood cutting a hazardous occupation, but Senj continued to cut and export a small amount of wood throughout the century. When regulations against raiding were strictly enforced, there was little alternative for some of the uskoks but to chance their luck felling timber in the hinterland.[62] Plans for the reform of the uskoks often sought to substitute the exploitation of this rich natural resource for the proceeds of piracy in Senj's economy, pointing out that the sale of Velebit wood products would benefit all those involved by providing the uskoks with an honest income, sparing the Habsburgs the expense incurred in the upkeep of the garrison, and ensuring a reliable source of building material for the Venetian Arsenal.[63] But the very real Ottoman threat was not

[59]Franco Borlandi, ed., *El libro di mercatantie et usanze de' paesi* (Turin, 1936), pp. 51–52.

[60]In Laszowski, *Monumenta habsburgica*, vol. 1, pp. 172–73.

[61]When it appeared that no more oars would be forthcoming from Senj in 1527, both because the town had sworn fealty to Ferdinand and because of Ottoman raids, there was consternation in the Arsenal lest no alternative source could be found (Sanuto, *I diarii*, vol. 45, p. 392; *Commissiones et relationes venetæ*, vol. 2, pp. 38–39).

[62]It was claimed that this industry was abandoned when the Turks crossed the Una in the 1550s (Leva, *Legazione di Roma*, p. 140); however, in 1577 wood products were still accorded great importance in Senj's tariff list (Herkov, "Carinski cjenik grada Senja," pp. 64, 66). See also Captain Denti of Bakar on the export of wood only during truce with the Turks in 1554 (in *Commissiones et relationes venetæ*, vol. 3, pp. 63–64); Ledenice was raided by Venetian forces in 1600 while the garrison was in the mountains cutting wood (Lopašić, *Acta historiam confinii*, vol. 1, p. 274; *Commissiones et relationes venetæ*, vol. 6, p. 100); and the Senj garrison, forced to cut wood for sale to keep from starving in 1642, was attacked by Turks (Lopašić, *Acta historiam confinii*, vol. 2, pp. 259–60). After about 1618 there are many references to Dalmatian barks going to Senj to purchase wood in the dispatches of Venetian commanders from the Zadar area (for example, in A.S.V., Provveditori da Terra e da Mar 60: dispatches of A. Zorzi, Rector of Zadar, 1619–20). See also W. von Valvasor, *Die Ehre des Herzogthums Krain*, 4 vols. (Laibach, 1689; reprint, Rudolfswerth, 1877–79), vol. 3, p. 89, for references to the Senj wood trade.

[63]An early version of this plan was proposed by L. Renaldi of Krk, (in A.S.V., Capi del Consiglio dei Dieci: Lettere Rettori, 282: 12 Oct. 1581). Marc'Antonio de Dominis, Bishop of

the only impediment to the development of a full-fledged wood trade in Senj. Habsburg distress at the loss of tariff income caused by the shift of trade away from Rijeka in the late sixteenth and early seventeenth centuries led to vigorous attempts to channel all timber exports through Rijeka, to the detriment of rival ports such as Bakar. Senj was also a potential rival to Rijeka's trade, and it was not at all in the interests of its lord, the Archduke of Styria, to encourage any revival of Senj's earlier success as a port.[64]

Many observers blamed the arrival of the uskoks in Senj for the decay of Senj's trade, contrasting the honest labors of earlier merchants with the indolence of uskoks who lived only on their ill-gotten gains: "All are intent on piracy, so that, as could be forseen from the beginning, every commerce, every art, every industry has been extinguished, and the land around is deserted and uncultivated; there remained only a few vines outside Senj in its little plain, which too have been removed because the land on which they were planted was needed for an earthwork and for the walls above the sea, and so this city has been made infamous and impracticable, living solely from theft and from the blood of others."[65] Another Venetian repeated the same judgment: "All reputation for business and for foreign commerce has been extinguished."[66]

But it was not true that concentration on raiding resulted in an abandonment of commerce. What is piracy, after all, but the exchange of goods by force rather than purchase? Not all plundered goods could be consumed in Senj—what would be done with the cargo of ostrich feathers worth 2400 ducats seized in a 1597 raid on a ship coming from Zante?[67] To profit from such plunder the uskoks had to sell it on the

---

Senj, would have used the forests to support Senj in a slightly different manner—the Habsburgs should sell the rights to the wood to Venice and use this sum to pay the garrison. In spite of much negotiation this scheme was never realized. See in particular the documents in Ljubić, "Prilozi za životopis Markantunu Dominisu," pp. 1–260.

[64]For the slow decline of Rijeka and Habsburg efforts to improve its trade, see Gestrin, *Trgovina*, pp. 112–19; and for relations between Rijeka and Bakar, see Gigante, "Rivaltà fra i porti di Fiume e Buccari," pp. 154–91. The excise officials of Rijeka sometimes employed the uskoks as customs guards to seize ships taking cargoes of wood or grain to Venice from Bakar. According to the Captain of Rijeka, such exports constituted tax evasion and contraband because they had not paid the customary excise duties at Rijeka, "with the greatest damage to the Treasury of His Most Serene Highness and this poor city" (A.S., Deželni stanovi za Kranjsko, 293: 1829 [23 Nov. 1611]; see also ibid.: 1795 [21 Nov. 1611] [complaint by the Provveditore di Krk]; ibid., 293a/1: 307–10 [3 Mar. 1612] [complaint by Čikulin, Zrinski's overseer in Bakar]; Lopašić, *Acta historiam confinii*, vol. 2, pp. 24–27 [complaint from Nikola Zrinski]). The Venetian authorities monitored such incidents carefully, using them as a pretext for blockading the Croatian Littoral in 1611 and 1612 (A.S.V., Provveditori da Terra e da Mar, 425: 6 Feb. 1612; 426: 3 March 1612; 427: 26 Jan. 1612; A.S., Deželni stanovi za Kranjsko, 293: 1921 [11 Dec. 1611]).

[65]In H.A.Z., Fond Šime Ljubića, 2/33: 281.

[66]In *Commissiones et relationes venetæ*, vol. 6, p. 103.

[67]Tenenti, *Naufrages*, p. 202.

marketplace. Rather than extinguishing commerce, the raids of the uskoks moved it into new channels. The wax, hides, honey, and coarse cloth from the hinterland; the wine, salted fish, figs, and coral of the coast; the finer cloth, grain, and more exotic goods of the Adriatic and Levant trade: much of the uskoks' booty from raids on shipping and caravans went into the hands of merchants. The captives sold as slaves also contributed, on a smaller scale, to Senj's market economy. It could be argued that it was, in fact, largely the plunder brought back to Senj by the uskoks' raids which preserved the economic life of the port at all. One anonymous author even went so far as to imply that uskok involvement in trade could wean them away from their role as border soldiers: "These valorous warriors have become most avaricious merchants of stolen goods, devoting themselves to nothing else than the sale of their plunder in Croatia, in Carniola, in Styria, in Hungary, even across the sea in Apulia and the Marches, and even in Venice itself, so that having abandoned the military arts they are applying themselves to one that is sweeter, that is, to profit."[68]

There was a grain of truth in this statement. Some of the uskoks were in touch with a wide economic network and did manage to parlay their share of the booty into larger enterprises. Matija Daničić, a member of an illustrious uskok family, raided together with the other uskoks, but he also became a wealthy merchant and was able to pay off an Ottoman ransom by importing grain on a large scale from the Metlika area and selling it to Venetian traders through Bakar. (The Daničić family also profited from another aspect of the grain business, for they owned mills in Žrnovnica, where the grain for the Senj soldiers was ground.)[69] Usually, however, the uskoks were less successful in parlaying their booty into wealth. They could rarely choose their markets and were often forced to take whatever price they could get for their plunder—if they managed to sell it at all. In 1601 Ivan Budanović and his band of renegade uskoks went to Rijeka trying to sell illicit booty (barrels of salted sardines they had seized from a Hvar fishing boat). When the Rijeka merchants, worried by the severe new regulations restricting the purchase of plunder, refused to buy, the uskoks had to hide the barrels under vines and bushes in Trsat before going home empty-handed.[70] This refusal was unusual, for more often the merchants were accommodating. Nev-

[68]In Horvat, *Monumenta uscocchorum*, vol. 1, p. 388.
[69]See Gestrin, *Trgovina*, pp. 51, 118; Horvat, *Monumenta uscocchorum*, vol. 1, p. 37. King Rudolf had granted Žrnovnica to Juraj Daničić in 1583 (Lopašić, *Acta historiam confinii*, vol. 1, p. 118). The mills were burned by Venetian forces in 1612 in retaliation for uskok raiding (A.S.V., Provveditori da Terra e da Mar, 426: 4 Sept. 1612; Sarpi, *La Repubblica di Venezia*, p. 49; Tamaro, "Episodi di storia fiumana," p. 19).
[70]Horvat, *Monumenta uscocchorum*, vol. 1, pp. 400, 402–3.

ertheless, it does show that the uskoks were at the mercy of the local markets in trying to profit from their plunder. As a rule, however, it was not the uskoks themselves who peddled Senj's plunder throughout local markets but rather those who made it their business to supply the uskoks' day-to-day needs.

Because the uskoks had no regular income, they depended on the merchants and artisans for credit until they could take a rich booty or until the pay commissioners arrived in Rijeka. Giovanni of Fermo, a merchant himself, told how this credit was arranged, describing the business of Vicenzo de Santi (Desantić), one of the wealthiest merchants in Senj:

> He could be called the father of this country, for he has oil, wine, and other goods brought from Apulia, and he aids the poor in their needs, although he takes care to have their pledges in his hands. . . . He gives his goods in this way: whoever is in need goes to him and asks for grain, wine, and oil to leave with his family while he is out after booty; as soon as he returns the merchant is paid; and he leaves as a pledge more than enough silver to secure the debt, and in this way he does a good business.[71]

Giovanni noted that Vicenzo held more than 30,000 ducats' worth of pledges of this sort and made a great deal of profit from them, for those who died in action could not redeem their pledges, and they remained his property.[72] Often, however, the uskoks could not cover their debts with a pledge and a promissory note was given instead:

> It happens that one of them may take money on loan, or more likely goods on credit; if he who takes the goods does not know how to write, the merchant or friend who is loaning the goods makes out a note according to the usual form, adding at the end, because the borrower does not know how to write, he will seal this document with his seal (for however poor a man may be, he has one made of silver), or not having a seal he will make a cross (†) by hand, swearing to the Holy Lord that he is this debtor. . . . They will say "When I return from the raid, fifteen days later I will pay, or else at that time I will give satisfaction in plunder" and this word they inviolably observe.[73]

Nearly all of Senj's domestic economy revolved around this system of credit against booty, from the small merchants and artisans, the pros-perous middlemen like de Santi, and even the company that employed

---

[71] In Rački, "Prilog za poviest hrvatskih uskoka," pp. 238–39.
[72] Ibid., p. 239.
[73] In Ibid., p. 240.

Giovanni of Fermo, which supplied the Military Frontier itself on credit, providing the Senj *fondaco,* or storehouse, with grain to the sum of six, eight, or even ten thousand ducats before they were paid by the Military Frontier commissioners, who then began a new account.[74] As a result of this pervasive indebtedness, as soon as the uskoks brought in any plunder, or as soon as they were paid, their gains immediately went to pay off their debts. "It has never been heard that any uskok has become rich," Archbishop Minucci wrote, and went on to tell the story of "an old uskok, maimed, lying all the time in bed, destitute of any aid, who confessed that he had participated in so much booty in his day that the shares due him had certainly exceeded 80,000 ducats; yet he was wretched and a beggar."[75] Although the wealth of the Adriatic trade might pass through their hands, the uskoks themselves were rarely able to capitalize on it.

Merchants such as Vicenzo de Santi were not simply providing a service to the uskoks whose wages did not stretch far enough. Their loans were an investment in the prospect of uskok plunder. They were not the only inhabitants of Senj to invest in this way, for the expenses of an uskok expedition were divided among many shareholders, only a few of whom actually participated in the raids. Vettor Barbaro described the system that developed as a collective enterprise involving most of Senj:

> Everyone shares in [the booty], for those who because of age or infirmity are not able to go themselves maintain servants at their expense and send them on their account, or they keep boats which they give to the uskok companies, and for each boat they receive two parts of the booty. To uskoks who are unable to provision themselves for their journeys they give each 30 loaves of bread and a ducat, and receive a half share; and finally the friars and priests go in person and attend to this traffic, and also the women who have sufficient commodity to be able to do this, so that as all of them live in this way, all other exercises are forgotten.[76]

When a raid returned to Senj with booty, it was divided into shares

---

[74]Ibid., pp. 192–93.

[75]Minucci, *Storia degli uscocchi*, p. 225.

[76]In H.A.Z., Fond Šime Ljubića, 2/33: 281. Minucci gives a similar description of the process: "Some who were ashamed to mix with the rogues would keep a servant in the house to go out with the others on the raids and bring back a part of the plunder to his patron; and others gave the poor supplies or other necessities, agreeing that they should have a part of the booty, and so everyone had an interest in it" (*Storia degli uscocchi,* p. 222). See also Friedrich von Hurter, *Geschichte des Kaiser Ferdinands II und seiner Eltern,* 11 vols. (Schaffhausen, 1850–64), vol. 2, p. 136; Sarpi, *La Repubblica di Venezia,* pp. 52–53; Rački, "Prilog za poviest hrvatskih uskoka," p. 240. Various details on the ways in which the Senjani invested in uskok raids appear in the 1558 dossier of interrogations from Cres and Lošinj (A.S.V., Provveditore Sopraintendente alla Camera dei Confini, 243: Processus Chersi i Ausseri, 1558).

and distributed to the Captain and the officers of the border, to those who had been present on the raid, and to those who had helped finance the expedition. This method of spreading the costs and the risks of a raid, repeated in corsair communities throughout the Mediterranean in the sixteenth century, ensured the town's active interest in uskok success.[77] It also meant that most uskok booty quickly passed into the hands of middlemen, whether as payment of a debt, as shares obtained through investment, or as purchase of an uskok share.

It was for the most part these middlemen who exploited the trade in marketable booty, if they were citizens or nobles of Senj availing themselves of the tax exemptions enshrined in the city statute and the tariff list.[78] Although the volume of trade passing through the city was negligible in comparison with that of past centuries, the Senjani still zealously preserved the privileges and exemptions they had acquired earlier, and they did what they could to nurture Senj's role as a northern Adriatic marketplace, using whatever means were to hand. Uskok booty was a welcome addition to the few hinterland goods that still found their way to the port. It also appears that the Senjani tried to use the uskoks to increase traffic through the town more directly. Although happy enough to cooperate in the Habsburg harassment of the Bakar trade with Venice by sending uskok patrols to seize "contraband" ships that had not paid the Rijeka excise, the Senjani were not content to see Rijeka alone profit, and they attempted similar strong-arm tactics to bring ships to their own port in the seventeenth century.[79]

---

[77]Descriptions of the division of uskok booty given by former inhabitants of Senj and visitors from Baška on Krk appear in A.S.V., Provveditore Sopraintendente alla Camera dei Confini 243: Processus Vegliæ, 1558. Similar syndicates of private investors, each receiving a share of the booty, funded Algerian and Maltese corsair ships in this same period (Earle, *Corsairs of Malta and Barbary*, pp. 73–74, 123–24).

[78]The tariff list, drawn up in 1577 in Vienna to regulate the collection of the excise taxes, gives an idealized picture of the character of the traffic through Senj in the late sixteenth century. It does, however, illustrate the determination of the Senjani to protect their part in whatever trade survived by incorporating nearly all of the privileges specified in the 1388 statute (Herkov, "Carinski cjenik"). The actual volume of trade is impossible to estimate in the absence of excise records. The annual income of the excise taxes between 1605 and 1612 was around two hundred florins (as compared to the 2843 florins taken as the Rijeka excise (*quarantes*) between January and September 1594) (Lopašić, *Acta historiam confinii*, vol. 2, p. 28; Gestrin, *Mitninske knjige*, p. 344). In a bad year, such as 1600, when the Venetian fleet blockaded Senj, this income would not even pay for oil for the three lamps kept burning in the fortress, the citadel, and the town (Lopašić, *Acta historiam confinii*, vol. 1, p. 280).

[79]In the State Archives in Ljubljana there is an extensive correspondence on the diversion of a Perast ship laden with wine, oil, cheese, iron, and nails from the Rijeka harbor to Senj in 1611. The Senj excise officials and merchants refused to surrender it to the Rijeka customs (the Rijeka tax had not been paid), stubbornly insisting that Senj's port taxes and privileges were as valid as Rijeka's, and collected pledges for the patron's security, in the face of Habsburg displeasure (A.S., Deželni stanovi za Kranjsko, 293: 135–38 [14 Dec. 1611]; 1901–14 [8 Dec. 1611]; 1911–16 [10 Dec. 1611]; 1931–34 [12 Dec. 1611]; 1965–68 [22 Dec. 1611];

But not even the merchants of Senj managed to parlay the booty that came into their hands into sufficient resources to establish Senj as an Adriatic trading emporium, a rival to Rijeka (or even Bakar) in buying and selling. In spite of a brief early flowering as an outlet for goods plundered anywhere in the northern Adriatic, not just by uskoks but by other pirates as well,[80] Senj remained essentially a warehouse—one that housed many varied goods, it is true, but did not succeed in profiting by them fully. Senj was no Algiers. The reasons are not difficult to find. Booty came into the city only irregularly and unpredictably, even when the uskoks were most active. It may have been enough to satisfy the requirements of the uskoks and the Military Frontier, at least most of the time, but the volume of plunder was not large enough to sustain a large commercial center through the lean periods between raids. If the uskoks were short of plunder, so were the merchants short of goods to tempt foreign buyers. Nor could such buyers be certain that they would find the articles they sought. It was an experienced slave trader who took the precaution of supplying himself with chains and manacles in Trieste before going on to look for galley slaves in Senj.[81] Furthermore, the reasons for Senj's decline as a trade port at the beginning of the century continued to hinder any revival of its former success. Merchants could take little advantage of Senj's favored position on the coast beneath a pass linking the Adriatic with the hinterland while Ottoman troops still threatened the roads and while shipping could be interrupted at any time by Venetian galleys.

These pressures meant that Senj was often forced to sell its goods cheaply. Particularly when the uskoks were under pressure from Venice or from their own masters, they could not choose their markets. As always, it was the receivers of the plunder who took the profits. Giovanni of Fermo described the financial killing made by Venetian subjects who bought up booty in cloth when the uskoks could not sell it elsewhere. "They sold their merchandise at the meanest price; I am ashamed to tell it; for they sold their goods to the rectors of Krk, Pag, Rab, Cres, Osor and to those of Istria. The velvet, worth four ducats a *braccio* was sold for one ducat; and the scarlet cloths and the others; and these rectors took it back to Venice on their return, reselling to the Turks or to others."[82] Not only rectors bought from the uskoks at a good price:

293a/1: 15–32 [3 Jan. 1612]; 1513, 1516 [20 Dec. 1612]). See also Gigante, "Rivaltà fra i porti di Fiume e Buccari," pp. 175–76, 178, 180.

[80]See *Commissiones et relationes venetæ*, vol. 3, pp. 193–94.

[81]Molmenti, *Venice*, vol. 2, pt. 2, pp. 306–8.

[82]In Rački, "Prilog za poviest hrvatskih uskoka," p. 242. (A short Venetian *braccio*, used for measuring precious textiles, was about 638 mm.; Herkov, *Mjere Hrvatskog primorja*, p. 100.)

according to an anonymous proposal to reform the uskoks written in 1601, other Venetian subjects "do business with them in plundered goods, so that the warehouses in Venice have been filled with them in the past, and perchance still are today."[83] Trade with the uskoks was nearly always officially forbidden to Venetian subjects, however. Some tried to evade these prohibitions: "Under the pretext of taking goods to the islands of Your Serenity they go idling along until, having encountered some of these uskoks, they allow themselves to be overpowered and conducted to Senj, having force for an excuse." There they exchanged supplies for cloth and other things plundered by the uskoks, at an advantageous price.[84] Even so, such buyers ran the risk of having their bargains confiscated by the Capitano contra uscocchi.

The Hasbsburg subjects living on the Zrinski estate in Vinodol north of Senj also often traded for booty in Senj when they themselves had not received a share as participants in the uskoks' raids. Even the lords of Vinodol had a part in this traffic, supplying their extensive export-import trade not only with goods bought from Venetian and Triestine merchants, but also "from the profits of Senj." As Count Juraj Zrinski became more involved in the Venetian trade toward the end of the century, however, his relations with the uskoks became cooler, and in 1599 he ordered his agent in Vinodol to punish his subjects' contacts with the Senjani. He repeated this order the following year, with the specific admonition that all his subjects should "keep clear of Senj plunder."[85]

More than the Dalmatians or the people of Vinodol, it was the merchants of Rijeka, and to a lesser extent of Trieste, the two Habsburg trading cities of the northern Adriatic, who profited from the plunder of the uskoks, buying it up cheaply and reselling it to Venetian buyers or merchants from the hinterland, as a Venetian noted in 1591: "They take away the goods that the uskoks rob secretly, and if it were not for the merchants of Fiume [Rijeka] who buy them and export them, the uskoks would not know where to sell these goods off."[86] Rijeka, rather than Trieste, was the most active in the commercialization of uskok booty. Although Trieste had taken over much of Rijeka's trade in the sixteenth century, Rijeka was better placed to exploit the goods that came through Senj. Up to the end of the sixteenth century, the city authorities encouraged trade with Senj, exempting Senj ships from the tax paid for mooring at the city quay, for example.[87] Even when the Habsburgs made

---

[83]In Horvat, *Monumenta uscocchorum*, vol. 2, p. 393.

[84]In A.S.V., Provveditori da Terra e da Mar, 922: 3 Apr. 1599.

[85]In Laszowski, "Urbar vinodolskih imanja," pp. 74, 82, 84; Laszowski, "Izbor isprava," pp. 15–16. See also Adamček, "Zrinsko-Frankopanski posjedi," pp. 35–37.

[86]A.S.V., Senato, Secreta, Materie miste notabili, 27: 11 June 1591.

[87]H.A.R., Zapisnici sjednica općinskog vijeća u Rijeci, 1593–1607: 46 (4 Nov. 1595).

a show of forbidding trade in uskok goods in Trieste to appease the Signoria, the merchants of Rijeka paid much less attention to such restrictions. One report from the Papal nuncio in Venice from 1597 is typical: "In Trieste the punishment for selling or buying goods taken by the uskoks is the gallows, but in places nearby all the merchants sell them publicly at the lowest prices, and the same is true not only in Senj but also in Fiume [Rijeka], and all these people laugh at the demonstrations made by the Emperor and the Archduke, which shows that they believe them made only for appearances."[88]

Nevertheless, the opportunity to market uskok booty was not an unmixed blessing for Rijeka, and at the end of the sixteenth century the city council was to question whether uskok booty was worth the trouble it brought. Even more than Senj, Rijeka bore the brunt of Venetian blockades of the Croatian Littoral. The pretext may have been retaliation for uskok raids, but the blockades were also a convenient way for the Signoria to damage a rival's trade in the Adriatic, and in this aim the Venetian commanders were very successful.[89] When the immediate threat of Venetian attack had passed, the city fathers worried that uskok raids in the northern Adriatic were limiting the number of ships coming to trade in the port.[90] Toward the end of the century Rijeka authorities began to issue orders restricting contact with the uskoks, though individual merchants quietly continued their lucrative dealings with Senj. Even Rijeka, anxious for any trade that would prop up its failing fortunes, found uskok booty a shaky foundation for prosperity.

In the sixteenth century Senj's economy was based almost entirely on plunder. To supply the town, the uskoks needed regular and profitable raids—or regular payments from tributaries in exchange for refraining from such raids. This need for booty helped to determine the type of actions the uskoks initiated, the areas they raided, and, to a degree, their victims. Of necessity, raiding was partnered by trade. Yet, neither the uskoks individually (except in a few cases) nor the town as a whole succeeded in making trade in booty the foundation of a broader commercial enterprise. Both the uskoks and Senj remained dependent for their livelihoods on a constant supply of plunder.

---

[88]In Horvat, *Monumenta uscocchorum*, vol. 1, p. 165.

[89]The surviving records of the city council (from 1593 to 1607, at the height of the Venetian blockades) repeat endlessly the same complaints to the Archduke against the Venetian seizure of Rijeka ships on the pretext of revenge for uskok actions. (H.A.R., Zapisnici sjednica općinskog vijeća u Rijeci, 1593–1607: 1, 19', 41, 62–62', etc.).

[90]The Rijeka council complained to Archduke Ferdinand in 1611, for example, of a possible drop in tariffs should merchants transfer their custom to other ports for fear of uskok attack (A.S., Deželni stanovi za Kranjsko, 293: 1965–68 [22 Dec. 1611]).

CHAPTER FIVE

Military Authority and Raiding

Military authority within Senj can be seen as arising from local circumstances, for until the turn of the century uskok leaders came to power through their ability to command a following—a quality that rested primarily on success in raiding. But uskok military hierarchy was also imposed by the administration of the Military Frontier, which distributed pay and offices according to its own criteria, originally merely confirming uskok decisions but increasingly attempting to control the actions of the uskoks, both directly and through the appointment of their leaders. An analysis of authority among the uskoks throws some light on the changing patterns of raiding.

According to Paolo Sarpi, the population of Senj could be divided into three groups: the natives, the paid uskoks, and the venturini.

The natives [casalini] are those, born or brought up in the city, who have had a firm domicile there for several generations. These are also called citizens [cittadini] and number about one hundred. Another two hundred are paid [stipendiati], more in title and name than in reality, and are divided into four companies of fifty each, with four captains, whom they call vojvodas. But besides these four there are other uskok leaders [capi], which is what all those who can arm a bark to go pirating are called. The vagabonds and those who have recently left Turkey, or those banished from Dalmatia or Apulia, who do not have a permanent residence in Senj, join with these and are grouped in bands. All of these latter are called venturini, and are under the command of the leaders while they are assigned to the barks in which they go out, now in small, now large numbers, robbing and plundering the neighborhood.[1]

---

[1]Sarpi, La Repubblica di Venezia, p. 52.

Sarpi's description gives a reasonably accurate picture of Senj's military organization in the sixteenth and early seventeenth centuries: a citizenry involved in the actions of the uskoks; a salaried uskok garrison, rarely paid (and a small garrison of "German" soldiers as a guard for the fortress, though Sarpi does not mention them under the rubric of "uskok"); and a large force of unpaid auxiliaries with their own leaders, all under the command of several superior uskok officers, subject to a Captain of Senj appointed by the Military Frontier.

Senj Citizens and Uskoks

The city of Senj was not simply a military installation, unlike towns such as Karlovac, which had been founded in 1578 to serve the Military Frontier. A civil society with a long tradition existed alongside the garrison. Senj was simultaneously the headquarters of a captaincy, under the authority of the Military Frontier and the Archduke, and a free royal city, subject directly to the Croatian-Hungarian King. In theory, most of the uskoks, either as immigrants to Senj or as members of the garrison, were not legally a part of Senj civil society. Although this division between civil and military spheres retained a symbolic significance, in practice the uskoks were closely integrated into the political and social life of the city.

Civil society in Senj had been organized according to its own traditions, codified in a statute written down in 1388, before Matthias Corvinus proclaimed Senj a free royal city and while the town still acknowledged the Frankopans as its lords. After the town was made the center of a captaincy in 1469, administrative power gradually accumulated in the hands of the Captain, who became not only the military but also the civil authority.[2] Yet in spite of the changes in Senj's status over the succeeding centuries, its social and political organization was still largely regulated according to the provisions of the 1388 statute.[3] In addition to establishing an administrative and legal code, the statute mapped out Senj's

[2]This change was formalized in the statute of 1640 but can be traced in the relations between the town and the Military Frontier over the previous two centuries. See Čulinović, *Statut grada Senja*, pp. 56–58.

[3]That a copy was still in official use during the uskok period is shown by the additions made to it in 1608. The reformed statute of 1640 is largely a word-for-word copy of the 1388 version. The statute of 1388 was published by Ivan Mažuranić, ed., "Statut grada Senja od godine 1388," *Arkiv za povjestnicu jugoslavensku* (Zagreb), 3 (1854): 141–70; and in a Croatian version by M. Zjačić, ed., "Statut grada Senja iz 1388. godine," *Rad JAZU* (Zagreb), 369 (1975): 39–116. The 1640 version was published by Mile Magdić, ed., "Statut kralja Ferdinanda III od godine 1640 za grad Senj," *Vjesnik Kraljevskog hrvatsko-slavonsko-dalmatinskog zemaljskoga arkiva* (Zagreb), 2 (1900): 78–97.

social structure, detailing the privileges and obligations of the inhabitants. According to this document, society was divided along several lines. As in other commune statutes of the period, the inhabitants of Senj were grouped into two categories, natives and foreigners. Native inhabitants were further divided into nobles and non-nobles. All non-nobles who lived within the city were citizens; subjects were those who lived in the district of the city. The statute details the rights and obligations of nobles and non-nobles of Senj. It touches on the rights and duties of foreigners only briefly, for the most part in reference to the regulation of their economic relations (most foreigners in Senj were probably Italian merchants at the time the 1388 statute was written down). The 1640 version of the statute records a third category that had gained importance in the meantime: *incolæ*, permanent residents of the town with no special rights, who are included with nobles and citizens in clauses regulating relations with the Captain of Senj.

Uskoks who came to Senj from outside the district were foreigners, or *incolæ*; they were outside the hierarchical order of Senj society and so they neither partook of the privileges of the nobles, even if they possessed an alien title, nor were subject to the obligations of the citizens, even if born a commoner elsewhere. Thus the uskok immigrants, though living in the city, in theory remained legally outside Senj's civil society, subject only to the military authorities (a fact the descendants of these uskoks emphasized in the eighteenth century in response to attempts by Senj nobles to assert prerogatives over them).[4] As "foreigners," uskok immigrants had no formal role in the political organization of the community, for they could not participate in the organs of communal government. In theory, uskoks coming to Senj from beyond its district could become full participants in Senj's civil society only by being received as nobles or citizens of Senj by a proclamation of the Council of Nobles.

Some tension between civil and military Senj contributed to the preservation of distinctions between the citizens of Senj and the uskok militia. Ever since Senj had been made a captaincy there had been civil resistance to the power of the captain and the Military Frontier in the city.[5] The preservation of Senj's autonomy against the encroachment of

---

[4]Drago Roksandić, "Bune u Senju i primorskoj krajini (1719–1722)," *Radovi Instituta za hrvatsku povijest* (Zagreb), 15 (1982): 42.

[5]At first it came primarily from the Church, whose empty lands were settled by the Military Frontier with military colonists who were freed from any obligations to the ecclesiastical landowners. In 1526 this conflict exploded into a battle between the Captain and the Bishop of Senj—the Bishop was attacked and beaten in his own church, and in retaliation placed the entire Senj area under an interdict, affecting the civilian population as well as the military (Farlati, *Illyricum sacrum*, vol. 4, p. 134). Somewhat later, in 1543, the Senj canons resisted attempts to make them take part in the city watch, protesting that "we are free, and not required to serve any but the Church" (Kukuljević-Sakcinski, ed., *Acta*

the military authorities meant maintaining the distinction between civil and military obligations and privileges. There is some evidence that citizens of Senj tried to maintain legal distinctions between themselves and the military personnel in Senj, particularly in reference to economic rights. In 1528, for example, they secured promises from Ferdinand I that when the citizens of Senj took Ottoman captives or other booty without the cooperation of the men under the command of the Captain they be allowed to divide their booty without interference (and presumably without giving up the required portion of plunder to the Captain).[6] This promise could not have conferred overwhelming financial advantages, for uskoks and citizens are regularly found raiding together in later years, but it did emphasize the Senj citizens' immunity from one particular type of military obligation.

The citizens and nobles of Senj also preserved statutory economic privileges that differentiated them from military personnel—mainly reduced or eliminated tariffs, set out in the statute and confirmed and augmented many times by the Habsburgs. The statute specifically provided for attempts by foreigners to circumvent their exclusion from these privileges. These rights were reasserted in the Senj tariff list of 1577, which contains an entire section detailing the exemptions and reductions due the citizens and "gentlemen" (*sintellemene*) of Senj, as well as those of other specially privileged groups (merchants from Ancona, for example), but does not mention privileges for the members of the garrison or the nonnative uskoks living in the town at all.[7] Such privileges seem to have been primarily of symbolic importance in distinguishing between citizens and newcomers in the uskok period, although of little practical relevance either to uskoks living on the proceeds of booty or to Senj merchants acting as their middlemen.

The physical organization of the town reinforced the image of a separation between civil and military society in Senj. The citadel (*kaštel*), originally built as a fortified domicile for the lords of Senj, had become the headquarters of the Captain of Senj after 1469. It formed a separate walled complex in the northeast angle of the city wall, with living quarters for the Captain or his representatives, storerooms, a dungeon, and an enclosed space for military drills. (See Figure 2.) This complex was fortified not only against attack from outside the city. While repairing the fortifications of Senj in 1550 Captain Lenković had been concerned about the weakness of the citadel walls on the inner side and had spent 250

Croatica, vol. 1, p. 244). Well into the eighteenth century there would also be secular opposition to the authority of the Military Frontier in Senj.

[6] Mile Magdić, "Regesta važnijih i znamenitijih izprava senjskih arkiva" *Vjesnik Kraljevskog hrvatsko-slavonsko-dalmatinskog zemaljskoga arkiva* (Zagreb), 2 (1899): 147.

[7] Herkov, "Carinski cjenik grada Senja od godine 1577," pp. 47–77.

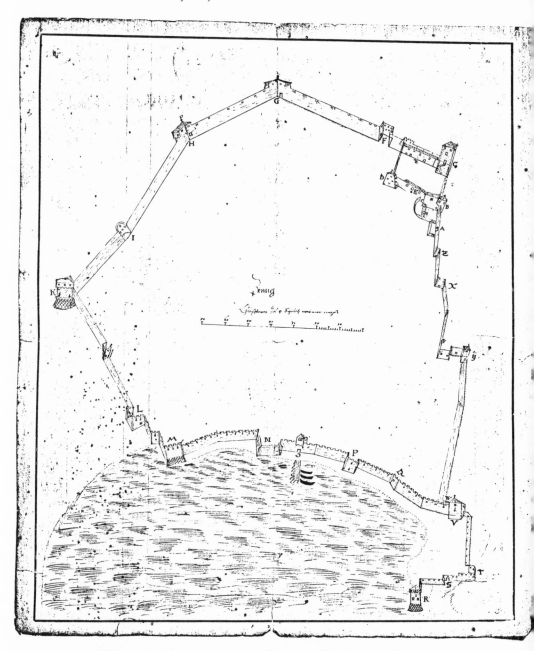

2. Diagram of the Senj fortifications (1619). This sketch was made to accompany a Military Frontier report on the conditions of the Senj fortifications. The letters B to E in the upper right designate the citadel, the area used as a command post by the Captain of Senj. (Reproduced from Arhiv Slovenije, Deželni stanovi za Kranjsko, 162/2: 76–90 [Beschreibung der Grenzfestung 1619].)

florins to improve the tower that faced the town, making it easier to defend the citadel against attack from within the city walls.[8] (Even so, the citadel could not stand up against a cannon used against it in 1601 during an uskok rebellion against Commissioner Rabatta, who had withdrawn to the citadel; the story of this attack and Rabatta's murder is told in Chapter 8.)

In 1550 Lenković also proposed building a fortress on the hill outside the walls of Senj, to prevent an enemy from taking advantage of this high position. This fortress, called Nehaj (Fear Not), was completed by 1558 and became a second stronghold for the Military Frontier forces in Senj, with its superb site and defenses and its enclosed cistern and supply stores. Here the German guard was stationed, well away from the town, probably partly by design, for successive Captains of Senj were concerned to keep their German troops strictly under their own control as loyal subordinates, uncontaminated by the conflicts of interest engendered by involvement in the town's affairs. Judging by their testimonies in an investigation of relations between the Captain and the uskoks in 1582, many of these troops were able to serve out their posting in the fortress in complete isolation from the life of the town, only ten minutes away at the bottom of the hill. When asked what he knew of recent events in Senj, Veitt Mallner, one of these guards, was reported as replying that "he knows nothing, because he pays attention to his work in the fortress, and seldom goes into the town."[9] Doubtlessly at that time this state of affairs was reinforced by the fact that, as many of Mallner's companions noted, they did not understand Croatian. Later Military Frontier officials would complain that the German guards had been supplanted by Croats, whose loyalty to the Captain was suspect because of their greater ability to assimilate in Senj. Even so, as late as 1611 a bookkeeper in the citadel, Stefan Cirfus, claimed under interrogation in a similar case of uskok insubordination, "God knows that I don't know anything about these matters, for I have my office in the citadel, and so I don't pay any attention."[10]

The physical division of Senj into civil and military zones had only a minimal influence on the relations between townspeople and uskoks, however. The uskoks, whether venturini with no official positions in the garrison or stipendiati with a wage from the Military Frontier, lived cheek by jowl with the townspeople in Senj's narrow streets. Uskok families rented houses from citizen landlords, while the wealthier uskoks acquired buildings in the center of town. In life, immigrants and citizens

[8]Lopašić, *Acta historiam confinii*, vol. 3, p. 400.
[9]In I.Ö. H.K.R., Croatica, fasc. 4, 1584, Apr. No. 2: 98.
[10]In Lopašić, *Acta historiam confinii*, vol. 2, p. 14.

prayed together, thinking ahead to their deaths they purchased burial sites next to one another, and both, concerned for life after death, solicited the prayers of the whole community in wills leaving their property to the churches and monasteries of the city. Vignettes preserved by chance in the documents record snatches of their casual conversations, their visits to taverns, the parties they attended together, their marriages. Perhaps more important, their economic lives were firmly intertwined. The town of Senj had welcomed a strong garrison as protection from the Ottoman incursions, but the raiding activities of the uskoks also offered a way to renew Senj's abruptly stifled economy. Both uskoks and natives of Senj agreed on the necessity of uskok raiding and plunder to their economic life. In this activity nearly all distinctions between town and garrison disappeared. Very soon all those living in Senj shared an interest in the uskok expeditions and were involved in some way with the economic enterprise of the uskoks.

There is little evidence that the townspeople of Senj had interests beyond and apart from those of the uskoks throughout the sixteenth and early seventeenth centuries. After the Ottoman peace of 1606, Senj was divided on what the role of the uskoks should be, in the face of Venetian blockade and Military Frontier pressure. Opinion did not split along the lines of town and garrison, but cut across these categories. Some townspeople, uskok leaders, and rank-and-file uskoks (including both recent arrivals in Senj and Senj "gentlemen") joined to denounce the raiding bands, whose actions threatened to draw reprisals down on Senj, while other townspeople and uskoks wanted the raids to continue.[11] This community of interest found expression in political action. In spite of the lack of formal statutory structures through which the uskoks could participate in the political process in Senj, the higher uskok leadership did take part in decisions that touched matters of general interest. This participation is reflected in the documents issued by the Senj commune. "The judges, the commune and the vojvodas of Senj" regularly issued joint declarations over the seal of the city of Senj and sent out emissaries in the name of "all the soldiers and the inhabitants of this town."[12]

There is also evidence of a degree of mutual solidarity between the uskoks and townspeople in the face of a threat to one or the other. When

[11]Longworth claims that in 1608 the Senjani were against the uskoks ("The Senj Uskoks Reconsidered," p. 354), using the evidence of Venetian officials who refer to "the good Senjani" in opposition to the uskoks (A.S.V., Provveditori da Terra e da Mar 423: 8 July 1608; see also Oct.–Nov., 1608). In fact, the conciliatory letters to the Ventian commander were signed by the "judges, the vojvodas, and the entire community of Senj" (e.g. A.S.V., Provveditori da Terra e da Mar, 423: 5 Nov. 1608). See also Chapter 8.

[12]See, for example, Lopašić, *Acta historiam confinii*, vol. 1, pp. 135–36; A.S.V., Provveditore Sopraintendente alla Camera dei Confini, 243: 8 Dec. 1579; Magdić, "Regesta važnijih i znamenitijih izprava," p. 149; Horvat, *Monumenta uscocchorum*, vol. 2, pp. 1–2.

in 1601 Habsburg Commissioner Rabatta introduced his harsh reforms, "all the knights and the honest soldiers in Senj" who wrote to the Archduke detailing their complaints did not dwell only on the injustices done to themselves but also pleaded for the townspeople, whose privileges had been disregarded; for various artisans and tradesmen sent to the galleys "who had honorably extended the soldiers every aid in food and drink and whatever they needed"; and for the prior of the monastery of St. Nicholas sent, as they claimed, to the galleys.[13] The commune of Senj and the garrison joined together to explain the uskoks' murder of Rabatta.[14] The townspeople of Senj also defended the soldiery from accusations by Military Frontier officials in various trials of uskoks for misconduct, especially during the trials of leaders Ivan and Miho Vlatković between 1609 and 1612. These uskoks, accused of raiding against orders by the Military Frontier authorities, were defended in numerous letters and petitions from the judges, nobles, and commoners of Senj[15] and from the Senj Cathedral Chapter, which specifically noted that Ivan and Miho "have always been of benefit to this city."[16]

Senj in the sixteenth century was a small town, probably never with many more than 4500 inhabitants. Within this society there were factions and divisions, the most obvious being the lines between full citizens and recent immigrants and between civilians and members of the Military Frontier. These distinctions lessened with time, but they did not vanish. Nevertheless, they had no decisive influence on the relations between Senjani and uskoks during the uskok period. The community of interest between the uskoks and the townspeople, the need for plunder, and the need for an economic network through which to dispose of it bound them closely together.

Uskok Rank-and-File: Venturini and Stipendiati

On arriving in Senj a new recruit would join the venturini. The word comes from the Italian *ventura* (fortune) and seems to be a Venetian variant of *venturiere*, a soldier of fortune.[17] The name was adopted by the

---

[13]In Lopašić, *Acta historiam confinii*, vol. 1, pp. 300–305.

[14]Horvat, *Monumenta uscocchorum*, vol. 2, pp. 1–2.

[15]Lopašić published some of these in *Acta historiam confinii*, vol. 2, p. 21. There are more in I.Ö. H.K.R., Croatica, fasc. 13, 1612, July No. 2: 1–94. See also Chapter 8.

[16]In Lopašić, *Acta historiam confinii*, vol. 2, p. 27.

[17]That is, one who fights for a portion of the booty. Sanuto uses *venturieri* in this sense for the Ottoman *akincis*, or irregular soldiers, "venturieri, so to speak, who are not paid by their lord." Vettor Barbaro makes the derivation of the word explicit: the venturini are *homini di ventura* (men of fortune) (in H.A.Z., Fond Šime Ljubića, 2/33: 279'). Venetians use both variants for the unpaid uskoks of Senj (e.g. A.S.V., Provveditori da Terra e da Mar, 1262: 3 Aug. 1593; *Commissiones et relationes venetæ*, p. 205).

Habsburg Military Frontier, and the unpaid uskok auxiliaries in Senj styled themselves *vinturini,* domesticating the Italian term. When they first came to Senj, according to Vettor Barbaro, these recruits were "admitted to the custody and ordinary guards of the city, as new men, whose loyalty cannot so easily be trusted; they substitute in the operations abroad and with time and valor they come to the wages and the prerogatives of the others."[18] The many part-time uskoks, so to speak, who lived near Senj on the islands and the coast and who regularly joined uskok forays for a share in the booty should also probably be considered venturini of a kind. Native citizens of Senj who raided as uskoks without holding a paid position in the garrison were also included among the venturini, in contradistinction to the stipendiati.

Reports always cite more venturini in Senj than paid uskoks—understandably, as the Military Frontier limited the number of paid places. There are few statistics for the number of venturini in Senj before 1577, though their presence is often mentioned. New uskok recruits continued to arrive in Senj well into the 1600s. It is with the 1580s that the number of venturini suddenly grew, as many more immigrants from the borders came into Senj (see Table 1). From this period the venturini played a more important role in discussions of the uskoks, particularly in analyses of uskok raiding and in plans for controlling it. From the mid-1580s, when many recruits began to come to Senj either from Dalmatia or through Venetian service in Dalmatia, some observers equated the venturini specifically with those Venetian subjects and saw in them the reason for a change in the nature of uskok raids. Archbishop Minucci specifically linked the influx of Venetian adventurers to indiscriminate raiding: "These [venturini] were not only Turkish subjects, but also subjects of the Venetian domains, either fugitives from the galleys or those who retired to this asylum, fearing a well-deserved punishment for their crimes, or those who came here naturally, through their evil natures or through a desire for robbery. . . . The art of robbery became by then so common that even the very citizens of Senj, accustomed previously to live modestly, or from their own labors, began to carry on this trade."[19]

---

[18]In H.A.Z., Fond Šime Ljubića, 2/33: 280.

[19]Minucci, *Storia degli uscocchi,* p. 222. For an earlier example of this view (1577), see also *Commissiones et relationes venetæ,* vol. 4, p. 205: "These *venturieri* are nearly all either exiles from the places of Your Serenity, or deserters from your galleys, fled to Senj for various crimes committed on your territory, and greater damages are sustained at sea from these than from the uskoks from Senj themselves." Giovanni of Fermo also equates the venturini with Venetian subjects, but to him the venturini seem to be islanders who do not live in Senj and raid only occasionally. "They are worse than the others, often massacring sailors whom they take, to make them confess whether they have money" (in Rački, "Prilog za poviest hrvatskih uskoka," p. 189).

Table 1. Stipendiati and venturini in Senj, 1571–1600[a]

	1571[b]	1585[c]	1588[d]	1593[e]	1598[f]	1599[g]	1600
Stipendiati	150	200	200	300	400	150	150[h]
Venturini	(250)	800	(1800)		600	(250)	(550)
Total	400	1000	2000	3500	1000	400	700[i]

[a]It is difficult to assess the relative numbers of paid uskoks and venturini over the century, for the pay lists naturally do not include venturini, and the estimates of various Military Frontier officials and Venetian observers provide the only other evidence. This table summarizes the available data on the numbers of venturini relative to the paid garrison for forty years. (The numbers in parentheses are inferred from the sources; the others are quoted directly.)

[b]*Commissiones et relationes venetæ*, vol. 4, p. 205 (Venetian estimate).

[c]Hurter, *Geschichte des Kaiser Ferdinands II*, vol. 2, p. 133 (Archducal commissioner to Imperial Council—Military Frontier figures).

[d]*Commissiones et relationes venetæ*, vol. 6, pp. 18–19 (Venetian estimate; the writer may be referring to the number of uskoks in the entire captaincy—his meaning is not clear).

[e]Leva, *Legazione di Roma*, pp. 140–41. These figures are for the entire captaincy.

[f]*Commissiones et relationes venetæ*, vol. 5, p. 243 (Venetian estimate).

[g]Ibid., vol. 5, p. 280 (Venetian estimate; reacting against exaggerated claims of the number of uskoks in Senj, the writer gives a very low estimate of the number of venturini).

[h]Lopasic, *Acta historiam confinii*, vol. 1, pp. 278–80. (Captain Barbo's correspondence with Archduke Ferdinand—Military Frontier figures).

[i]De Dominis' estimate of the number of soldiers in the city, in Ljubić, "Prilozi za životopis," p. 19.

The implicit reasoning here has already been mentioned in the discussion of the origin of the uskoks. To these observers, since the Venetian venturini had not fled from Ottoman oppression but rather from Venetian justice, they were criminals and adventurers rather than avengers, and their raids were prompted by nothing other than greed for booty—particularly when these raids harmed Venetian as well as Ottoman interests. But the motives of Venetian recruits to Senj were little different from those of the subjects of the Porte. They shared a hatred of the Turk as the primary enemy to be faced on the border, and they were no more or less likely than Ottoman subjects to be common adventurers. Furthermore, the venturini were by no means all Venetian subjects. Like the paid uskoks, they came from all the areas of the border, reflecting in their ranks changing conditions along the frontier.[20] Many of the venturini the Serenissima claimed as her subjects in the 1590s were originally Ottoman subjects who had served briefly in Dalmatia before fleeing to Senj. Venetian concern for Dalmatians among the uskoks was certainly stimulated in this period by the Habsburgs, who tried to evade responsi-

[20]Of the thirteen leaders among the venturini named in 1599 by Nicolò Donà, only three were from Venetian territory—the rest were from Ottoman areas (A.S.V., Provveditori da Terra e da Mar, 922: 12 Mar. 1599).

bility for uskok raids by emphasizing the role played by Venice's own subjects.[21]

The criticisms of these observers did hold a kernel of truth. As soldiers of fortune the venturini had neither official standing nor wages and they lived entirely from their share of plunder. The character of the venturini and their need to raid explains a great deal about the leaders they chose and the extent to which they would willingly obey authority. Their ranks contained the most recent arrivals in Senj, those who had the most fragile ties with the rest of the uskok organization, and those who were the least assimilated into the uskok community. As this was the first step in an uskok career, the venturini also included the young unproven bachelors, those not yet grown to military experience and family responsibilities. Such men were anxious to prove themselves, as well as provide for themselves, in successful and glorious actions. A leader of the venturini needed to be able to plan and carry out such raids, and it is the qualities of shrewdness, courage, and daring that are most stressed among such men. Conversely, the venturini were unwilling to follow those who demanded that they sit quietly at home when the Habsburg authorities so desired. They were likely to rebel against such orders, and were difficult to punish—unless in their persons—for they had no pay to withhold. Whenever the Hofkriegsrat and the Archduke wished to reform Senj and exert greater control over uskok operations, it was these venturini, the most unstable elements among the uskoks, who were expelled or removed to the outlying fortresses, while those who were left in Senj were the older, paid uskoks and those with wives and children, who were less likely to rebel.[22]

The venturini might have been restrained by a judicious distribution of supplies (and on occasion this was attempted, in contravention of Military Frontier rules, though never on a scale that would have allowed them to stop raiding entirely). But when the Hofkriegsrat could not even pay the stipendiati regularly there was little money for the venturini. A steep rise in the number of recent recruits in Senj from the late 1580s (and therefore a relatively greater number of venturini dependent on raiding

[21]Some Venetian officials remained skeptical. See the negotiations over a plundered Venetian *saettia* (a lateen-rigged merchant ship) in 1600: "The archducal ministers would have it that the uskoks who plundered the *saettia* are separate people, banished from the company of the real uskoks, and for the most part subjects and exiles of the Signoria, but there is reason to believe that this is a fiction, and that in the end they are all in accord in these raids" (in Horvat, *Monumenta uscocchorum*, vol. 1, p. 293).

[22]In 1582 Commissioner von Dorimberg advised Archduke Charles that a reform of Senj should begin by prohibiting the settlement of "any other exiles and vagabonds, who are called venturini, and live solely from plunder" (in Hurter, *Geschichte des Kaiser Ferdinands II*, vol. 2, p. 139). Another such plan, this time involving the resettlement of the venturini, was proposed in 1597 (I.Ö. H.K.R., Croatia, fasc. 9, 1597, Oct. No. 45: 5) and carried out in 1601 by Rabatta's commission (H.A.Z., Fond Šime Ljubića, 2/33: 283).

for their income) did increase the number of raids that came out of Senj. Of all the uskoks, the venturini depended most directly on frequent, successful raids.

The stipendiati differed from the venturini by definition in that they were enrolled on the Miltary Frontier muster roll and were supposed to receive pay for their service in the Senj garrison. The wages and pre-rogatives of a position in the garrison could come to an uskok through "time and valor." Ultimately these were at the discretion of the Muster Commission. In practice, however, an uskok's advancement was depen-dent on the recommendation of the local representative of the Military Frontier (the Captain or Vice Captain) or of the vojvoda under whose command he would be placed.[23] Valor and experience were the obvious qualities a position in the garrison required, but since the distribution of places was controlled by a few highly placed officers, other qualities (such as obedience or even less obviously military qualifications) could play a role.

A position in the garrison brought the uskok prestige and some pre-rogatives, including a share in the grain or cloth distributed by the mili-tary stores, the possibility of a pension for the uskok or his family, and the hope of an official ransom should he be captured. The basic wages of the stipendiati, as discussed above, were low, though those who dis-tinguished themselves were paid a little more.[24] The paid uskok could rise in rank with success in battle, becoming a harambaša or vojvoda, positions of leadership that brought greater prestige and higher wages. But the question of pay was largely academic for, as Sarpi pointed out, the stipendiati were differentiated from the venturini "more in name and title than in reality" since they were so seldom paid. Under such circumstances the stipendiati were often obliged to support themselves on booty like the venturini, "for since they are rarely given their wages, neither the one group nor the other can sustain themselves for long without robbery."[25] On raids there was little distinction made: both might take part in the same expedition under the same leader, who might himself be either paid uskok or venturino. Thus, like the venturini, the stipendiati looked to leaders who could win them glory and booty in successful raids and grumbled when their commanders kept them at home within the walls.

The stipendiati, however, were less independent in their raiding than the venturini. Their positions and prestige made them vulnerable to the

[23]I.Ö. H.K.R., Croatica, fasc. 13, 1609, June No. 17: 5 July 1609 (Captain Gušić's complaints about problems in finding paid places for a number of uskoks under the command of Ivan Vlatković and Perica and Juriša Lučić [Hajduk]).

[24]Lopašić, *Acta historiam confinii*, vol. 1, pp. 77–78.

[25]In *Commissiones et relationes venetæ*, vol. 5, p. 16.

demands of their superiors, whose disapproval could mean dismissal from the garrison or withdrawal of the promise of pay, as well as physical punishment. During the times when there were few restrictions on their raiding, this difference had little practical meaning. But when the Habsburgs ordered the curtailment of uskok operations, the stipendiati were more easily disciplined. The venturini were more likely to take the initiative in independent raiding for their own support, even when the Military Frontier authorities forbade it. The view of one Provveditore Generale toward the venturini was phrased intemperately but was still basically accurate:

> Maintaining themselves without a stipend, and gathering together without any skills and without any income of their own on which they could live, and support themselves and their families, they unite at their own pleasure and commit the notorious crimes from which, however, their maintenance depends. These, as I have said, more than the others [the stipendiati], scorn to obey the Emperor, care little to execute the orders of the ministers sent for that purpose by His Imperial Majesty, esteem even less the sham orders of their Captain (as he shares with them in the booty they take), and expose themselves to any danger, holding their own lives of little account, out of greed for profit.[26]

Although in the 1590s and early 1600s Habsburg-Venetian relations in the Adriatic were such that the uskoks were pressed to limit their raiding, the venturini were no less in need of booty, and no more able to find other sources of support. Moreover, when the number of venturini in Senj increased, neither the established uskok leaders nor the Military Frontier officers could effectively control venturini raiding. New to Senj, with no long ties of loyalty to the established uskok leaders, these recent recruits had little reason to heed arguments that they should tighten their belts to assuage the critics of Senj. Nor did such men need to wait for an authorized raid under an uskok leader licensed by the Hofkriegsrat. Many had come to Senj as preexisting bands, with experience in raiding and with their own leaders, perhaps even their own boats. Why should they not raid independently, with or without the approval of Senj or the Hofkriegsrat?

Uskok Commanders

From 1597 we have a glimpse of an otherwise unknown uskok commander who had been captured by Venetian mercenaries: "a man of fine

[26]In ibid., vol. 5, p. 243.

stature with a thick beard and black hair with a tuft of hair on top of his head, well dressed in the uskok manner, in breeches of scarlet cloth, aged—so far as can be discerned from his appearance—about thirty-six." Responding to interrogation he stated, "My name is Zorzi Vachsich, son of Zuane of Podstrana, previously an inhabitant of Trogir, but I am from the Primorje, and was a Turkish subject before I came to the devotion [of Venice], and my profession was to work the land, and it is three years since I went with the uskoks." In these three years he had apparently demonstrated considerable prowess, for when asked what company he belonged to he replied, "I have a company of thirty uskoks and I am, so to speak, their true leader, but now I have dismissed them, so that I have no more than fifteen, but they are not with me because they have gone ashore to plunder."[27] The uskoks called such leaders harambašas; these led bands of ten to thirty uskoks, usually the number necessary to man one of the barks used for raids. Records of the 1590s, when uskok numbers were at their height, mention twenty-five to thirty harambašas or commanders of barks.[28]

The ability to "arm a bark to go pirating" stressed by Sarpi as a qualification for uskok leadership may have been partly economic. The harambašas are sometimes referred to as the owners of their vessels, and some uskok leaders even had barks built to their own specifications in Rijeka or Trieste. In 1585 the Capitano contra uscocchi seized three particularly large such barks, "of great beauty, and perfectly in order, two with sixteen oars and the third with twelve. The uskoks often went out in these three barks, for they are convenient, and suitable for taking booty because of their size, and because fifty of these scoundrels can embark in each of them."[29] A harambaša who did not have the funds to buy a suitable bark or build one to order could always try to commandeer one somewhere on the coast.

Like wealth, social status was a means to office in Senj, but it was no guarantee of authority or honor. In the earlier years of the captaincy, the Military Frontier authorities had filled the officers' places in the garrison with members of the Senj nobility and career soldiers from Inner Austria, as can be seen from the pay lists. Among the harambašas who commanded the uskok bands, however, there were a few Senj nobles later in the century. A few prominent refugees from outside Senj also reached high rank in the Senj hierarchy, possibly aided by the Military Frontier practice of granting the leaders of refugee groups higher wages

---

[27]In A.S.V., Provveditori da Terra e da Mar, 1263: 11 June 1597.

[28]Ibid., 1319: 11 June 1591; 1263: 31 May 1597; 922: 12 Mar. 1599. The term 'harambaša' is from the Turkish *harami*: robber, and *baş:* leader.

[29]In A.S.V., Archivio dei Baili Veneti a Constantinopoli, 305: 18 Apr. 1585.

and greater privileges.[30] But there were many harambašas, like Zorzi Vachsich, quoted above, who had worked the land for a living.

From a dossier on the principal uskoks compiled for the use of the Provveditore Generale in 1599, it can be seen that leadership did not necessarily depend on seniority, for some of the harambašas, including Vachsich and Martin Posedarski, had been in Senj only two or three years, yet they commanded considerable followings. Nor was a paid position in the garrison necessary for the command of an uskok band— of the thirty-two harambašas in the dossier, only eighteen were stipendiati (paid from four to twelve florins per month). The Military Frontier did reward the successful commander: those with higher salaries were well-known uskoks who had led many raids, and one had been a leader on the attempt on Klis. But some of the less well paid were also noted leaders, such as Miloš Slavičić (noted as a "well-esteemed man") and Juriša Hajduk. Fourteen of these harambašas were venturini with no stipend. These too included some well-known names—Miloš Bukovac ("a famous commander of the venturini") and Mirko Domazetović (who had been a Venetian commander under General Almorò Tiepolo).[31] The most important qualification for the rank of harambaša, as this list makes clear, was military prowess. All these men appear over and over in dispatches recounting uskok actions, distinguishing themselves in raiding and in battle. The harambaša needed to attract investors to supply his bark and to recruit uskoks to man it, and so had to demonstrate military capability, force of personality, knowledge of the terrain, and similar qualities. Skill in battle and success in planning and executing raids were the most important factors in a leader's rise to authority and his continued hold over his following. Most of the initiative for plundering expeditions lay with these harambašas, who thus constantly affirmed their worth as uskok leaders.

This Venetian list of harambašas, almost equally divided between venturini and stipendiati, also confirms that the rank of harambaša depended far more on popular success among the uskok rank-and-file than on Military Frontier recognition. It is quite clear that the Military Frontier authorities could not easily strip popular and influential uskok commanders of their positions and followings—much as they may have desired to do so in some cases. Juriša Hajduk (noted in the 1599 dossier as a "man with a following," though with a low wage) was long a thorn in the side of the Military Frontier officials for his insubordination, yet because of his popularity it was difficult to remove him. When banished from

[30]As in the cases of Damian and Tadija Petrović, leaders of the Krmpoćani, for example. See Lopašić, *Acta historiam confinii*, vol. 1, p. 349.

[31]A.S.V., Provveditori da Terra e da Mar, 922: 12 Mar. 1599.

Senj for plundering in Istria against orders, he merely retired to the countryside with his band and continued to raid, secure in the knowledge that his friends in the town would continue to aid him. When a rumor came in 1601 that he had been captured by the Turks, Bishop de Dominis, whose plans for reforming Senj had been badly set back by the raids of independent uskok leaders, noted hopefully that "if he does not wish, or is not able to ransom himself, it would be of great benefit if his death could be procured."[32] Two years later the Military Frontier authorities offered him a position as vojvoda of Otočac, but he was said to have seen this as another attempt to get rid of him: "He doesn't want to accept this position because the Turks raid those parts daily," and he continued to raid from Senj.[33] Miloš Bukovac, "famous commander of the venturini," was of a similar character. More than once Habsburg commissions banished him from Senj, yet to no lasting effect, for he and his band would spend long periods in the field, finding a safe refuge with friends on Venetian and Ottoman territory. In the early 1600s both Bukovac and Juriša Hajduk raided as renegades, plundering Venetian targets in defiance of Military Frontier orders. In spite of the disapproval of some of the uskoks in Senj, who feared Venetian retaliation or disagreed on the legitimacy of such targets, these commanders did not lack for loyal followers as long as they were successful in their expeditions.

Nor could the Military Frontier officials always impose harambašas successfully on Senj. The uskoks bitterly resented Commissioner Rabatta's attempts to reform their ranks in 1600 by appointing new leaders whose military skills they clearly doubted. The second of a long list of the uskoks' complaints to the Archduke after Rabatta's murder read: "[Rabatta] deprived many old, trustworthy harambašas, commanders, and many other old loyal soldiers of their positions without cause, and in their places put shopkeepers and other artisans, who had never even seen the border otherwise, and several of these were not even from Senj, but lived outside."[34] Such unwanted or unsuccessful harambašas found that they could neither recruit a following nor command the uskoks assigned to them.

"Almost every uskok behaves as he will, for knowing full well how much they are needed, and having an extremely haughty opinion of themselves, they are promised and permitted everything for their bravery. They have, however, certain higher officers, believed by them to be of remarkable valor, whom they call vojvodas . . . and from these all the

---

[32]In Ljubić, "Prilozi za životopis Markantunu Dominisu," p. 32.

[33]Interrogation of a captured uskok, in A.S.V., Senato, Secreta, Materie miste notabili, 126: 23 Jan. 1603.

[34]In Lopašić, *Acta historiam confinii*, vol. 1, p. 301.

others depend," a knowledgeable observer reported in the early 1600s.[35] The term 'vojvoda' is a common Slavic word meaning military leader, or *dux belli*. It was not peculiar to Senj, but was widespread among the South Slavs and was adopted by both the Habsburg and the Venetian Military Frontier systems. In Senj the term was used for uskok commanders who united all the uskoks, venturini as well as stipendiati, under their control, and who mediated between the uskoks and the representatives of the Military Frontier, in particular the Captain of Senj. This office appears to have developed on the basis of successful uskok leaders who could command the respect of all the uskoks and the trust of the Military Frontier authorities. One of the earliest uskok vojvodas to be recorded in Senj was Miloš Parizević, the same Miloš who had distinguished himself as a youth in a duel with an Ottoman opponent before Klis. In 1540 he was taken onto the Senj pay list for the first time as a replacement, at a very high salary (eighteen florins), presumably in recognition of his status among the uskoks. When the Venetians captured him in 1548 he was hanged in Zadar as "commander of all the uskok harambašas."[36]

At first the Military Frontier merely confirmed vojvodas chosen by the uskoks themselves and granted them a stipend. It was in these terms that Giovanni of Fermo described the careers of two of the most famous vojvodas of the sixteenth century, Juraj Daničić the elder and his son, also called Juraj, whom Giovanni had known well. The elder Juraj had fled from the Ottoman occupation of his home in the 1540s, "as a Catholic, abandoning all his relations and his belongings and retiring to Senj as a soldier, and went together with the others to molest the Turks by land and by sea." He married in Senj and had three sons and a daughter. "And with his long experience his valor was more and more recognized, so that all the soldiers elected him as their captain general. And some of the principal captains of the uskoks took him to Emperor Ferdinand and told him of his valor, and he confirmed him in that position, in confor-

---

[35]Report to Sarpi made some time after 1614, in H.A.Z., Fond Šime Ljubića, 2/32: 1'.

[36]Minucci describes him as having accepted the challenge of one of the Ottoman beseigers of Klis, in spite of his youth, saying that if he lost it would do "little dishonor to the Christians should a Turk of such renown succeed in defeating a mere boy" (in Rački, "Prilog za poviest hrvatskih uskoka," p. 219). Klaić reports that an enormous votive candle he was alleged to have dedicated to the Virgin after his unexpected victory could still be seen at Trsat at the end of the seventeenth century (Klaić, *Povijest Hrvata*, vol. 5, p. 649). See also Lopašić, *Acta historiam confinii*, vol. 3, p. 394; A.S.V., Senato, Secreta, 66: 19 Jan. 1549. Pariževič was well enough known for his death to merit a note in Fra Simun Glavić's sixteenth-century chronicle with no further explanation: "1549: At this time Milos Pariževič was hanged on the feast of St. Simon the Elder, January 3, in Zadar" (In Ivan Kukuljević-Sakcinski, ed., "Kratki ljetopisi hrvatski," *Arkiv za povjestnicu jugoslavensku* (Zagreb), 4 (1857): 41).

mity with the status that the uskoks had conferred upon him."[37] This probably took place between 1551, when Daničić was receiving a moderate wage in the garrison, and 1566, when he is reported by the Venetians as the head of all the uskoks.[38] Vojvoda Daničić was active leading uskok raids throughout the 1560s, but in 1571 he was killed, possibly as a result of Ragusan treachery, during a raid across Dubrovnik's territory. (See Chapter 4.) Ragusan dispatches immediately after the incident describe the retaliatory raids led by his son Juraj, who by the late 1570s had become the second vojvoda of that name in Senj.[39] According to Giovanni, he was chosen to succeed his father immediately after his murder.

When the uskoks saw the head of their general and the cruelty and treachery that had been used, they fled with their barks. . . . Since Giorgio [Juraj], his eldest son, eighteen years of age, was in this company, and since he was a spirited youth, of good appearance and fine promise, all the soldiers who had been at this spectacle, shouting, created him their general, swearing to obey his commands; swearing also, all together, to avenge the general and their brothers. . . . The principal captains took the aforesaid Giorgio to the Emperor, telling him of the treachery of the Ragusans and asking His Majesty to confirm the office which they had given to his son, which His Majesty did.[40]

In interpreting the selection of Juraj Daničić as a vojvoda, Giovanni of Fermo stressed his experience and his valor in raids and noted his son's promise of similar qualities—which when they were proven in battle brought him the same authority. His parentage alone was not sufficient to qualify him as a vojvoda. Among the clans of Montenegro and Hercegovina, and among the later Dalmatian uskoks of the seventeenth and eighteenth centuries, the office of vojvoda was hereditary in certain distinguished families. In Senj there were a few families in addition to the Daničićes which provided several successive vojvodas, but this was not a hereditary post. The rank had to be earned. In spite of his spontaneous election, Juraj was required to prove himself in battle, and although he is frequently reported among the raiders in the years following his father's death, it is only after several years that he is found in the company of the other vojvodas. By 1591 he was the supreme vojvoda, described by a Venetian spy as "a very ugly man, about fifty-five, with

[37]In Rački, "Prilog za poviest hrvatskih uskoka," p. 184.
[38]A.S.V., Provveditori da Terra e da Mar, 1318: 4 Mar. 1566.
[39]H.A.D., Diplomata et acta 16 st., 11: 450–i/22 (3 Aug. 1571); 450–d/8 (5 Aug. 1571).
[40]In Rački, "Prilog za poviest hrvatskih uskoka," p. 185. According to contemporary estimates of his age, Juraj was probably older than eighteen at the time.

one ear missing, but a man very much revered and obeyed by these people."[41]

The vojvodas' authority was strongest in military matters, as the etymology of the term suggests. They organized and led raids, gathered information, and decided on tactics and fields of operation. We find the younger Daničić leading many uskok raids on Ottoman flocks and on shipping as well as more conventional military actions, such as the attack on Ottoman Klis in 1582.[42] Daničić also demonstrated the qualities that made him a respected uskok leader in negotiating on behalf of the uskoks with Venetian officers (over the return of plundered goods and the possibility of joining Venetian service), with Ottoman commanders (over fixing ransom rates), and with Christian Ottoman subjects (over the payment of tribute).[43] The vojvodas were also responsible for discipline among the ranks. The organization of the Senj watch was one of their responsibilities, a matter that became an issue in the investigation of vojvodas Juraj Daničić and Matija Tvrdislavić in 1582. Testimony from the uskoks themselves at that time provides an illustration of the ways in which the vojvodas exercised their authority (and their prerogatives) through a mixture of force and personal example. The vojvodas did not always take watch duty themselves. Sometimes they would "come to the watch, and when they had made an appearance, they would then go home and lie down to sleep."[44] Often they appointed substitutes to take their places, though some uskoks testified that the vojvodas performed their duties as sentries "more diligently than the Captain."[45] Witnesses noted that Daničić and Tvrdislavić did not tolerate laxity among their subordinates, however. Men who failed to appear for their shifts or, in one case, who were found drunk on duty, found themselves thrown into the tower by the vojvodas "so that they would be more diligent on their watch next time."[46]

The vojvodas' power over the uskoks was by no means absolute. Like other autonomous frontier military organizations, the uskok bands of Senj nurtured an ideal of collective responsibility for decisions, in which all the uskoks participated—a primitive democracy.[47] Subjects of public

[41]In A.S.V., Senato, Secreta, Materie miste notabili n. 27: 11 June 1591.

[42]Klaić, *Povijest Hrvata*, vol. 5, pp. 440–41.

[43]For negotiations with Venetian officers, see A.S.V., Provveditore Sopraintendente alla Camera dei Confini, 243: 18 Feb. 1580 (Nicolò Surian), 24 May 1580 (Alvise Balbi); I.Ö. H.K.R., Croatica, fasc. 4, 1584, Apr. No. 2. With the Sancak-bey of Lika: A.S.V., Archivio dei Baili Veneti a Constantinopoli, 305: 13, 14, 16, and 31 Jan. 1589 (m.v.). With the subjects of the Porte: I.Ö. H.K.R., Croatica, fasc. 4, 1584, Apr. No. 2.

[44]In I.Ö. H.K.R., Croatica, fasc. 4, 1584, Apr. No. 2: 64 (Deopunti).

[45]In ibid., 62' (Previnovitsch); 104 (Castanitsch).

[46]In ibid., 83 (Sakholitsch), and 69 (Podovadovitsch); 89 (Vukhavitsch); 102 (Floritsch); 104'–5 (Vogavatz); 106' (Lacvitsch).

[47]Cf. Gordon, *Cossack Rebellions*, pp. 83–88.

importance and of common interest were discussed publicly, as a matter for the uskok community as a whole to decide.[48] As far as can be seen from the records, however, the mechanisms of uskok democracy were somewhat amorphous. If the uskoks did have institutionalized modes of public discussion, like the village councils or the regional leagues current in Dalmatia, few details have survived in the evidence beyond descriptions of the crowds that came together in the city square in times of crisis. Even if the uskoks did possess more highly developed democratic mechanisms, in practice the vojvodas had a good deal of executive autonomy. They represented the uskoks in civil matters, joining with the other administrative officers of the town (the judges and the city council) to act on behalf of the community. Perhaps more important, they also controlled decisions that affected raiding and the distribution of booty. One captured uskok, for instance, reported that the uskoks often did not know in advance where raids would be directed—their commanders and guides kept the details secret.[49] When another uskok, Žarko Nikolić, was interrogated about the disposition of booty taken by his band, he claimed that "the leaders don't wish to trust us others, but when they take something, they take it wherever they please, without telling any of us."[50] This delegation of authority to the vojvodas was accepted without complaint for the most part, for the uskok rank-and-file always possessed the sanction of disobedience or outright rebellion.

The vojvodas' influence and authority also had limits because they were chosen by the ranks (at least until the 1590s) and because they depended for their authority on the support of the uskoks. Without effective outside support they could not impose measures unacceptable to the community as a whole, and particularly to the uskoks. While the uskoks still chose their own commanders, those commanders achieved position and authority through military skill and personal qualities. Although that respect might derive from family background or noble birth and although a fortune with which to outfit a raiding bark was helpful, privilege itself had to be balanced by skill and courage. Any uskok could aspire to the power, prerogatives, and the titles granted to successful vojvodas by initiating successful and profitable raids, by demonstrating military prowess, and by gathering a following.

When uskok raiding served the interests of the Military Frontier, the authority of the vojvodas was not questioned. From the mid-1500s, however, the Emperor, the Archduke, and the Hofkriegsrat increasingly

[48]This discussion was especially the case in times of crisis, such as the rebellion against Commissioner Rabatta, when, following his murder, the uskoks consulted together on the steps to take to govern themselves. See for example Minucci, *Storia degli uscocchi*, p. 259.
[49]In A.S.V., Senato, Secreta, Materie miste notabili 126: 23 Jan. 1603.
[50]In H.A.Z., Arhiv Trogira 25/11: 1494–95 (21 Sept. 1599).

demanded the control or halting of raiding because of the demands of Habsburg foreign policy. Through the 1580s the Senj vojvodas successfully ignored or resisted these demands, largely because of their influence among the uskoks. As will be seen in the trial of Juraj Daničić (discussed below), the authorities were not yet willing to provoke open rebellion in Senj by retaliatory measures against the uskoks' leaders, nor were they ready to remove the uskoks from Senj. However, when Juraj Daničić was reported missing in action in 1591 after an expedition near Ogulin, the General of the Frontier immediately ordered that the vacant post be filled with "a well-qualified person."[51] From then on the Captain of Senj and the authorities of the Military Frontier took a much more active role in the selection of the vojvodas. By the 1590s it had become usual for there to be four vojvodas in Senj. These were still selected from the ranks of active uskok leaders who had proved their worth in raids and who could command the respect of the uskok ranks. Now, however, the vojvodas also had to be acceptable to the Military Frontier authorities, proving their loyalty by their willingness to execute their superiors' orders. The Captain and the Hofkriegsrat procured higher salaries and more extensive privileges for favored vojvodas, attempting to exert greater control over the actions of the uskoks by assimilating their leaders, eroding the democratic character of uskok decision making, and driving a wedge between the leaders and the ranks. In the midsixteenth century many vojvodas had held their posts for years, even decades, but by the early seventeenth century there was a rapid turnover, with many more names appearing in their ranks, many for only short periods.

As the vojvodas' offices began to depend to a larger degree on official support, the vojvodas were put in a difficult position. Mediators between the uskoks and the Military Frontier hierarchy, they were caught between the needs of the former and the demands of the latter. Ignoring or resisting official pressures could bring on retaliation from the Captain or the Military Court in Karlovac. On the other hand, if the vojvodas tried to enforce the requirements of the Military Frontier authorities, particularly when no other provisions were made for the uskoks' support, their attempts were resisted in Senj, they lost the trust, respect, and obedience of the ranks, and the gap between the vojvodas and the uskoks widened. Disagreement among the vojvodas themselves over what constituted legitimate raiding further weakened their authority over their troops, who demonstrated their rebellion by increased private raiding. By 1601 Barbaro had noticed that although the four vojvodas were "uskoks elected by the Emperor himself, in earlier times they were accustomed to be much more esteemed and obeyed."[52] By 1618 the disintegration of an autonomous uskok organization was almost complete, following the treaty that ended the war between Venice and the Habsburgs, and none of the uskok leaders wanted to accept a Military Frontier commission because of the impossible burden of responsibility without authority the position had come to represent. A Venetian observed that "everyone is avoiding becoming a leader in order not to suffer."[53]

Captains of Senj

The Captain of Senj, the Military Frontier representative in Senj, was the titular commander of the uskoks. He was a Military Frontier officer chosen, after the 1578 reorganization of the Frontier, by the Hofkriegsrat from candidates proposed by the Estates of Inner Austria. The Captain's duties, as described in 1601, were to "pay and increase or dismiss the stipendiati, to assign captains to the fortifications in his jurisdiction at his discretion, to order and execute raids at his pleasure; but he recognizes as his superior the General of Croatia, who resides in Karlovac." He was also responsible for discipline among the uskoks and was expected to carry out official policies in this regard.[54]

Although the Hofkriegsrat or the General in Karlovac usually dictated the character of the military operations organized by the Captains of Senj, the Captains were not always reliable instruments of central policy. They were often absent from Senj, seeing to the needs of their own estates, traveling to Karlovac or to the Habsburg courts, leaving Senj under the command of a subordinate (the Vice Captain or the administrator of the fortress, who was sometimes a vojvoda, sometimes a Senj official). During these lengthy absences the uskoks acted as they thought fit, without the restraint of a direct representative of the Military Frontier. But even when the Captain was in residence, there were often reasons for him to wink at uskok actions that were not entirely in accord with the instructions he had received from the Hofkriegsrat.

The Captain of Senj often took the uskoks' part in relations with the central authorities, not merely in pressing for wages or supplies but in defending the uskoks' acts in the face of official censure. In daily contact

[52]In H.A.Z., Fond Šime Ljubića, 2/33: 281.

[53]In A.S.V., Provveditore da terra e da mar 1315: 8 Apr. 1618.

[54]In H.A.Z., Fond Šime Ljubića, 2/33: 281. Military Frontier instructions to newly appointed Captains describe the duties of the post in more detail but along much the same lines, though with additional urgings to limit the actions of the uskoks (I.Ö. H.K.R., Croatica, fasc. 4, 1585, Dec. No. 20 [instructions for Furio Molza]; fasc. 12, 1606, Nov. No. 6 [instructions for Sigismund Gušić]).

with the uskoks and their dilemmas, he could be more inclined to respect the immediate problems of border warfare than the more distant claims of policy. Such disobedience, wrote one of Archduke Ferdinand's advisers in 1593, was that of a good commander. With the Turks plundering daily up to the walls of Senj, "should our men remain locked up in the place like old women, or should they not sally forth also and earn the bread they eat?"[55]

But there were other, more mercenary reasons for the Captains' attitudes toward the uskoks' raids. The Captain of Senj, like the other officers of the Frontier, was paid from the subsidies raised by the Estates of Inner Austria—and like the other salaries this pay came irregularly. Besides this source of income, the Captain received a part of the uskok booty, an amount that varied over the century. In 1558 the share taken by representatives of the Military Frontier was a quarter of any booty worth over fifteen ducats, a part going to the border officials and a part to the Captain. Later in the century the Captain's share was fixed at one-tenth, though he might be given a particularly fine piece of plunder as a gift. In 1600, in a reform of Senj, the Captain was denied a share in the booty, and he then petitioned to have his pay increased proportionately.[56]

The uskoks somewhat resented the Captain's share in the booty, particularly when he did not actively participate in the raids. In 1558 one Piero of Šibenik, whose *fregata* had been attacked by the uskoks, testified that "these uskoks complained that they put their lives in jeopardy, but nevertheless they had to give the better things that they looted to the Captain of Senj."[57] This resentment was voiced repeatedly.[58] But in spite of the uskoks' natural reluctance, it was in their interest to acquiesce, for as one Venetian pointed out, "The greater part of the booty goes into the hands of these officials, and with this security the uskoks make their own Mont'Albano," that is, they ensured their superiors' continued patronage of their actions.[59]

Certainly the prospect of personal gain affected the Captain's relations with the uskoks and his support of their actions, including the encouragement of profitable raids. Early in the seventeenth century, Barbaro noted that "the Captain has a tenth of the booty and the captives and other

[55]In Horvat, *Monumenta uscocchorum*, vol. 1, p. 73.

[56]In Lopašić, *Acta historiam confinii*, vol. 1, p. 278.

[57]In A.S.V., Provveditore Sopraintendente alla Camera dei Confini, 244 (summary of processes from the Rectors of Dalmatia, 1558).

[58]The uskoks were particularly enraged that Rabatta, for all his other reforms, retained this privilege of the commander, reporting that "out of every profit the soldiers took on a raid, they had to give him a share, as though he had gone with them on that raid" (in Lopašić, *Acta historiam confinii*, vol. 1, p. 304).

[59]In *Commissiones et relationes venetæ*, vol. 6, p. 50. "Mont'Albano" apparently refers to one of the *monti* or common funds dedicated to various purposes.

advantages when he permits the uskoks to go out to sea, and thus enriches himself. He gets no more than 80 florins a month as pay, which, even if it were paid on time, would not be enough for his wine, so that of necessity he makes good company with the uskoks, and drinks it in great quantity together with them."[60] Some Captains were suspected of placing a share in plunder above all other considerations. Furio Molza, Captain from 1585 to 1591, is described as having been anxious to reform the uskoks and accommodate Venetian complaints when he entered his captaincy, but with time and participation in their booty his interests turned in other directions. By 1588, for example, he was doing everything in his power to rescind the tribute paid to the uskoks and the Habsburgs by Ottoman subjects for protection, so that the uskoks would be free to plunder them once more, reportedly so that his own share of the booty would thereby be augmented.[61] The Captain's economic interest in uskok raiding raised obvious problems of uskok discipline, for he could hardly be trusted to enforce restrictions on uskok actions wholeheartedly. More than one Captain was censured by the Hofkriegsrat for disobeying orders in regard to booty. Such disobedience could sometimes be taken too far. In 1576 Johann Fernberger, a Tyrolean who had been made Captain of Senj as a reward for his service against the Ottomans and the French and who had been the subject of Venetian complaints over his complicity in uskok raiding, was dismissed from Senj after a special commission investigated his involvement in uskok raids against Venetian shipping.[62]

But even if a Captain wished to prevent or restrict uskok raiding, how could he do so? He might supplement orders banning raiding with concrete measures. In 1598 General Lenković had a gate cut in the sea wall, drew all the uskok barks up within the city walls so that they could be kept under guard, and locked the oars in the citadel.[63] Still, a band of

---

[60]In H.A.Z., Fond Šime Ljubića, 2/33: 281.

[61]"In the first days, when he entered into the governance of his captaincy, he showed himself anxious to give the greatest satisfaction to Your Serenity by his command; but afterward, I have discovered, it has all been to the contrary, for he not only assents to the uskoks' operations, but he himself acts to the same ends, sometimes sailing with them, and participating in the booty both when he is there and when he is absent" (in *Commissiones et relationes venetæ*, vol. 6, p. 14). Habsburg interest in appeasing Venice had waned somewhat during Molza's captaincy (Lopašić, *Acta historiam confinii*, vol. 1, p. 157; *Commissiones et relationes venetæ*, vol. 6, p. 15).

[62]Horvat, *Monumenta uscocchorum*, vol. 1, p. 11; Sarpi, *La Repubblica di Venezia*, p. 408; Grünfelder, "Senjski kapetan Kaspar Raab i senjski uskoci," *Senjski zbornik* (Senj), 9 (1981–82): 164. He may have been a token sacrifice to Venetian opinion, as Klaić suggests (*Povijest Hrvata*, vol. 5, p. 416). There is a short biography and portrait in Khevenhüller, *Conterfet Kupfferstich*, vol. 2, p. 398.

[63]*Commissiones et relationes venetæ*, vol. 5, p. 244. In later years the uskok barks were often ordered burned. See Theiner, *Vetera monumenta Slavorum meridionalium historiam illustranti*, vol. 2, p. 113, and Sarpi, *La Repubblica di Venezia*, p. 34, for examples.

uskoks could easily steal a bark in Dalmatia. Such measures could be effective only if the uskoks too could be kept within Senj. Three years after the sea gate had been opened, Vettor Barbaro noted that the other subsidiary gates had been walled up "to deprive the uskoks of the freedom of going out, and to avoid the trouble and expense of keeping German guards there." Both the main land gate and the sea gate were under guard, and a watch of stipendiati was kept on the walls, "not with rounds, for there is no path or corridor by which these could be made, but with permanent guards in the towers, which call to one another, every moment of the hour, with cries as loud as their voices can manage."[64] Even Turkish captives, however, had evaded these guards in poor weather by scaling the walls, so it was not surprising that the uskoks themselves easily escaped.

Other regulations also aimed at checking uskok raids, for example, the authorities regularly sequestered booty as it came into the city and passed judgment on whether or not it was licit plunder before dividing it. All plunder was to be registered in Senj and divided under the supervision of the Captain or some other official.[65] This practice originated to ensure that the representatives of the Military Frontier received their allotted share, but the system also made it possible for the Captain to return disputed goods to pacify Venice or the papacy and to punish uskoks for prohibited raiding by withholding the booty. Enforcement was difficult, for the uskoks could simply divide the booty before returning to Senj or refuse to surrender their plunder for assessment.[66]

Another possibility was to regulate raids, with the targets and routes carefully specified to prevent contact with Venetian territories or subjects. On such raids, the number of uskok commanders, usually the vojvodas, was expanded to enforce restrictions. These attempts to control uskok raids were extended into a system of licenses, based on the safe conducts issued to uskoks to protect them from Venetian harassment at sea.[67] Toward the end of the sixteenth century, such documents

[64]In H.A.Z., Fond Šime Ljubića, 2/33: 284.

[65]Regulations governing this process are given in Lopašić, *Acta historiam confinii*, vol. 2, pp. 14–15: the uskok should hand the booty over to the Captain or Vice Captain in the citadel, and it should not be divided until it had been examined. When the Venetians sacked Karlobag in 1592, they found bales of plundered merchandise, "in the custody of the imperial commander, with special ledgers recording not only its consignment but also the procedure for distributing it" (in A.S.F., Mediceo del Principato, 3086: 490 [11 July 1592], 500 [25 July 1592], quoted in Tenenti, *Piracy and the Decline of Venice*, p. 159).

[66]See Ivić, "Prilozi za povijest Hrvatske i Slavonije," pp. 302–3, for a letter from the uskok vojvodas justifying just such an action.

[67]One of these safe conducts has been preserved in the Provveditore Generale's papers: "Vojvoda Vragnin is leaving here with a few barks to carry out some of his duties without doing any damage to any person. I request that he be allowed to pass freely, and as evidence of the truth [of this] we have issued the present document in our own hand and over

were issued by the Captain or his representative only to approved expeditions and were increasingly specific in noting the purposes and area of the raid. Usually approval was limited to raids for supplies. As the Captain of Senj explained in 1606, he had to allow the uskoks out "to give them some way of getting themselves some sort of booty, since without this they cannot live." On this occasion their license specified that they were not to harm Venetian subjects or possessions.[68] These documents were intended not only to serve as safe conducts for officially permitted raids when Venetian patrols challenged the uskoks but also to reduce forbidden raiding, for those who raided without licenses, or beyond the terms of a license, received no official protection. Commissioner Rabatta issued explicit orders in 1600 that uskoks raiding without a written license from the Captain could be taken prisoner and executed.[69]

The use of safe conducts and licenses was not completely effective, for once issued, these pieces of paper could be used in ways the authorities had not intended. In 1570 a band of uskoks used the safe conduct they had been issued by the General of the Frontier, which announced that the bearers "were seeking nothing but goods belonging to Turks," to board a ship from Kotor in a Ragusan port. Once on board they began to demand the bills of lading, saying, "You have goods belonging to Turks and Jews on this ship." The two leaders obviously saw this document as legitimating their search for Turkish goods.[70] Licenses could also be forged or saved for later use without permission. Some uskoks didn't even go to that much trouble. In 1612 Bože Milovčić, the leader of a band raiding around Makarska and the Neretva delta, was reported to be showing "a sheet of folded paper, which appeared to have a big seal, and he said that this was a license from the Venetian Senate that he could make raids in the territories of the Turks," but he would not let anyone read it.[71] Inasmuch as the lack of a license made an uskok expedition vulnerable to Venetian retaliation, the system may have had some deterrent effect. But uskok raids at sea had always been in peril from Venetian patrols, and the lack of a license had little effect on those who were used to the risks of independent raiding. Futhermore, even an expedition approved by the officers of the Military Frontier did not always find a license an effective protection from Venetian commanders, who remained skeptical of any uskok raid.

---

our own seal. Issued in Senj, 25 September 1603, Daniel Francuol, Captain" (in A.S.V., Senato, Secreta, Materie miste notabili, 126: 9 Oct. 1603).

[68]A.S.V., Provveditori da Terra e da Mar 420: 18 July 1606 (quoted in report by Contarini).

[69]In Horvat, *Monumenta uscocchorum*, vol. 1, p. 329.

[70]In H.A.Z., Arhiv Korčule, 808: 392–400 (July 1570).

[71]He wasn't the only one using this ruse. In the same letter another uskok leader was reported doing the same thing (in A.S.V., Provveditori da Terra e da Mar 1314: 24 July 1612).

Physical coercion and punishment of disobedient uskoks would perhaps have been the most effective means for the Captain of Senj to
enforce his will, and certainly these were courses constantly urged by
the authorities in Graz and Vienna. But such punishment could threaten
the Captain with uskok rebellion. More often punitive measures were
associated with Military Frontier commissions. These were repeatedly
sent to Rijeka or Karlovac (usually not to Senj itself, for it was difficult
to guarantee the commmissioners' security there) with orders to investigate complaints of illicit raiding and punish the disobedient uskoks.[72]
The commissioners, supported by troops from other parts of the border,
would carry out interrogations, seize and burn uskok barks, and execute a handful of prisoners, afterward distributing pay to the chas-
tened stipendiati. But the Military Frontier had only limited means for
enforcing direct coercion. The commissions came and went, and with
them went their soldiery. They were hampered by the same constraints
as the Captains of Senj—their measures could be effective only as long
as they had men and arms to enforce them or funds to purchase uskok
obedience.

The experiences of Kaspar Raab illustrate the difficulties faced by a
Captain in his relations with the uskoks and the Military Frontier.[73]
Raab, sent to Senj in 1576 to replace the compromised Johann Fernberger,
was a reforming Captain. His appointment had been made with the
explicit purpose of reorganizing the uskoks and preventing their raids at
sea, and Raab immediately began to carry out this commission by retaliating against uskoks who had been involved in raids on Venetian territory or shipping (particularly the plundering of Ottoman trade carried
on Venetian ships). At the same time he began to expand operations
against the Turks on land, rebuilding the fortifications in Bag (renamed
Karlobag in honor of Archduke Charles), placing a garrison there, and
sending raids into Lika to attack newly settled Ottoman colonists.

These measures, however, could keep the uskoks under control only
for a short time. So long as the Military Frontier could not provide some
other source of income for the uskoks, Raab could not be successful in
forbidding their plundering raids. As far as the Captain's authority was
concerned, discipline was a function of the prompt payment of wages
and delivery of supplies, and Raab (like other Captains) repeatedly linked
the irregular pay of the garrison to its frequent insubordination. Raab
informed the Hofkriegsrat that the best way to prevent uskok piracies

---

[72]The first such commission was sent in 1548 to investigate Venetian complaints over
uskok raiding. Similar commissions were sent in 1559, 1565, 1575, 1579, 1582, 1589, 1592, 1597,
1600, 1607, 1610, 1612, 1613, 1614, 1618, and 1619.

[73]For a more detailed account of Raab's career in Senj, see Grünfelder, "Senjski kapetan
Kaspar Raab," pp. 163–81.

completely would be to pay the uskoks more regularly.[74] This advice was not taken, for in 1580 he was complaining to Archduke Charles that the Senj garrison had not received their pay or provisions for three months and was in severe want. Under such conditions it was useless for the Archduke to demand, as Charles did that same month, that the uskoks obey their Captain and show him the respect he was due.[75]

It was also impossible to prevent the uskoks' resulting expeditions to take much-needed booty. Raab was able to channel uskok raids at this point into Ottoman territory, even leading some of the expeditions himself. His measures could not, however, prevent forbidden raids at sea against Venetian and Ragusan vessels, including an attack on a Venetian merchant ship off Hvar, in which booty was taken "regardless of the fact that they could clearly tell from the books shown to them by the ship's clerk that it belonged to Christians," according to Venetian complaints.[76]

If he could not prevent raids, Raab tried to maintain discipline by punishing the offenders. His initial methods were not unusual: "If any [uskok] has opposed my will, I have punished them in accordance with justice: some I have had quartered, and ordered their quarters hung in many places as an example to others; many have been banished on pain of death, with a price on their heads; and many who have committed lesser crimes have been punished by imprisonment." Banishment was not a satisfactory measure, for it merely removed the offenders from close surveillance in Senj, as Raab himself admitted.[77] Corporal punishment was effective only when he could command sufficient strength to impose it. The German garrison alone was not strong enough to keep Senj in order; its numbers were kept low to minimize the expense (and even so, Raab complained that he had been forced to pay the guards at the gate out of his own living allowance).[78] Unaided or with only a few loyal troops at his command, he found it dangerous to act against the combined opinion of the uskoks and found himself forced to rely on troops from elsewhere on the border—when they were available.

In 1580, when the Archduke demanded the arrest of the Daničić brothers for their part in raids on Venetian shipping, Raab answered that he

[74]In Lopašić, *Acta historiam confinii*, vol. 1, p. 53; I.Ö. H.K.R., Croatica, fasc. 3, 1580, Jan. No. 46 (20 Nov. 1579). See also *Commissiones et relationes venetæ*, vol. 4, pp. 203–4.

[75]I.Ö. H.K.R., Croatica, fasc. 3, 1580, Jan. No. 46 (3 Feb. 1580); Lopašić, *Acta historiam confinii*, vol. 1, p. 94.

[76]In I.Ö. H.K.R., Croatica, fas. 3, 1580, Jan. No. 46: 2. Some of this booty was later returned as a result of negotiations with Venice (Lopašić, *Acta historiam confinii*, vol. 1, p. 97).

[77]In I.Ö. H.K.R., Croatica, fasc. 1, 1578, Feb. No. 41 (14 Feb. 1578); Lopašić, *Acta historiam confinii*, vol. 1, p. 55.

[78]In I.Ö. H.K.R., Croatica, fasc. 4, 1585 Feb. No. 25 (11 Feb. 1585).

could do nothing against the vojvodas without outside support.[79] The Military Frontier commission sent to Senj in 1581 to deal with the matter found that the uskoks who had been sentenced to death as ringleaders in Venetian raids (over loud protests from Vojvoda Daničić) had escaped from prison. They hesitated to act against the Daničić brothers, fearing to provoke a rebellion (*tumultt*).[80]

Personal qualities might have succeeded in gaining the cooperation of the uskoks where force failed. Raab had himself led the uskoks on successful raids in Ottoman Lika, and one might expect that his military skills would have won him some influence among the uskoks, as other Captains of Senj had enjoyed the respect of the uskoks through loyalty born of shared experience. Giovanni of Fermo mentions, for example, the affection Senj had for Baltazar Lamberger, who was Captain from 1569 to 1571.[81] But there seems to have been little respect for Raab's authority, either among the vojvodas or among the rank-and-file, an attitude clearly revealed in the 1582 proceedings of the military tribunal in Karlovac against Vojvoda Juraj Daničić, his brother Matija, and Vojvoda Matija Tvrdislavić.[82]

These proceedings were based on Raab's charges of insubordination. Since he could not count on the Hofkriegsrat to back up his reform efforts with force, he attempted to use the authority of the Military Frontier indirectly to assert his control of Senj. The charges against the vojvodas centered on questions of authority: they had opposed Raab's efforts to punish attacks on Venetian shipping and had acted without his authority in negotiations with Venetian representatives and Ottoman subjects; they had undercut Raab's efforts at military discipline, "always belittling it" and encouraging the uskoks to ignore his orders; and they themselves had disobeyed Raab's commands. Investigators were appointed and a tribunal was constituted. Testimony taken from 137 Senj witnesses reveals a great deal about the attitudes of the uskoks and their vojvodas toward the nature and locus of authority in Senj, at the very time when the Hofkriegsrat was beginning to tighten its own control over the military organization of the uskoks.

Raab's complaints called attention to several trials of uskoks accused of piracy against Venetian ships in which the vojvodas had intervened on behalf of the accused. One of these incidents, the case of Juraj Subaša (Subwäschä), was investigated in detail. The vojvodas had been accused

---

[79]In ibid., fasc. 3, 1580, Jan. No. 46 (6 Jan. 1580); Lopašić, *Acta historiam confinii*, vol. 1, pp. 97–98.

[80]Lopašić, *Acta historiam confinii*, vol. 1, 95; I.Ö. H.K.R., Croatica, fasc. 3, 1580, Jan. No. 46 (21 Mar. 1580); fasc. 4, 1584, Apr. No. 2 (28 Sept. 1581; 3 Jan. 1582).

[81]Rački, "Prilog za poviest hrvatskih uskoka," p. 197.

[82]In I.Ö. H.K.R., Croatica, fasc. 4, 1584 Apr. No. 2.

of breaking into the Subaša trial under arms, and Juraj Daničić in particular was supposed to have declared that he would seize the accused from the executioner with his own hands to keep him alive. The issue was not Subaša's guilt or innocence, but rather the legitimacy of the trial. Witnesses agreed that Daničić, accompanied by the other vojvodas, had entered the room in the fortress where the trial was proceeding under Raab's supervision and had asked the Senj magistrates "what they intended to do with this poor sinner." They answered that they would do "what the judgment and the law allow." Daničić, as the spokesman for all the vojvodas, then disputed the court's right to pass judgment, and the court discontinued the trial.

The witnesses cited a number of reasons why the vojvodas objected to the trial. They did not overtly oppose the grounds for the trial—raids on Venetian shipping—though the uskoks often criticized the protection extended to Venice by the representatives of the Military Frontier in Senj. There was a sense that Subaša had been unfairly singled out as a scapegoat and that he could not in fairness be tried alone but that, as a witness observed, "many more should be summoned here, for there were many in the game."[83] A more important issue was the way in which the trial was held. A few witnesses (most of them on the magistrates' bench) described the trial as having been held "according to the Senj custom," but the site, the size of the court, and the character of the people present were all called into question, according to the depositions. Frane Blagajić [Francist Blaggei], the city watch-master (and later to be a municipal magistrate himself), was quite clear on the requirements of custom: "The Captain had convened the court in the fortress with a few persons . . . which is not however customary, for a criminal trial like that should take place openly on the square." Daničić and the other vojvodas had demanded that "the Captain should hold the trial as customary in the town hall or on the open square, and should include the vojvodas and other qualified persons."[84] The city statute did in fact require that such trials take place in public.[85] Other witnesses agreed that Daničić had objected that none of the soldiery was present and that in a case when "sentence was to be passed on flesh and blood, the whole common crowd should participate."[86] In effect, the vojvodas were objecting to the usurpation of the power to judge uskok actions by an

---

[83]In ibid.: 69' (Valtschitsch).

[84]In ibid.: 76–76' (Blaggei).

[85]Either in the City Loggia on the Little Square (*Mala placa*) or next to the salt warehouse (Zjačić, "Statut grada Senja," pp. 63, 94; Magdić, "Statut kralja Ferdinanda III," p. 84). Not until after 1640, with the growing civil power of the Captain in Senj, were trials officially moved to the fortress (Čulinović, *Statut grada Senja*, p. 179).

[86]In I.Ö. H.K.R., Croatica, fasc. 4, 1584, Apr. No. 2: 112' (Radonitsch).

outside authority and arguing that in the first instance this power be
longed to the Senj community as a whole—not only the duly chosen
magistrates but also the uskoks and townspeople whose lives were affected by such judgments. Inasmuch as the bench discontinued the
hearing, it appears that they may have agreed with this line of argument.

As his subsequent accusations indicate, Raab clearly perceived Daničić's statements as a challenge to his own authority and that of the
Military Frontier officials. He paced up and down the hall saying, "Daničić, you have always been vexatious to me," and made an offensive
gesture toward Daničić ("gave Daničić the fig under his nose"), to which
Daničić answered, "You are the Captain, and I am a vojvoda of Senj. I
am as good as a vojvoda as you are as a Captain."[87] The vojvodas, as
Daničić's speech implied, recognized the authority of the Captain, and
beyond him of the Hofkriegsrat. They were, after all, soldiers in the
service of the Habsburgs and Christendom, as they themselves frequently pointed out. Although relations between them were strained in
1582, Daničić and the other vojvodas accepted Raab's right to command
and urged him to punish soldiers who disobeyed him.[88] The vojvodas'
also saw the Military Frontier authorities in Karlovac as a higher military
authority: Daničić was ready to appeal Raab's actions to Karlovac if he
could not stop Subaša's trial in Senj.

The real question was where the limits of centralized state authority in
Senj lay, and the fundamental answer was that the state and the Hofkriegsrat could command obedience to the extent that they could dis-
charge their responsibility toward the uskoks by guaranteeing the uskoks'
livelihood. Raab's inability to extract the uskoks' long-overdue pay from
the Hofkriegsrat made his authority in Senj negligible, particularly when
it was not backed up by any other effective authority. The vojvodas are
quoted as telling the uskoks, "Why should you concern yourself with
the Captain, when he has told you that he cannot help you?" and, "He
can do you neither harm nor good," because he was incapable of obtaining the uskoks' overdue pay.[89]

In the period when these hearings took place, the vojvodas' interests
and loyalties were still very closely connected with the uskoks and with
Senj. When necessary, the vojvodas took an active role in leading raids
that would supply Senj with booty (even if it was sometimes of dubious
character) and, as these hearings show, also strongly defended the interests and rights of the Senj uskoks against the demands of the Captain
and the Hofkriegsrat. It is no wonder that the uskoks were more inclined

[87]In ibid.: 53′–54 (Stipanovitsch); 62–62′ (Previnovitsch); 83′–84 (Prachaim); 89–89′ (Millaschin).
[88]In ibid.: 55 (Stypschitsch).
[89]In Ibid.: 74′ (Vuschitsch); 75′ (Lasynovitsch).

to obey the vojvodas, according to many of these witnesses, and respected them more than they did the Captain.[90] Although it had not been proved that the vojvodas had actively fomented mutiny, it was clear that they were not following the central government's changing views of Senj's role in the frontier system. Nevertheless, in this case the Hofkriegsrat did not try to impose a new, stricter discipline on the uskoks. The charges against the vojvodas were eventually dismissed for lack of evidence and the costs were assessed against Raab, though it was later decided that the hearing had been handled incorrectly and the entire case was to be liquidated.[91] Nevertheless, when the court did not find the vojvodas guilty, what effectiveness Raab had commanded was further shaken and the uskoks, ignoring his orders, began to raid more widely. In 1585 he submitted his resignation, citing his inability to control the uskoks without effective and consistent support from the Hofkriegsrat and the government.[92]

The case of Kaspar Raab shows the weapons available to the Captain of Senj when he tried to restrain the uskoks from raids that conflicted with the interests of the state, and the limits of their effectiveness. The authority of the Captains, particularly in reforms that went against the grain of uskok custom, ultimately rested on support from the military authorities in Karlovac, Graz, and Vienna. They gave Raab very little of the help he needed to tame Senj, delaying the pay commissions, dismissing his charges against his rivals for power in Senj, and failing to strengthen the German garrison, the only troops he felt he could trust completely. In his letter of resignation, Raab made it quite clear that without this necessary aid, the Captain of Senj could do little to prevent Senj raiding. "Both the paid and the unpaid Senjani are seized by a stubborn spirit, for they feel and sense that I have no one to deal with the disobedient, or to send to their town, so that they give little attention or obedience to the urgent decrees so often issued."[93]

The distribution of power and authority among the uskoks in Senj was largely a function of their own particular type of military organization: experience and success in raiding brought with it booty and a following. Because uskok leadership was based on a democracy of military prowess, the authority of the leaders was limited, requiring a measure of consent from the rank-and-file. Although the vojvodas were nominally a part of the Military Frontier and had a lively awareness of the benefits

---

[90]Ibid.: 71' (Milodict); 77 (Blaggei); 52' (Lasynovitsch).
[91]I.Ö. H.K.R., Croatica, fasc. 4, 1584 Apr. No. 2: 26'.
[92]In ibid., fasc. 4, 1585, Feb. No. 25 (11 Feb. 1585).
[93]In ibid. Raab continued to act as an adviser on uskok affairs, urging the suppression of their piracies (ibid., fasc. 9, 1597, Aug. No. 7 [20 Aug. 1597, Raab to Archduke Ferdinand]; Ljubić, "Prilozi za životopis Markantunu Dominisu," p. 21).

they could gain by using its processes to their own advantage, their primary loyalty was to Senj and the uskoks. The Captain of Senj, however, was always a creature of the Military Frontier, appointed from outside Senj. In spite of his strong economic interests in successful uskok raiding, his position was ultimately dependent on the pleasure of the central military authorities. Like military commanders anywhere, the Captain might be more or less successful at capturing the uskoks' loyalty through his military prowess, his personal courage, or his ability to milk the system for the benefit of his troops. This relationship, however, depended on the extent to which the current policy of the government matched the needs of the uskoks. The Captain could assert his authority over the uskoks only so far without forceful assistance from the central military administration.

The Habsburgs and the Military Frontier Administration

Why did the Habsburgs and the military administration of the Frontier not take consistent measures against uskok insubordination? The border wars, with their sporadic mobilizations and major operations preceded and followed by constant small raids, called for troops who were easily raised and easily dismissed, who could keep the Ottoman forces well back from the borders with raids of their own, and who were not overdependent on the treasuries of the Estates, the Archduke, or the Emperor for their support. The uskoks in Senj proved ideal for these Habsburg needs. In spite of the irregular pay the Senj garrison was always full, and the venturini provided a sizable force of auxiliaries who made few financial demands. The uskoks also provided a large force of experienced troops whenever conventional military operations were planned. Their raiding expeditions kept the Ottoman forces in check and hindered frontier settlement that might have provided a base for Ottoman expansion. For many years the Venetian ambassadors protesting the actions of the uskoks and demanding their removal received the same reply: "His Majesty told me that he could not remove them under any circumstances, even if I were to do him every possible service in the name of Your Serenity, knowing that he has no subjects in all his dominions more suited to his needs and to his borders than these. . . . If he wanted to employ Germans, or any others, he would have to agree to pay them more and they would not be so valorous, nor so fit to operate at sea."[94]

Nevertheless, diplomatic pressure from Venice, especially when sec-

[94]In Turba, *Venetianische Depeschen vom Kaiserhofe*, vol. 3, pp. 236–37 (1559).

onded by allies in the papal court, sometimes effectively moved the Habsburgs to check uskok raids, although usually the uskoks were convenient pawns in Habsburg quarrels with the Serenissima. But the Archduke of Styria was vulnerable to economic threats from Venice, particularly to blockades of shipping on the Croatian Littoral, and more than once a serious threat to the revenues of Rijeka and Trieste led the Archduke, as Commander of the Military Frontier, to send a commission to Senj to restrain the uskoks.

Ottoman diplomatic pressure was a more effective stimulus to imperial action. Although war on the frontier may have seemed never-ending and the periodic truces and peaces virtually meaningless, in the capitals, where ambassadors were discussing a cessation of hostilities, a peace or truce could seem vital, offering a chance to turn troops elsewhere or to reduce expenditures swollen by war. Under such circumstances unauthorized raiding could threaten precarious negotiations.

The negotiations for the Habsburg-Ottoman truce concluded in 1547–48 are a representative example. In the autumn of 1546 Charles V and Ferdinand were suing for peace with the Ottomans. The constant raids of the uskoks in Senj and Vinodol were an obstacle to the process—in spite of Ferdinand's warning to Ban Zrinski to curtail them in Vinodol.[95] The final version of the truce issued in Ferdinand's name specifically mentioned the uskoks at the insistence of the Porte: "That the brigands from both sides who have made the other's fields dangerous by their robberies, such as the hajduks, martoloses, and uskoks, should be restrained and punished by each party."[96] Anxious that the uskoks not disturb the peace until the decision had been made whether to renew the war with France or to return to an offensive against the Ottomans, Ferdinand took steps to keep the uskoks under control, warning their commanders to restrain them and sending a commission to proclaim the truce to the uskoks.[97] In March 1548 two commissioners arrived in Senj to ensure that the provisions of the treaty with the Ottomans were carried out. The venturini, "unstable men, who have no settled lodging but live in Senj and other places, plundering the subjects of His [Habsburg] Majesty as well as others," were to be dismissed, and not permitted to live in Habsburg territory. The others, particularly those with families in Senj, were allowed to remain, "to serve against the Turks in time of war," "because [His Majesty's] ministers are able to ensure that they will do nothing against the will of His Majesty," probably by using threats to withhold their pay. The uskoks' barks were also to be confis-

---

[95]Barabás, *Zrinyi Miklós*, vol. 1, pp. 65–67.

[96]*Monumenta Hungariæ historica*, vol. 2, p. 144. The version issued in the name of the Sultan promised to keep Ottoman irregulars from harming Senj (ibid., p. 147).

[97]Barabás, *Zrinyi Miklós*, vol. 2, pp. 192–204.

cated. In the following months news came that the remedies taken against the uskoks had included the imprisonment and execution of some of the offenders. All of these measures were reported in full to the Venetian ambassadors—for impressing Venice with the sincerity of the Habsburg desire to keep the uskoks at peace was not the least important of the commissioners' roles.[98] In spite of his anxiety to maintain peace with the Porte, however, Ferdinand explained to the Venetian ambassadors who insisted that the only solution was for "His Majesty to chase them out of all his territories, and not permit that similar sorts of men be given asylum in the state of a Prince so just," that he could not do so, because there was no peace with the Ottomans, only a five-year truce, and the uskoks, "who are most valiant enemies of the Turks," were necessary to defend his borders.[99] The next year, with the Ottoman armies engaged in Persia, the uskoks were again raiding unrestrained.[100] The Habsburg negotiations and treaties with the Porte in 1562, 1568, 1575, and 1606 all followed the same pattern. To appease the Ottomans, orders were sent to restrain the uskoks, and clauses prohibiting raiding were written into the treaties.[101]

To curtail uskok raiding completely, the Habsburgs would either have had to provide for the uskoks' support or to remove them from Senj entirely. The difficulties encountered in paying the uskoks have already been touched upon. The problems in removing the uskoks were no less great—the most obvious being that it would be difficult and expensive to defend Senj without the uskoks. Nonetheless, the possibility of removing the uskoks was considered seriously several times when the demands of imperial foreign policy made the question of controlling uskok raids particularly pressing. As often as this plan was proposed it met with opposition, either from the Hofkriegsrat in Graz or from the Archduke of Styria himself. These supporters stressed the necessity of maintaining the garrison as a barrier to Ottoman incursions, the unique suitability of the uskoks to conditions in Senj, and the great expense of keeping a regular garrison there. They also cast doubt on the motives of the plan's supporters—particularly the Venetians—claiming a conspiracy to deliver Senj into the hands of Venice and the Porte.[102] However, because the

---

[98]For documents on the commission see A.S.V., Provveditore Sopraintendente alla Camera dei Confini, 243 (dispatches of Alvise Mocenigo, Lorenzo Contarini, and Francesco Badoer, Augsburg, 1548).

[99]In A.S.V., Provveditore Sopraintendente alla Camera dei Confini, 243: 28 Mar. 1548 (Alvise Mocenigo and Lorenzo Contarini).

[100]Laszowski, *Monumenta habsburgica*, vol. 3, p. 323.

[101]Turba, *Venetianische Depeschen vom Kaiserhofe*, vol. 3, p. 199; *Libri commemoriali*, vol. 13, p. 44; Horvat, *Monumenta uscocchorum*, vol. 1, p. 17 ff.; G. Noradounghian, *Recueil d'actes internationaux de l'Empire ottoman* (Paris, 1897), vol. 1, p. 104.

[102]See, for example, Lopašić, "Prilozi za poviest Hrvatske XVI i XVII vieka," vol. 17,

Signoria was so anxious to be rid of the uskok irritant, the plan for removing the uskoks became a valuable negotiating card for the Habsburgs, played in response to any Venetian attack.

A second part of the problem in imposing limits on uskok raiding lay in the difficulty of achieving a consensus among all the parties responsible for the uskoks. The facts that Senj, as a free royal city, was subject to the Croatian-Hungarian King (who was usually also the Emperor) and that the garrison, as a part of the Military Frontier, was the responsibility of the Archduke of Styria, were often used by the Habsburgs to shift blame for the uskoks' actions in the face of Venetian protests.[103] The interests of the Inner Austrian Estates, the Hofkriegsrat in Graz, and the archducal court on the one hand and the imperial courts at Vienna or Prague on the other, often differed over the threat posed by the Ottomans and by Venice, as their sometimes conflicting policies toward Senj reflect. While Maximillian II and his successor Rudolf II were anxious not to extend the hostilities with the Porte, Archduke Charles and later his son Archduke Ferdinand needed the uskoks as troops in the constant "little war" of the borders and as a weapon in the equally constant diplomatic struggle with the Serenissima. Others with interests in uskok affairs also contributed to the debate. Magnates such as Zrinski, with extensive lands in Vinodol and interests in Venetian trade, officials such as the Governer of Pazin, and trading towns such as Rijeka or Trieste all found that they had a direct interest in checking uskok raids and avoiding Venetian retaliation against their own exposed territories. It was often claimed that nobles in Inner Austria or in the Military Frontier administration supported the uskoks out of an interest in their booty; it was also sometimes suggested that the Protestant nobility of Inner Austria used the uskok issue against the Archduke and the Emperor, hoping to win religious concessions should war break out.[104] In such circumstances, it was rare that complete agreement could be reached on the limits to be placed on the uskoks.

For most of the sixteenth century effective restraint of uskok raiding was attempted only in exceptional circumstances and was enforced intermittently and without much consistency. The central military administration was unconcerned by its failure to achieve complete control over the uskoks. As long as the benefits to the Frontier and the Habsburg monarchy as a whole outweighed the disadvantages of uskok raiding, the authorities were content to intervene only when policy so demanded. From the end of the 1590s, however, with more direct Venetian pressure,

---

p. 202; Turba, *Venetianische Depeschen vom Kaiserhofe,* vol. 3, pp. 174–75.

[103]See, for example, Horvat, *Monumenta uscocchorum,* vol. 1, pp. 3–6, 236–38.

[104]H.A.Z., Fond Šime Ljubića, 2/33: 285.

particularly in the form of blockades of archducal ports, backed by interests at the papal court, and with negotiations over the conclusion of the Long Turkish War, uskok actions began to cost more than they were worth. The need for effective and consistent control over the uskoks developed into a concern that affected both the Archduke and the Emperor, as well as other, private interests. More and more frequently, Senj was subject to pressure to mend its ways, exerted both directly through the Captains and commissions and indirectly through Hofkriegsrat attempts to control the uskoks' leaders.

CHAPTER SIX

Legitimating Raiding:
The Uskok Code

In the view of Venetian officialdom, the uskoks of Senj were pirates and bandits, their profession of religious motivation pure hypocrisy, if not a cynical manipulation of the appearance of religion to sway public opinion.[1] To the Habsburg authorities they were a convenient soldiery on the ramparts of Christendom, although when uskok raiding conflicted with the interests of the moment they agreed among themselves that this was a lawless rabble motivated by greed. Both groups looked at the uskoks from the standpoint of their own interests. But what was the uskoks' own vision of their role on the border, and what sources did it derive from? Certainly the uskoks were not entirely without self-interested economic motives for their raids, as has already been discussed. Yet to concentrate solely on this aspect would be to ignore a significant part of the uskoks' mental world. Any evaluation of their actions must give serious consideration to the uskoks' own beliefs and ethos.

The Uskok *antemurale Christianitatis*

The uskoks' explanation of their warfare was simple and explicitly formulated: they were fighting a holy war against the Muslim infidel in defense of the borders of Christendom. This role accorded well with the uskoks' alleged origins as refugees from Ottoman conquest and Turkish tyranny. It was given added encouragement by the Habsburgs and the Catholic Church.

[1]See especially Sarpi, *La Repubblica di Venezia*, p. 57; Contarini, *Le historie venetiane*, pp. 325-26.

The defense of the borders of Christendom in the Balkans was one of the main justifications for the Habsburgs' claim to the Croatian crown. On the basis of pledges of a vigorous response to Ottoman encroachment the Croatian Diet had accepted Ferdinand I as King of Croatia and had agreed to the organization of the Military Frontier as a separate entity. This Habsburg frontier in Croatia was not legitimated solely in military and political terms. Faced as it was with Muslim antagonists, the border was permeated with a strong sense of religious obligation—a war of the faith against the infidel. The initiatives to raise the Balkan Christians in support of the Habsburg military advances were expressed in these terms—the aim was their liberation from the yoke of a religious tyrant. Any shortcomings in material support for the Frontier were compensated by a strong Habsburg emphasis on the Frontier's duty to defend the "Republic of Christ." Throughout the sixteenth century, Habsburg officials never ceased reminding the uskoks in Senj that they served as outposts of Christendom, even when attempting to subordinate the uskoks' acts against the infidel to the demands of political expedience. References to Senj in official documents constantly blended military and religious metaphors: Senj is a bulwark of the faith, the ramparts of Christendom, a *propugnaculum adversus infideles*, and the *antemurale Christianitatis*. In turn this vocabulary helped to shape the uskok self-image.

The Holy See and the local Catholic clergy reinforced the Habsburg formulation of the *antemurale Christianitatis* as the framework for uskok activities. Papal commitment to the crusade against the infidel was sometimes muted in the sixteenth century by the claims of other conflicts, but a number of popes (particularly Adrian VI, Pius V, and Clement VIII) made energetic attempts to unite Christendom against the Turk. In particular, the lower Catholic clergy on the Croatian and Dalmatian borders supported papal efforts against the infidel consistently and militantly. Many of these clergymen had strong ties with the uskoks, using their influence to regulate relations between the uskoks and their flocks. Some, approving uskok raids against the infidel, passed them information and hid their booty, and in return received a generous share, as one Provveditore Generale remarked venomously, "under the guise of alms."[2] Others joined the raids themselves. The important part played by these priests and friars in raising the Dalmatian and Ottoman population to support the uskoks was dramatically shown in the context of the 1596 uskok attempt on Ottoman Klis. Many Venetian subjects, interrogated afterward, claimed that they would never have disobeyed the prohibitions of the Signoria had it not been for the crusading enthusiasm of the

---

[2]In *Commissiones et relationes venetæ*, vol. 5, p. 134.

friars. One of these, Fra Simon Urmaneo, had gone from house to house visiting those who were reluctant to join the uskoks and rebels, bearing a distaff and a spindle and saying, "Take this, sluggard, put down your arquebus and sword and take these as your arms. These are the exercises that suit you. Put on a woman's dress and stay at home spinning in shame. Don't you see that your contemporaries are at war and are fighting for the faith?"[3] This militancy reached such a height that the Zadar Synod of 1598 was driven to issue an ordinance prohibiting clerics from appearing in church in military dress.[4]

The clergy of Senj was no exception to this anti-Ottoman attitude. Senj was the seat of a bishopric, with a cathedral and chapter and a number of smaller churches, as well as two monastic foundations, one Franciscan, the other Dominican. Like the rest of Senj, the clergy was extremely poor, having little in the way of benefices after the loss of Church lands to the Ottoman conquerors. The bishopric received payments in kind from lands in Vinodol and a small income from a Rijeka tithe and archducal grants, and some money was earmarked for the churches and monasteries from the income of the Senj tariffs.[5] This was scarcely enough—in 1583 the Cathedral Chapter had six canons, but only sufficient funds to support one.[6] Some of the uskoks' booty went to support the Senj churches, which were described as furnished with the gifts and alms of the uskoks. Their booty also helped to support the clergy. On returning from a raid, Giovanni of Fermo reports, the uskoks "immediately go humbly to the church, and thank the Lord for the prosperous journey they have had, and for their safe return home; then they share out the booty, together taking out a donation, which seems to them to be in conformity with the plunder they have made, and they distribute it to the clergy, all of these being poor and mendicant."[7] The participation of the clergy in uskok booty led Venetian observers to believe that monetary benefit was the sole reason that the priests of Senj approved the uskoks' raids and that their sermons were calculated to incite the uskoks to bring in still larger hauls.[8] Whether or not self-interest was a deciding factor, the ecclesiastics of Senj, like their brethren elsewhere on the

---

[3]In A.S.V., Provveditori da Terra e da Mar, 417: 30 July 1596.

[4]In Farlati, *Illyricum sacrum*, vol. 5, p. 146.

[5]Edo Pivčević, "Kako je de Dominis postao senjski biskup," *Crkva u svijetu*, 18/2 (1983): 185, 188; Lopašić, *Acta historiam confinii*, vol. 1, pp. 18; 120–21; vol. 2, p. 23; Manoilo Sladović, *Povesti biskupijah senjske i modrŭske ili krbavske* (Trieste, 1856), p. 174.

[6]Sladović, *Povesti biskupijah senjske*, p. 174.

[7]In Rački, "Prilog za poviest hrvatskih uskoka," p. 241.

[8]"Because their priests and the bishop receive a tenth of their robberies in cash, their actions are not only approved, but covered with religion, so a way is found to mantle each greater evil with the title of good" (in Contarini, *Le historie venetiane*, pp. 325–26). See also *Commissiones et relationes venetæ*, vol. 5, p. 66.

border, enthusiastically supported the holy war against the infidel, not only preaching the necessity of defending the faith through the raids of the uskoks but also joining in themselves. Bishop Frane Živković and other clerics who were enrolled on the muster register of 1551 received pay from the coffers of the Military Frontier, probably honorary stipends, but it was not at all unusual for the clergy of Senj to join the uskoks on their forays, like the priest who was captured raiding near Omiš in 1566 as part of an uskok band.[9]

Ecclesiastical confirmation of the uskoks' appointed place on the ramparts of Christendom also came from Rome itself. The Holy See long saw the uskoks not only as defenders against Ottoman incursions into Croatia and Friuli, and even Italy as a whole, but also as troops who figured prominently in each new plan to liberate the Balkans from the Muslim yoke. Material aid accompanied papal exhortations to stand firm against the infidel. First Klis and then Senj received bounty as well as blessings from Rome. The large round tower that defended Senj's walls to the north was built by Leo X (1513–21), whose memory was kept alive in the town by a bas-relief and the papal arms set into the wall, as well as by the familiar name of the "Pope's Tower."[10] Papal aid helped raise Nehaj ("Fear Not"), the fortress that still stands above Senj. Money from Rome sometimes paid the stipends of the uskoks, most notably for a time in the 1580s, and grain sent from the Papal States fed the garrison in Senj more than once in times of need. Was it any wonder that the uskoks should have proclaimed themselves as specially chosen agents of the Holy See, and their raids on the Ottomans as blessed by the Pontiff himself? On their expeditions, Archbishop Minucci of Zadar reported in 1601, "The uskoks go spreading the rumor . . . that they have been blessed by His Grace, and that they are winning merit by their actions."[11]

The precise quality of Christian belief is no easier to measure among the uskoks than it is among the common people elsewhere in Europe at this time. They were not the least devout of Christians, despite the accusations of their opponents. Supporters of the uskoks naturally emphasized their religious observances and the high moral standards of their daily life.[12] Giovanni of Fermo explicitly contrasts their piety with con-

---

[9]The Venetian captors immediately hanged his lay companions but hesitated to hang a priest. When the captain wrote to his superiors for advice, they initially complained that he should have hanged the priest as well, claiming ignorance of his station, but eventually agreed to take the matter up with Rome (*Nunziature di Venezia*, vol. 2, p. 53).

[10]Rački, "Prilog za poviest hrvatskih uskoka," p. 175.

[11]In Horvat, *Monumenta uscocchorum*, vol. 1, p. 338.

[12]See Leva, *Legazione di Roma*, vol. 1, p. 141. An ecclesiastical investigation into de Dominis's candidature for the Senj bishopric provides a few details of the religious observances in Senj in 1600: the cathedral was in a ruinous state and badly needed repair; services were held daily, usually in the "Illyrian" language (Croatian) but also in Latin; the

temporary Italian practices, to the great disadvantage of the latter.[13] More tellingly, perhaps, Vettor Barbaro, a well-informed critic after his sojourn in Senj as Provveditore Generale Pasqualigo's representative in 1601, admitted that the uskoks showed every evidence of public and private piety. "They frequent the churches, and at times the uskoks are seen on their return from a raid, making their way on the ground from the quay to the churches on their bare knees to give thanks for having been delivered from some danger or conflict."[14] Even Paolo Sarpi agreed that at least the uskoks were not heretics. "They are not Lutherans, nor are there any other churches than those of the Catholic religion in Senj, nor can it be said that they are misbelievers in any of the articles that are disputed with the Protestants."[15]

It is not the depth of the uskoks' piety, however, or the degree of their Catholic orthodoxy, but another aspect of their belief that is important for an understanding of uskok values. The uskoks' religiosity had a special flavor, one given it by the frontier, one that can be detected elsewhere in this period and in earlier centuries along the borders between Islam and the Christian world. This was a crusading creed, with military elements inextricably incorporated into religious life. The Church and its symbols played an essential role in uskok war, and so too the accoutrements of battle entered the life of the Church. The clergy preached the holy war from the altars of Senj; held services for those about to go to the garrisons of the frontier, blessing their weapons;[16] accompanied the uskok bands to their barks in processions, carrying crosses and sprinkling the barks with holy water, even on high holy days;[17] stored booty from their raids in the chapels;[18] and even fought alongside their flocks. The very churches in Senj were shrines celebrating the uskoks' commitment to the defense of Christianity against the Turk. Symbols of uskok battles adorned the two monastery churches, the Dominican St. Nicholas and, in particular, the Franciscan St. Francis. Here were the banners, dedicated by the Senj standard bearers, that had flown above famous victories. Here were the plaques that memorialized the military skill and devotion of the uskoks whose bones were interred nearby. They bore

---

people were pious and held to old ways in church practices, holding various prayers and processions at different times of the year (Pivčević, "Kako je de Dominis postao senjski biskup," pp. 178–92). In 1615 the newly appointed bishop of Senj reported that "they believe in the Holy Roman Church, but are completely ignorant of Christian doctrine" (in Jačov, *Spisi tajnog vatikanskog arhiva*, p. 30).

[13]In Rački, "Prilog za poviest hrvatskih uskoka," pp. 34–36.
[14]In H.A.Z., Fond Šime Ljubića, 2/33: 281'.
[15]Sarpi, *La Repubblica di Venezia*, p. 57.
[16]Horvat, *Monumenta uscocchorum*, vol. 1, p. 416.
[17]Fiedler, *Fontes rerum Austriacarum*, vol. 24, pp. 36–37.
[18]Ivić, "Prilozi za povijest Hrvatske i Slavonije," p. 302.

such inscriptions as "Jakov Suminich, honored soldier, murdered by the Turks, lies here. 1556." Above this inscription there was a coat of arms showing a hand holding a bare saber. Other such heraldic imagery was similarly warlike: a mace, an ax, a winged lion holding in its paws a sword and a Turk's head.[19] "Even the pictures of the saints in the churches have the air of ruffians and assassins, if Our Lord will pardon me," commented Barbaro after his return from Senj.[20] The frescoes in the churches have vanished now, but we know that Senj's iconography gave pride of place to St. George, that martial dragon slayer, who was the patron of the city itself and appeared on the personal seal of at least one of the uskoks, as well as on that of the city. Certainly the minds of the uskoks and of their clergy found no incongruity in the spectacle of an uskok praying on his knees in the Church of the Holy Ghost, with his battle ax in his hands, though the Habsburg commissioner who witnessed this scene was appalled.[21] Nor does it seem incongruous, if we look at the uskoks' behavior beyond the walls of Senj, that their cry while joining battle with Ottoman forces should have been "Jesus! Jesus!"[22]

In justifying their attacks on the Turks, the uskoks presented them first and foremost as religious opponents, "the enemies of the name of Christ" or "traitors to the Christian faith," who should be pursued and plundered wherever they were found. Jews, infidels of another variety, were routinely bracketed with the Turks by the uskoks who ransacked ships' cargoes for their goods and demanded heavy ransoms for their persons. The uskoks' relations with the Christian subjects of the Turk were less clearcut. Although they were Christians, the uskoks (and their patrons in Vienna or Rome) often argued that they were legitimate targets. If they fought as Ottoman irregulars (as martoloses, for instance) they were branded enemies of the Christian cause, and if they were Orthodox they might be stigmatized as schismatics. Even the fact that they had remained under Ottoman rule could be enough to cast doubt on the sincerity of their adherence to the Christian faith. To the extent that the uskok was defined as a soldier on the ramparts of Christendom, his enemy was also defined primarily in religious terms, as the infidel, the unbeliever, and the schismatic, fitting easily into categories that had legitimated corsair plundering long before the uskoks adopted them.[23]

[19]"IAKOV SVMINICH HONORATVS MILES A TVRCIS INTEREMPTVS HIC IACET MDLVI" (in the Church of St. Francis) (Kukuljević-Sakcinski, *Natpisi*, pp. 244–48).

[20]In H.A.Z., Fond Šime Ljubića, 2/33: 281'.

[21]Horvat, *Monumenta uscocchorum*, vol. 1, p. 405.

[22]A.S.F., Mediceo del Principato, 3084: 482 (20 Apr. 1586); A.S.V., Materie miste notabili, 126: 24 Dec. 1602.

[23]The uskoks were not the only ones to rationalize the plunder of Turks, Jews, and even Christians in this way. This was the common practice of the crusading orders, the Knights of St. John and the Knights of St. Stephen, and of the corsairs of the Christian states. Even

If it is easy to characterize the uskoks' enemies, it is more problematic to say what the uskoks were fighting for. There is little evidence that the uskoks themselves developed any coherent project of Balkan liberation, apart from their recurrent dream of retaking Klis, that earlier uskok stronghold. Throughout the sixteenth century plans to seize Klis had circulated among those in the West who believed that the Balkan Christians were ready to rise against the infidel yoke and needed only an appropriate occasion and the promise of Western support. The uskoks were invariably cast in the role of the troops who would set these plans in motion by liberating this once-Christian fortress. As we have seen, schemes to liberate Klis had circulated throughout the sixteenth century. Attempts were made in the 1540s and the 1580s, and in 1596 Klis was briefly recaptured.[24] Their part in these attempts reinforced the uskoks' commitment to the idea of holy war against the infidel and his allies (while Venetian punishment meted out to the Klis conspirators in the 1580s and the 1590s helped give uskok resentment of the Republic a religious justification). Because of their contacts with conspirators working on plans of Balkan liberation, the uskok vojvodas were aware of other movements against the Turk. After the Ottoman peace of 1606, when it appeared that the Habsburgs might withdraw their support for border warfare, Vojvoda Ivan Vlatković learned of Spanish plans to raise Bosnia, Hercegovina, Serbia, and Albania against the Ottomans under the leadership of Grdan, Christian vojvoda of Ottoman Nikšić, and volunteered the support of the uskoks. (Once again Klis was the focus of his scheme.)[25] But the uskoks themselves were only rarely the organizers or instigators of these undertakings. Even if the uskoks were committed to the struggle against the Turk, and if some uskok leaders saw the possibility of joining forces with other allies under the rule of Venice or the Ottomans, the uskoks were not visionary leaders or revolution-

papal protests were not always enough to protect Greek Orthodox Christians and Jews residing in the Papal States from the raids of Christian corsairs (see, for examples, Tenenti, *Piracy and the Decline of Venice*). Even Venice, during the wars of 1539–40 and 1570–73, seized Christian shipping on the pretext that it was carrying the goods of Turks or Jews (*Nunziature di Venezia*, vol. 132, pp. 280, 349).

[24]For 1541 see Theiner, *Vetera monumenta Slavorum meridionalium historiam illustrantia*, vol. 1, p. 651, and Alexandre Tausserat-Radel, *Correspondance politique de Guillaume Pellicier, ambassadeur de France à Venise, 1540–1542* (Paris, 1899), p. 277; for the events of the late 1570s and 1580s see A.S.V., Capi del Consiglio dei Dieci, 306: 2 July 1578; ibid., 301: 4 Nov. 1572, 5 June 1573, 23 July 1582, 26 Aug. 1582; and L. Jelić, "Isprave o prvoj uroti za oslobodjenje Klisa i kopnene Dalmacije od Turaka g. 1580–1586," *Vjesnik Kraljevskog hrvatsko-slavonsko-dalmatinskog zemaljskog arhiva* (Zagreb), 6 (1904): 97–113. For the plans of the 1590s and the recapture of Klis, see Chapter 7. Peter Bartl, *Der Westbalkan zwischen spanischer Monarchie und osmanischen Reich* (Vienna, 1974), contains a general overview of such schemes.

[25]Tomić, *Grada za istoriju pokreta na Balkanu protiv Turaka*, pp. 361–62, 377, 409; Fiedler, "Versuche der türkisch-südslawischen Völker," pp. 288–300.

aries. In general the uskoks were only foot soldiers in insurrectionary projects concocted by other dreamers.

It should not really come as a surprise that the uskoks never placed themselves at the head of popular revolt against Ottoman rule. The idea behind the image of the *antemurale* was, after all, the defense of Christendom, not a program of liberation. But not only the shortcomings of an ideology hindered the uskoks from mobilizing a Balkan resistance to Ottoman rule. These potential leaders were dependent on their putative allies for plunder. The uskok defenders of Christendom did not necessarily see themselves as the protectors or defenders of their unfortunate coreligionists under Ottoman rule, although they may have felt some sense of responsibility for these Christians, particularly when they were bound together by kinship or tribute relationships. The two roles of defenders and of raiders coexisted uneasily, neither the one nor the other wholly predominating. In their own eyes, however, for the uskoks to claim the title of the bulwark of Christendom it was enough that they devote themselves to fighting the Turk, constantly risking their lives in the endless war of raid and counterraid.

Honor and Vengeance

To the idea of the uskok *antemurale Christianitatis* as a guide to action, the uskoks added other elements, in particular a preoccupation with honor. This ideal was not unique to the uskoks but was part of the common mental equipment of the people of the border (and indeed, served to regulate social relations throughout much of the Mediterranean where state power was weak).[26] In Senj honor and associated values were elevated to a central place in the uskok code. We find them expressed in the vocabulary of the South Slavic oral epic, that great compendium of cultural attitudes. It is characteristic that the Senj Cathedral Chapter's defense of the "heroes" Ivan and Miho Vlatković is couched in the epic metaphors for honor and shame, good faith and treason: the illustrious and the tarnished countenance or reputation (*svijetao* or *crn obraz*). "Never has it been heard in this city that he or his brother have done any villainy or treason that could tarnish their countenances; but they have always shown an illustrious countenance before the lords and the knights."[27]

---

[26]See J. G. Peristany, ed., *Honour and Shame: The Values of Mediterranean Society* (Chicago, 1966); J. Schneider, "Of Vigilance and Virgins: Honor, Shame and Access to Resources in Mediterranean Societies," *Ethnology* (Pittsburgh), 10 (1971): 1–24.

[27]"Nigdar na ouom gradu ny cuueno, da bi ni on ni brat gniegou kakouy lotry ally neuery radilly, cim bi se mogal gnih obraz pogrubiti, nego uazda suital obraz pokazali pred gospodu i vitezovy" (in Lopašić, *Acta historiam confinii*, vol. 2, p. 27). For the concepts of honor

Honor was the most important attribute of a hero, the title all uskoks aspired to. The other testimonials submitted by the Senjani in support of Ivan and Miho Vlatković enumerate the qualities and behavior that enhanced heroic honor: loyalty to their city, army, and band; "honorable attention to every knightly obligation"; readiness to lay down their lives or spill their blood in time of war; experience in warfare; ability to benefit their city; success and glory in duels with the Turks and other "enemies of the Christian faith"; severity in punishing those who were disobedient or rebellious.[28] Similarly, a hearing intended to assess Antun Mikulanić's performance as commander of Otočac reveals the uskoks' views of qualities that detracted from or negated one's honor: reluctance to shed one's own blood; failure to engage the enemy in battle; ground-less boasting; avoidance of risks on the frontier; failure to take prisoners, trophies, or booty; meanness in rewards to comrades or spies; the ab-sence of any general recognition of one's manliness; the lack of battle scars or wounds.[29]

As these assessments testify, the effective use of force (in the service of Senj and the *antemurale* and in the pursuit of personal prestige) was a central aspect of honor among the uskoks. Strength and arrogance were admired, weakness and cowardice were despised. Almost as soon as they began to walk, so the report went, boys were taught to compete in tests of strength and dexterity, racing and fighting, even throwing stones at one another until the blood ran.[30] The uskok's weapons were an emblem of his manliness as well as a means of demonstrating it in combat, and every uskok carried sidearms—usually a dagger or sword—as a necessary part of his daily dress. Commissioner Rabatta's order that the uskoks give up all their arms was treated as an unheard-of dis-grace.[31] Physical force, the ability to coerce, to intimidate, to impose one's own will were essential, first to win honor, then to defend it.[32]

---

and shame in southeastern Europe see Traian Stoianovich, *A Study in Balkan Civilization* (New York, 1967), pp. 47–49; and Jovan Brkić, *Moral Concepts in Traditional Serbian Epic Poetry* (S'-Gravenhage, 1961), pp. 96–98, 133–37.

[28]Lopašić, *Acta historiam confinii*, vol. 2, pp. 20, 21–22, 27. Cf. Kleut, *Ivan Senjanin u srpskohrvatskim usmenim pesama*, p. 24.

[29]I.Ö. H.K.R., Croatica, fasc. 12, 1607, Nov. No. 25 (2 Oct. 1607).

[30]*Commissiones et relationes venetæ*, vol. 5, p. 279; ibid., vol. 6, p. 255.

[31]Horvat, *Monumenta uscocchorum*, vol. 1, p. 405.

[32]The concept of honor discussed here is that which governed masculine conduct. Women also possessed honor but, as in other Mediterranean societies, it was linked above all to their chastity. Rather than win honor, a woman could only lose it, damaging the honor of her menfolk in the process. In this sphere, too, masculine honor in Senj (and beyond) revolved around claims to power—in this case the man's ability to control and protect the chastity of women in his family—and in theory any stain could be cleansed only by blood. Giovanni da Fermo discusses the example of an uskok who was dishonored by the abduction and subsequent release of his wife by a Rijeka gentleman. Not able to reach her captor, he killed her to preserve his honor. See Rački, "Prilog za poviest hrvatskih uskoka," pp. 235–36.

The preoccupation with honor involved a concomitant stress on loyalty and good faith (*vjera*), particularly within the bonds of the community, whether defined by kinship or some larger unit (the band, the city, Christendom). This was a society in which the given word was sacred, as Provveditore Generale Donà found to his surprise, after having tried to bribe an uskok leader to send him information secretly: "For all the wicked assassinations they commit, these scoundrels have this much good in them, that they are most observant of their word, not only among themselves, but also with their enemies, so that they will do every other evil thing except to fail a companion or use treachery."[33] Pledges of good faith committed the honor of the swearer. Any betrayal was dishonorable (and any refusal to accept such a pledge was an affront). Outsiders repeatedly noted that "there is not a one among them who would use treachery, however great the gain" or that "a betrayal of faith is so abominated by these people, when they have been joined by a vow, that they would rather suffer any penalty, even death, than betray this faith."[34] The uskoks themselves stressed this aspect of honor in their assessments of their vojvodas, dwelling on the fact that they "had never been a traitor to the city," "had never betrayed the city, the army, or their bands."[35]

Human nature being what it is, these principles were not observed invariably. Oaths were broken, safe conducts ignored, and the substantial prizes offered to those who delivered up their companions to Venetian hands did result in cases of uskok treachery.[36] But the uskok belief in the moral imperative of revenge did much to enforce these standards. According to Giovanni of Fermo, the uskoks were "a vengeful people, even to four times [the original damage], and woe to those who incur their revenge, for the vendettas they execute are remembered for centuries."[37] Any betrayal of faith could provoke a violent vengeance, illustrated in the case of uskoks who did succumb to the temptation of a

---

[33]In A.S.V., Provveditori da Terra e da Mar, 922: 25 Jan. 1598 (m.v.).

[34]In *Commissiones et relationes venetæ*, vol. 5, p. 279; Horvat, *Monumenta uscocchorum*, vol. 1, p. 415, in a report probably by de Dominis. Similar observations were often made, for instance, see Rački, "Prilog za poviest hrvatskih uskoka," p. 235.

[35]In Lopašić, *Acta historiam confinii*, vol. 2, pp. 20, 21–22.

[36]For examples of Venetian successes of this sort (often provoked by specific circumstances in Senj), see the case of Matija Daničić, who defected briefly from Senj and led a Venetian attack on his companions in revenge for some unspecified mistreatment (A.S.V., Provveditori da Terra e da Mar, 1261: 23 Jan. 1592 [m.v.]; 18 May 1593; Minucci, *Storia degli uscocchi*, p. 240); and that of Juraj Bodotina, an uskok who had been implicated in a series of rapes and who was betrayed by three other uskoks to the Capitano contra uscocchi, for which they received stipends (A.S.V., Archivio dei Baili Veneti a Constantinopoli, 305: 21 June, 1582; H.A.Z., Arhiv Trogira, 75 [Registrum literarum et proclamationum secundus]: 88'–89, 29 Nov. 1584).

[37]In Rački, "Prilog za poviest hrvatskih uskoka," p. 209.

Venetian reward. When Sule Bosotina, a Muslim who had converted to Christianity in Senj, defected to Venice, an elaborate charade of capture was arranged to forestall uskok reprisal against his family in Senj.[38] His anxiety can be explained by an incident of the previous year, in which uskoks killed Juraj Bersković of Brač and other members of his household "because Pavle Bersković, son of this Juraj, having become an uskok, had abandoned Senj and had come into [Venetian] service, readmitted by the illustrious [Provveditore Generale] Bembo. From this Your Serenity can see how they persecute those who commit such a betrayal of faith, as they call it."[39] Nor were these standards and sanctions restricted only to the uskok community. The code of honor encompassed the silence over uskok movements exacted from the rural population, the adherence to the rules of dueling and ransom negotiated with the border Turks, and the observance of the pledges of safe conduct granted by border commanders. The uskoks used the idea of honor to coerce the weak, to maintain a balance of power with their equals, and to mitigate their disadvantages against the strong. It could also be a pretext and a justification for raiding.

Among the many accounts of acts of revenge on outsiders in return for a perceived betrayal or affront to honor, perhaps the best-known case is that of the vengeance taken on Dubrovnik for the murder of Vojvoda Juraj Daničić in 1571, in violation of the word of honor or oath (*fede* or *vjera*) allegedly given him by the Ragusan authorities. The uskoks under his command had been raiding the territory of the Republic of Dubrovnik, with the tacit encouragement of the Venetians, who were at war with the Ottomans and who saw a chance of harming their small rival in the process. (The uskoks had apparently wounded Ragusan honor by planting flags on their territory, proclaiming their sovereignty over land near the Church of the Holy Trinity, to the Ragusans' "great shame and prejudice.") This uskok band, returning from Brgat with plunder from a Ragusan caravan, had been confronted by Ragusan troops near Rijeka Dubrovačka. Daničić defended his actions to the Ragusan commander, saying that they had come only to attack the Turks and that spies had told him that the caravan contained Turkish goods. He excused an earlier clash in the Ragusan village of Vitaljina by saying that the uskoks had been desperate for food and had wounded the villagers only when they had tried to resist, and he agreed to return the Ragusan merchandise from the caravan. In the meantime, however, a scuffle broke out, several on both sides were killed, and a number of uskoks were drowned trying to embark in haste. Exactly how Daničić died was unclear; however,

---

[38] A.S.V., Provveditori da Terra e da Mar, 922: 23 July 1599; 14 Aug. 1599.
[39] In ibid.: 12 Mar. 1599; H.A.Z., Arhiv Trogira, 25/11: 1480 (15 Mar. 1599).

rumors persisted that the Ragusan commander had given Daničić his word of honor to come and parley in safety and that Daničić had then been seized and killed.[40]

Whether or not the Ragusans had indeed deliberately murdered Daničić, the uskoks assigned a corporate responsibility to the Ragusans for this breach of faith. The vendetta against Ragusan merchants and officials continued for several years until it was resolved through the mediation of the Pope.[41] In the meantime, however, it justified raids on Ragusan shipping and incursions across Ragusan territory. This vendetta became a model of righteous uskok vengeance, repeatedly cited by observers and by the uskoks themselves. Some ten years after Daničić's death a group of uskoks wrote to the Rector of Trogir, who had seized one of their company in violation of a pledge of truce, to threaten him with Daničić's example and to emphasize the importance they ascribed to the idea of honor and good faith. "Fifty of us have made a sacrament that as long as one of us remains, we will avenge him as well as we can, and as God allows, as was done to the Ragusans for Daničić, because you well know that if you were to call all of us to come ashore under oath (*sopra la fede*), we would come, and henceforward your oath (*fede*) will be worth nothing, as is the Ragusans.' "[42]

Uskok revenge was not haphazard; it followed certain rough rules. The uskoks had a collective duty to avenge injuries or insults to one of their number. It was not strictly necessary for the original malefactor to be the victim of vengeance; if this were impossible, members of his family, or some other equivalent group, could suffer in his stead. Who was liable to vengeance could be a matter of dispute, as the patron of a *fregata* commanded by the captain of the Candian guard found to his relief in 1577. He had been stopped in a cove by a bark of sixteen uskoks: "They took me alone to a wood nearby . . . and told me that they would cut off my head, and three times they made me put my head on a stone, while their captain, called the harambaša, said 'your Captain has hanged my son, and I want you to bear the penalty for him.' " A priest who was with the uskoks objected to this resolution and sent for a cousin of the harambaša, who successfully interceded for the patron's life.[43] The uskoks

---

[40]The Ragusan Senate was enough concerned about the damage to its reputation abroad that it composed and circulated a memorandum on the affair, made up of the testimony of foreign witnesses to the battle and signed by the French and Venetian representatives in Dubrovnik (H.A.D., Diplomata et Acta XVI st., sv. 16, 466/36, 4 Apr. 1572).

[41]Rački, "Prilog za poviest hrvatskih uskoka," pp. 185–87; for the full tale, see Jorjo Tadić, "Pogibija uskočkog vojvode Djura Daničića 1571." *Novosti*, (Belgrade), 24 Jan. 1931: 8; Vinko Foretić, *Povijest Dubrovnika do 1808* (Dubrovnik, 1980), vol. 2, pp. 61–63.

[42]In A.S.V., Archivio dei Baili Venti a Constantinopoli, 305: 26 Aug. 1581; Capi del Consiglio dei Dieci, Lettere, 281: 26 Aug. 1581.

[43]In A.S.V., Capi del Consiglio dei Dieci, Lettere, 306: 25 Sept. 1577.

did not strictly follow a principle of equivalence in that, as Giovanni of Fermo remarked, the vengeance exacted could far outweigh the original injury, but retaliation did conform to a rough calculation of comparability. The report of the Candian *fregata*'s patron did not specify why his life had been spared, but possibly the harambaša was eventually convinced that he was not an appropriate substitute for the guilty captain.

The society of the Dalmatian and Ottoman hinterland (and uskok society) was only lightly and intermittently constrained by the authority of the state, whether represented by the Habsburgs, the Signoria, or the Ottomans. In the absence of effective state sanctions, and in a semimilitarized, largely pastoral society, social relations were governed according to the code of honor and vengeance, which had strong roots in pastoral life. Violence played an important role in this code, for a man's reputation was acquired, his honor maintained, and his virility vindicated through the use of physical force. This was not only a matter of constant warfare, though the endless raids on both sides did much to spread a martial ethos. Any dispute might lead to bloodshed. The cult of arms—the weapons so lovingly described in the epic songs and so proudly carried as evidence of manliness—doubtless made assaults more lethal.

Was the level of violence also affected by the russet wine (*rujno vino*) so often poured for the heroes in the epic ballads? Wine was a basic necessity of life in the region, no less so than bread and meat. Drunk in too great quantity, however, it might lead to foolhardiness and aggression. In 1605 a company of uskoks assaulted the galley of the Capitano contra uscocchi, with much loss of life among the attackers—twenty dead and forty wounded, and a terrible lament among the women of Senj when the survivors returned. An observer from Rijeka in Senj reported that in this case there would be no attempts at avenging this loss: the uskoks blamed themselves, for they had been drunk when they heard the news of the captain's approach and made a vow to destroy him. They had set out in great disorder, and escaped complete destruction only because of the cover of darkness.[44]

In such circumstances, violent death was familiar. There is little evidence of revulsion against the bloody deeds and cruelty that frequently accompanied it. The bodies of the living were subject to torture, while the bodies of the dead provided trophies. After a battle near Senj in 1532 the noses of the slaughtered Turks were sent to the Emperor together with the captives that had been taken.[45] Both sides collected the severed heads of their enemies to display on stakes, dishonoring their victims and gaining glory for themselves. It was not that life was cheap or the

---

[44]A.S.V., Provveditori da Terra e da Mar, 1321: 28 July 1605.
[45]Sanuto, *I diarii*, vol. 56, p. 807.

individual's fate of no consequence. (Uskoks went to great pains to regain the heads of their comrades for Christian burial.) It seems, rather, that such violence was accepted as a normal part of existence.

But the violence that sprang from the frontier code of honor was not irrational or aimless. On the contrary, it was structured according to more or less explicit guidelines, and it was carefully calculated to evoke fear and respect. Such purposeful violence was seen as necessary, even praiseworthy, and as such it was sanctioned and justified. The ability to use violence effectively in the pursuit of one's goals was a virtue, bringing with it honor, prestige, and a claim to leadership. Girolamo Giustinian, the Venetian ambassador to the Habsburg court in 1618, exaggerated, but he perceived the link between the use of violence and uskok leadership accurately: "They elevate to higher degrees and honors those who carry out their trade the best, and those who are able to commit greater and more atrocious cruelties, such as eating human flesh, drinking blood, roasting and devouring the hearts of their captives, are elected vojvodas and harambašas."[46] Understanding all these factors can help explain not only the prevalence of violence in the local culture but also the attitude toward it, both among the uskoks and among the people of the hinterland who shared this code. While outside observers, particularly Venetians, were aghast at uskok looting, ransom, arson, and vengeance killing, the people of the border seem rather to have accepted these aspects of honor, even to have celebrated them as an integral part of the uskok image.

Here we might look more closely at the uskok atrocities on which Venetian reports dwell with such horrified fascination. Some of these tales are straightforward reports of uskok vengeance and retaliation, in which uskoks kill their victims, burn their dwellings, and loot their villages. Some of these stories were embroidered by rumor, malicious or not. One series of reports, for example, gradually exaggerated the way in which uskoks allegedly terrified one victim into paying an enormous ransom: beginning with a report that his servant had been killed, followed by a tale of the servant's heart being roasted and eaten, culminating in the accusation that the uskoks responsible had made straps for their leather moccasins (*opanci*) from his skin.[47] Such tales passed into wide circulation, providing grisly illustrations for popular histories.

The descriptions of many of these atrocities, particularly those inflicted on enemies killed as an act of vengeance, center around blood. The victim's blood is drunk, bread or cloth is dipped in it, his wounds are sucked

---

[46]In Fiedler, *Fontes rerum Austriacarum*, vol. 26, pp. 36–37.

[47]Horvat, *Monumenta uscocchorum*, vol. 1, pp. 310, 311, 341. The reports from the area at the time of the incident do not mention any of these acts (A.S.V., Provveditore Sopraintendente alla Camera dei Confini, 296: 17 Oct. 1600; 11 Nov. 1600).

3. An engraving from *Die neueröffnete ottomanische Pforte* (Augsburg, 1694) illustrating a variety of uskok atrocities. It accompanied text describing uskok bloodthirstiness which was adapted from *Memorie storiche de monarchi ottomani* (Venice, 1688) by the Venetian historian G. Sagredo. (By permission of the School of Slavonic and East European Studies, University of London.)

or his flesh is devoured. Rabatta was murdered "for our honor" as the uskoks said, and his blood was allegedly lapped up by the wives of the uskoks he had killed.[48] (See Figure 3.) It was reported that similar acts were perpetrated on the corpse of the Venetian Christoforo Venier, decapitated in retaliation for a betrayal of a pledge of safe passage given to the uskoks by the Provveditore Generale, his relative.[49] These patterns bring to mind the ritual aspects of bloodshed to purge an affront to

[48]Horvat, *Monumenta uscocchorum*, vol. 2, pp. 2, 3; *Die neueroffnete ottomanische Pforte* (Augsburg, 1694), p. 355 (a translation of Sir Paul Rycaut's and Giovanni Sagredo's histories of the Ottoman Empire). In Corsica, women are reported to have "sucked the wounds of victims of violence" in a similar context of feud and honor (Wilson, *Feuding, Conflict and Banditry*, p. 408).

[49]Rački, "Prilog za poviest hrvatskih uskoka," pp. 214–16; and see Chapter 8.

honor recorded in the later feuds of the Balkans.[50] Blood was the central metaphor in these patterns as well—the blood that flowed through the veins of the kin who bore the responsibility for vengeance, and the spilled blood that called out for vengeance. It seems likely that the uskoks' actions, if they did in fact occur in the forms described, were not simply gruesome aberrations of—literally—bloodthirsty savages, as they were seen by the Venetians. Rather they appear to be rituals that must be placed within the coherent system of uskok beliefs and values if they are to be understood.

To a Venetian this seemed a topsy-turvy world, where to steal was not a sin, and living in peace was cowardice: "Those who do not go [on raids] are considered by the elders, and by everyone else, to be cowardly and disgraced; as on the other hand, the most honored families, and those considered of greatest merit, are those who for the longest time have traced their origins in a continuous descent from those hanged, cut to pieces, and foully massacred in other ways in their pursuits; and it is difficult in the churches, among the banners hung to the memory of these, their glorious heroes, to find the inscription of anyone who died a good death in his own bed."[51] But such a death was not admired in Senj. The uskok code required that a hero of the frontier should fall in battle with the Turk and his allies. This code may not have been much to the taste of outsiders, and may have appeared incomprehensible, even perverse in some aspects, but it was consistent—and its influence can be seen in many of the uskoks' actions.

Solidarity and Conflict

Uskok society in Senj was heterogeneous. The uskoks had no ties of common origin, coming as they did from many different parts of the border, with varying cultures, traditions, even ethnic and linguistic backgrounds. Although prolonged association would minimize diversity among those who had long been in Senj, the constant influx of new recruits meant that such differences were always being renewed. For the same reason, kinship ties could not bind the uskok community into a cohesive whole (though marriage and ties of fictive kinship were used to incorporate an outsider into uskok society). Other divisions, too, marked uskok society: the divisions between native Senjanin and immigrant;

---

[50]This connection is discussed by M. E. Durham, *Some Tribal Origins, Laws, and Customs of the Balkans* (London, 1928), pp. 159–61.

[51]In H.A.Z., Fond Šime Ljubića, 2/33: 281–81'.

between those with a Military Frontier post and the unpaid venturini; between rich and poor; leaders and rank-and-file; young and old.

Nevertheless, the uskoks did form a self-conscious unit with a distinctive uskok identity. This was perhaps most obvious to outsiders in their dress and appearance, which could immediately identify them as uskoks. In 1613 the captain of an armed Venetian bark reported his attack on a group of men: "I believe they were uskoks of Senj because of their clean white shirts and the *gecerme* [Cr.: *ječerme*, sleeveless jackets] which they wear on top, according to their usage, so that the sleeves of the shirts show on the outside."[52] Giovanni da Fermo gives a more detailed description of uskok dress: They wore a pair of breeches, "though from the knee down not too narrow, split from the calf to the heel, without gaiters, made of cloth and fastened with iron or silver buttons; and a pair of cloth stockings, with *opanci* [leather sandals] on their feet; a jacket to a little below the waist, with half-sleeves, over a shirt with short, wide sleeves, so that their arms are half bare, and over this they wear a long gown in the Hungarian style."[53] (See frontispiece.) Many uskoks wore their heads partly shaven, with their hair in a single long lock, a style called *all'uscocca* in the area.[54] These, however, were merely external signs of the solidarity the uskoks strove to maintain in their relations with the outside world.

The bonds that created and nurtured this sense of community derived substantially from the ideas discussed above as the "uskok code." The interlocking concepts of honor and vengeance were an important integrative force in uskok society. As the Capitano contra uscocchi noted shrewdly in 1597, "The uskoks make a particular profession of avenging every injury, no matter how minor, done to one of their brothers (they use this name for each other, though they scarcely know one another); but I believe that they wish this exercise of robbery to hold them bound and joined together under the name of brotherhood, and that they are obliged to act thus from this reason."[55] The duty of mutual responsibility not only required that uskoks avenge one another but also that they attempt to ransom their fellows from Ottoman captivity and give aid to the wives and children of uskoks who had been captured or killed. The sense of brotherhood among the uskoks, and the responsibilities that

[52]In A.S.V., Provveditori da Terra e da Mar, 427, 21 Jan. 1612 (m.v.).

[53]In Rački, "Prilog za poviest hrvatskih uskoka," 191–92. See also Cesare Vecellio, *Habiti antichi et moderni* (Venice, 1590), who confirmed that the uskoks kept their arms bare and also noted their splendid decorative buttons: "They fasten their jackets with buttons of gold or silver, which they usually do not do up" (p. 348a). See also M. Gušić, "Nošnja senjskih uskoka," *Senjski zbornik* (Senj), 5 (1971–73): 9–120.

[54]"Zuffo in testa all'uscocca" (Bertoša, *Epistolæ et communicationes rectorum histrianorum*, vol. 1, p. 98).

[55]In *Commissiones et relationes venetæ*, vol. 6, p. 53.

this imposed on them, is one of the themes dealt with in the epic songs of Senj and the uskoks, particularly in the narratives of imprisonment and liberation. In these tales, heroes captured by the Turks languish in captivity for long years, unable to pay their ransom, until their faithful companions resolve to free them (or are shamed into the attempt by the hero's aged mother); either by trickery or by courage they deliver the prisoner and return victorious to Senj.[56] That the duty to free a captured comrade was not simply a poetic convention but a real obligation is illustrated by the story of Vicko de Santi (Desantić), taken prisoner by the Turks. His father offered to pay a high ransom for him, but his fellow uskoks decided instead to free him from the tower in which he was being held captive, carrying out a daring raid.[57] Their responsibilities to their fellows extended even beyond the threshold of death. More than one priest on Venetian territory reported a nocturnal visit from a group of uskoks who broke into the church to bury one of their number, demanding that the usual ceremonies be carried out and the bell for the dead be rung.[58] The uskoks were known to risk their lives to recover the bodies of fallen comrades and to give them proper burial: in 1597 one uskok was captured by Venetian forces while trying to redeem from some Morlachs the bones of the uskok Vukdrag Bukovac, who had been killed the previous year below Klis. His nephew and the leader of the expedition, Miloš Bukovac, intended to return the bones to Senj or bury them in sanctified ground.[59]

The uskoks were also bound together by their image of themselves as soldiers on the frontier of Christendom. This ideal cemented the bonds of group solidarity against their common enemies, "the enemies of the name of Christ," as they themselves phrased it, and differentiated them from those who were not animated by this same purpose. This image can be seen most clearly, perhaps, in the words the uskoks used to refer to themselves, never using the term 'uskok,' with its literal meaning of refugee and its slightly pejorative ring, but preferring the more warlike collective title of knights, soldiers, or heroes; *vitezi, soldati, valent'huomeni, junaci.*

The uskok code as it has been described here, with its diverse religious, moral, and cultural elements, was a prescriptive ideal: it provided a framework for uskok action and defined the uskoks' relations with the

---

[56]For early examples see Gesemann, *Erlangenski rukopis*, #72 (pp. 97–99), #119 (pp. 170–71); V. Bogišić, *Narodne pjesme iz starijih, najviše primorskih zapisa* (Biograd, 1878), #108 (pp. 296–300), #109 (pp. 301–3).

[57]Rački, "Prilog za poviest hrvatskih uskoka," pp. 196, 237.

[58]A.S.V., Archivio dei Baili Veneti a Constantinopoli, 305: 10 Jan. 1581 (m.v.); Provveditori da Terra e da Mar, 1263: 11 June 1597.

[59]A.S.V., Provveditori da Terra e da Mar, 1263: 11 June 1597.

outside world. Its main outlines—the defense of Christendom, an ideal of honor, the duty of vengeance—were not disputed in Senj (nor, indeed, on much of the border). Some uskoks overstepped the boundaries of the code and found themselves facing uskok sanctions. Such punishment was most commonly meted out for transgressions that injured the community: theft or persistant refusal to pay debts (for which the culprit was shamed by being dressed as a woman and led through the town carrying a distaff)[60] or treachery against Senj (punished by death). Uskoks were also punished or ostracized by their fellows for acts that offended against the ideal of the *antemurale* (raiding Christian shipping, for example).[61]

But general acceptance of these ideas did not guarantee complete consensus or conformity of action among the uskoks. For one thing, what people do and what they ought to do are not always the same. Indiscriminate raids against all and sundry, with no attempt to legitimate their actions, carried out by bands outside Senj (sometimes claiming the uskok name) are not considered here, for these men did not also claim the Senj uskoks' *antemurale* ethos. But many raids from Senj harmed Christians and yet went unpunished, partly because of the ambiguity and flexibility of the uskok ethos. Individuals could apply it in very different ways, according to the circumstances and their own interests. Because the code was open to many potential interpretations, differences of opinion over its meaning and requirements resulted.

Conflict in Senj most often arose in attempts to differentiate between licit and illicit victims and plunder. Although the logic of the *antemurale* idea made Muslims, as infidels, the primary targets of uskok raids, contradictions within the uskok code could put even this principle in doubt, when honor conflicted with the duty to battle the infidel, for example. Thus there could be dissension in Senj over the correct way to deal with a wealthy Muslim, come to Senj in 1607 on business without requesting a safe conduct in advance. A council of ten uskok elders convened and decided that he was liable for capture and ransom; yet another group of uskoks with ties to the man demanded that he be released on their pledge of his good conduct. Should he be held captive or not?[62] The ideal of the uskok *antemurale* did not prevent the uskoks from recognizing other obligations imposed by kinship or the pledge of honor.

Many more difficulties arose, however, when the uskoks needed to decide when and how it was permissable to attack or raid Christians, putative allies in the struggle against the infidel. The character of Adriatic trade and of uskok warfare required that this problem be faced

---

[60]Rački, "Prilog za poviest hrvatskih uskoka," p. 240.
[61]See Chapter 8 for examples.
[62]A.S.V., Provveditori da Terra e da Mar, 1313: 29 Sept. 1607 (report of Quadrio to Moresini).

continually. Were goods belonging to Turks and Jews carried on a vessel belonging to Christians legitimate booty? What about the goods and ships of Ragusans, vassals of the Sultan? How much should Christian subjects of the Porte be liable to uskok raids? To what degree could Venice's Dalmatian subjects be expected to aid the uskoks, and how should they be treated if they refused? Should Venetian commanders who patrolled against the uskoks be considered allies of the Turk? The answer to all these questions depended on the context in a given situation and on the interests of the actors. At one time or another uskoks were able to justify raids on all of these groups in terms of honor or their duty to defend Christendom against the infidel without causing dissension within Senj. Unsurprisingly, the victims of these raids usually did not agree with claims that they were justified. Similarly, the Military Frontier authorities frequently differed with the uskoks over the legitimacy of their booty. However, the uskoks could disagree among themselves on the distinction between licit and illicit raiding, their views dependent on their own calculations of the relative demands of duty, honor, and self-interest.

Clearly the uskok codes of behavior do not completely explain uskok actions. Other factors were also at work: economic necessity; the changing political requirements of their masters, allies, and enemies; a variety of alliances (or antagonisms); complex local circumstances—all these influenced to a greater or lesser extent the ways in which the uskoks related to the world of the border. But material considerations were not the only factors in the equation. Necessity and ideology were constantly balanced against each other. The uskoks interpreted their circumstances in terms of the imperatives of holy war, the ideal of honor, and the right to vengeance. These ideas must have affected their actions. If nothing else they gave the uskoks a clear sense of right and wrong—and for the most part the uskoks believed that they were in the right. It would be a mistake to ignore the influence of this conviction of righteousness, justifying their raids and their use of violence. The inscription Sebastian de Sachi placed over one of the windows of his Senj house while he was Vice Captain summed up the uskoks' attitude: "Si Deus pro nobis quis contra nos" ("If God is with us, who will oppose us?").[63] Who can doubt that this belief was one of the reasons the uskoks were able to survive so long?

[63]In Kukuljević-Sakcinski, *Natpisi,* p. 246.

CHAPTER SEVEN

Allies and Victims

The uskok code, with its diverse political, religious, and cultural elements, provided a framework for uskok action and defined the uskoks' relations with the outside world. What were the relations of the uskoks with the infidel, with the Christian subjects of the Ottomans, with the subjects of Venice? The uskoks advanced the ideal of the *antemurale*, the need to defend Christendom against the infidel Turk, as the public justification and legitimization of their relationships, but to what degree did their actions correspond to this ideal, and to what degree were they a product of other forces?

Relations with the Infidel

It would serve no purpose to attempt to list uskok actions that took Muslims as their victims. The brunt of uskok attack was always borne by the Ottomans and their subjects: the wealthy and privileged Muslims, the administrators, the townspeople, merchants, artisans. Jews, too, infidels of another variety and often Ottoman subjects, suffered heavily. The success of their Adriatic trade drew the unwanted attentions of other pirates as well as that of the uskoks. But the goods and money of the wealthy and powerful were not the only forms uskok booty took. In theory, no Muslim or Jew, even if destitute, was entirely safe from uskok attack. Up and down the Adriatic, from one end of the border to the other, the uskoks seized their goods, held the merchants themselves for ransom, pillaged towns, and carried off cattle and captives. The uskoks' antagonism against the Ottomans was also articulated in formal warfare under the command of the officers of the Military Frontier; in smaller military actions led by the Senj Captain and vojvodas, and in countless independent expeditions. Some of these attacks—the firing of mosques, for example—reflect the ideological basis of the uskoks' enmity with the Turk.[1] Others had more conventional military objectives: battles with Ottoman troops or the destruction of Ottoman ports or garrison outposts.

How effective was the warfare against the Ottomans? The uskoks' supporters claimed that if it were not for the uskoks, the border would not be safe from Ottoman attack as far as Trieste and Friuli. Each new proposal that the uskoks be removed into the interior in response to Venetian complaints was met with the argument that the uskoks held the Ottomans in check on the maritime border and that to remove them would open the way for an Ottoman invasion of Inner Austria and Italy.[2] But perhaps the assessment of the uskoks' contribution in the long border wars against the Ottomans should come not from their supporters, who often exaggerated their worth, but from one of their Venetian critics. In his detailed critique of the uskoks in Senj at the beginning of the seventeenth century, Vettor Barbaro, the secretary to the Provveditore Generale, summed up the benefits the Republic of Venice received as a result of the uskoks' activities.[3] Most of these have to do with the uskoks' services against the Turk in preventing both their military and economic expansion in the Adriatic.

First of all, according to Barbaro, the uskoks ensured that not only much of Lika, but also the Ottoman territories close to the shore near Skradin, Omiš, and the Neretva were kept free of Ottoman settlers, who feared exposure to uskok raids, and, second, the uskoks restrained the insolence of the border Turks. This claim that the uskoks had made the border uninhabitable by the Turks, particularly in Lika, was often repeated, both by uskok supporters and Venetian critics. Lika was easily reached by land from Senj and had long been a target of raids for cattle and captives, though as its fields and villages were despoiled by constant warfare it offered less in the way of booty. In the late 1570s the Ottoman authorities began to settle the deserted fields of Lika with Orthodox Vlach stockherders from the Balkan hinterland. Archduke

---

[1]In 1594 Derviş-çavuş, an emissary from the Sultan, objected to the Venetian Doge that compaints arrived at the Porte almost daily about the mosques burned by the uskoks, including one of the best known, the mosque of Sultan Mehmed (Lamansky, *Secrets d'état de Venise*, vol. 1, pp. 491–92). For another example, see J. Radonić, *Acta et diplomata Ragusina*, Zbornik za istoriju, jezik i književnost, section 3, vols. 5, 8, 9 (Belgrade, 1935–39), vol. 3, pt. 1, pp. 158–61.

[2]A good example of these arguments is the "Discursus de non removendis ex Segnia Vskokis," a report circulated in Prague in 1580 in response to proposals to curb the uskoks (A.S.V., Provveditore Sopraintendente alla Camera dei Confini, 243: 24 May 1580 [enclosed in A. Badoer's dispatch]). See also Hurter, *Geschichte des Kaiser Ferdinands II*, vol. 2, pp. 146–47. For similar arguments from uskok supporters, see Leva, *Legazione di Roma*, p. 141; Rački, "Prilog za poviest hrvatskih uskoka," pp. 182–83.

[3]In H.A.Z., Fond Šime Ljubića, 2/33: 289–89'.

Ernest (regent of Hungary and Croatia), General Andreas Auersperg, and the Military Council in Vienna immediately ordered the prevention of a permanent establishment of an Ottoman population so close to the border by repeated raids from Senj against the Lika Vlachs. The Captain of Senj was ordered to kill as many settlers as possible and to sell the captives over the sea as slaves.[4] Throughout the 1580s and 1590s the Senj uskoks redoubled their raids on Lika, both under Military Frontier leadership and independently.[5] In one typical incident in 1586, the uskoks raided through Lika taking 240 head of cattle and skirmishing with the Bey of Lika. They killed the Bey's standard bearer, captured the Turkish standards, and impaled the heads of some of the Ottoman dead on the border as a taunt and a warning. When the commander of a Venetian galley intervened on seeing the impaled heads, both the Captain of Senj and Archduke Charles protested, noting that such raids on Lika were necessary to prevent the Turks and Vlachs from settling the area to the detriment of imperial and archducal interests.[6] The uskoks were not able to prevent some Ottoman settlement in Lika (a fact that worked to their advantage, ensuring a source of booty nearby). Nevertheless, their constant raids did much to ensure a steady trickle of emigration from Lika into the Habsburg lands, and at the same time their attacks on the towns prevented the expansion of Ottoman garrisons there.

Lika, as the inland territory most easily reached from Senj, was an extreme case, but Barbaro's claim that uskok raids also hindered Ottoman settlement in border territories farther removed from Senj was repeated by other observers, including the Sancak-bey of Klis, who reported that the borders toward Šibenik and Trogir were deserted because of the fear of uskok incursions.[7] It is hard to judge how far uskok raids restrained the insolence of the border Turks. Venetian and Ragusan authorities both argued that such raids in fact provoked the Ottomans to retaliation against the border. Much of the population, however, seems to have held the firm belief that without the fear of the uskoks the Ottomans would be bolder in their attacks on Christian territories.

Barbaro went on to note that the uskoks, more than anyone else, ensured that the Turks were unable to use their Adriatic ports to arm a fleet. The Republic of Venice, anxious to forestall any naval rivalry in its gulf, had negotiated agreements that the Porte would not arm vessels in

[4]Lopašić, *Acta historiam confinii*, vol. 1, pp. 28–32, and Ivić, "Migracije Srba u Hrvatsku," p. 47.

[5]See for example A.S.V., Archivio dei Baili Veneti a Constantinopoli, 305: 16 Mar. 1581; 11 July 1582; Ivić, "Migracije Srba u Hrvatsku," pp. 50–52; Lopašić, "Prilozi za poviest Hrvatske," *Starine*, vol. 19, p. 62.

[6]A.H., Građa Karlovačke krajine: Spisi Like i Krbave, 1: 28 Aug. 1586; 17 Sept. 1586; A.S.F., Mediceo del Principato, 3084: 48.

[7]In *Libri commemoriali della Repubblica di Venezia*, pp. 59–60.

the Adriatic, but they were not always able to prevent the local Ottoman authorities from attempting to contravene them. The role of the uskoks in thwarting such attempts can be followed in the fortunes of shipbuilding in Obrovac, a small port on the Zrmanja River above Zadar. The area around Obrovac was rich in timber suitable for shipbuilding, and occasional attempts were made to establish an Ottoman fleet there. This was first tried in the 1530s, with plans to use the fleet against Senj, but one June night an expedition from Senj burned the four *fustas* and the galley that were being built there and sacked the town.[8] Plans to build *fustas* in Obrovac were revived in the 1560s and 1580s, only to be forestalled by uskok raids.[9] Obrovac remained a garrison town and a small-scale merchant port, but it was unable to take full advantage of its site in the face of constant uskok attack. Similarly, the small ports of Skradin and the Neretva delta were never able to overcome the combined forces of the uskoks' raids and the Venetians' diplomacy to expand their naval role. The uskoks were also successful in preventing the construction of Ottoman fortifications controlling the sea routes, most importantly at Dračevac, overlooking the Novigrad Strait at the end of the Velebit Channel. (Barbaro also remarked that the uskoks' frequent raids against the Turks provided an excuse and a cover for the injuries caused to the Ottomans by Venetian subjects—and here it is perhaps worth pointing out that not all the damage done to Ottoman naval preparations was committed by uskoks. In 1582, for example, a confidential report to the Council of Ten in Venice described in jubilant detail the way in which a Turkish vessel which had been raiding the Vrana area had been sunk by Venetian citizens on a stormy night, in a manner that had thrown all the suspicion on the uskoks.)[10]

The final point Barbaro made was that the uskoks contributed to the growth of Venice's ports by destroying the merchant trade of the Ottoman ports (and that of Venice's rivals). It was clear that Ottoman merchant shipping was very vulnerable to uskok attack. Gabela, the major Ottoman merchant port in the estuary of the Neretva, was an ideal place for the uskoks to hunt the cargoes of Muslim merchants: marshy and overgrown with luxuriant vegetation, approached by many shallow channels. The uskoks had only to arrange an obstruction across the channel and then wait in ambush for their prey, or to descend on the quays by

---

[8]Sanuto, *I diarii*, vol. 70, pp. 164, 217, 238, 257, 294, 332.

[9]In 1568 the uskoks both planned to burn the *fustas* being built in Obrovac and informed the Venetian authorities that Venetian subjects were involved in the supply of oars to the Ottoman shipyard (A.S.V., Capi del Consiglio dei Dieci, Lettere dei Rettori, 282: 14 Nov. 1568, 16 Nov. 1568). Again in 1585 uskoks burned the town and a *fusta* being built there, and stole its sails (A.S.V., Archivio dei Baili Veneti a Constantinopoli, 305: 25 June 1585).

[10]In A.S.V., Capi del Consiglio dei Dieci, Lettere dei Rettori, 306: 26 June 1582.

night to plunder the ships and the warehouses. The Sancak-bey had ordered fortifications built there as a defense against uskok attack, but these did not prevent the uskoks from raiding the Neretva port of Gabela and plundering the Ragusan salt warehouse on more than one occasion.[11] In 1592 Ottoman merchants were complaining to the Sultan about the attacks the uskoks were making on traffic on the Neretva River, "not only ruining and spoiling the domain of Your Imperial Highness, but also causing great damage and shortfalls in your income."[12] Shortly afterward the Porte sent Derviş-aga of the Neretva district as an emissary to Venice to complain of this drop in revenue. "It was the custom," he told the Doge, "to auction the income of the Neretva excise tax for seventy purses of aspers. Now this income is lost because of the damages done by the uskoks."[13]

Uskok action also contributed to the fall in trade through the Neretva estuary in an indirect way. Their raids could never halt the flow of Ottoman goods to the markets of the West, but they did much to affect the ways in which this trade developed. From the 1560s Daniel Rodriguez, a Portuguese Jew active in the Levantine trade, had promoted the expansion of the port of Split as the link between Venice and the commerce of the Ottoman lands, choosing Split, a hitherto minor port, mainly because the approaches both by sea and by land could easily be guarded against the uskoks.[14] This safety was important to the Jewish trading communities of the Adriatic, which were particularly vulnerable to uskok piracy, but was equally attractive to anyone involved in the Ottoman trade. From Split, Ottoman merchants could send their goods to Venice in an armed convoy. With the success of Venetian Split as a transit port in the 1590s, the Ottoman Neretva area rapidly declined. Dubrovnik's role as a transit port for the Ottoman trade was also threatened by this new competition, much to the distress of the Ragusans, who sent an emissary to the Paşa of Bosnia to warn that Split was "a nest of uskoks and evildoers" and that its success would mean that Dubrovnik would be unable to pay its tribute to the Sultan.[15]

Paolo Sarpi, writing with a polemical purpose in 1613, on the eve of

[11]S. Nodilo, *Annales Ragusini anonymi item Nicolai de Ragnina*, Monumenta spectantia historiam Slavorum meridionalium, 14 (Zagreb, 1883), pp. 104–5. In 1591 uskoks took a substantial sum in Ottoman currency (18,300 *akçi*) from the the Ragusan salt vendor in the Neretva (H.A.D., Acta Consilii Rogatorum, 71: 148–48′, 167′–68).

[12]In Lopašić, *Acta historiam confinii*, vol. 1, pp. 171–73.

[13]In Stanojević, *Senjski uskoci*, p. 136. For further details on uskok raids into the Neretva see Bogumil Hrabak, "Uskočki zaleti u Neretvu, 1537–1617," *Pomorski zbornik* (Rijeka), 17 (1979): 323–39.

[14]For the influence of the uskoks on the development of Split as a merchant port in the sixteenth century, see Morpurgo, "Daniel Rodriguez i osnivanje splitske skele," pp. 185–248; Contarini, *Le historie venetiane*, pp. 340–41.

[15]H.A.D., Lettere di Levante, 37: 289–89′.

war with the Habsburgs over the uskoks, would pour scorn on the uskoks' guerrilla war against the Turk, depicting their actions since 1540 as those more of pirates than of soldiers, of little moment against the Ottoman foe.[16] Barbaro's assessment of the importance of uskok actions against the Turk, meant solely for the information of the Signoria, gives the lie to Sarpi's words (though to an extent Barbaro may have been influenced by a desire to console the Signoria for its failure to extirpate the uskoks). But the many Ottoman firmans (decrees) dealing with the threat posed by the "uskoks and other evildoing dustlike misbelievers" confirm the importance attached to their actions by the Ottoman government itself.[17] It is impossible to quantify the cost of uskok raids to the Ottomans, both to individuals and to the state, yet over the eighty-odd years of their existence it was substantial.

This unrelenting Senj hostility against the Turk was not always the most salient factor in the uskoks' relations with the border Muslims, however, and these relations were not always solely destructive. Although they were enemies, the uskoks and the border Muslims lived in a shared world, and in practice a wary coexistence was often more important than mutual destruction. A number of factors moderated the antagonism between uskok and Muslim, buttressing the balanced—though often violent—economic system that was border warfare and helping to maintain the equilibrium of border society.

Among these factors were certain cultural patterns, particularly the shared concepts of honor, of heroism, of vengeance, and of the responsibilities of real and fictive kinship. In one of the most elaborated expressions of the congruence of these codes of behavior, uskok and Muslim met in formal duels, competing to acquire honor for themselves and for their side. Vojvoda Ivan Vlatković's duel with a Muslim challenger was emphasized by the Senj Cathedral Chapter as an outstanding event in his career, reflecting glory on Senj and on the Military Frontier. Vlatković's dramatic blow, severing the left hand of Ahmet-aga Cukarinović at the wrist, his magnanimous concession of the aga's life, and his triumphant return bearing the bloody trophy, seem to have made a deep impression in the popular mind, for versions of the story were still being retold into the twentieth century.[18] The institution of the duel ritualized

---

[16]Sarpi, *La Repubblica di Venezia*, pp. 54–56.

[17]Ottoman firmans in the Venetian Archives dealing with the uskoks are discussed in A. Bombaci, "La collezione di documenti turchi dell'Archivio di Stato di Venezia," *Rivista degli studi orientali*, 24 (1949): 102. Several examples are given in full in N. H. Biegman, *The Turco-Ragusan Relationship* (The Hague, 1967), pp. 167–68; summaries of various Ottoman communications with both the Republic of Venice and the Habsburg Emperor on the subject of the uskoks are printed in *Libri commemoriali della Repubblica di Venezia*.

[18]For contemporary descriptions of the incident see Lopašić, *Acta historiam confinii*, vol. 1, p. 27; and J. Božitković, ed., "Kratki ljetopis Tome Juričića iz godine 1596. i 1599.," *Narodna*

and circumscribed the armed conflict between Christian and Muslim, for though the troops of each side attended such duels, under normal circumstances only the two protagonists actually fought, not to the death but to a victory determined by the rules of chivalry. Nevertheless, although it reduced bloodshed on the border, the ritual of the duel did not conceal or obscure the conflict between Islam and Christendom which lay at the heart of frontier relations. Instead, such duels presented this clash in the simplest, most graphic way, with the two combatants representing the opposing forces, their victory or defeat bringing honor or shame to their fellows and to the border as a whole. The townspeople of Zadar, who crowded the walls and the roofs of the houses to watch six of their men break lances with six Turkish cavalrymen in October 1571, during the War of the Holy League, were watching a piece of theater with a message about the eventual triumph or conquest of the warring faiths as explicit as that of the *moreska*, a mimed battle between Christians and "Moors" danced in coastal towns every year during carnival.[19]

Other, more intimate bonds also connected the uskoks with their Ottoman enemies—particularly those of kinship. The strength and longevity of these relationships can be glimpsed in the pleas sent by Ottoman dignitaries to Venetian officials on behalf of captured uskoks. In 1588 the Capitano contra uscocchi, thinking to please a visiting Ottoman delegation, proposed to execute six recently captured uskoks in their presence. Instead, the delegation asked that they be spared, in part because one of the uskoks was a close relative of an eminent Ottoman captain.[20] The responsibilities that ties of kinship entailed persisted, modifying border antagonisms. Where such ties did not exist, they were sometimes manufactured, in the institution of *pobratimstvo*, or blood brotherhood. A bond of this sort, across the boundaries of religion and political allegiance, could act as an instrument for controlling socially and economically destructive conflict. Blood brotherhood between Christian and Muslim is a familiar motif in the uskok cycle of oral epics. Duelers, for example, are often presented in this way, their very conflict

---

starina (Zagreb), 10 (1931): 118. Other, poetic versions, including Kačić-Miošić's, are discussed in Mijatović, *Uskoci i krajišnici*, pp. 12–14. It is largely unproductive to attempt to pin the oral epics too closely to fact. Their interest for the historian lies rather in the changing attitudes they reveal. Still, in the powerful song "The Death of Senjanin Ivo," in which the dying Ivo returns from a raid carrying his right hand in his left, it is tempting to see the singer transforming Ahmet-aga's severed left hand into Ivo's own hand, a conceit that perfectly mirrors the tragic dislocation of logic in the rest of this epic. A version is given in Mijatović, *Senjski uskoci*, pp. 117–18.

[19]Solitro, *Documenti storici sull'Istria e la Dalmazia*, vol. 1, pp. 159–60.

[20]*Commissiones et relationes venetæ*, vol. 6, p. 24. See also A.S.V., Archivio dei Baili Veneti a Constantinopoli, 305: 14 Jan. 1581 (m.v.) for a similar incident, in which the Ottoman administrator of the Neretva and Makarska regions and the Sancak-bey of Hercegovina interceded with the Venetians for the life of a captured uskok.

treated as a device that bound them together, and not merely a literary device adapted by the singers to fill their dramatic requirements. That such ceremonies were not uncommon can be seen from the decision of the 1579 Synod of Zadar and Split forbidding priests to officiate at blood-brotherhood rites between Muslims and Christians, "this familiarity offering an occasion for many sins" in the eyes of the Church.[21]

These ties were sometimes deliberately contracted in attempts to minimize bloodshed and maintain stable relations across the boundary of faith. In 1588 the Ottoman government, hoping to decrease uskok raids, had ordered that captives no longer be ransomed from the uskoks, contrary to usual practice. This decree was to the taste of neither side, for the exchange of captives for ransom was an important part of the frontier economy and, in addition, ensured a minimal personal security. The uskoks therefore approached the Sancak-bey of Lika to propose an independent agreement. He, fearing the Porte's displeasure, preferred reaching an accommodation on a lower level. His brother Halil-bey, a military commander in the Zadar hinterland, came to the coast to negotiate with Vojvoda Juraj Daničić. Their discussions covered the continued practice of ransom and also set jointly approved levels of payment, for a recent mutual inflation of demands had created difficulties for poorer captives on both sides. A satisfactory agreement was reinforced by an exchange of gifts and a ceremony joining Halil-bey and Juraj Daničić as brothers-in-blood, after which they retired to sleep "in a single bed, in each other's arms."[22] Afterward mutual raiding was resumed according to the agreed rules. Here a contract of fictive kinship served to cement a commitment to limit hostilities, benefiting the warring parties equally.

Shared codes of honor, duels, ties of kinship and fictive kinship were all mechanisms through which the uskoks and the border Muslims could limit conflict, destruction, and bloodshed. The fundamental force that modified the inflexible opposition between uskok and Muslim implied by the ideal of holy war was that of local self-interest—whether it was primarily economic, as in the case of ransom agreements, or whether it rose more generally from a desire for a quieter life. Accommodation based on such interests could seem to ignore the requirements of the *antemurale* almost entirely. This outcome can be observed in the relations between the uskoks of Senj and Muslim administrators in Ravni kotari and Bukovica, areas on the border of Lika often raided by the uskoks, for they lay on the uskoks' route into the Ottoman interior. To reach Ottoman territory, the uskoks first had to cross through the narrow Novigrad

---

[21]In Farlati, *Illyricum sacrum*, vol. 5, p. 134.

[22]A.S.V., Archivio dei Baili Veneti a Constantinopoli, 305: 13 Jan. 1590; 16 Jan. 1589 (m.v.); 31 Jan. 1590 (Zadar) (copies also in A.S.V., Provveditori da Terra e da Mar, 416); I.Ö. H.K.R., Croatica, fasc. 5, 1589, Feb. No. 2: 9 Feb. 1589.

Strait, eluding the Venetian guard stationed there. The local Ottoman officials, when they could not retaliate against the uskoks, often vented their anger on this Venetian garrison.

One such raid in 1580 can be taken as a typical example. It was described in detail by Nikola Katić, the magistrate of Venetian Novigrad, who had been picked up by a band of uskoks as he returned from a journey to Rijeka to buy wine. Thirteen barks commanded by Vojvoda Juraj Daničić had left Senj and sailed down the Morlach Channel, passing through the Novigrad Strait. At dawn the uskoks landed and headed towards Ottoman territory, leaving a guard with the barks. In the middle of the same afternoon they returned, driving 250 animals plundered from below Učitelj in Ravni kotari. They loaded their booty into their barks and set sail for Senj, releasing Katić.[23] The Učitelj Turks, enraged at the raid and blaming the Venetian subjects for not warning them, vented their anger by pillaging the Novigrad area. Three of the local agas asked the Sancak-bey for permission to retaliate against Venetian territory in all such cases.[24]

This sort of conflict was deeply destructive for all concerned. The Ottoman subjects lost their flocks, the mainstay of their existence; Novigrad's lands and population were pillaged in retaliation; and on subsequent raids the uskoks found a formerly well-disposed population less inclined to tolerate their incursions. All parties saw advantages in recognizing their common interests and in finding another, less violent way of dealing with one another—and that is precisely what they did.

In 1582 the Capitano contra uscocchi received a tip that the uskoks and the agas of Karin in Ravni kotari had concluded a truce. He ambushed the messenger between the two parties and seized a letter from the vojvodas of Senj replying to a proposal from Saba-aga, the commander of Karin, and Mustafa-aga Kositerović. This document is worth quoting in detail, both for the terms of the negotiation and for its tone.

> To the greatly honored Saba-aga and Mustafa-aga, worthy of every praise and honor, and to all the other heroes of Karin, as neighbors and honored knights, obeisance and salutation. . . . We have understood your request that we be content not to visit your subjects as often as we have been doing up to now . . . and have also understood the promise that you, the agas and the other heroes of Karin, have made in these letters, pledging by your faith as Muslims that when our men need to pass below Karin you will not cause them any trouble or impediment, but will show them every courtesy and good fellowship, and further, if there arises the necessity of pursuit, during the chase we may count on you, knowing that both there and in any other

[23]A.S.V., Archivio dei Baili Veneti a Constantinopoli, 305: 23 Aug. 1580.
[24]Ibid.: 31 Aug. 1580.

place you will be quick to aid them and show them the right road, and to send their persecutors in the wrong direction. As for your suggestion that we should not take it ill if we find that you are forced to let off one or two gunshots for your honor when you have news of us: all this you may do, if it will not damage your honor, and you will be excused in this case with no damage or prejudice to yourselves. If this is true and agreed, we, the vojvodas of Senj, with all the other heroes, pledge our faith as Christians that we will uphold your proposal honorably.

The letter was signed by "vostri buoni amici in ogni conto," Juraj Daničić, Pavle Lasinović, and Matija Tvrdislavić, vojvodas, and "all the other heroes of Senj."[25]

Thus, according to this agreement the Ottoman officials of Karin agreed to allow the uskoks to cross their territory freely in order to plunder other Ottoman settlements and to mislead any troops (Ottoman or more probably Venetian) sent to pursue the uskoks (in terms that irresistibly bring to mind the "they went that-a way" of the Westerns). In return the uskoks promised not to harm Karin.

That the interests of the uskoks and the agas coincided is clear. A desire to reduce friction in an area in which they were in constant contact could lead to cooperation between these sworn opponents. The letter also demonstrates that communication between these representatives of ostensibly opposed civilizations could be based on a common understanding. A common language was only the most basic element in this exchange. The quotation given here is from an Italian copy sent to the Venetian Bailo in Istanbul, which had been translated from the original in "the Serbian tongue" (the phrase usually used by the Venetians to refer to Bosančica, the variation of Cyrillic used on the borders). The uskoks and the agas shared not only a common language but also a common culture, exemplified here by the concern for honor and dishonor. The uskoks, understanding that for the Muslims to preserve their honor in the eyes of the world they must appear to fight the uskoks, agreed to the proposed subterfuges (if, in an aside that sounds slightly ironic, these would not damage the agas' honor in their own eyes). For both sides, the ideal of honor was to guarantee this agreement, and both sides bound themselves by pledges on their respective—antagonistic—faiths. Honor provided a common idiom that could mediate their agreement.

This incident offers yet another indication of the subordination of political loyalty and ideology in the face of local self-interest. The messenger who had negotiated between the two groups was none other than

---

[25]In A.S.V., Archivio dei Baili Veneti a Constantinopoli, 305: 25 July 1582.

Nikola Katić, the magistrate of Venetian Novigrad. When the Capitano contra uscocchi interrogated him on his part in this shameful agreement, asking why he had not informed the Rector of Zadar, he replied that he had discussed it with Captain Kalabrujić of Novigrad and Matija Mamišić, captain of the armed bark, and they had concluded that it would be in the best interests of the town. Katić explained that the Ottomans had plundered Novigrad constantly over the past six years in retaliation for uskok acts and had taken captive at least forty-seven people (this from a population that four years later numbered no more than 105 adult males).[26] The Ottoman officials had "promised that after this truce between themselves and the uskoks of Senj they would no longer allow that we men of Novigrad should be damaged in our goods or our persons."[27] The Venetian officials of Novigrad, like the Ottoman officials of Karin, found their political loyalties modified by the desire for a measure of local security (at the expense, it is true, of their fellows, who would instead bear the brunt of uskok raiding).

In spite of the Venetian discovery of these negotiations, the agreement seems to have remained in force, and it was even extended to other nearby Ottoman settlements such as Obrovac and Učitelj. Shortly after this agreement was concluded there were several reports of uskok raids that had bypassed Karin to raid villages farther inland, allegedly with the cooperation of the local Ottomans.[28] The following year the uskoks were again reported to be raiding in the area, having strengthened their mutual agreement by bonds of blood brotherhood with the Muslims, eating and drinking with them "as if they were Turks themselves."[29] Even well after the Ottoman officials responsible for the truce were punished by their superiors, this arrangement seems to have operated to the mutual benefit of the uskoks and the Ottoman subjects. An anonymous report from the late 1580s, written by someone clearly familiar with conditions on the borders near Zadar, gives further details of the relations between the uskoks and the border Ottomans from a Venetian perspective:

> When they enter our borders, [the uskoks] nearly always disembark in the river of Obrovac, a place so confederated with them that a bark never enters that river without [the uskoks] going to seek the principal Turks of Obrovac,

---

[26]*Commissiones et relationes venetæ*, vol. 4, p. 373. Including men, women, and children, the population of Novigrad was about 305 in 1586.

[27]In A.S.V., Archivio dei Baili Veneti a Constantinopoli, 305: 25 July 1582 (interrogation of Katić enclosed).

[28]A.S.V., Archivio dei Baili Veneti a Constantinopoli, 305: 27 Aug. 1582; A.S.V., Capi del Consiglio dei Dieci, Lettere dei Rettori, 301: 18 Nov. 1582.

[29]In A.S.V., Archivio dei Baili Veneti a Constantinopoli, 305: 24 Mar. 1583; 7 May, 1583.

the Morlachs of Krmpote, and other neighbors, with whom they speak with every security, since they have been their tributaries and confederates already for many years. The Turks of the fortress of Karin and of Seddi-islam or Učitelj, with other villages of the neighboring area, are also among these confederates, conversing and trafficking with them as freely as if they were brothers or close relatives. . . . The animals of these confederated places graze right to the seashore, so that the uskoks could seize them at any time, but all the same these are safe, while those one or two days' march away are plundered by [the uskoks], a most evident sign of this confederation.[30]

This is one of the few examples of uskok-Ottoman collaboration for which, by chance, detailed evidence has survived. There are other, indirect references to similar arrangements—usually temporary, meeting the needs of both sides, underpinned by a balance of power but regulated by mutual pledges of honor and cemented by ceremonies of blood brotherhood and the sharing of hospitality. It is perhaps too easy, at this chronological and cultural distance from the uskoks, to see these arrangements as a betrayal of the holy war. Little more than a century after the uskoks had been removed from Senj, an epic warning against judging the acts of the uskoks according to alien standards was recorded on the border. The "Ban," the Venetian governor of Zadar, reproached two uskoks for sparing Glamoč, an Ottoman town, from their raids and listed the "good friends" each uskok had among the Muslims there. The answer comes back:

> Gospodine mlad zadarski bane
> lasno ti je ladno vino piti
> na kapiji Zadru bjelome
> sedeći ljepo u debelu ladu. . . .
> ali mučno čuvati krainu
> krvavom se obrisući rukom. . . .
> ljepo ti je pomučati Bane
> pomučati ne govorit mnogo
> jer ovdi ima detca samovolnih

---

[30]In H.A.Z., Fond Šime Ljubića, 8/21 ("Relatione intorno ai confini della Dalmazia"). The uskoks raided Obrovac in 1585 and burned a *fusta* being built there, as noted above, but more cordial relations were soon reestablished, to the point that in 1592 the Provveditore Generale complained to the Paşa of Bosnia that the Turks of Obrovac and Učitelj collaborated with the uskoks, "keeping spies for them and accepting them into their houses" (A.S.V., Provveditori da Terra e da Mar, 1261: 23 June 1592). The Provveditore Generale's suspicions about too-friendly relations between the uskoks and the border Turks were confirmed by the warm testimonials sent him by the Ottoman commanders of Obrovac, Karin, Nadin, and Učitelj (Seddi-islam) on behalf of Matija Daničić, a temporary defector to Venetian service from Senj (ibid., 1262: 18 May 1593). In 1603 the Turks of Obrovac, Karin and Seddi-islam once again renewed their relations with the uskoks, agreeing to pay them for protection from raids (A.S.V., Senato, Secreta, Materie miste notabili, 126: 3 Nov. 1603).

koi nemaju ni oca ni majke
puška i sablja otac i majka. . . .

("Noble Lord, young Ban of Zadar, / it is easy for you to drink cool wine / at the gateway to white Zadar / sitting pleasantly in the deep shade. . . . / But it is hard to guard the border, / wiping off hands wet with blood. . . . / It would be better for you to keep quiet, Ban, / keep quiet and not talk so much, / for there are self-willed children here / who have no father and no mother. / Gun and sword are their father and mother. . . .")[31]

Frontier warriors on both sides can be seen as concerned largely with making a livelihood from the border, an attitude that made warfare a matter of exchange and reinvestment—forcible, but not always mutually destructive, and certainly not anarchic. Common interests in these matters led to pragmatic decisions such as those discussed above—a degree of cooperation achieved by border soldiers acting independently of their superiors and governments. Shared beliefs and values, regular communication, a common hope for a marginally more peaceful existence, and above all a sense of self-preservation could go a long way in moderating the naked struggle for survival. Nevertheless, the inevitability of warfare between Christian and Muslim remained an unquestioned assumption. This was indeed a holy war in the eyes of the uskoks, justified by the obligation to defend Christendom, even when it was not entirely geared toward destruction. The exigencies of warfare could sometimes achieve a sort of balance on the border. But one should not overemphasize the prevalence of mutual communication and interest. The equilibrium between uskok and infidel was based as much on the balance of power and fear as on any reciprocity of respect or tolerance.

Uskoks and Ottoman Christians

The uskoks' relations with the subjects of the Porte, whether Muslim or Christian, were essentially those of soldiers with an enemy population. Venetian observers often noted the damage done by the uskoks to the subjects of the Porte, protesting that they harmed Christians more than they did Muslims, the uskoks' stated foes. Marc'Antonio Pisani, Capitano contra uscocchi, reported in 1588 that the Habsburgs permitted the uskoks "to go pirating and plunder the persons and the goods of the Turkish subjects and Jews by land and by sea. But since the principal vein of their depredations consists of the Morlachs, whom they make

[31]In Gesemann, *Erlangenski rukopis*, pp. 81–82.

slaves, and the animals they take from them, the effect is to render their acts immediately illicit, since these Morlachs (whom they capture) are all Christians, and the goods they take from them those belonging to Christians."[32]

The uskoks did not dispute the bond of common religion, but the fact of their Christianity alone was not enough to preserve the subjects of the Porte from uskok plunder. The right to raid all subjects of the Turk was vigorously defended by the uskoks (and by their Habsburg superiors). As early as 1535, as has already been mentioned, Captain Petar Kružić of Klis announced that he considered all those who lived beyond the coastal mountains (in Ottoman territory) to be Turks and therefore vulnerable to uskok plunder.[33] This principle continued to guide uskok raiding throughout the century. As Vojvoda Ivan Vlatković stated in a letter of 1604 to the Rector of Split, the uskoks claimed not only the Turks as legitimate victims but also "those who serve the Turk."[34]

The ideal of a common Christian duty to oppose the infidel does seem to have influenced uskok antagonism toward some subjects of the Porte. Later writers reported that those Christians who served the Turk in a military capacity as martoloses were particularly hated by the uskoks, their betrayal of Christianity acting as an aggravating factor. A seventeenth-century description, based on information from Pavao Vitezović, a native of Senj, claimed that for the martoloses alone the uskoks had adopted the Ottoman custom of impaling their enemies on a sharpened stake to execute them.[35] The earliest recorded oral epics about the uskoks contain tales involving conflict between the Senj uskoks and bands of Christian adversaries, some of them specifically described as being in Ottoman service. Ivan Senjanin (often identified with Ivan Vlatković), for example, is described demanding of Mujo Jelečković, Muslim vojvoda of a "Turkish band" and his blood brother, that Mujo betray a Christian member of his company, Vite Marinčić, to the uskoks.[36] Contemporary sources also yield a few incidents involving martoloses or Christian renegades. But these were certainly not the only Christian subjects of the Porte the uskoks' raids affected. Nor were the uskoks invariably hostile to Christians in Ottoman service. Accommodation leading to mutual benefit was more common with this population than with the Muslims— not surprisingly. Ottoman officials constantly complained that their

---

[32]In *Commissiones et relationes venetæ*, vol. 6, p. 19.
[33]Laszowski, *Monumenta habsburgica*, vol. 1, p. 456, and see also ibid., vol. 2, p. 264.
[34]In Tomić, "O Senjaninu Ivu," p. 103.
[35]W. von Valvasor, *Die Ehre des Herzogthums Krain* (Laibach, 1689; reprint, Rudolfswerth, 1877–79), vol. 4, p. 92.
[36]Gesemann, *Erlangenski rukopis*, pp. 196–97.

Christian subjects were in league with the uskoks.[37] This cooperation could extend to joining the uskoks in Senj. As already discussed, martoloses and other privileged Ottoman Christians provided one of the sources of uskok recruitment.

The uskoks may well have justified their raids on some Christian subjects of the Turk through their claims as defenders of the faith. The new immigrants from the Ottoman hinterland who settled on the borders were largely Orthodox believers. Giovanni of Fermo, for example, reported that the martoloses, the enemies of the uskoks, were of the "Greek faith."[38] The uskoks' superiors did not hesitate to point out the Orthodoxy of the Ottoman population, claiming that the schismatic character of their Christianity, added to their Ottoman dependence, rendered them legitimate victims of the uskoks. As Faust Vrančić, adviser at the court of Rudolf II, noted, "Most of the people who live in those regions are men of the Greek faith, who can be hunted by [the uskoks] without offence."[39] As early as 1549 the Habsburgs were inquiring whether the Pope might not lift the prohibition against the sale of Christians in the case of schismatics on the Ottoman borders.[40] In 1598 Bishop de Dominis reiterated this proposal in a letter to Minucci, Archbishop of Zadar: "It would mean a great deal if the uskoks could be permitted to capture and sell as slaves the Morlachs, Turkish subjects, although they are Christians, for in this case the name is extended to the most wicked men, much worse than the Turks themselves, who have as Christians nothing but baptism."[41] The same plan is made more explicit in a plan of 1601, probably also originating with de Dominis, which proposed that the Pope allow the uskoks to seize and sell Ottoman subjects "excepting only the Catholics and those loyal to the Apostolic See of Rome."[42] In spite of the petitioning nature of these plans, their acceptance would merely have legitimated a practice that had been common earlier but was no longer openly accepted. Among the captives sold by uskoks from Senj in the Split marketplace while Venice was at war with the Porte in 1537–40 there were both Muslims and Ottoman subjects "of the Rascian faith"—in other words, Orthodox.[43]

---

[37]In one incident in 1591 the Sultan complained to Hasan, Beylerbey of Bosnia, that various Christian subjects of Klis and Krka, although required in return for privileges "to impede the passage of the uskoks onto Turkish territory, instead unite with them to attack it" (*Libri commemoriali della Repubblica di Venezia*, pp. 60–61).

[38]In Rački, "Prilog za poviest hrvatskih uskoka," p. 200.

[39]In Lopašić, *Acta historiam confinii*, vol. 1, p. 151.

[40]Friedensburg, *Nuntiaturberichte aus Deutschland*, p. 404.

[41]In A.S.V., Provveditori da Terra e da Mar, 922: 27 Oct. 1598.

[42]In Horvat, *Monumenta uscocchorum*, vol. 1, p. 388. See also the corrupt version dated 1581 in H.A.Z., Fond Šime Ljubića, 8/18: 5.

[43]In H.A.Z., Arhiv Splita, 83/88, 1/II and 1/IV. There was a formal distinction between the

Although this confessional division between the uskoks and the Ottoman subjects clearly had an influence on the direction of uskok raids, the
uskok bias against the Orthodox does not seem to have been consistent.
The line between the uskoks and the Orthodox subjects of the Porte was
increasingly blurred in the course of the sixteenth century, particularly
after the 1590s with the increased immigration from the Ottoman interior
to Habsburg and Venetian territory. Certainly Orthodox were among the
recruits to Senj. Areas known to be settled with Orthodox from the
hinterland (the Klis district, for example) sent many immigrants to Senj,
where they seem to have been absorbed into its Catholic structures
without difficulty.[44] Toward the end of the sixteenth century further
evidence suggests that the uskoks were willing to reach an accommodation with Orthodox communities in the Ottoman hinterland, promising
not to raid them in return for tribute.[45] The difference in confession
could have justified the raids of these soldiers of the faith, but it was not
necessarily a source of lasting enmity. Catholics under Ottoman rule
were also victims of uskok attack—"those who serve the Turk" was a
rubric with a broad meaning, one that did not much discriminate on the
basis of confession.

Some historians have interpreted uskok raids on the Christian population on Ottoman territory as a conscious attempt to weaken the Ottoman military and administrative system, of which the Christian subjects
were an important part.[46] The attacks on Christians were certainly a part
of Habsburg policy on the Military Frontier, particularly in regard to
Lika. But how much the uskoks' attacks on the Lika settlers were motivated by the desire to shake Ottoman control of the frontier is uncertain.
The extent to which independent uskok raids concentrated on plundering rather than on direct military confrontation suggests that an attack
on Ottoman government was secondary.

Although the uskoks' need for booty was one of the most important
influences on their actions, eventually the requirements of the holy war
were to moderate the uskoks' raids in Ottoman territory. When Muslim
goods and captives were not to be had, the most abundant source of

---

two types of transactions: the Muslims were sold outright as slaves, but only the services of
the Orthodox Christians sold, and only for a specified number of years. In practice, their
experiences probably differed little.
    [44]In just one example, there were Paštrovići from the Boka Kotor area among the uskoks.
By the beginning of the seventeenth century the Archbishop of Bar described the Paštrovići
as nearly all members of the Orthodox Church and under the jurisdiction of the Patriarchate
of Peć. (Franjo Rački, ed., "Izvještaj barskog nadbiskupa Marina Bizzia o svojem putovanju
god. 1610 po Arbanaškoj i staroj Srbiji," *Starine* [Zagreb], 20 [1888]: 60).
    [45]Lopašić, *Acta historiam confinii*, vol. 1, pp. 161–62. For further details on tribute see
below.
    [46]For example, see Vinaver, "Senjski uskoci," p. 66.

plunder was the Ottoman Christian population, whether Orthodox or Catholic, and these Ottoman subjects provided the uskoks with much of their income. Nonetheless, there was a sense on both sides that this state of affairs was not ideal, that the uskoks and the Christian subjects of the Porte *ought* to be on good terms.

Certainly cooperation between them was not uncommon. The Christian peasants and shepherds of the Ottoman border, if given the choice, were fully prepared to aid the uskoks, particularly when the raids were directed against their own enemies, above all the Ottoman administrators, landlords, and towns. Without the aid, information, and reinforcements provided by their collaborators on Ottoman territory, the uskoks would scarcely have been able to inflict the damage on the Ottomans which they did. This theme was continually repeated by the Venetians, anxious to shift the blame for the depredations of the uskoks from their own shoulders. "When they go to do damage in the Turkish lands, they go with as much safety as if they were visiting their own homes, for in every place they have friends and relatives, who not only support them, aid them, and keep them hidden, but also give their prey into their hands."[47]

Tribute. Links with friends and relatives left behind may have provided a basis for common action with many Ottoman subjects, but not all areas enjoyed such close ties with Senj. Other ways of formalizing relations were found. One of the most common bases for accommodation was the tribute agreement. From the 1570s a series of such agreements, balancing the uskoks' need for plunder and the common desire for cooperation, regulated the relations between the uskoks and Christian subjects of the Ottoman territories in Bukovica and Ravni kotari, the hinterland of Trogir and Šibenik, Makarska Krajina, Poljica, and the Biokovo-Neretva region. In return for a certain tribute or tax, the uskoks were to refrain from indiscriminate plundering. The earliest agreements seem to have been based on informal negotiations between the uskok vojvodas and prisoners taken for ransom or to have risen out of arrangements to limit mutual destruction, as in the case of Karin, which began to pay a tribute to the uskoks in the 1580s.[48] As the benefits of such arrangements became clear, the local clergy proposed others. Still other agreements seem to have arisen out of agitation among the Ottoman population for uprisings against their Ottoman rulers and were contracted with the Habsburgs themselves, rather than with the uskoks.

---

[47]In *Commissiones et relationes venetæ*, vol. 5, p. 16.
[48]A.S.V., Archivio dei Baili Veneti a Constantinopoli, 305: 7 May 1583.

These resulted in letters and patents issued to Senj by the Habsburg authorities, prohibiting the uskoks from harming the groups in question.[49]

The villages of Vratkovići (the common name given to a group of villages in the Ottoman hinterland of Trogir) provide a good example of the tribute relationship between the uskoks and Ottoman subjects. Together with Trogir itself they had passed into the hands of Venice in 1420, only to be overrun by Ottoman forces with the invasion of the Dalmatian hinterland. Sovereignty over the villages was disputed throughout the sixteenth century—though they were inhabited largely by newly settled Ottoman subjects from the interior, primarily pastoral Vlachs, the Venetian state and the landowning families of Trogir still claimed dues on their land in Vratkovići, and in fact received them intermittently.[50] The uskoks often raided this area, for they could easily reach it by sea without drawing the attention of Venetian garrisons in the two nearest towns, Trogir and Šibenik. The grain and the cattle of the inhabitants offered a lucrative source of booty, as did their ransoms. In 1576 the Sancak-bey of Klis wrote to inform the Rector of Šibenik that the uskoks had taken nine captives from Vratkovići and Gradac.[51] Apparently at about this time the payment of protection money was first discussed. According to the testimony of witnesses from Vratkovići and Trogir, Vojvoda Daničić was the chief instigator of the scheme, suggesting the arrangement to the villagers who were being held for ransom in Senj. The annual tribute, amounting to one-half a ducat per household, was shipped to Senj from the little port of Rogoznica near Trogir in the form of grain and was accompanied by the gift of a horse and carpet for the uskok vojvoda.[52]

---

[49]See for example the documents dealing with the Trogir hinterland, Lopašić, *Acta historiam confinii*, vol. 1, pp. 81–89; Jelić, "Izprave o prvoj uroti za oslobodjenje Klisa," p. 102; Šišić, *Acta comitalia*, vol. 5, pp. 107–9.

[50]Pavao Andreis, *Povijest grada Trogira*, trans. V. Rismondo 2 vols. (Split, 1971), vol. 1, pp. 308–16; vol. 2, pp. 384–92; *Commissiones et relationes venetæ*, vol. 2, p. 209; vol. 4, p. 429; A.S.V., Provveditori da Terra e da Mar, 424: 11 Mar. 1611.

[51]Tomić, "Sedam srpskih pisama," p. 12.

[52]This information comes from a series of interrogations made by the Rector of Trogir in 1580, forwarded to the Signoria in 1583 in response to a request for information on tribute negotiations (A.S.V., Capi del Consiglio dei Dieci, Lettere dei Rettori, 281: 18 Jan. 1582 [m.v.]). According to one witness, the tribute had been paid for some four years. Piero Crastovazich of Bristivica (30 July 1580), as a Venetian subject closely involved in dealings with the uskoks, was understandably vague about the details of the negotiations, but other, less compromised witnesses were more explicit (Nicolo Pistor and Simon Opatovich, both of Trogir [1 Aug. 1580]; and letter of Rector T. Marin [28 July 1580], all enclosed in a letter of T. Marin, A.S.V., Capi del Consiglio dei Dieci, Lettere dei Rettori, 281: 18 Jan. 1582 [m.v.]). Some years after this arrangement was made, Vojvoda Daničić was accused of having taken Ottoman villages under uskok protection and collecting tribute from them without informing the Captain of Senj or asking his permission. Testimony taken from the uskoks in this connection was vague about the circumstances under which the agreements had been made, but generally implied that the previous Captain of Senj, Johann Fernberger, had approved (relieved of his post in 1577) (I.Ö. H.K.R., Croatica, fasc. 4, 1584, Apr. No. 2: 55′

Shortly afterward Fra Benedetto Rottondo, Archdeacon of Trogir, tried to formalize this arrangement, proposing that the Christian villages of this area pay an annual tribute of two gulden for each household to the Habsburgs, in exchange for which they would be protected from uskok attack and would once again be considered subjects of the Croatian-Hungarian crown (as they had been before 1420).[53] Venice opposed this plan, mistrusting the establishment of Habsburg jurisdiction so close to its own borders, and the agents of the Republic appear to have done their best to prevent Rottondo from carrying out the terms of the agreement.[54] In spite of their actions and some difficulties in collecting the tribute, the arrangements seem to have been extended to further villages and were reconfirmed along the same lines in 1586.[55]

The links between the uskoks and their tributaries in Vratkovići extended beyond the payment of money to protect the villagers from raids. In 1588, when the uskoks looted through the Vratkovići area, they killed and captured Muslims there with the aid of the Christian inhabitants—a collaboration that brought an immediate punishment from Ottoman forces.[56] Throughout the 1590s Venetian representatives collected evidence that the villagers of Vratkovići collaborated with the uskoks: "They make company with the uskoks when they are few in number, taking the booty they gather with them, and there are more who hide them in their houses for weeks and months at a time, concealing them and supplying them, so that the uskoks, whether few or many, stay there with as much confidence as if they were in Senj."[57] That this complaint was not baseless was demonstrated by an incident in 1591, in which a band of uskoks plundered the flocks of the village of Mirilović in the sancak of Klis and, pursued by Venetian troops from Šibenik, took refuge in Vratkovići, where the villagers joined in their defense against the Venetians.[58] It was only a short step from plundering with the uskoks

[Stypschitsch]; 58′ [Floritsch]; 60–60′ [Sehiltkhovitsch], etc.).

[53]Lopašić, *Acta historiam confinii*, vol. 1, pp. 81–85, 88–89; I.Ö. H.K.R., Croatica, fasc. 2, 1579, May No. 11: 12–14′.

[54]A.S.V., Capi del Consiglio dei Dieci, Lettere dei Rettori, 281: 18 Jan. 1582; Lopašić, *Acta historiam confinii*, vol. 1, p. 105.

[55]Jelić, "Izprave o prvoj uroti za oslobodjenje Klisa," p. 102; Ivić, "Migracije Srba u Hrvatsku," p. 51.

[56]Sarpi, *La Repubblica di Venezia*, p. 412; A.S.V., Archivio dei Baili Veneti a Constantinopoli, 305: 29 Jan. 1587 (m.v.).

[57]A.S.V., Senato, Secreta, Materie miste notabili, 27: 12 Mar. 1591. Similar complaints in A.S.V., Archivio dei Baili Veneti a Constantinopoli, 305: 25 Apr. 1590; *Commissiones et relationes venetæ*, vol. 5, pp. 17, 32.

[58]A.S.V., Provveditore Sopraintendente alla Camera dei Confini, 243: 5 Dec. 1591 ("IX Comandam.ti et altro circa li confini di Dalm.a . . ."). Other evidence of Vratkovići participation in uskok raids: A.S.V., Provveditori da Terra e da Mar. 1263: 18 May 1597; H.A.Z., Arhiv Trogira, 25/11: 1478′ (17 Dec. 1598); 1481 (31 Mar. 1599); 1488–88′ (9 June 1599); 1489 (8 Aug. 1599).

to going to Senj as an uskok. Dragoslav Poplaković and Milos Slaviči were both well-known uskok harambašas who came to Senj from Vrat-kovići in the early 1590s, probably as a result of the ties formed by the tribute arrangements. Both would later be found raiding in the area, relying on their local contacts for support.

The privileges granted by the Habsburgs to various areas under Otto-man rule were regularly accompanied by letters to the Captain and soldiers of Senj, stressing their duty to protect and aid those who had been granted imperial protection.[59] Evidence suggests that the uskoks saw their responsibility for these tributary villages as something greater than merely refraining from pillaging them. In 1598 the uskoks pressed their superiors to intercede with Venice on behalf of some of their Otto-man tributaries who, they claimed, had been condemned to row on the Serenissima's galleys in chains for joining the uskoks in fighting the Turk.[60] Whether they were able, even if willing, to protect their tribu-taries against Ottoman or Venetian retaliation, except by offering refuge in Senj, is doubtful.

Nevertheless, of the three protectors and rulers Vratkovići recognized and paid, the area seems to have derived the most direct benefit from the uskoks, and they returned the favor, as a Provveditore Generale com-mented in 1591: "They acknowledge the Great Turk, and also Your Seren-ity, but most of all the uskoks, giving them aid and favoring them in every season."[61] In return for their taxes the Ottomans had done little to protect the villages. Nor could their landlords in Venetian Trogir give them much aid, and the Venetian authorities had not even been able to prevent their own subjects from raiding Vratkovići. The uskoks took an annual tribute, but they at least shared the subsequent plunder. The uskoks also kept their word to their tributaries. Those villages who paid the promised sum were immune from uskok raids, while other Ottoman subjects were not, as Nicolò Surian reported in 1580:

Vojvoda Daničić has the authority to protect all the borders of the Turkish lands from the district of Zadar to the mouth of the Neretva, ensuring that no village of these frontiers close to the shore can be harmed by the uskoks if they pay a certain tribute. He keeps this promise if these Turkish subjects pay the part of the tribute they owe, as is seen by experience, for it has happened that when the Morlachs from the upper territories descend to the shore in the winter to pasture their animals, if in plundering the Morlachs the uskoks have also taken a Morlach or Turk who has paid the *haraç*, and

[59]See for example Šišić, *Acta comitalia*, vol. 5, pp. 107–9.
[60]A.S.V., Provveditore da Terra e da Mar, 1263: 15 Mar. 1598.
[61]In *Commissiones et relationes*, vol. 5, p. 17.

who is known by Vojvoda Daničić, this vojvoda has had them restored, and there have been many such restitutions.[62]

The tributaries did not hesitate to protest any ill usage. In 1597 one hundred uskoks plundered many cattle from the river bank across from the village of Kukalj on the border of the Zadar district, and also took captive a Morlach called Frletić and his son. Since Kukalj was a tributary village, the two captives were at once released—but Frletić's son immediately announced his intention of demanding the restitution of their flocks as well from the authorities.[63]

Perhaps, as has recently been suggested, the willingness of the Ottoman subjects to pay this tax to the uskoks is connected to the breakdown of feudal dependency in this area—the uskoks benefiting from the peasants' growing resistance to the obligations demanded by their landlords.[64] A change in attitude toward the landlords' traditional rights can be traced over the sixteenth century among the villagers of Vratkovići. Before the Ottoman invasion of the hinterland, some of these lands had belonged to various noble families of Trogir, and others had been in the possession of the archbishopric of Split, the commune of Trogir, or the Venetian Republic itself. The tenant farmers (*coloni*) worked the land in exchange for a variety of obligations. Over the first few decades of the sixteenth century the area was depopulated by the Ottoman wars and the great plague of 1527—and then resettled, largely by Morlachs from the interior but also with a good number of original inhabitants who returned to their ancestral hearths. Throughout the century these villages were the subject of repeated Venetian-Ottoman jurisdictional disputes. Even when Venice was recognized as their sovereign, Ottoman subjects still largely worked and pastured the lands because of the diminished population of the Venetian territory. These Ottoman subjects paid the Ottoman state a *haraç* (or more accurately the *cizye* or poll tax) and were also expected to render the obligations connected with the lands to their Trogir owners. These were the *terratica* or *zemljarina* (the land tax, usually one-sixteenth of the wheat or other produce) and the *regalia* (a goat at Christmas, a lamb at Easter, one cheese, and six loads of wood) to be paid annually by each household.[65] By the 1540s the peasants of

[62]In A.S.V., Provveditore Sopraintendente alla Camera dei Confini, 243: 1 Feb. 1580 (N. Surian). This pattern was confirmed by testimony from the Habsburg court as well (Lopašić, *Acta historiam confinii*, vol. 1, pp. 161–62).

[63]A.S.V., Provveditore da Terra e da Mar, 1263: 13 Dec. 1597.

[64]Pederin, "Gospodarski i ideološki pristup," p. 187. He describes the uskoks, who by collecting a tax with the help of the people themselves, filled the gap left by the peasants' refusal to pay the old feudal dues.

[65]See Andreis, *Povijest Trogira*, vol. 1, p. 316; vol. 2, p. 389.

Vratkovići were resisting the payment of their obligations to Trogir land-lords. This move was not, however, a concerted or complete rejection of these dues. On the contrary, even when the Venetian-Ottoman border commission of 1574 recognized the loss of part of Trogir's territory to the Ottomans, some of the obligations on these lands continued to be dis-charged voluntarily.[66] The villagers did not entirely reject the idea of paying a tax to the owners of their land. However, rather than recognize the traditional rights of the landowners, they seem to have seen the tax as a tribute paid to the state or its representatives in return for protec-tion. This process had been noted as early as 1553, when a Venetian syndic had reported that the Ottoman subjects paid a small subsidy on their lands and also a levy to the treasury of St. Mark, but they resisted paying what was "right and proper," their feudal obligations to the landowners.[67] The uskoks, then, were not rendered the dues formerly paid to the landowners—rather, they represent a power whose aid, in the minds of the villagers, might appropriately be secured by a tribute. Indeed, Venetian reporters stress that at times Vratkovići simultane-ously paid a tribute to all three powers—the Porte, the Republic, and the uskoks—to ensure their own well-being.[68] The villagers were far better disposed to the uskoks, who at least shared their booty, than they were to the Ottoman officials, who "imposed extraordinary burdens on them in order to extort their incomes," according to a Rector of Trogir report-ing in 1593 to the Ventian Senate.[69]

Payment of protection money to the uskoks could have been justified on the grounds of political tradition as well as political function. The uskoks may well have enjoyed a certain allegiance in this area as represen-tatives of the Habsburgs and the Croatian-Hungarian crown. Certainly Fra Benedetto Rottondo's phrases as he negotiated a tribute agreement suggest that such a tradition may have legitimized the arrangement in the eyes of the villagers, "who were anciently subjects of the Kingdom of Hungary and desire to become vassals of Your Highness, and to return to their former state."[70] Precisely how widely this tradition was pre-served it is difficult to say, particularly as Vratkovići had been largely resettled. One factor may have been the influence of the remaining indigenous inhabitants, among whom the tradition of allegiance to the Croatian-Hungarian crown was strong enough to be commented on, worriedly, by numerous Venetian officials. Perhaps by paying a tribute to the uskoks, the representatives of the Habsburgs, the villagers were

---

[66]Ibid., vol. 2, pp. 92, 390, 392; *Commissiones et relationes venetæ*, vol. 4, p. 149.
[67]*Commissiones et relationes venetæ*, vol. 2, p. 209.
[68]Ibid., vol. 4, p. 429; vol. 5, pp. 17, 32, 62–63.
[69]In Ibid., vol. 5, p. 63.
[70]In Lopašić, *Acta historiam confinii*, vol. 1, p. 82.

making their own claim to a choice of political identity. (It was clearly as a deliberate political choice that the Catholic, Orthodox, and Muslim population of Zažablje and Popovo in Hercegovina, "seeing our ruin" after discussing the matter in a general assembly in 1604, offered to submit themselves to the Habsburg Emperor and began to pay the uskoks a tribute.)[71] The Venetians certainly feared that such was the case, objecting in particular to the idea that this jurisdiction should be institutionalized in the payment of tribute, "a word and title most important in infinitely many respects, and most prejudicial to the interests of Your Serenity."[72] In this connection it is significant that the Ottoman subjects, in paying their tribute, are described as treating Vojvoda Daničić, who had come to collect the tribute at the Novigrad Strait, "in such a way that it can be said that they received him in these deserted places much better, and with more honor than if the Sancak, their natural lord, should have come."[73] But the Christian villagers, with a tradition of better times under the Croatian crown, might well have denied that the Ottomans were their "natural lords" and turned instead to the uskoks, and through them to the Habsburgs.

An equally important element in tribute arrangements seems to have been the desire both of the Ottoman subjects and of the uskoks to reduce the uskoks' pillaging raids against a potentially friendly Christian population. The position of the Ottoman subjects is clear—their petitions explicitly state that they wish to be freed of the attacks of those "in whom we ought to be able to trust, and through whom we ought to receive every grace from His Most Serene [Habsburg] Highness."[74] The uskoks themselves were not always primarily concerned with the amount of their booty. That they too desired to limit these destructive raids can be inferred from their defense of the tribute arrangements when the Captain of Senj and the officers of the Military Frontier wished to end the practice on the grounds that it did not produce as much booty as did unrestricted raiding.[75] Far from acceding to these plans, the uskoks made new treaty arrangements with the Ottoman Christians without

---

[71]Truhelka, "Nekoliko mladjih pisama," p. 478; H.A.D., Lettere di Levante, 41: 52'; H.A.D., Lettere di Ponente, 9: 156', 165. A similar combination of political tradition and desire to free themselves from Ottoman rule can be seen in the 1609 letter of the local Christian leaders of Lika and Krbava, which begged military aid against the Ottomans and offered to submit "the land of Ivan Karlović" (Croatian Ban and the last Christian lord of Krbava-Lika) to Habsburg rule (Theiner, *Vetera monumenta Slavorum meridionalium historiam illustrantia*, vol. 2, pp. 101–3).

[72]In H.A.D., Fond Šime Ljubića, 2/33: 287.

[73]In A.S.V., Archivio dei Baili Veneti a Constantinopoli, 305: 24 Jan. 1587 (m.v.).

[74]In Theiner, *Vetera monumenta Slavorum meridionalium historiam illustrantia*, vol. 2, p. 102.

[75]*Commissiones et relationes venetæ*, vol. 6, p. 15; Lopašić, *Acta historiam confinii*, vol. 1, pp. 98, 157, 160.

informing their Captain (an example of a sense of community which modified the uskoks' economic interests).[76]

Although the uskoks and their tributaries and collaborators often reached an accommodation based on common interests and values, they did not negotiate on an equal footing. The threat of force was always implicit in these relations, and the fear of uskok retaliation played a large part in maintaining this equilibrium. In this connection, the report of Provveditore Generale Donà suggests that the Christian subjects of the Porte may have viewed the appeal of a common Christianity, so often stressed by the clerical initiators of many of these proposals, with some skepticism. He noted that "the Morlachs call this tax a *zadusbina* [Cr. *zadužbina*, a charitable bequest], meaning it ironically, as alms for the soul of the Emperor."[77] Venetians, though reluctant to speculate on the existence of other ties between the uskoks and the border population, were quick to emphasize the uskoks' power to terrorize. It was the uskoks' armed extortion that the tribute arrangements were intended to regulate, and the fear of renewed raids that ensured prompt payment. In 1599 the Provveditore Generale believed that "if [the uskoks] were to be removed, or impeded in their navigation, the fear [they inspire] ceasing, the tribute would cease as well."[78] Accordingly, over the following few years Venice deployed forces not only to prevent uskok voyages collecting tribute but also to hinder Ottoman delegations attempting to deliver it to Senj.[79]

By 1602 the villages of Vratkovići had not paid their annual tribute for several years, either because they no longer felt a need to pay off uskoks whose raids had been limited by Venetian patrols and Habsburg commissions or because they had been prevented from doing so by Venetian vigilance. Their history of cooperation with the uskoks did not protect them from retaliation. Just before Christmas the uskoks of Senj stormed through Vratkovići, seizing captives and animals in Britivica, Prapratnica, Blizna, and Ljubitovica, "because for three years they had not received the tribute these villages had been accustomed to give." When Vojvoda Ivan Vlatković was told that Venice would demand the return of the booty, he responded that it was in place of the tribute owed to Senj and that he would fight to defend it, though a conflict between Chris-

---

[76]The collection of this independently negotiated *harač* was an issue in the investigations of both Juraj Daničić in 1582 (I.Ö. H.K.R., Croatica, fasc. 4, 1584, Apr. No. 2) and Ivan Vlatković in 1611 (Lopašić, *Acta historiam confinii*, vol. 2, pp. 8–10).

[77]In *Commissiones et relationes venetæ*, vol. 5, p. 281.

[78]In ibid., vol. 5, p. 281. This attitude was shared by other observers, including Vettor Barbaro (H.A.Z., Fond Šime Ljubića, 2/33: 287), and Furio Molza, the Captain of Senj in 1590 (Lopašić, *Acta historiam confinii*, vol. 1, p. 157).

[79]A.S.V., Senato, Secreta, Materie miste notabili, 126: 3 Nov. 1603; Rački, "Prilog za poviest hrvatskih uskoka," pp. 209, 213.

tians was no way to celebrate Christmas Eve.[80] This was not an isolated in-cident—other areas too were subject to the same means of persuasion. The inhabitants of Ravno, in Popovo Polje above Dubrovnik, were pillaged in 1605 "although in the past tributaries of the uskoks who found, it seems, the tribute promised them too small," according to a Ragusan official.[81]

Their actions imply that the uskoks viewed these Christian villages with the eyes of conquerors. The bonds of a common Christianity did not lead them to ignore the rights conferred on them by their superior might, any more than a triumphant general would dismiss the tax obligations of newly liberated Christian borderers. Theirs was the legitimacy of superior power, as they themselves described their relationship with the tributary Christians. In a letter of 1607 to Rudolf II, uskok vojvodas and leaders asked permission to collect their dues from Ottoman territory in spite of the truce with the Porte. "We, the ever faithful and constant militia of Senj, with our skill and prudence, with great risks and valiant arms, spilling our blood, have acquired . . . certain villages and possessions, and they with their subjects, for fear of our valor, pay tribute."[82]

The rural population of the Ottoman hinterland differed from that of Venetian Dalmatia and the Croatian Littoral largely in being ruled by the Sultan. This difference provided the uskoks with a justification for raiding them. Nonetheless, their common Christianity, given a special meaning by the uskoks' claims to be defenders of the faith, imposed certain mutual obligations and expectations on their relations, though it did not prevent the uskoks from exploiting the Ottoman subjects. Yet power did not all run one way. As we will see, the uskoks' relations with the rural Ottoman subjects were very similar to those with the villagers of Dalmatia. Like bandits elsewhere, the uskoks were in many ways dependent on the local rural population—for booty, yes, but also for protection and support. The uskoks made themselves respected in the hinterland and in Dalmatia through the use of force, but uskok terror was impossible to sustain for long. In the end, a less violent accommodation was achieved, partly on the basis of threats, but partly too through the promise of benefits: a measure of stability, the prospect of booty, the satisfaction of striking a blow against the infidel conqueror.

Christian Neighbors: Venice and Dubrovnik

Uskok actions also threatened citizens of the Christian states that traded in the Adriatic—from the Papal States, Naples, Tuscany, and far-

---

[80]In A.S.V., Senato, Secreta, Materie miste notabili, 126: 24 Dec.1602; 23 Jan. 1602 (m.v.).
[81]In H.A.D., Lettere di Levante, 41: 52'–53.
[82]In Lopašić, *Acta historiam confinii,* vol. 3, p. 437.

ther afield—and the subjects of neighboring Christian states, such as Dubrovnik and especially Venetian Dalmatia. These states were not at war with the Habsburgs or with the uskoks. The governments of Venice and Dubrovnik were, for the most part, carefully neutral in the battles between the West and the Ottoman Empire. It might seem, in terms of Senj's *antemurale* ideology, that none of the subjects of these Christian states should have been vulnerable to uskok attack in the same way that subjects of the Porte were. Still, the uskoks ransacked the cargoes of Western ships, whatever flag they flew, and raided the villages of the Dalmatian coast and islands. Venice was particularly affected by these uskok activities. Nearly all uskok actions against the Ottomans infringed Venetian jurisdiction. Unless the uskoks took the long overland route to Ottoman territory, they could reach the Ottoman hinterland most easily by striking through Dalmatian territory (only a mile or two wide in some places). The raids at sea, with their ambushes of coastal traffic and searches for infidel merchandise, involved long, armed cruises on the Serenissima's gulf, as well as anchorages on the Dalmatian islands and coast to take on supplies and pick up information. But the uskoks also did direct damage. Certainly the insurance claims for Adriatic shipping and the judicial records of the commune archives seem to support a view of the uskoks as common brigands. In addition to Muslims and Jews, Christian merchants of all states claimed recompense for uskok losses; Venetian officials reported attacks on the galleys of the Signoria in which the uskoks killed troops and seized dispatches and supplies; shepherds, fishermen, and peasants registered innumerable small thefts of provisions; and a few reports concern bloody uskok murders in the villages. Nonetheless, as on Ottoman territory, the uskoks also had allies who protected and supported them.

The Ottoman threat was at the foundation of the relations between both the Republic of Venice and the Republic of Dubrovnik on the one hand and the uskoks on the other. As long as their interests demanded peace with the Turk, neither state could afford to countenance the uskoks' actions. When diplomatic attempts to force the uskoks' Habsburg masters to restrain them failed, both governments took direct action against the uskoks themselves. The uskoks, in turn, saw these acts as a betrayal of the Christian cause, particularly in the case of the Serenissima, and thus started an escalating spiral of uskok defiance, Venetian punishment, uskok revenge, and Venetian retaliation, which grew constantly more violent.

Yet Venice's attitude toward uskok raiding fluctuated according to the state of Venetian relations with the Porte. During the sixteenth century Venice warred openly with the Porte three times: the war of 1499–1503; the War of the Holy League, 1537–40; and the War of Cyprus, 1570–73.

During these periods, the Signoria used uskoks for its own purposes, encouraging the independent raiding of Ottoman subjects and attempting to enlist uskok bands in Venice's armed forces.[83] Uskoks took advantage of Venice's need for recruits, raiding the Ottomans as they had before, but now under the protection of the Republic. Many such uskoks, nominally in Venetian service, retained their own organizations, with their own leaders chosen from within their own ranks rather than appointed by the Signoria, and with their own forms of warfare. Such bands were never completely assimilated into Venice's military system. Their ideas of correct behavior were not those of Venice—when peace came they did not stop raiding. If they were caught, they were punished. If they were dismissed from service, one Venetian representative noted after the War of Cyprus, "not knowing how to live, they go to Senj and become assassins. It is these who are constantly giving Your Serenity so much trouble."[84]

Although a number of incidents have been put forward as the first in which the uskoks and Venice came into conflict,[85] the conditions that generated this antagonism had existed from the earliest appearance of uskoks on the border between Christian and Ottoman territory. By the 1530s the raids of the Klis and Senj uskoks were provoking Ottoman retaliation against Venetian subjects for their alleged complicity.[86] The report to the Senate by Antonio da Mula, Rector of Zadar, in about 1543, might equally well have come from any of Venice's officials in Dalmatia for the following eighty years.

> The greatest troubles I have had from [the Turks] have been caused by the men of Senj, who pass in their barks beneath Morlacchia [the Velebit mountains] toward Obrovac, come ashore, and do great damage to the Turks, who say that Your Serenity is responsible for guarding them from the sea, and demand that we give them recompense. And so I have chased the

[83]For uskoks in Venetian service from 1499 to 1503, see Sanuto, *I diarii*, vol. 2, p. 1277; vol. 3, pp. 217, 297, 777–78, 785. For recruitment of uskoks in the War of the Holy League, see *Commissiones et relationes venetæ*, vol. 2, p. 116; Sarpi, *La Repubblica di Venezia*, p. 405; Lamansky, *Secrets d'état de Venise*, vol. 2, p. 557; and for the War of Cyprus, see Horvat, *Monumenta uscocchorum*, vol. 1, p. 6; Sarpi, *La Repubblica di Venezia*, p. 408; A.S.V., Senato, Secreta, reg. 78: 153' (15 Oct. 1572). The subject is treated in more detail in Bracewell, "Uskoks in Venetian Dalmatia," pp. 84–92.

[84]In *Commissiones et relationes venetæ*, vol. 4, pp. 171–72.

[85]Magdić proposed the seizure of the ship *Contarina* in 1573 (*Topografija*, p. 108); N. Klaić suggested 1563, when she dates the Republic's serious claims to hegemony over the Adriatic (*Društvena previranja i bune*, p. 184); Šišić advanced 1557 and the first Venetian blockade of Senj (*Pregled povijesti hrvatskog naroda*, p. 309); Pederin placed it in 1547, when the uskoks were forced to raid southward because of the Habsburg-Ottoman treaty of that year forbidding raids on the border ("Gospodarski i ideološki pristup," p. 185).

[86]Sanuto, *I diarii*, vol. 57, p. 517; see also Laszowski, *Monumenta habsburgica*, vol. 2, pp. 258–59; 264–66; 277–79; etc.

Senjani and the said uskoks as much as I have been able, and many times I have sent . . . the Captain of the Fustas . . . to pursue them, and on occasion he has recovered Turkish prisoners, and sometimes he has taken the Senj barks, to the Turks' great satisfaction.[87]

Venetian officials not only pursued the uskoks and seized their captives and barks but also blockaded Senj itself to prevent their excursions, punished uskok supporters, and sent their Ottoman neighbors information on their whereabouts and plans. When uskoks were taken captive they were usually executed summarily—if possible in the presence of an Ottoman representative—and their heads displayed publicly, both as a warning and as evidence to the Ottomans that Venice was indeed keeping its pledge to keep the seas free of the enemies of the Turk—all, as da Mula had said, "to the Turks' great satisfaction." Still, with all its might, the Republic of Venice found it impossible to keep the coasts and seas clear of the uskoks. As Archbishop Minucci wrote, using a metaphor drawn from familiar Dalmatian images, "the battle for the most part ends up like that between the Lion and the Mosquito, for no matter how the Lion lashes out with his teeth, his paws, and his tail, he only rarely hits the Mosquito, while it constantly buzzes about his ears, annoying and irritating him."[88] When all the Republic's might proved inadequate against these small but persistent adversaries, Venetian representatives sometimes turned to desperate stratagems. In 1599, during the long Venetian blockade of Senj, a Venetian commander hoped to use the uskoks' thirst to settle the conflict for once and all by allowing them to capture a cargo of poisoned wine provided by the Council of Ten in Venice, thus achieving "what cannot be done by the sword."[89] There is no record that this attempt succeeded, but in spite of their fearsome reputation, the Council of Ten's poisons were not always reliable.

Dubrovnik was equally plagued by Ottoman retaliation for alleged complicity with the uskoks but, less powerful than the great republic to the north and more vulnerable to uskok vengeance, for many years the government responded to uskok actions by diplomacy rather than by force. It sent letters and emissaries to the Habsburg courts, to the officers of the Military Frontier, and to the Pope, begging that the uskoks not provoke the Turk to retaliate against Dubrovnik. Emissaries were also sent to the uskoks themselves when they appeared in Ragusan waters, warning them against infringing Dubrovnik's neutrality. Such contacts were kept secret, for fear of further Ottoman accusations of collabora-

---

[87]In *Commissiones et relationes venetæ*, vol. 2, p. 175.
[88]Minucci, *Storia degli uscocchi*, p. 238.
[89]In A.S.V., Capi del Consiglio dei Dieci, 306: 12 Mar. 1599.

tion. A few instructions to such messengers are recorded in the surviving fragments of the Secreta Rogatorum, the secret minutes of Dubrovnik's ruling body which were usually so carefully destroyed. As early as 1535 the Ragusan authorities, rather than punishing uskoks captured on their territory, explained the problems they caused for Dubrovnik, asked them to leave the area, and set them free, with the gift of a barrel of wine, a sack of bread, and a sheep to see them on their way. The Ragusan emissaries entrusted with this task were threatened with death if word of this agreement leaked out.[90]

In spite of this initially conciliatory attitude, relations between the uskoks and the Ragusan Republic had deteriorated badly by the end of the sixteenth century. The Daničić affair, when the uskok vojvoda had met his death on the Republic's territory, apparently from Ragusan treachery, had put them at odds for almost a decade, and in spite of the Pope's mediation in 1580 new clashes invariably brought up the old dispute. Although by the 1590s the Senate was still sending emissaries to dissuade the uskoks from crossing Ragusan territory, they were now accompanied by a substantial armed guard, and a bloody fracas was as likely to ensue as an agreement. In early 1596, for example, a number of uskok harambašas were killed when they refused to heed the Senate's messengers. Their heads were cut off and nailed above the Ploče gate, both to reassure Ottoman opinion and to vent Dubrovnik's own irritation with these persistant nuisances.[91] In 1604 and 1605, when the Senate's reaction to vigorous uskok activity can be traced both in diplomatic instructions and in the clandestine measures recorded in another fragment of the Secreta Rogatorum, it can be seen that although the Ragusan authorities maintained contact with the uskoks whenever possible, the mobilization of troops against violation of their territory was a constant preventive measure.[92]

It was hardly surprising, under such circumstances, that the uskoks often regarded Venice and Dubrovnik as open allies of the Ottomans and therefore as their own enemies. The Ragusan Senate reported as much after their violent clash with the uskok harambašas in 1596: "They regard us as they do the Turks themselves."[93] (This was an attitude no doubt reinforced by Dubrovnik's legal position as a protectorate of the Ottoman Empire.) Throughout the sixteenth century the uskoks maintained

[90]H.A.D., Secreta Rogatorum, 1: 113; Lettere di Levante, 21: 21–22, 24.

[91]H.A.D., Lettere di Ponente, 8: 1–3 a tergo; Lettere di Levante, 39: 43–44.

[92]H.A.D., Secreta Rogatorum 3: 36'; 10–10'; and compare Acta Consilii Rogatorum 57: 62–64; 80: 52–53'. For reactions to Dubrovnik's attempts to win aid against the uskoks through diplomatic action, see I.Ö. H.K.R., Croatica, fasc. 12, 1604, Feb. No. 37; Lopašić, *Acta historiam confinii*, vol. 1, pp. 320–23; Horvat, *Monumenta uscocchorum*, vol. 2, p. 66.

[93]In H.A.D., Lettere di Levante, 39: 43'.

that the agents of Venice and Dubrovnik were not their real enemies—it was not until the early seventeenth century that uskok antagonism toward Venice began to smack of political opposition to the Republic's hegemony in the Adriatic. Instead, it was only to the extent that these agents came between the uskoks and their true enemy, the Turk, that they were subject to uskok violence. As Christian states, the Republics of St. Mark and St. Blaise ought to have aided the struggle against the infidel, or so the uskoks claimed, ignoring the political and economic pressures that made such a policy impossible. Ingenuously or not, the uskoks operated under the assumption that their ideal of the *antemurale* was shared by their Christian neighbors and that the infidel was the common enemy. Writing to the Ragusan Senate about some gunpowder that had been confiscated from them, the uskoks protested, "We were not keeping the said powder for any act of treachery against your lord-ships, but were holding it for our enemy and for yours, that is [the enemy] of the Christian faith."[94] This attitude would be most clearly expressed at the turn of the sixteenth century in a series of uskok pro-posals and pledges that they would not harm Venetian subjects if they were not prevented from raiding against the Turk. When these putative allies failed to accept the uskoks' methods of dealing with the common enemy, and in fact took up arms to prevent uskok actions, the uskoks reacted as to a betrayal of the Christian (and uskok) struggle against the Ottomans.

This uskok formulation of their relations to the neighboring Christian states is reflected—on the whole—in uskok actions. They rarely directed their raids primarily against the territory or subjects of Venice or Du-brovnik but, rather, in passing through these territories on their way to Ottoman areas, they provoked retaliation. Direct attacks on Venetian or Ragusan representatives and troops were most often a reaction to suc-cessful actions against the uskoks and were expressed in terms of righ-teous vengeance for an affront to uskok life and honor (as in the Daničić affair), as well as for the betrayal of the Christian cause. Revenge as an obligation to those who had been killed or captured was the justification for many of the attacks on Venetian officials or Venetian subjects—from an incident in 1542, when sixty uskoks tried to capture the Rector of Šibenik, "wishing to avenge themselves for the death dealt to nine of their relatives from Senj,"[95] to the 1612 kidnaping of the Provveditore of Krk, in retaliation for the seizure of an uskok leader.[96]

A certain sense of social injustice in the face of their wealthy and

[94]In H.A.D., Diplomata et Acta XVII st., 71/1–2126/1 (28 May 1610).

[95]In *Commissiones et relationes venetæ*, vol. 2, p. 158.

[96]A.S.V., Provveditori da Terra e da Mar, 1313: 6 June 1612; 17 Aug.1612. See Chapter 8 for further details.

powerful opponents can occasionally be heard in the uskoks' remarks. In 1569 uskoks boarded a ship bound for Hvar, and loaded with biscuit on the account of the Signoria. One of the passengers reported the scene: "They began to ask if there were Turks or Jews aboard, and seeing that there were not, asked who owned the biscuit. When they were told it was on the account of St. Mark, they said, 'St. Mark is rich, he has plenty of money, and we are poor men . . . and are dying of hunger' and they began to unload the biscuit in sacks."[97] There is more than a little sarcasm in these remarks. The imperial winged lion of Venice and St. Mark was scarcely a symbol of the equitable redistribution of wealth in the Adriatic. Yet this attitude is not often heard—more often the uskoks' acts were expressed in terms of religious and political opposition to the Republic of Venice.

The standard of St. Mark and other symbols of Venetian power looted from state galleys were more than once burned on Senj's main square in a display of contempt. At first a reaction to specific circumstances and rising out of Venetian intervention in the uskok struggle with the Turk, hostility to Venetian authority in the Adriatic had become a constant element in uskok attitudes by the end of the sixteenth century. In 1616 the Provveditore Generale recorded his concern that the children of Senj, some five hundred under the age of thirteen, growing up in a period of warfare between Venice and the uskoks, would acquire "an evil disposition toward the interests of the Republic, as can easily be imagined."[98] But by 1616 this "evil disposition" toward the Republic had long been ingrained among the uskoks. The memory of Venetian blockades, battles, and executions joined with the idea of revenge for a betrayal of Christianity had become a more than adequate justification for attacks on Venetian authority in the eyes of the uskoks. "They believe the damages they inflict on the possessions and subjects of Your Serenity to be justified," Vettor Barbaro reported in 1601, "because Venice prevents them from going to attack the Turks, and they hold this doctrine because it is taught and preached to them by their friars and priests, who are ignorant and iniquitous rogues."[99]

Their anti-Ottoman stance and their distrust of Venetian and Ragusan authority in the Adriatic made the uskoks obvious allies for any movement against either. On several occasions Ragusan renegades planning an attack on the Ottomans sought uskok aid, both to fight the Turk and to punish Dubrovnik for its lack of enthusiasm for such crusades. In 1547 a Ragusan, Miha Bučinčić (Bucignola), was to have led an attack on the

---

[97]In H.A.Z., Spisi zadarskih knezova, Ettore Tron, 1569–71: 440–41' (12 Apr. 1570).
[98]In *Commissiones et relationes venetæ*, vol. 6, p. 255.
[99]In H.A.Z., Fond Šime Ljubića, 2/33: 281'.

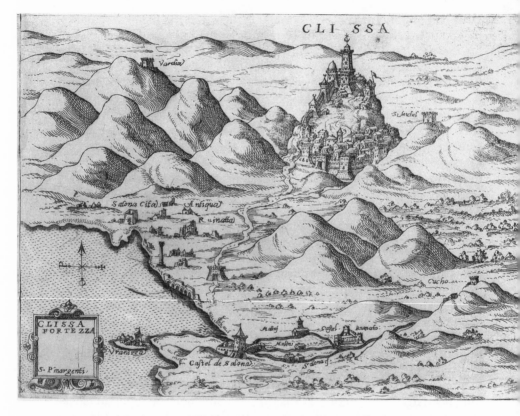

4. A view of the fortress of Klis in Ottoman hands (crowned by the crescent) and its
environs, from *Isole che son da Venetia nella Dalmatia et per tutto l'Arcipelago* (Venice:
Simon Pinargenti, 1573). (By permission of the British Library.)

Neretva estuary and Ragusan Ston at the head of some seven to eight
hundred uskoks, with the blessings of the Habsburgs. Again in 1611–12
two noble Ragusans, Marin Rastić (de Resti) and Jakob Đorđić (Giorgi)
imprisoned in Dubrovnik for their part in smuggling arms to rebellious
Christians in Hercegovina, fled to Senj, whence they returned to pillage
Ragusan and Ottoman territory at the head of uskok bands.[100] But the
uskoks' most dramatic involvement in such a movement came in 1596,
when opposition to both Ottoman and Venetian rule was united in the
attempt to retake Klis.

Just before sunrise on Palm Sunday, 7 April 1596, Ivan Alberti, a Split

---

[100]H.A.D., Lamenti politici, 6: 22–25'; Foretić, *Povijest Dubrovnika*, vol. 2, p. 76; A.S.V.,
Provveditori da Terra e da Mar, 1313: 16 Apr. 1612; 8 Aug. 1612.

patrician, with some forty supporters from Split and Trogir and a unit of eighty uskoks from Senj were secretly admitted to the fortress by co-conspiritors in Klis. They succeeded in completely overwhelming resistance within the fortress by the next day, with the aid of a further three hundred uskoks. These then returned to Senj with the Ottoman captives, leaving some seventy uskoks and a force of men from nearby Poljica to hold Klis. The Habsburg standard and a banner with the cross were unfurled over the ramparts, and the uskoks further adorned the walls with the heads of the Ottoman defenders killed in the attack.[101]

The people of Dalmatia and of Bosnia hailed the success of the conspirators with joy, but the Ottomans reacted quickly. By May some ten thousand Ottoman troops had gathered below Klis. In addition, the Signoria, concerned for good relations with the Porte and not at all pleased at the prospect of a Habsburg stronghold controlling access to the newly expanded port of Split, closed the Dalmatian borders to all supplies and reinforcements for the Christian troops in Klis and sent a fleet to observe the proceedings. Furthermore, Venice issued strict orders forbidding the inhabitants of Dalmatia to aid the uskoks and their allies in Klis in any way. The occupiers of Klis were soon desperate, with few supplies, little water, and no way of obtaining reinforcements, for no effective plan of operation had been conceived beforehand. A hastily recruited relief force, made up of uskoks from the Croatian Littoral and troops from Karlovac under the command of General Lenković, was badly beaten by superior Ottoman forces. Seeing the Christian rout, the Ottoman subjects on whose revolt the Klis plan was predicated failed to rise. Those who had been pressed into the Ottoman camp made no effort to aid the relief forces. Klis could no longer hold out against overwhelming odds, and by 29 May the garrison was forced to withdraw. Many of the Venetian and Ottoman subjects who had aided in the venture, fearing retaliation, fled with the uskoks to Senj. The next day the Ottomans again entered Klis.

The extent of Dalmatian participation in the Klis conspiracy and the reactions of its subjects to the capture and loss of the fortress opened the Signoria's eyes to Dalmatia's willingness to aid the uskoks and the Habs-

---

[101]The most important documents have been published in Tomić, *Građa za istoriju pokreta na Balkanu protiv Turaka*; Lopašić, *Acta historiam confinii*, vol. 1; H. Noflatscher and E. Springer, "Studien und Quellen zu den Beziehungen zwischen Rudolf II. und den bosnischen Christen," *Mitteilungen des österreichischen Staatsarchivs* (Vienna), 36 (1983): 31–82. Monographs include Tomić, *Grad Klis*; Gunther Rothenberg, "Christian Insurrections in Turkish Dalmatia, 1580–1596," *Slavonic and East European Review* (London), 40 (1961–62); E. Springer, "Kaiser Rudolf II., Papst Clemens VIII. und die bosnischen Christen: Taten und Untaten des Cavaliere Francesco Antonio Bertucci in kaiserlichen Diensten in den Jahren 1594 bis 1602," *Mitteilungen des Österreichischen Staatsarchivs* (Vienna), 33 (1980): 77–105.

burgs against the Turk and against Venice. The Republic was determined to put a stop to sentiments so detrimental to its interests. In the aftermath of the siege, the Provveditore Generale took only moderate measures against those rebellious Venetian subjects who had participated in the affair, balancing the need to show the border Ottomans the depth of official disapproval against the fear of inciting further opposition in the province.[102] Nevertheless, the Venetian authorities vigorously pursued the clergy who had been involved with the uskoks and the Klis conspirators against the orders of the Signoria, both because of their disobedience to the secular authorities and because their support reinforced the uskoks' claims to be fighting a holy war, giving them added prestige in the eyes of Dalmatia. The bishops of Šibenik and Korčula were expelled from their sees, and several priests and friars were arrested for their ties with the uskoks. Whatever the justice of Venetian charges that these priests had defied secular authority and merited punishment, the general opinion was that the Signoria was "persecuting those who had supported the conquest of Klis and who desired to see the Turks driven out of the borders," according to the Ventian emissary to Rome.[103]

The events around Klis in 1596 had a powerful emotional impact on Senj. Long afterward, the most valued items in the Senj cathedral treasury were the great keys to the Klis citadel, carried away in the final retreat and kept as a pledge of an eventual return. At least eighty-four uskoks, including both stipendiati and venturini, had died in the final clash with the Ottomans under the walls of the fortress, the most prominent among the dead being the Bishop of Senj himself. Those who survived, especially those who fled to Senj and joined the uskoks in fear of Ottoman or Venetian punishment, retained their prestige years later. Such warriors were distinguished by the honorific "of Klis" and remembered for their "services to Christianity."[104]

Perhaps Venice's opposition to the liberation of Klis, the obstructions placed in the way of the Western forces, and the subsequent punishment of Venetian subjects involved in the conspiracy left an even greater impression on the uskoks. These events seemed the clearest possible proof

[102]Most of those who were convicted of aid to the uskoks at Klis were sentenced to the galleys. Some of their sentences are recorded in H.A.Z., Arhiv Splita, 140/9: 385'–89, 392–92', 404'. Those ringleaders who survived the fall of Klis escaped Venetian punishment by fleeing to the Habsburg courts.

[103]Tomić, *Grada za istoriju pokreta na Balkanu protiv Turaka*, p. 238; see also A.S.V., Provveditori da Terra e da Mar, 417: Aug. 1596, 29 Aug. 1596, 19 Sept. 1596; A.S.V., Capi del Consiglio dei Dieci, 302: 26 Sept. 1596. The issue is discussed in Tomić, *Grad Klis*, pp. 249–72, and Ante Belas, "Sukob između šibenskog biskupa Bassusa i mletačkog providura Mora zbog murterskog župnika godine 1596," *Jadranski dnevnik* (Split), 4/, no. 84 (1937): 2–3.

[104]Horvat, *Monumenta uscocchorum*, vol. 1, p. 372; Ljubić, "Prilozi za životopis"; Lopašić, *Acta historiam confinii*, vol. 2, p. 38.

of the Signoria's complicity with the Ottoman enemies of Christendom, and the uskoks blamed the loss of Klis on Venetian betrayal. After 1596 uskok infringements of Venetian authority redoubled and the uskoks' anti-Venetian acts and attitudes acquired more obviously political over-tones. By the early seventeenth century, perhaps partly under the influ-ence of Habsburg and papal claims to freedom of navigation in Venice's gulf, some uskoks openly began to contest the right of the Republic to control the Adriatic. In opposition to the Venetian claim of *mare nostrum* the uskoks asserted their own right "to defend and to hold our Adriatic sea," which the Venetians rule "by force." Not only did they contest Venice's supremacy in the Adriatic, both in their acts and in words, but at the same time they echoed the statements of the Croat nobles of the coastal communes in advancing a claim to Dalmatia as "our homeland" and previously a part of the Croatian-Hungarian kingdom, "although for the time being in [Venice's] power."[105]

In spite of the uskoks' deeply held distrust and resentment of the Serenissima's hegemony in the area and a corresponding impatience in Dalmatia with the rule of Venice and the threat of the nearby Ottomans, the uskoks never led a rebellion against the authority of Venice. Their success in the attempt to seize Klis in 1596 had brought them widespread respect, admiration, and aid from all ranks of Dalmatian society and from a large part of the Ottoman Christian population. For a short time the hope of changes in the rule of the hinterland and in Dalmatia united these people—regardless of other tensions—in support of the uskoks and their masters, the Habsburgs. Yet the uskoks could not survive without constant plunder—and this coalition could not hold together once uskok raids alienated the citizens and merchants of the coastal towns. The Rector of Šibenik, the year after the failure to free Klis, reported the collapse of this union with evident relief. The common people, he noted, were eager to proceed against the Turks, "but never against the uskoks; and if the uskoks had not begun to abuse and offend the townspeople of substance, even to their death, they would be mas-ters of their wills as well; but because these have been touched in their goods and on occasion in their lives, now they are somewhat disgusted; but had things been different the well-being of the uskoks would have been the same as their own to them."[106]

Merchants and Cities

In the sixteenth century, the Adriatic, the uskoks' hunting ground, formed a great south-north passage linking the markets of the Muslim

[105]In Lopašić, *Acta historiam confinii*, vol. 3, p. 437.
[106]In *Commissiones et relationes venetæ*, vol. 5, p. 223.

East with those of the West—Venice above all. Land and sea routes from the Levant converged here. Through the Straits of Otranto came galleys and roundships from Smyrna, Alexandria, and Constantinople with foodstuffs, spices, fine textiles, and all the wares of the East; at the estuary of the Neretva and later at Split the overland caravan routes unloaded not only the wax, honey, and hides of the Balkan hinterland but also raw material and goods from farther afield in the Ottoman Empire. As well as flowing north from the Ottoman territories, goods were also carried south, bringing Western manufactures and materials to Ottoman markets and beyond. It was not only Venetian merchantmen that carried these goods to and fro. All the Christian fleets that plied up and down the Adriatic had a stake in trade with the infidel. Venice's two great rivals in the Adriatic were the Ragusans, orchestrating caravan trade out of the Balkan hinterland and shipping it under the flag of St. Blaise, and the subjects of the Pope, sailing out of Ancona. The Serenissima's trade with the Turk, abruptly halted in the war years of 1571–73, was quickly taken over by Ragusan ships, to Venetian dismay. Who could afford to reject the profits of this flourishing trade with the infidel? Even the popes, with an eye to their tariffs, repeatedly extended their protection to the Levantine Jews who shipped their merchandise through Ancona.[107] In 1586, when these Jews threatened to remove their trade because Christian pirates repeatedly seized their cargoes, Sixtus V declared that both Jews and Christians trading with the Ottomans should be permitted to ship their merchandise without impediment as long as they were not dealing in contraband.[108]

Regardless of the extent of Ottoman trade or even the papal protection extended to it, the uskoks considered the infidels' merchandise fair booty. Like the Knights of Malta, the Tuscan Knights of St. Stephan, and the Spanish ships out of Naples and Sicily, it was above all the cargoes of Turks and Jews that the uskoks sought in their raids on Adriatic shipping, whether they were carried on Christian ships or not.[109] Their answer throughout the century to the protests of Christian merchants and their governments would be that of Captain Ivan Lenković of Senj in 1542: "The Illustrious Signoria has neither art nor part in this affair, because the goods all belong to the infidels, and the infidel prisoners are

---

[107]*Libri commemoriali*, vol. 25, pp. 51–52, gives the papal briefs of 1543, 1581, and 1586.

[108]In *Magnum bullarium romanum*, vol. 4, pt. 3, pp. 265–67; A.S.V., Provveditore Sopraintendente alla Camera dei Confini, 303: 18 June 1588. See also Tenenti, *Piracy*, pp. 38–39.

[109]Their hunt for cargoes owned by Jews, in particular, is graphically illustrated in the insurance claims published by Tenenti, *Naufrages, corsaires et assurances maritimes*. Identifying the Jewish merchants with the aid of the analysis in B. Blumenkranz ("Les juifs dans le commerce maritime de Venise," *Revue des études juives*, 120 (1961): 143–51), one discovers that although Jews represented only 3.5 percent of all the insurees in these records, they appear in at least 25 percent of the cases of uskok raids.

also subjects of the Turk. . . . As far as I am concerned, the subjects of the Signoria will not be molested, but the infidel Turks and their subjects will not be safe, wherever they may be." He goes on to state an attitude that would also be expressed by the uskoks in response to Habsburg claims of political necessity. "My king can command me to do whatever His Majesty pleases, but if he orders me not to harm the infidels, and to give back that which I have taken and intend to take whenever and wherever I can, I would rather lose my head than obey him."[110]

The uskoks boarded ships wherever they could stop them: at sea if these ships were slow to flee, but more often at anchor in a bay or port. Resistance merely aroused their suspicion of the passengers. "If you are Christians don't fight, if you are Turks take up your arms!" cried out the sixty uskoks who approached a ship sailing from Kotor in July 1599. When the Kotor crew replied that they should stand off, they immediately began to fire on their victim.[111] On boarding, the uskoks demanded to know who owned the cargo, whether it belonged to Christians, Turks, or Jews, so that they could make their choice of the booty. Sometimes they even presented a document, issued by the Captain of Senj or some other official of the Military Frontier, permitting them to go out to raid the infidel, as proof of their license to plunder Turkish goods.[112]

The uskoks seem to have expected the Christian captains and passengers both to cooperate and to share their belief that such plunder was not only permissible but praiseworthy. Some in fact did, even if prudence forbade an open expression of support. There is a burlesque air about some of these encounters, with the uskoks and the mariners settling the transaction between themselves with a minimum amount of inconvenience, over the protests of the merchant passengers. (And if the cargo was insured, why should they risk their lives in its defense?)[113] Some captains were openly in league with the uskoks. For a time the sailors of Perast were notorious for delivering their cargoes into the hands of Senj, where there were a number of their countrymen. In January 1581 a Perast ship, which had failed to take the precaution of sailing with the Venetian galleys from point to point, was boarded by uskoks. The Muslim merchants on board wanted to flee, but the captain, Nicolò de Stefano of Perast, said, "Don't worry, we have made a treaty with the uskoks and the Turks." The nature of this treaty was revealed soon enough—the ship sailed to Senj, where the Muslims were made captive and tied up and all their goods seized, while the sailors disem-

---

[110]In *Commissiones et relationes venetæ*, vol. 2, p. 163.
[111]In A.S.V., Provveditori da Terra e da Mar, 922: 3 July 1599.
[112]H.A.Z., Arhiv Korčule, 808: 392–400 (July 1570).
[113]See Alberto and Branislava Tenenti, *Il prezzo del rischio: L'assicurazione mediterranea vista da Ragusa (1563–1591)* (Rome, 1985).

barked to eat, drink, and celebrate with the uskoks. When Venetian authorities picked up the Perast captain some time later, he confessed that he had received 473 hides and a bale of wool as his share in the booty. (He then had the insolence to write to Ancona asking the Muslim merchants, by then released, to intercede on his behalf. They refused indignantly.) The Provveditore dell'Armata noted in his report that "it isn't the first time that these [Peraštani] have done something of this sort."[114] Other captains and crews cooperated from fear, and some resisted, braving the uskoks' wrath. When in 1591 a group of uskoks boarded a Ragusan ship returning from Ancona, they took some goods belonging to Jewish merchants and slit open all the letters they found with their daggers (looking for money or information, the witnesses thought). When the captain complained that not even Turks would act in such a way, one uskok, deeply offended, gave him several heavy blows.[115]

It would be foolish to expect, under these conditions, that the uskoks took only plunder that was strictly legitimate—though in their eyes legitimacy may have had a considerably looser definition than plunder belonging only to Muslims and Jews. The goods of Christian merchants when taken on Ottoman territory were always claimed as just booty by the uskoks (though sometimes against the protests of their superiors). The claim to loot Muslims and Jews, however, was by no means merely a transparent excuse to raid all and sundry alike. Often there are references to the uskoks' demands to see the bills of lading (*libro del carico*), which they used to separate out the goods they would take.[116] Repeatedly the merchandise belonging to Christians was left aside, returned, or stored in Senj until it could be either reclaimed or pronounced just booty. In 1594, Folco Portinari, a Florentine merchant, received nineteen bales of cordovan and two sacks of wax from a Ragusan ship plundered by the uskoks: "The insurers guess that because this was Florentine merchandise, the uskoks didn't wish to meddle with it, but they took all the rest."[117]

The uskoks were sometimes skeptical of the captain's identification of his cargo and of his bills of lading. Uskoks boarded one small vessel in a

---

114In A.S.V., Archivio dei Baili Veneti a Constantinopoli, 305: 11 and 27 Jan. 1580 (m. v.); 11 Feb.1580 (m.v.); 4 Apr. 1581.

115H.A.D., Diversa Cancellariae, 181: 114–15' a tergo (30 Dec. 1591).

116Giovanni of Fermo describes the plunder of the roundship *Contarina* on Christmas Eve in 1575, when the uskoks used the bills of lading to identify the goods of Turks, Jews, and Ragusans (with whom they were feuding at the time) (Rački, "Prilog za poviest hrvatskih uskoka," p. 193).

117In T. Popović, ed., *Pisma Bartolomeu Borđaniju (1593–1595)*, Spomenik Srpske akademije nauka i umetnosti, 124, Historical Sciences section, 3 (Belgrade, 1984), p. 95; for other examples, see Horvat, *Monumenta uscocchorum*, vol. 1, p. 79; Ivić, "Prilozi za povijest," pp. 302–3; and Lopašić, *Acta historiam confinii*, vol. 2, pp. 14–15.

port of Mljet in 1570 and told the captain, "You have goods of Turks and Jews on board." They demanded the bills and, so the captain testified, "having seen them, without having understood them, or even having read them," began to unload the cargo into their barks. The captain protested that the bales of merchandise belonged to men of Kotor and Dubrovnik, but the uskoks claimed not to believe him.[118] This seems a straightforward case of the deliberate flouting of uskok standards of legitimate plunder—their claim to seek only the goods of Turks and Jews a mere sham.

Nevertheless, a close look at cases in which the uskoks seem to plunder Christian merchants in defiance of this code may reveal motives other than greed for loot. "We well know," wrote Fra Cipriano Guidi, a Dominican monk sent to Rome as an uskok representative in 1592, "that in the markets of Italy the sacred cross is placed on the bales belonging to Turks and to Jews; we well know that the clerks have two books, one real and one falsified."[119] Such subterfuges were often used in an attempt to preserve these merchants from uskok attentions. In April 1590 uskoks from Senj climbed aboard a galleon sailing from Hvar, asking, "Where are the goods of the Turks?" The captain insisted that only fifty-three bales in the hold belonged to Turks and that the rest of the cargo was in the names of Christians. "They didn't wish to believe me, but wanted to see the cargo lists, and finally had the goods unloaded into their barks, and then, after much discussion between the uskoks and their leaders, returned forty bales belonging to Ottavio dall'Oglio and five bales of Antonio Facchinotto." The uskoks had been right to be skeptical. Their final booty included the fifty-three bales first identified as belonging to a Turk, Josuf of Mostar, as well as fifty-seven bales of wax and cordovan belonging to another Muslim, some unspecified goods, the property of a Jewish merchant, and twenty-four bales apparently belonging to two Christians, Marco da Rado and Ivan Matijašović.[120]

"However, we think that if the occasional bale contains goods belonging to Christians," said the same uskok representative in 1592, "nevertheless our justification does not lose its vigor."[121] Other, farther-reaching reasons, the uskoks felt, justified their seizing Christian merchandise. Every year, according to Fra Cipriano, the Bishop of Senj publicly read the bull on excommunication, *In Coena Domini*. After the article excommunicating and anathemizing "pirates, corsairs, and bandits of the sea,"

---

[118]In H.A.Z., Arhiv Korčule, 808: 392–400 (July 1570).

[119]In Leva, *Legazione di Roma*, p. 141. The sacred crosses placed on the bales refer to the merchants' identifying marks. Many Muslim and Jewish merchants used ciphers incorporating symbols such as the crescent or the Star of David.

[120]A.S.V., Archivio dei Baili Veneti a Constantinopoli, 305: 22 Apr.1590.

[121]In Leva, *Legazione di Roma*, p. 141.

there was a section that the uskoks felt had more relevance to their raids, excommunicating all those who "export and convey to the Saracens, Turks, or other enemies of the name of Christ . . . horses, arms, iron, cordage, iron implements, tin, steel, every other sort of metal, or instruments of war, ship timbers, hemp, ropes, either of that same hemp or of any other sort of material, or material of any other kind, with which [these enemies] could attack Christians and Catholics."[122]

This threat of excommunication could not prevent the development of a flourishing contraband trade with the Levant, a trade that because of its nature appears in the records only fragmentarily. In 1574, for example, a ship from Venice for Syria was forced by a storm to put into Ancona, where she was found to be laden with contraband copper to the value of 150,000 ducats.[123] This was contraband on a large scale, but there was a smaller trade in prohibited goods on the Balkan border, particularly in arms. The Ragusans were especially suspected of supplying their Ottoman suzerain with Western implements of war, and for this reason sometimes found it difficult to make a large purchase of such goods. In 1573 the Ragusan Senate, finding Ancona unwilling to supply the city with arquebuses and halberds, reassured the Pope that the weapons were for the city's own defense and that care would be taken that they not leave the city.[124] Nevertheless, the uskoks claimed that "as far as Senj along the Adriatic coast the Turks are armed with Italian arms by the Ragusans, and in particular we know certain merchants who will give so many guns for so many oxen."[125] Contraband of this sort—guns, metals, war matériel—was certainly legitimate spoil for the defenders of the Christian border.

The bull *In Coena Domini*, however, was open to a wider interpretation: any material that could be used against the Christians was prohibited merchandise. In this light, Fra Cipriano could portray textiles, grain, practically anything as supplies that strengthened the Ottoman Empire to the detriment of the Christian West. "We understand from our priests that it is permissible to take the provisions that are exported to the aid of the enemy. . . . Since the Jews and the Christian merchants carry supplies to our enemy . . . we do not believe that in taking these supplies which go to the enemy we commit any error."[126] His analysis goes on to justify the interruption of commerce with the Ottomans by claiming that

---

[122]In Lucius Ferraris, *Prompta Bibliotheca Canonica*, 8 vols. (Venice, 1766), vol. 3, pp. 280–81.
[123]Braudel, *The Mediterranean*, vol. 1, p. 555. See also Kravjanszky, "Il processo degli Uscocchi," pp. 262–65, for further details on Venetian contraband.
[124]H.A.D., Diplomata et Acta XVI st. 466/16: 3 Jan.1573.
[125]In Leva, *Legazione di Roma*, p. 141.
[126]Quoted in Kravjanszky, "Il processo degli Uscocchi," pp. 260–61, a section of Fra Cipriano's report not printed in Leva, *Legazione di Roma*.

such trade did nothing but weaken the West in comparison with the Ottoman Empire. "Ask yourself what the merchants give to the Turk? Gold, silver, cloth, iron, steel, and other things that serve the military. What do they bring to the West? Cotton, pepper, cinnamon, cloves, jewels, pearls, and such things."[127]

Although this legalistic interpretation served as a justification for their raids, it seems unlikely that the uskoks themselves shared the suspicion of international trade which Fra Cipriano voiced. After all, the entire economy of Senj was based on trade. The Christian merchants on whom they preyed were Senj's competitors for the resources of Adriatic commerce, and the forcible seizure of their cargoes served, in a way, to redress the disadvantages under which the uskoks operated. How should they resist looting these ships when by doing so they not only lined their purses but also carried out the duties of the *antemurale Christianitatis* preached to them by such pastors as Fra Cipriano?[128]

Not surprisingly, the merchants of the Adriatic viewed the actions of the uskoks with alarm, although a few entrepreneurs turned uskok activities to their own benefit. Some acted as brokers between the uskoks and their victims; for example, traveling between Senj, Dalmatia, and the Ottoman territories they negotiated on behalf of Ottoman captives in return for a percentage of the ransom price. Others made a profit by buying up uskok booty at low prices and reselling it. In general, however, the merchants of the border area were more likely to lose than to profit from the uskoks' actions. Furthermore, it was not only direct uskok attack that harmed those who lived by trade. The slackening of Ottoman exports through the Dalmatian towns in the face of uskok attacks on the caravans also injured Dalmatian merchants. These raids

[127]In Leva, *Legazione di Roma*, p. 142. Fra Cipriano goes on to develop this theme in more detail: "What need do the Christian religion and the Western princes have, to preserve the Catholic faith and their states, of such merchandise, which serves for nothing but lust, gluttony, and pride, three mortal sins? . . . As many men in the west are occupied in making these goods salable as are occupied in wars against the infidels, in agriculture, and in other exercises more necessary to republics. . . . On the other hand, who does the Turk occupy in producing the pepper, cloves, and the other things he exports to the Christians, if not women and children, reserving the men for the army and for agriculture?" (ibid.)

[128]It was said in 1593 that Fra Cipriano had been sent to present this argument to the Pope by the uskoks themselves, without having a commission from the Archduke. He was seized by the office of the Inquisition, apparently at the instance of the Signoria, which found this use of canon law to defend the uskoks extremely disturbing, but he either escaped or was released, and he returned to Croatia with a Venetian price on his head. There he continued to act as an uskok advocate, gaining influence with the Hofkriegsrat. The Venetian Council of Ten tried to have him assassinated, apparently with little success. He was involved in the plans to take Klis in 1596, but his later fate is unknown. See Kravjànszky, "Il processo degli uscocchi," pp. 260–62; Minucci, *Storia degli uscocchi*, pp. 234–35; Contarini, *Le historie venetiane*, p. 328; Lamansky, *Secrets d'état de Venise*, vol. 1, pp. 105–8, 488–90; Springer, "Kaiser Rudolf II., Papst Clemens VIII. und die bosnischen Christen," p. 95; Ljubić, "O Markantunu Dominisu," p. 166.

could not be regarded with equanimity by the Dalmatian cities, whose very survival, after the loss of most of their agricultural districts to the Ottomans, depended on trade from the hinterland. In spite of their fear of and hostility toward the Muslim conquerors, the merchants of Dalmatia knew that their daily bread was contingent on peace with their Ottoman neighbors. The raids of the uskoks, no matter how great an emotional response they aroused among the border Christians in times of crisis, put their commerce and their livelihood in peril. Dalmatia's complaints to the Signoria about the uskoks were formulated in these economic terms. As Gregorio Grisogono, noble and merchant of Zadar, lamented to the Venetian board of trade, the Cinque Savii alla Mercanzia, in 1588, the uskoks caused trade between Venice and the Levant to avoid the Dalmatian coast; the income from the islands was reduced by their attacks; the tariffs of the ports of Zadar, Šibenik, Trogir, Split, and the Neretva delta were no longer abundant; the Ottoman caravans, fearing the uskok-infested passes, had diminished.[129] Others pointed out that uskok raids had devastated the hinterland economy, making less grain and fewer cattle available for export to the Dalmatian cities. In some cases Ottoman subjects sent what grain there was as ransoms or tribute to Senj, "valuing it at a higher price than that current," according to the Rector of Zadar, with serious consequences for the coastal towns that depended on this grain trade for their sustenance.[130]

Few urban merchants of Dalmatia put their hopes in a crusade against the Turk, even during the Klis affair. Mavro Vetranović, a Ragusan Benedictine (and the son of a merchant), saw the uskoks as potential soldiers in a war of liberation, but his views on this subject were shared by few. His Vlach sybil was not echoed by the Dalmatian merchants when she sang:

> U istok spravite, vodite uskoke,
> ter Cipar branite i ostale otoke
> i s vašom vojnicom, višnjega boga rad,
> oružnom desnicom primite Carigrad.

(Turn to the East, lead the uskoks, defend Cyprus and the other isles, and as the work of God on high, with your army and strong right hand, seize Constantinople.)[131]

The Dalmatian merchants were more likely to have recognized their own apprehensions in the words of Petar Hektorović when, in a greeting

[129]A.S.V., Senato, Secreta, Materie miste notabili, 27: Zadar, 1588.
[130]*Commissiones et relationes venetæ*, vol. 5, p. 107.
[131]In Vetranić [Vetranović], *Pjesme Maura Vetranića Čavčića*, pp. 219–20.

to Nikola Nalješković (another Ragusan merchant), he spoke of the uskoks as merely one of a number of other robbers and evildoers whose acts brought inconvenience rather than salvation:

> Uskoci daše trud i zlocinci ini
> Hvala ti na svem bud', moj bože jedini
> koji nas od njih ruk milo obdarova . . .

(Uskoks and other evildoers cause trouble; thanks be to Thee, my only God, who mercifully preserves us from their hands.)[132]

The ports and cities of Dalmatia shared this hostility to the uskoks; as we shall see, the uskoks were more likely to find support among the rural population than in the towns, apart from the allies the uskoks found among the disaffected urban patriciate. The importance of trade to the cities did not allow much sympathy for the uskok threat. Even the ports of the Habsburg Littoral, which tried to use the uskoks against their trade rivals for a time, would eventually find the uskoks a two-edged weapon, harming trade more than they benefited it. The city council and the Captain of Rijeka did not hesitate to use the uskoks as a private army when it was convenient—commissioning uskok barks to harass shipping from their rival, Bakar, or hiring eighty-odd uskoks to strengthen the city's defenses in the face of Venetian attack.[133] But both Trieste and Rijeka found that they paid dearly for the use of the uskoks against Venetian trade competition when blockades and embargoes were raised against them in the 1590s and early 1600s, as well as when Venice took direct action against them with the outbreak of war between the Archduke and the Signoria.[134] Under such circumstances, Rijeka tried to cut its ties to Senj, forbidding uskoks to enter the city to collect supplies or to transport grain from the warehouse to Senj. Rijeka shipbuilders were ordered not to build boats for the uskoks any longer. Rijeka even issued orders to pull down the little ferry house on the other side of the river, to prevent the uskoks from meeting there, presumably to offer

---

[132]In Hektorović, *Ribanje i ribarsko prigovaranje i razlike stvari ine*, p. 244.

[133]A.S., Deželni stanovi za Kranjsko, 293: 1829 (23 Nov. 1611); 293a/1: 307-10 (3 Mar. 1612); H.A.R., Zapisnici sjednica općinskog vijeća u Rijeci, 1593-1607: 79 (7 Feb. 1599).

[134]For Trieste's use of the uskoks in connection with its trade rivalry with Venice and Venetian retaliation, see Tamaro, *Storia di Trieste*, vol. 2, pp. 102, 104ff., and T. Fanfani, "Il sale nel Litorale austriaco dal XV al XVIII secolo: Un problema nei rapporti tra Venezia e Trieste," in *Sale e saline nell'Adriatico (secs. XV–XX)*, ed. A. di Vittorio (Naples, 1981), p. 157. Braudel perhaps overestimates the part Trieste played in encouraging the uskoks (*The Mediterranean*, vol. 1, p. 131). For the relations between Rijeka and Senj, see Gigante,"Rivaltà fra i porti di Fiume e Buccari," p. 178; Fest, "Uskoken und Venezianer in der Geschichte von Fiume;" *Povijest Rijeka* (Rijeka, 1988), pp. 115-19.

their booty to those Rijeka merchants who still found the uskok trade profitable, even if it brought down ruin on the city.[135] The uskoks reacted violently to such insults, abusing and threatening the citizens, picking fights in the streets when they came to Rijeka, and exacting a petty revenge by damaging vines and fruit trees in the fields outside the city.[136] If by their angry actions the uskoks "rendered themselves ungrateful and odious in return for the favors they had received," as the city council put it,[137] they too felt that the citizens of Rijeka had acted ungratefully in accepting armed help in their struggles against their rivals, Venice and Bakar, but scorning the uskoks once their raids became an inconvenience.

The Rural Population of Dalmatia

Venetian records of uskok activities in Dalmatia reveal an apparent paradox. They reported that the uskoks raided throughout Dalmatia, "with no discrimination whatsoever, infesting the sea, the fleets, and the shores, so that no land, village, or island is safe from their hands; killing and pillaging the rich and the poor to their injury and ruin."[138] Nevertheless, year after year, Venetian officials charged with extirpating the uskoks from Dalmatia protested that their task was impossible, not because of the uskoks' numbers or their strength, but because of the support they received from Venice's own subjects in Dalmatia. In 1580 Nicolò Surian, Provveditore dell'armata, reported to the Council of Ten, "Your Excellencies should understand that however many damages of this sort occur, they are all with the knowledge and participation of your own subjects, and that the desire to favor the uskoks is so rooted in their minds that it will be impossible to remedy these injuries completely unless some other provision is made."[139] This "desire to favor the uskoks" found expression in a collaboration between the uskoks and Venice's subjects in Dalmatia, a collaboration that provided the uskoks with shelter, supplies, transportation, information, and reinforcements in their raids, in spite of constant official prohibitions. By 1613, according to Filippo Pasqualigo, Provveditore Generale in Dalmatia, the ordinary

---

[135]H.A.R., Zapisnici sjednica općinskog vijeća u Rijeci, 1593–1607: 63' (21 May 1597), 64' (18 June 1597), 69 (22 Jan.1598, 20 Feb., 1598), 245 (24 Sept. 1605), 251' (3 Apr. 1606), 253' (28 Apr. 1606), 278 (18 July 1607).

[136]Ibid.: 49–49', 63, 102, 245, etc. See also Fest, "Uskoken und Venezianer in der Geschichte von Fiume," for details of uskok relations with Rijeka in the 1590s and 1600s.

[137]In H.A.R., Zapisnici sjednica općinskog vijeća u Rijeci, 1593–1607: 64'.

[138]In *Commissiones et relationes venetæ*, vol. 5, p. 223.

[139]In Horvat, *Monumenta uscocchorum*, vol. 1, p. 388.

inhabitants "are without a doubt more obedient to a single uskok than to the public representatives; so that it can truly be said that excepting the walled cities little sign of the jurisdiction and patronage of Your Serenity remains in the rest."[140] How is one to reconcile this popular support for the uskoks with the widespread reports of their indiscriminate and violent actions in Dalmatia?

The injuries done by the uskoks and the support they received paralleled to a great extent the cleavages in Dalmatian society. Venetian observers did not overlook the element of social differentiation in uskok relations in Dalmatia. They repeatedly noted that although the city people feared the uskoks, the villagers were "so much in league with these wicked people . . . that they go out and traffic with them freely in the fields, completely without suspicion."[141] Another observer, Andrea Gugliemi, linked this differentiation to the social origins of the uskoks: "If the peasants [*contadini*] of the place [Krk] wished to defend themselves with arms they could, but they don't wish to because, as I have said, they are all related, and [the uskoks] do no damage to them, but rather only to those with whom they are not related, who live in the city—the citizens [*cittadini*]."[142] In Dalmatia, as in other bandit-ridden societies from Corsica to China, the uskoks recruited primarily from the countryside, and it was largely the rural population that aided the uskoks against the demands of official authority. Although the uskoks cannot easily be seen as champions of social justice, in their relations with the peasantry of Dalmatia and the hinterland they do to a certain extent fit Hobsbawm's description of social bandits, "peasant outlaws whom the lord and state regard as criminals, but who remain within peasant society, and are considered by their people as heroes . . . , and in any case as men to be admired, helped and supported."[143]

It is the structured social inequalities between privileged and unprivileged, between rich and poor, between town and country, which are usually identified as the basis for "social" banditry, but this is not the only conflict that can divide a community in its attitudes toward crime or brigandage. Political conflict also divided Dalmatian society. In Dalmatia, Venice needed to keep the peace with the Ottomans at all costs. The deeply held hatred for the Muslim conquerors of much of Dalmatian society was in contradiction with this policy. In some ways social cleavages reinforced this division. The wealthy and the urban elite allied with Venice depended for their position and their prosperity on peace and on Ottoman trade. These people were most harmed by uskok attacks and

---

[140]In *Commissiones et relationes venetæ*, vol. 6, p. 188.
[141]In ibid., vol. 5, p. 225.
[142]In A.S.V., Senato, Secreta, Materie miste notabili 27: 11 June 1591.
[143]Hobsbawm, *Bandits*, p. 1.

were most active in opposing them. The rural population, on the other hand, both regularly exposed to the raids of neighboring Ottomans, and subjected to the increasing demands of their landlords in the Dalmatian towns, was united with the uskoks to retaliate against the Ottomans and their allies. But social and political divisions were not entirely identical: as we have seen, many Dalmatian nobles resented their loss of power under Venetian rule. They opposed the alliance between Venice and the Ottomans and looked to the uskoks as allies. Patrician Ragusan rebels, impatient of the policies of their government, also formed ties with the uskoks. Apart from brief alignments, however, the uskoks' interests were usually at odds with those of the wealthy and the politically powerful in Dalmatia—who, after all, were those whose resources made them targets for plunder. Unlike bandit groups elsewhere, forced to seek alliances with the local elites to survive, the uskoks, secure in their position on the Military Frontier, could afford to hold aloof from other patrons. It was more often with the peasants in the countryside, the shepherds, and the fishermen that the uskoks had their closest ties.

But Andrea Gugliemi was exaggerating when he claimed that the uskoks did no damage to the peasantry. The uskoks did cause suffering among the common people of Dalmatia, though to a lesser extent than in the Ottoman hinterland. When the uskoks took bread, wine, one or two sheep, or commandeered a bark, their owners did without. When a villager was reported to the Venetian authorities for sheltering or aiding the uskoks, he was severely punished. The people of Dalmatia, however, were often unwilling to denounce uskok requisitions to the authorities. Shepherds' and fishermen's judicial reports of small-scale plundering in Dalmatia sometimes appear to have been entirely pro forma—to cover themselves against Venetian accusations of complicity with the uskoks. Typically these informers made their reports before the Venetian rector, through a court interpreter, some time after the incident, giving as little information as possible—they did not know who the uskoks were or where they were from. If they admitted to taking money for supplies, it was only because the uskoks had paid "by force."[144] Some of these denunciations, denying any complicity or even acquaintance with the uskoks, strain the reader's credulity. What must the Venetian officials have made of a Trogir night guard's declaration that fifty uskoks had secretly made their way into port without being recognized or challenged and had taken a fully equipped bark—leaving in exchange the precise one they had "stolen" two years previously?[145]

[144]See A.S.V., Provveditori da Terra e da Mar, 1261: 20 July 1592; ibid., 1262: 6 Oct. 1593; H.A.Z., Arhiv Trogira, 25, 27/11, a collection of reports of uskok acts from the 1590s.
[145]H.A.Z., Arhiv Trogira, 25/11: 1481–81' (5 Apr. 1599).

Like people elsewhere, caught between the demands of the state and the pressures exerted by bandits, the Dalmatians recognized the virtues of keeping silent, although this practice was not dignified by any special term, like the *omertà* of the Sicilians. In the face of such sullen lack of cooperation a Venetian representative in Dalmatia complained that "the inhabitants . . . not only make no resistance to their landing, nor pursue them as they ought, but rather hide them, and when they are required by the representatives of Your Serenity to pass on news [of the uskoks], they deny any knowledge, and never reveal it unless after these uskoks have left, a fact that can be seen clearly from the denunciations given to the rectors of the cities, which are all after their departure, which they do either out of fear, as they claim, or more likely because of the benefits and rewards they receive from them."[146] The villagers' silence spoke loudly to those who wished to understand where power resided in the province: it was the uskoks, not the Venetian rectors and provveditori, who were most scrupulously obeyed. But why should this be so?

Observers did not always dismiss the fear inspired by uskok threats. "If you oppose us and our company and persecute us we will burn your houses and massacre you," a group of uskoks asking for supplies told the villagers of Pupnat on Korčula.[147] It was not an empty threat— people the uskoks regarded as traitors were indeed killed and their houses burned, as in a case described by Giovanni Michiel, Capitano contra uscocchi, in which a suspected informer, his wife, and young son were all slaughtered and their cottage leveled by vengeful uskoks.[148] A Dalmatian villager convicted of aiding the uskoks could expect an equally harsh Venetian sentence, yet according to Venetian representatives it was the uskoks' threats that prevailed and forced cooperation: "They would rather suffer exile, the burning of their houses, and the persecution of justice as miscreants; this seeming a lesser punishment to them than to be, as they fear, burned together with their entire family and goods suddenly one night by the uskoks."[149] Uskok retribution was

---

[146]In A.S.V., Senato, Secreta, Materie miste notabili, 27: 12 Mar. 1591. This would not be the only such complaint. Provveditore Generale Nicolò Donà noted in 1599 that "it is not possible to imagine a greater inclination toward these scoundrels among the inhabitants [of Dalmatia], for the uskoks are always perfectly informed of my whereabouts, and I cannot ever extract from them any sure news, and if they do bring me any, it is always too late, and out of step" (in A.S.V., Provveditori da Terra e da Mar, 922: 3 Apr. 1599).

[147]In H.A.Z., Arhiv Korčule, 812: 392–94; 427–27' (28 Jan. 1597).

[148]In *Commissiones et relationes venetæ*, vol. 6, p. 53. Other examples of uskok vengeance are similar: a woman killed and her house burned because she betrayed an uskok hiding place to the Provveditore dell'armata (A.S.V., Provveditori da Terra e da Mar, 417: 26 Sept. 1596); murder of a man on Brač who opposed the uskoks, and threats of arson as vengeance for the release of uskok captives (A.S.V., Capi del Consiglio dei Dieci, Lettere dei Rettori, 301: 6 Jan. 1595).

[149]In *Commissiones et relationes venetæ*, vol. 3, p. 191.

more certain—and the Venetian state could offer little protection. But the uskoks did not pursue an indiscriminate reign of terror in the Dalmatian countryside. Uskok violence was selective, calculated to elicit respect and ensure neutrality, at least, in any conflict with the authorities. No doubt uskok revenge did reduce the temptation to profit by betraying an uskok to the Venetian government. Whether uskok intimidation could command constant, widespread, and active support from the Dalmatian population is another matter.

Terror was not the only principle at work in uskok relations with the rural population. A popularly accepted code of behavior, with limits recognized by both sides, can also be observed. Uskok requisitions provide an example of these principles and of the way they worked in practice. In theory, the uskoks had no desire to harm the inhabitants of Venetian Dalmatia, but they felt that they could justifiably demand supplies for their services in fighting the Turk. In a letter that set out their view of their relations with Venetian Dalmatia in 1600, the vojvodas specified that they would take provisions only when they were "necessary to human life, in case of great need," when they would be paid for.[150] And indeed, the authorities agreed that the uskoks often did pay, "either well or poorly, according to the the resources available to them from their most recent plunder."[151] One Provveditore Generale described the uskoks of Senj, who "go out only to plunder the Turks . . . taking from the subjects of Your Serenity nothing, unless they need it for their own use and sustenance—bread, wine, and similar things—for which they pay more often than not," and distinguished these sharply from the independent Dalmatian uskoks and brigands who rob "with no respect nor distinction whatsoever."[152] In any case, supplying these uskoks with food and wine was strictly prohibited by the Signoria, which made association with the uskoks a capital offense.

A judicial investigation of Francesco Boschaino [Frane Boškin/Baš-čanin?] of the village of Novalja on Pag reveals some of the stresses in the relations between the uskoks, the people who aided them, their neighbors, and the Venetian authorities.[153] In May 1557 shepherds shearing their flocks in the fields on Pag saw a bark and its crew come ashore at the

[150]In a proposal by the vojvodas and the "whole militia of Senj," in A.S.V., Provveditori da Terra e da Mar, 923: 25 Apr. 1600 (enclosure).

[151]Minucci, *Storia degli uscocchi*, p. 223. Dalmatians reporting uskok encounters in the Venetian records repeatedly describe the uskoks' paying for their provisions (see, e.g., A.S.V., Provveditori da Terra e da Mar, 1262: 6 Oct. 1593; other examples in H.A.Z., Arhiv Trogira 25, 27/11).

[152]In *Commissiones et relationes venetæ*, vol. 5, p. 211.

[153]All of this evidence on Francesco Boschaino and his dealings with the uskoks comes from a large collection of testimony accumulated as part of an investigation, dated 14 June 1557, in the papers of Antonio Canale, Rector of Rab (H.A.Z., Arhiv Raba, 1).

inlet called Vojska. They feared that the strangers were the Turkish corsairs who had seized two barks a few days previously farther north up the coast. After several days, when a band of men led by the Vice Rector cautiously approached to investigate, they found that these were uskoks who had been in pursuit of the corsairs and who had been driven ashore by the *bura,* the strong northwest wind. The uskoks had been four days without wine and wished to buy some from the villagers, but no wine was to be had in Novalja, except that belonging to Boschaino, a well-off peasant. He, however, had already refused to sell his wine either to his compatriots or to the patricians in the city. (This was spring, when most of the local wine would have already been consumed, and well before the new harvest. Boschaino could have been keeping it for his own use or hoping to get a better price for it later.) Although he had earlier been on good terms with the uskoks and they had visited his house in Novalja, the uskoks of Senj were harboring a grudge against him. Sometime earlier he had been involved in the capture of an uskok who was then turned over to Venetian justice, and as a result he had been granted permission to bear arms to defend himself against uskok vengeance. When summoned by the uskoks, Boschaino feared to go, but they sent word that there was a relative of his among them and pledged on their honor not to harm him. Boschaino then went and made peace with the uskoks, and returning to town asked the magistrates and the Vice Rector for permission to send them some wine, saying that otherwise they threatened to come and take it themselves. The testimony as to whether this permission was granted is contradictory, though it is clear that the Vice Rector did not want to face battle with the uskoks—"they fight like devils," he told the court. In any case, Boschaino sent a donkey loaded with wine back to the uskoks. No payment was accepted—the gift of wine acted to seal their renewed friendship. The uskoks left at dawn the next morning, when the village was already buzzing with gossip about Boschaino's pact of friendship with the Senjani and the wine he had sent them, in violation of Venetian law and in contradiction of his earlier refusal to sell to the local people of Pag or Rab.

This publicity precipitated the charge against Boschaino—his contacts with the uskoks were public knowledge, and it was impossible to keep the matter quiet, though his previous relations with the uskoks had caused no action (on one earlier occasion he had spent a whole day eating and drinking with them in his house and, in view of several witnesses, had embraced the leader and bid them Godspeed as brothers). The document charging Boschaino denounced the uskoks as "public and most capital enemies of our illustrious lords and banned from their domain, most famous rogues, murderers, and pirates who keep watch constantly, day and night, circling about in order to offend and damage this country and its inhabitants as enemies," and the witnesses paid lip service to the Venetian regulations against the uskoks, but there seems to have been little real aversion to these uskoks among the villagers. When the villagers suspected that the uskok bark held Muslim corsairs, they sent a messenger to recall a departing Venetian brigantine, but when they learned that these were uskoks, they made no attempt to get armed reinforcements from the city, though more than one hundred men could have been put in the field. If there were corsairs in the area, having a bark of uskoks nearby was no bad thing. It was even hinted that others might have sold the uskoks provisions, for several lambs were missing from the Vice Rector's flock, and one shepherd (who had spent the night with the uskoks in amiable conversation, to make sure that they didn't make off with any of his sheep), noted that they were eating roast lamb, which he did not believe was stolen. No one suggested it had come from Boschaino (though some thought he had also sent them bread). Had it been sold to them by another shepherd?

All the witnesses recognized that Boschaino was acting from a mixture of fear and friendship, though they disagreed about which was predominant in this instance. (Attitudes toward Boschaino probably influenced their interpretation of his motives—and the emphasis on his refusal to sell his wine on Pag hints that he had irritated some of his neighbors.) Although he may initially have been acting under compulsion, once it became clear that "all the heroes of Senj who used to wish him ill now wish him well and are friends with him,"[154] the balance of fear and friendship in his dealings with the uskoks could well have tipped the other way. Even if he had not been charged, Boschaino would now have had more to fear from the Signoria, while he could expect to find his dealings with the uskoks rewarded in booty or other favors. Under such circumstances, Boschaino might have been happy to support the uskoks clandestinely. Other similar men and women, more discreet in their contacts with the uskoks and therefore less well recorded in the judicial archives, did aid the uskoks in this way.

As Boschaino's case shows, profit was not the only factor in the relationship between villagers and uskoks. The villagers had to balance the relative weights of profit and loss, fear and friendship, the satisfaction of plundering the Turk and the threat of Venetian retribution, among other factors. In practice, the uskoks often relied on the threat of force, rather than payment, in obtaining supplies, and the villagers of the nearby islands and the coast found their flocks treated as a convenient larder for bands of uskoks who had not been successful in taking Ottoman plun-

[154]Ibid., testimony of Antonio Christophoro de Dominis, noble of Rab, who subsequently had this news from some men of Senj.

der and who could not pay for their provender. This was the main complaint of the villagers of Ražanac, on the border of the Zadar district,
where the uskoks often passed on their way to the Ottoman hinterland.
They did no harm to the village, they reported, except that they ate
without paying. "When they take booty, they pass through our village
with it, and take it all with them, and on those occasions they give us
no trouble; but when they haven't got anything, then they take our
goods."[155] Still, they tolerated the uskok incursions.

Beyond certain limits, however, this behavior would not be accepted.
A telling indication of the existence of mutually recognized limits can be
seen in the accounts of shepherds traveling angrily to Senj to denounce a
wrongdoer before the justices and the assembled uskoks for plundering
an entire flock, rather than only one or two sheep, in the expectation that
justice would be done. This was the case with one Helena of Baška on
Krk, who traveled twice to Senj to complain about excessive uskok raiding, and won the support of a Senj magistrate.[156] An examination of two
uskoks accused of stealing goats and cheese on Rab in 1592, during a
Venetian blockade of Senj, made it clear that such requisitions could be
justified only by necessity. Asked if he knew why he had been arrested,
Pero Crnojević replied that he supposed "it was for his sins over the last
year," which covered a whole series of petty thefts of cheese and livestock from the islands of Rab, Cres, and Krk, not for his own needs, but
to sell, with the profits going to his *patrone*. In particular, he had seized
sixteen animals on Cres, which he had then sold to a shepherd in Vinodol for two lire a head. In contrast, Matija Grmorčić, although he had
induced shepherds on Rab to give him goats and cheese when he found
himself outside Senj with no victuals, sometimes by boasting that he and
his companions were from the ships of Senj, emphasized that although
"this had happened several times, and he had taken the animals, nevertheless that which he did, he did from necessity, to eat and not to sell."
Both were to be punished, but it was Pero Crnojević who was thrown
from a window of the citadel above Senj's main square, "with a chain
around his neck, and left hanging there dead, as an example to the
wicked and a spectacle to the people."[157]

Perhaps we can discover where the limits to acceptable behavior lay by
looking at those who ignored them—for as we have seen not all uskoks
observed them scrupulously. Inevitably some were greedier, or more

[155]In A.S.V., Provveditori da Terra e da Mar, 1321: 8 Nov. 1602 (testimony of two men of
Ražanac).

[156]A.S.V., Provveditore Sopraintendente alla Camera dei Confini, 244: Processus Vegliæ,
Baška, 13 Mar. 1558.

[157]In A.S.V., Provveditori da Terra e da Mar, 1261: 24 Aug. 1592 (enclosing the letter of
General Lenković [6 Aug. 1592] and the two interrogations [5 Aug. 1592]).

sadistic, or primarily anxious to settle personal scores. Certainly there were out-and-out pirates among the uskoks, men who observed no distinctions or limitations. Such men, however, frequently did not last long as uskoks. Quite often they were dealt with by other uskoks, who did not approve of their acts and who could not allow them to endanger their own support among the people. This was the attitude of the vojvodas of Senj who warned the Provveditore Generale in 1598 that they were abroad for the purpose of tracking down "certain evildoers who are pillaging your ports and islands in Dalmatia under our name; when we find them we will take them bound to Senj."[158] Only while the uskoks retained the respect and support of the local people, as they very well knew, could they operate in Dalmatia with impunity.

Attempts to exact ransom from Venetian subjects in Dalmatia went well beyond the limits of acceptable action. Although it was customary for Ottoman subjects captured by uskoks to pay a ransom for their release, Venetian subjects were immune from this imposition.[159] Uskoks who seized Venetian subjects often released them on discovering their mistake[160] or else were warned to do so by more careful comrades ("Oh, leave them alone, they are Christians, and what would our Captain say?").[161] But the occasional Venetian captives knew their rights—and did not hesitate to demand that they be respected, appealing to the uskok vojvodas, the Captain and magistrates of Senj, and the Archduke and Emperor. The loud protests of the men of Poljica, convinced of their claim to immunity from uskok seizure, won them a formal patent, freeing all Poljica captives with no obligation to pay ransom.[162]

The people of Dalmatia sometimes took justice into their own hands against uskoks who were too greedy or too violent. When the uskoks demanded too much, their erstwhile supporters might well lose their patience and join together against them. This was the case with the villagers of Punta Križa on Cres, who had been subjected to repeated uskok demands during a Venetian blockade of Senj. When four uskoks openly plundered the village, going from house to house stripping the people of their "clothes, food to eat, money, and every other thing" and threatening to kill those who defended their poor possessions, the

---

[158]In A.S.V., Provveditori da Terra e da Mar, 922: 20 Feb. 1598. For a further discussion of dissension among the uskoks over the limits of acceptable behavior, see Chapter 8.

[159]This immunity was in several cases cited as evidence that particular villages were or were not under Venetian administration (*Commissiones et relationes venetæ*, vol. 4, p. 149; H.A.Z., Arhiv Trogira, 28/1: 251'–53).

[160]H.A.Z., Arhiv Trogira, 28/1: 252'–53; A.S.V., Provveditore Sopraintendente alla Camera dei Confini, 244, Processus Traugurii: 2 May 1558.

[161]In A.S.V., Archivio dei Baili Veneti a Constantinopoli, 305: 24 Mar. 1583.

[162]Koharić, "Nekoje dukale," pp. 228–32.

villagers banded together to kill them and hung their heads on the pillory.[163]

The usual uskok restraint in requisitioning provisions in Dalmatia could crumble in the face of a desperate need for supplies, and the uskoks could disregard previously recognized limits when they were blinded by rage, particularly when Venetian blockades and pursuit made raids on Ottoman territory impossible. "Since your masters will not let us go to take plunder in the territory of the Turk, we will plunder these islands," the uskoks told the people of Rab in 1598 during a severe Venetian blockade of Senj, "and we will take everything we find on them, and finally, after we have taken the goods, we will butcher you all, the gentlemen together with their sons, and make you slaves, however we please."[164] But not only gentlemen were the victims of these raids— some of the uskoks' fury could fall on their former allies among the peasants as well. Such attacks stripped the uskoks of their most basic claim to legitimacy among the peasantry: that their raids were directed primarily against the common Ottoman enemy. More and more often, from the end of the sixteenth century, the uskoks turned to Istria or the islands for supplies when they were unable to reach Ottoman territory, sorely trying the patience of the villagers. Even in the period of greatest pressure from Venetian forces in the 1590s and early 1600s, however, observers (and the uskoks themselves) continued to claim a degree of cooperation between the people of Dalmatia and the uskoks.[165]

What then was the basis of this long-lasting accommodation between the uskoks and the rural population both of Dalmatia and of the hinterland? Many Venetian observers stress their common natures, "both inclined to plunder and kill."[166] Nicolò Contarini went further in specifying the characteristics the men of the border shared with the uskoks: "Fierce, insidious, no great friends of toil, lacking in cultivation and those arts which serve society and are practiced in honest sweat; so the inhabitants [of Dalmatia and the neighboring regions] are commonly poor, fickle, given to piracy, and vague about blood and the property of others. . . . It is so much a part of their nature to pillage, and so instilled in them since birth, that those things which are universally detested as contrary to every humanity are always praised by them as proper to men of valor."[167] Such comments were often no more than the expression of

---

[163]A.S.V., Provveditore Sopraintendente alla Camera dei Confini, 243: 22 Oct. 1591 (Cres); Horvat, *Monumenta uscocchorum*, vol. 1, p. 64.

[164]In A.S.V., Provveditori da Terra e da Mar, 922: 2 Dec. 1598.

[165]The Venetian *relazioni* of this period continue to be full of such remarks. See for example *Commissiones et relationes venetæ*, vol. 6, pp. 53, 119, 223, 256.

[166]See ibid., vol. 5, p. 30; vol. 6, pp. 53, 119, for representative Venetian views of Dalmatian and uskok savagery.

[167]Contarini, *Le historie venetiane*, p. 324.

an exasperated urban superiority that had little understanding of border realities. But they do hint at a common culture, shared between the uskoks and rural subjects both of Venice and of the Porte, that admired heroism and accepted the use of violence in the pursuit and defense of honor and power. As I argued above, this frontier code owed much to weak state control over the peripheries of the empires and to the values of a pastoral society. Recent research has noted links between pastoralism and banditry in other societies, where aggressive competition over resources, habitual livestock raiding, and socially sanctioned violence provide a context that can breed brigandage.[168]

The uskoks certainly had much in common with the Vlach pastoralists, whose military organization, as we have seen, provided the pattern for the military frontiers under both the Ottomans and the Habsburgs. Many recruits to Senj came from the ranks of these pastoralists and military colonists, and the uskoks found collaborators among them both in Dalmatia and in the Ottoman hinterland. By 1588 cooperation between the uskoks and the recently settled Vlachs of Bosiljina, near Trogir, reached such levels, that the Rector of Trogir was forced to decree that no Vlach was to live in Bosiljina or its environs, on the pain of confiscation of his flocks, in order to break this alliance.[169] Another group of Vlach pastoralists, the Krmpoćani, had a long history of association with the uskoks. In the early years of the seventeenth century a large number of Krmpote families emigrated to the Senj area, where they continued to raid together with the uskoks and on their own. But relations between the uskoks and the pastoralists were not invariably cordial, in spite of their shared values. Even some of the Krmpoćani eventually turned against the uskoks, leaving Habsburg territory to settle in Istria.[170] The uskoks did not hesitate to prey on the Vlachs, whose transhumant flocks, when they descended to the shores in winter, were an important source of uskok booty. Nor did the affinities between the uskoks and the pastoralists prevent the uskoks from taking the side of the sedentary agricultural population on occasion. In 1602 the uskoks were reported to be planning a raid against the Šibenik hinterland because the flocks of the Vlach colonists newly settled on Ottoman territory were doing much

---

[168]D. Moss, "Bandits and Boundaries in Sardinia," *Man* (n.s.), 14 (1979): 477–96; Koliopoulos, *Brigands with a Cause*; Wilson, *Feuding, Conflict and Banditry.*

[169]H.A.Z., Arhiv Trogira, 25/3: 344′–45 (19 Apr. 1588). It appears that such measures were not enough to prevent the cooperation between Bosiljina and the uskoks, for two years later the Venetians were still receiving Ottoman complaints about the aid given to the uskoks by the village (A.S.V., Provveditori da Terra e da Mar: 414, 4 Nov. 1590). Other evidence suggests Bosiljina's ties with the uskoks; see, for example, an interrogation of a Morlach girl taken captive by the uskoks (H.A.Z., Arhiv Trogira, 25/1: 1491–93′ [7 Aug. 1599]).

[170]See Bogumil Hrabak, "Neuspjelo naseljavanje Krmpoćana na Kvarneru, u Istri i Dalmaciji, 1614.–1615. god.," *Jadranski dnevnik* (Split), 12 (1982–85): 365–94.

damage to the fields of the Šibenik district.[171] Shared culture and values did not always meaned shared goals and actions.

More to the point, perhaps, is the Venetian emphasis on ties of kinship between the uskoks and subjects both of the Ottoman Porte and of St. Mark. Many uskoks, particularly those who had only recently left their homes and emigrated to Senj, remained integrated in a network of family relations which retained meaning even after they had left their native villages, influencing not only the areas they raided and attacked but also where and with whom they could count on finding support and shelter. Reports on uskok incursions in Dalmatia, like those concerning the Ottoman hinterland, constantly refer to the aid given to the uskoks by those "who have friends and relatives among them." Venetian attempts at retribution occasionally make it possible to unravel these relationships. For example, an uskok attack on Makarska in 1556 was carried out with the aid of people from Brač, including one Vice Stipetić. When he was seized as an uskok spy, the explanation for his participation was that he had two brothers in Senj.[172] Women, too, acted as links between their uskok husbands and the families that they left behind in Dalmatia. They often played an important role as go-betweens, journeying from Senj to their native villages with a freedom their menfolk could not risk, passing under the noses of Venetian guards to collect ransoms, carry news, and gather information.[173]

Marriage also maintained and extended these family ties among the rural population. Paolo Sarpi claimed that the uskoks contracted these ties by force. "Wherever there was a marriagable daughter of good family on the islands or the maritime territories of Dalmatia, they came unexpectedly, by night or at other more opportune times, and forced the house, abducting her and marrying her to one of them. Then they made peace, and made excuses for the act with her relatives (who had no remedy when the damage had already been done), and tried to convince them to recognize [the uskoks] as relations, and to favor their affairs with information, warnings, and other help." (If the relatives refused to aid the uskoks, they were harassed with claims for the girl's dowry.)[174]

The dispatches of Venetian commanders in the Adriatic occasionally mention uskok abductions of marriageable girls from the Dalmatian islands, as in 1597, when a band of uskoks is reported as having "abducted

---

[171]A.S.V., Provveditori da Terra e da Mar, 1321: 28 Dec. 1602.

[172]A.S.V., Senato, Secreta, reg. 70: 6 Aug. 1556.

[173]A Venetian official summed up the advantages they had in this: "Because it is not so easy for their men to do so, the Senj women come under cover of their female sex, and under the name of relatives in the places of Your Serenity, where they make their contacts" (A.S.V., Senato, Secreta, Materie miste notabili, 27: 1591 [Contarini]).

[174]Sarpi, *La Repubblica di Venezia*, p. 20. See also Minucci, *Storia degli uscocchi*, p. 108, for the abduction and forced marriage of a "well-born girl" from the Zadar archipelago.

by force a young girl of marriageable age from her own house . . . and forced the priest of that village [Novalja] to wed her forcibly to one of them, and took her away with them in their bark."[175] As in this example, the emphasis in the incidents, as reported by the families of the girls, is usually on the uskok use of force. One better-documented case, however, hints that forcible abduction was sometimes a ruse for escaping the awkwardness a conventional courtship and wedding might bring upon the family (in much the same way that abduction [*otmica*] was used in other neighboring areas to bypass inconvenient marriage conventions). In 1606 a group of uskoks abducted Justina Vuković, daughter of Vicko Vuković of the village of Bol, on Brač. They wanted the village priest to perform a wedding then and there, but he had hidden in fear, so they carried her off to Senj, accompanied by Vicko Margitić, a relative, who went along with Justina to represent her family at the wedding in Senj. Venetian authorities presented this event as an abduction, but the presence of a relative for the ritual purposes of the wedding hints otherwise. It emerged that Justina and her uskok suitor had "long been in love, as he had already been asking for her hand in marriage for some time." Her father had refused a formal agreement (fearing Venetian penalties for collaboration with the uskoks). This "abduction" apparently provided a face-saving solution, allowing Justina to wed her lover with the quiet support of her family but without incurring Venetian retribution.[176] This was an exceptional case, documented because of its sensational nature, but there must have been many other unrecorded marriages or other ties contracted between uskoks and the population of Dalmatia and the hinterland. Such bonds of family and acquaintance did much to provide the uskoks and the rural population with common ground.

The importance of a common nationality is more difficult to assess. Venetian observers repeatedly stress this aspect in discussing the uselessness of the Croat militia in Dalmatia against the uskoks: "Your Serenity will never be well served against the uskoks by the Croats, because both the one and the other are of the same nation, and they share interests born of friendship, dependence, and kinship, and therefore will never resolve to offend their own blood."[177] These ties, like those of kinship, probably did contribute to the reluctance of Venice's Dalmatian subjects to fight against the uskoks, though there are only scattered

---

[175]In A.S.V., Provveditori da Terra e da Mar, 1263: 7 May 1597.

[176]The relevant documents are in A.S.V., Provveditori da Terra e da Mar, 1265: 21 Mar. 1606; Provveditori da Terra e da Mar, 420: 22 Mar. 1606; 15 Apr. 1606 (interrogation of Jeronim Pervaneo of Hvar and report of Mattio Pacifico Cenza, Split, noting that the General of the Frontier, Veit Khisl, had promised to punish those involved "according to their merits"). Tomić gave a highly colored version of the story in "Iz istorije senjskih uskoka," pp. 98–99.

[177]In *Commissiones et relationes venetæ*, vol. 5, p. 255. Also see ibid., vol. 3, p. 194; vol. 4, p. 332; Minucci, *Storia degli uscocchi*, p. 235.

references to a sense of ethnic or national community among the members of the rural population. When a Venetian captain captured an uskok harambaša in Bosiljina, near Trogir, the men of the village not only refused to help but went so far as to say that "they don't wish to capture, or to help to capture the said uskoks, as they are Christians and their brothers, and used other imperious words."[178] Was this an acknowledgment of a common origin? And were the references to a common political tradition under the Croatian kings evidence of a national heritage shared by the uskoks and the people of Dalmatia? Certainly both the educated urban elite of the coastal towns and the Venetian representatives in Dalmatia were explicit about the significance a Croat identity had for them. But even if ideas of national affinity or difference did influence relations between the uskoks and the rural population, they do not always seem to have been decisive. Cooperation and antagonism often floated free of such factors: uskok relations with the people of the border vary far more according to state sovereignty than according to any recognizable national pattern. Dalmatian Croats, hinterland Vlachs, Italian immigrants, and Albanian mercenaries are to be found both in conflict with the uskoks and among their supporters.

Far more than sentiments of shared national identity, the concrete advantages that derived from a common opposition to the Turk seem to have defined these relationships. One Venetian rector reported in the early seventeenth century that the people of Dalmatia did not wish to see the uskoks extirpated "because of the blood ties between them, because many of them do not lose in their traffic with the uskoks, and because it seems to them that the uskoks defend their territories from the Turks."[179] Mutual benefit and a common hatred of the Turk: these are the points emphasized over and over again. Raids on Ottoman territory, utterly prohibited to her Dalmatian subjects by a Venice concerned for peace with the Porte at any price, brought back substantial booty. The Sancak-bey of Klis complained to the Rector of Šibenik in 1576 that the uskoks and the people of the Šibenik district "had been eating and drinking together for an entire month, and coming here to plunder." As a result of such joint raids "there is not a single horse, or nag, or ox, or goat that has not been stolen or taken by force."[180] Such tempting booty was not easily resisted in Dalmatia's rapidly deteriorating economy, particularly in the aftermath of the Ottoman wars. Much of Dalmatia's agricultural land had been lost to the Ottomans; what was left yielded little, for the mass emigration had left few hands to work the land, even if fear

[178]In A.S.V., Capi del Consiglio dei Dieci, Lettere dei Rettori, 281: 26 Aug. 1581.
[179]In H.A.Z., Fond Šime Ljubića, 8/18.
[180]In Tomić, "Sedam srpskih pisama ćirilicom pisanih mletačkog arhiva," pp. 70, 72.

of Ottoman raids had not made the laborers reluctant to return to cultivation. More and more, Dalmatia was dependent on trade with the Ottoman Morlachs for grain and cattle to feed its cities. Even so, supplies were unstable. Famine was invariably the result if crops should fail, imports be impeded, or war break out. By the end of the sixteenth century, Dalmatia was already sinking into poverty, and poverty, as Provveditore Generale Donà reported in 1599, is always accompanied by discontent.[181] Accompanying uskoks on their raids of the Ottoman hinterland did little to relieve Dalamatia's deep-seated economic problems. By damaging Morlach agriculture and livestock rearing and by reducing the volume of trade to the Dalmatian cities, uskok raids contributed to Dalmatian economic instability, but the immediate promise of booty generally obscured such long-term considerations.

In addition, these raids were a blow against the hated conqueror of Dalmatia's hinterland territories—the cause of all the province's misfortunes in the popular mind—and a warning against further Ottoman attempts at conquest. Hence one Venetian noted the "voluntary and universal inclination of all Dalmatia to favor these scoundrels, for these people live by the heresy, so to speak, that the conservation and maintenance of this province depend on the raids of the uskoks."[182] Much of Dalmatia shared the uskok view of raids against the Turk as part of a Christian crusade against Islam. Hatred of the conquering infidel, encouraged by the preaching of the lower clergy, was firmly entrenched, endangering the Signoria's efforts to keep peaceful relations on their Ottoman frontier. Why should the people of Dalmatia prevent the uskoks from raiding the Turk?

At the same time, official attitudes saw aid to the uskoks as a challenge to Venetian authority, the alien law of the towns, and foreign rulers. All Dalmatian support for the uskoks could be construed as defiance of Venice. Under exceptional conditions, hatred of the Turk and discontent with Venetian rule could combine to overcome even the social divisions, so carefully nurtured by Venetian representatives in the towns of Dalmatia. In the 1596 attack on Klis nobles, citizens, and commoners all joined together in aiding the uskoks, in open opposition to Venetian orders. Not only had the time come to press to the gates of Constantinople and lift the Turkish yoke but also, said Venice's subjects, "now we will change our masters."[183] The Rector of Šibenik, when he returned to Venice in 1597, recalled in his report that "when Klis was stolen from the Turks . . . according to whether the news of [the uskoks'] progress was

[181]In *Commissiones et relationes venetæ*, vol. 5, p. 228.
[182]In ibid., vol. 5, p. 51.
[183]In Contarini, *Le historie venetiane*, p. 328; Tomić, *Grada*, p. 77.

good or bad, so either joy or sorrow could be discerned in everyone's faces, as though it was a matter of their own lives, or even their souls."[184]

Certainly the uskoks' part in the dramatic events around Klis in 1596, and the subsequent Venetian and Ottoman repression of the participants, particularly the lower clergy, helped to reinforce the popular image of the uskok in Dalmatia as a defender of the *antemurale* against the infidel Turks and their allies in Venice. The uskoks, reported Donà in 1599, "have acquired a great reputation as a result of the recent events and the successes at Klis; a place that a great part, if not the majority, of all the estates of Dalmatia desire with great avidity; and they are convinced that through these people they can enlarge their borders and improve their fortunes."[185] Although the uskok raids on Venetian shipping in the aftermath of Klis may have soured the views of some Dalmatian citizens and merchants, "touched in their goods and on occasion in their lives,"[186] other inhabitants of Dalmatia retained their belief that the uskoks were the true defenders of the border long afterward.

The uskoks also played a role both in Dalmatia and in the Ottoman hinterland as agents of protest and rebellion. Support for the uskoks could be an outlet for a broad variety of discontents. Their very existence, by itself, made one type of rebellion possible: the constant stream of dissatisfied Venetian and Ottoman subjects who joined the uskoks in Senj. The independence and the opportunities of uskok life offered the malcontent a social alternative—one familiar and readily attainable. My account has concentrated on opposition to the Ottomans and to Venetian authority, but other conflicts found expression through the uskoks as well. Until the middle of the sixteenth century, the inhabitants of Kaštela (and other parts of the Trogir district) were required to buy and sell wine and grain in the city at fixed prices, and until they could win a change in these regulations, clandestine trade with the uskoks provided a way to outmanuever the municipal laws they chafed against. (It may not be a coincidence that when the rectors of Dalmatia were asked to collect complaints against the uskoks in 1558, the Rector of Trogir was unable to find citizens of the district who were willing to make depositions.)[187] Another conflict was that between the older agricultural population of the coast, the peasants and fishermen, and the more recent pastoral usurpers of Ottoman-occupied or disputed lands on the border.

---

[184]In *Commissiones et relationes venetæ*, vol. 5, p. 223.

[185]In ibid., vol. 5, p. 282.

[186]The Rector of Šibenik, writing in 1597, quoted above (ibid., vol. 5, p. 223).

[187]A.S.V., Provveditore Sopraintendente alla Camera dei Confini, 244: 13 May 1558 (Processus Traugurii); A.S.V., Capi del Consiglio dei Dieci, Lettere dei Rettori, 281: 27 Feb. 1563 (m.v.); Vjeko Omašić, *Povijest Kaštela od početka do kraja XVIII stoljeća* (Split, 1986), pp. 148–49.

The antagonism between these different cultures and attitudes, perhaps exacerbated by religious and national differences and by contrasting levels of obligation, can be seen in the frequent involvement of the people of the Trogir and Šibenik districts in uskok raids on recent pastoral settlers from the hinterland in the disputed villages of the border.[188] It is against this background that we should see an incident from 1551, in which Jerko Sudinić, a fisherman from the coast accompanying some uskoks on a raid, grabbed their captive, a Vlach herdsman, by the beard and pulled him into the boat, saying, "You animal!" and punctuating his contempt with a blow from his ax.[189] Many such conflicts—the countryman's resentment of the city dweller, the commoner's antagonism toward the patrician, the small producer's rivalry with the large merchant and landowner, even the petty personal hatreds that developed in the small, circumscribed society of the villages and communes—all of these could be articulated in the company of the uskoks, whether or not the uskoks themselves shared these motivations.

The uskoks' activity was thus exploited for the expression of a range of protests generated by divisions in society. The peasantry, however, do not appear to have idealized the uskoks as champions of the oppressed, in spite of an undoubted respect for their prowess. Although the uskoks occasionally claimed community with the rural poor, the Dalmatian people seem to have had a healthy skepticism about the altruism of the uskoks' raids. Some of their comments are quite cynical (though it should be noted that they were addressed to Venetian officials): "It is quite true that when they find someone who has no goods they say that he is their brother, but when they find goods, they say that he is their enemy, and take everything from him."[190] "When they see that they cannot get anywhere, they send you with God, saying 'we do not wish to displease you,' but still they take your bread and wine."[191]

Not even popular mythology attempted to convert the uskoks into agents of social justice, unlike the legends of noble robbers in other societies. The earliest collected epic songs about the uskoks (written down in the early eighteenth century) depict them as motivated by the competitive struggle for honor and the desire for Ottoman plunder, rather than by any intention of helping others or righting wrongs. Although the uskoks usually war against the Turk, in these early epics their adversaries also sometimes include Christian bands. The uskoks of the epic

---

[188]See the complaints from this area in Tomić, "Sedam srpskih pisama," especially the December 1576 letter complaining about joint uskok and Dalmatian raids on Gradac and Vratkovići, p. 12.

[189]H.A.Z., Spisi zadarskih knezova, Antonio Civran (1551–53) 1: 32–37.

[190]In A.S.V., Provveditore Sopraintendente alla Camera dei Confini, 244: 2 May 1558.

[191]In ibid.: 4 May 1558.

songs are heroes, an epithet used constantly in the texts as in real life, but they are not romanticized. Their quarrelsomeness and boastfulness, their trickery and deceit, the wives and mothers they leave weeping are all presented with clear-eyed comprehension. The qualities of heroism embodied here are those of loyalty toward comrades, piety, skill and cunning, a rough compassion for worthy opponents and innocent victims, and above all personal bravery and strength. It is for themselves, not for the consequences of their actions for the poor or oppressed, that the uskoks are admired, and this admiration includes not a little fear. Although in other societies bandit legends, by idealizing the bandits, may have legitimated their use of force, in these songs the connection between uskok legend and reality seems to be much closer. Perhaps the uskoks expressed the cultural values of violence and honor so well that no fictional mystification was necessary for them to be accepted as heroes.[192]

The uskoks cannot be considered leaders of popular protests or conscious champions of movements of social or political rebellion. They themselves lacked any concrete program for change. They may have dreamed of driving the Ottomans from the Balkans, but they were content, in general, to wage war on their property rather than on their persons, let alone their system. Nonetheless, though some uskoks plundered the people of Dalmatia and the hinterland to the extent they could get away with it or when they had no readily available alternative, the uskoks' raids were not anarchic or indiscriminate. As a group they did not oppress the rural population systematically. They could not afford to do so, for they had no other network of support outside Senj. Their restraint, their moderate requisitions, their selective and limited use of violence were matters, at least in part, of pragmatic calculation, meant to ensure the minimum popular support necessary for their survival. At the same time, their commitment to war against the infidel led them to expect the support and approval of their fellow Christians. The uskoks' relations with the rural population of Dalmatia and the Ottoman hinterland are more ambiguous than the image of the noble robber might suggest, and they illustrate the difficulty of isolating the social element in the actions of bandits.

It is important, however, to distinguish between the acts and motives of the uskoks themselves and the political and social significance of support for them. The aspirations and dissatisfactions of Venice's subjects in Dalmatia, particularly the peasantry, but also some patricians,

---

[192]See for example Gesemann, *Erlangenski rukopis*, #64 (pp. 82–85), #72 (pp. 97–99), #80 (pp. 111–13), #94 (pp. 134–35), #97 (pp. 137–39), #106 (pp. 148–49), #119 (pp. 170–71), #122 (pp. 175–76), #127 (pp. 188–89), #131 (pp. 196–97), #135 (pp. 202–04), #143 (pp. 220–23), #164 (pp. 244–46).

were largely in conflict with the official law of Venice. Similarly, the complaints of subjects of the Porte on the frontiers set them in opposition to the Ottoman state. These attitudes found wide expression outside the law, in the company of the uskoks. Whatever the aberrations of uskok behavior, they provided a channel for popular protest, a means of voicing grievances for which there were no other outlets. They also embodied epic images of heroes, whose courage, recklessness, and violence inspired admiration, fear, and respect.

The uskoks, according to Nicolò Contarini's seventeenth-century sketch of their history, "pretended that they did not wish to seize anything but the goods of Turks and Jews; but tolerance only sharpened the boldness of these rogues, and they treated all alike."[193] Venetian complaints about the uskoks sometimes obscure the fact that the uskoks did not pretend to attack only the Turks and Jews: these were in fact always their primary targets. Nor is it true that the uskoks were indiscriminate. A set of rules, deriving in part from the uskoks' claim to be defending Christendom, guided and justified their raids. In the eyes of the uskoks themselves, as we have seen, these were not the random, wholesale attacks of pirates or brigands. Attacks on Muslims or Jews, or their property, needed no excuse, nor did warfare against the population of enemy territory, though this might be modified according to the claims of a common Christian religion and opposition to the infidel. Harm inflicted on non-Ottomans was justified to the extent that the victims collaborated with the enemy either openly, or implicitly (by opposing the uskoks). All such raids were licit in the framework of the holy war.

The idea of licit booty implies its opposite—illicit, forbidden plunder. The precise line between the two was not always clearly defined, nor did the uskok and his victim always see the distinction in the same way. In practice uskoks must often have stretched the definition to cover the circumstances of the moment, for the extent of the victim's collaboration with the Ottomans was not always the ultimate test. Conversely, although the imperatives of holy war made raiding the infidel a duty, relations between uskok and Muslim were not invariably hostile. The *antemurale* ideal did not adequately explain all uskok actions. The need to make a living, among other factors, was often more important. The form that uskok actions took, however, depended on a whole range of constraints and possibilities, among them the very real demands of uskok ideology.

[193]Contarini, *Le historie venetiane*, p. 326.

CHAPTER EIGHT

The Final Decades

In the quotation from *The Pleasant Conversation of the Slavic People* that stands as an epigraph to this book, Andrija Kačić-Miošić points out the difficulty of constructing a narrative out of a multitude of incidents, each much the same, each employing the same vocabulary: "heads chopped off, slaves carried away." Fra Andrija organized his tales of the frontier around individual heroes and battles. This book has tried to make sense of the uskoks by looking instead at separate aspects, focusing on themes that would be less clear in a chronological framework. To an extent, however, clarity has been gained at the expense of a sense of sequence, change, and causality. Now it is time to turn to the unfolding of events, to try to tell the story of the last few decades of the uskoks of Senj. In the period between the failure to regain Klis in 1596 and the "Uskok War" of 1616–18, the ideas, constraints, and forces analyzed in the previous chapters can be seen in action. In this chapter I do not attempt to give a comprehensive account of uskok actions throughout this period, fearing that more than a few readers would follow Fra Andrija's admonition to go off to sleep if the tales were not to their taste.[1] But the raids and counterraids that make up the stuff of the uskok tale in this period help us to understand how and why the uskok world was changing.

The turn of the century was a turning point for the uskoks. Some of the reasons have been touched on in the previous chapters: the shift in areas of recruitment; the increasing economic difficulties felt by the uskoks, both unpaid and paid; the Military Frontier impatience with

---

[1]Fairly comprehensive accounts can be found in Stanojević, *Senjski uskoci* (based on Venetian reports), and Grünfelder, "Studien zur Geschichte der Uskoken" (based largely on Military Frontier material).

uskok independence; the erosion of an uskok consensus on legitimate targets for raiding. In addition, the relations between the empires on whose borders they lived were shifting, challenging the very assumptions on which their world was built.

Deteriorating Relations with Venice

At the start of Holy Week, 1597, a fleet of uskok barks carrying more than five hundred men set out from Senj on an unusual raid. Although it had something of the character of a crusade, this expedition was not directed against the infidel, unlike the one that had set out to storm Klis on Palm Sunday the previous year. The flotilla sailed north to Istria, where the uskoks fell on the Venetian harbor of Rovinj by night, stripped the ships bare of their goods (to the sum of 400,000 *scudi*), took Venetian citizens hostage, and headed back to Senj, taking more prizes on the way. It was said afterward that to show their disdain for the Signoria and to complete their revenge they forced their way into Pula and danced on the public square.[2] Some weeks later the Provveditore Generale received a list of the commanders of the barks and the uskoks who had been involved: they included most of the best-known uskoks, many of whom had participated in the liberation of Klis.[3] This was far from the first uskok attack on Venetian subjects, but other such raids had at least had the excuse of seeking Turkish cargoes. The expedition to Rovinj was a blunt and self-righteous expression of corporate anger against the Republic. The attempt to take Klis from the Ottomans had failed the previous summer, and the uskoks had been incensed at Venetian aid to the Turks and at subsequent Venetian reprisals against uskok allies in Dalmatia. The execution of a number of uskoks captured by the Venetians, and the subsequent display of their severed heads in Venice, had further enraged Senj. Their act of vengeance opened a cycle of revenge and retaliation which would become virtually unbreakable over the coming years. In its course the uskoks would become divided among themselves, the character of their raids would change, and they would begin to lose popular support.

In 1597 the uskoks were not only of one accord in revenging themselves on Venice by their daring raid. They also stood side by side in the

[2]Horvat, *Monumenta uscocchorum*, vol. 1, pp. 156–57. The raid itself is described in a series of dispatches from Almorò Tiepolo and Zuane Bembo, who succeeded him as Provveditore contra uscocchi, in A.S.V., Provveditori da Terra e da Mar, 1263; and a full account based on these documents is given in Tomić, "Crtice iz istorije senjskih uskoka." See also Horvat, *Monumenta uscocchorum*, vol. 1, pp. 156–60.

[3]The list is in A.S.V., Provveditori da Terra e da Mar, 1263: 26 Apr. 1597 (report of Alessandro Busencolo, Zadar).

face of the subsequent reprisals against Senj—a Venetian blockade and an investigatory commission appointed by the Archduke and the Emperor. A Venetian spy in Senj who agitated among the paid uskoks in 1597, proposing that the solution to the uskoks' problems was to drive out the venturini, was told that the venturini were their brothers and that "what happens to them will also happen to us."[4] The Habsburg commission, headed by General Juraj Lenković, began severely, installing itself in Rijeka with a large contingent of troops and summoning the suspected uskoks to appear before it, then issuing a proclamation that the plundered goods were illicit booty and must be returned. Lenković banished several uskoks to Brinje, executed seven uskoks (some for crimes unconnected with the Rovinj affair), and expelled a number of deserters from Venetian galleys and other Venetian outlaws from Senj, but eventually capitulated to the uskoks on the issue of the booty and distributed two months' pay to the stipendiati. In spite of the complaints of the Provveditore Generale, Zuane Bembo, who blamed the venturini for the incident, Lenković was reluctant to single them out for special punishment, replying that he feared that events might take a sinister turn, particularly as the uskoks were "a most insolent race, and therefore, particularly at the present time, unite to govern themselves with much attention." Provveditore Bembo suspected that, in any case, any measures short of complete banishment would have little effect on the venturini, as they were not paid, and so had little cause to respect Habsburg authority.[5]

Having vented their rage against the Signoria, many Senjani were willing to agree that their raids be directed solely against the Ottomans, particularly if such agreement would protect them from continued Venetian reprisals carried out by the ships under Bembo. In early February 1598 a number of uskok vojvodas and harambašas (both paid and unpaid) signed a declaration promising not to inflict harm on any Venetian subject or territory and not to permit any individual raids, but to obey their Captain and vojvodas, on pain of forfeiting "head, wife and children, and property, honor and goods." The stated purpose of this pledge was to prevent "all injustice and dissension, and all harmful piracy" that could threaten the Habsburg lands with war at Venetian hands.[6]

[4]In A.S.V., Provveditori da Terra e da Mar, 1263: 2 Aug. 1597 (interrogation of Marin Obladina).

[5]Bembo's report, in *Commissiones et relationes venetæ*, vol. 5, p. 242. See also A.S.V., Provveditori da Terra e da Mar, 1263: 25 Nov. 1597 (Lenkovich); *Commissiones et relationes venetæ*, vol. 5, pp. 243–44, and for the acts of the commission see I.Ö. H.K.R., Croatica, fasc. 9, 1597, Oct. No. 45: 12 Dec. 1597.

[6]In I.Ö. H.K.R., Croatica, fasc. 9, 1598, Mar. No. 60: 5 Feb. 1598. At least nine of the fourteen signatories had been on the Rovinj expedition.

It is not clear whether the uskoks made this pledge voluntarily or whether it was extracted from them by their Captain. It is not surprising, however, that when Bembo attacked the uskok fleet ten days later, they reacted with aggrieved innocence. Eighteen barks of uskoks had disembarked near Šibenik, crossed into Ottoman territory, and rounded up 8000 head of livestock, which they drove back to the coast. The uskoks were outraged when Bembo and his Albanian troops blockaded them in rainy weather in the shallow bay of Rogoznica, south of Primošten. The Captain of Senj had licensed their expedition to go out in search of provisions, and the uskoks had carefully restricted themselves to Ottoman booty. The vojvodas and harambašas wrote politely to Bembo, who was waiting for the weather to clear before attacking. They distinguished between their expedition and the indiscriminate raids by banished uskoks who had not agreed to respect Venetian interests. They informed Bembo that they had gone out "to try whether we can win anything from our enemies on the mainland" and to track down renegade uskoks who had been raiding in Dalmatia. They had thought that they were at peace with Venice, but seeing that Bembo intended to do them harm, they had avoided the Venetian patrols, "so not to spill Christian blood." They protested that they had no intention of doing any harm to the islands and ports of the Signoria and asked Bembo to leave them in peace. If not, they would do their best to defend themselves, and Bembo would have to answer to God for the result.[7] The uskoks saw their raid as completely legitimate. They had a license, and they had attacked only Ottoman subjects, doing no harm to Venetian subjects, according to the terms of the oath signed by their vojvodas and harambašas. But Bembo could not afford to look through his fingers at such expeditions, primarily because of the consequences they were likely to have for Venice. Not only did they embolden the uskoks to attempt less carefully controlled raids, but, more important, they gave the Porte an opportunity to accuse the Republic of neglecting its duty to keep the Adriatic free of pirates or worse, of cooperating with Ottoman enemies.

Bembo did not deign to reply to this letter, and the uskoks did not wait for the weather to improve so that he could attack. Trusting to a stormy night with the *bura* blowing hard, they reinforced their barks with gunwales made from planks taken from the doors and windows of the houses in the port and chanced their lives in an escape past the Venetian ships. In the dead of night, when the storm was at its height and the sentries on the galleys would be able to hear nothing but the roar of the wind and the slap of the waves, the uskok barks slipped out one by one

---

[7]In A.S.V., Provveditori da Terra e da Mar, 1263: 15 Feb. 1598 (written by the vojvodas and harambašas in the port of Rogoznica, enclosed in Bembo's dispatch of 20 Feb. 1598).

into the open sea and set sail for home.[8] The uskoks' pledge to avoid conflict with the Venetians during their supply raids on Ottoman territory had ended badly, with the uskoks confirmed in their distrust of the Serenissima's motives. When on their journey these uskoks found a group of Bembo's Albanian troops in the harbor of Krk they slaughtered them in a bloody revenge, at the same time releasing some of their comrades from captivity on the galleys; and when they came across some Venetian barks with provisions and arms, they plundered them as recompense for their lost Turkish livestock. Bembo took his revenge by sacking Novi Vindolski and strengthening the blockade of the Croatian Littoral. Uskok-Venetian relations deteriorated further.[9]

An anonymous observer, probably Bishop de Dominis, looking back on this period, tried to explain the causes of this escalating spiral of violence by emphasizing how strengthened Venetian patrols had the unintended effect of increasing uskok raids for supplies in Dalmatia.

> As the uskoks sometimes passed the limits of discretion in their plunder and robbery, so too the ministers of the most serene Republic began to hinder not only illicit stealing and robbery, but also all just plunder carried out by land, militarily, in Turkish territory, as well as the traffic in ransoms and in the usual tribute owed by the Turks to the militia in Senj. These unusual and extraordinary impediments, bitter, hard, and troublesome to the uskoks, were the cause of great evil, because they gave the uskoks, anxious and famished, a real reason to be enraged, and to turn their thoughts to iniquities; and they gave the predators covering and prextext enough to palliate their misdeeds. And so they began to turn from despairing attacks to open harm to the nearby islands and to the neighboring subjects of the most serene Republic, and to multiply their plunder and robbery at sea, spoiling indifferently as much as they conveniently could, with regard neither to sect nor religion, nor to nation.[10]

In their own complaints, the uskoks also emphasized their need to find provisions. In 1598 they protested that the Venetians, while protecting the Ottomans by pursuing all uskok expeditions, were reducing the uskoks to starvation, "not being able to sustain ourselves in the territo-

[8]Bembo was enraged at losing a quarry that had no chance against his superior forces (*Commissiones et relationes venetæ*, vol. 5, pp. 245–46; A.S.V., Provveditori da Terra e da Mar, 1263: 20 Feb. 1598). Other writers of the time retold the story as an example of uskok daring or recklessness (Minucci, *Storia degli uscocchi*, p. 238; Rački, "Prilog za poviest hrvatskih uskoka," pp. 203–4).

[9]See A.S.V., Provveditori da Terra e da Mar, 1263 : 2 Mar. 1598; I.Ö. H.K.R., Croatica, fasc. 9, 1598, Mar. No. 56 and No. 60; and *Commissiones et relationes venetæ*, vol. 5, pp. 245–46. Tomić gives a description of the bloody attack on the Albanian troops in "Crtice iz istorije senjskih uskoka," pp. 43–47.

[10]In Horvat, *Monumenta uscocchorum*, vol. 1, p. 397.

ries of the Turks, our common enemies."[11] The Captain of Senj informed the General of the Frontier that "if we cannot obtain other provisions, such as meat, wine, bread, and other necessities, we suffer great hardship and dearth . . . which would not be the case if the Venetians allowed my subordinates to pass home peacefully with the cattle they have obtained." The Captain was particularly concerned that the venturini might raid against his orders if no provision was made for them: "They, and especially the venturini, protest against me loudly when I will not let them go out, in spite of their need, and keep them constantly imprisoned in the fortress. I ought to give them [the venturini] some form of maintenance as well, for otherwise they won't be able to endure; some of them are ready to leave secretly and go out again."[12]

In spite of the anonymous analysis quoted above, not all the uskoks were prepared to raid Christian subjects indiscriminately, even under the pressures of the blockade. Through most of 1598 many tried to preserve the fragile peace in the Adriatic by limiting their raids in accordance with the pledge. Although the Provveditore Generale was patrolling the waters before Senj, with orders to seize all vessels entering or leaving the ports of Senj, Rijeka, Bakar, and Vinodol, and the city was in great need, especially of wine, the vojvodas, harambašas, and most of the stipendiati remained quietly in Senj. The main reason for their patience was the hope that some improvement in their circumstances would come out of the plans for the support of Senj being orchestrated by the Pope, with the help of Archbishop Minucci and Bishop de Dominis.[13]

Many of the venturini, however, were less sanguine about the prospects of peace, not least because these plans would have removed many of their number from Senj. Distress eventually drove these venturini to rebellion, and eight barks left Senj, the men declaring that since they had no other means to live they would rather risk anything than die of hunger in Senj; a Venetian emissary reported that "they said that they would like to cut the Bishop of Senj in pieces, as he had kept them inside for so long under the pretence of reaching an agreement."[14] The venturini reserved their worst hatred for the Venetians who wished to prevent them from raiding the Turk. Many of them, led by Juriša Hajduk, retired to Vinodol and then to Lika, where they remained for several months, raiding wherever they could find booty. A Venetian subject they

[11]A confidential report to Provveditore Generale Bembo from Senj on the uskoks' complaints to their superiors, in A.S.V., Provveditori da Terra e da Mar, 1263: 15 Mar. 1598.

[12]In I.Ö. H.K.R., Croatia, fasc. 9, 1598, Mar. No. 56: 31 Mar. 1598.

[13]A.S.V., Provveditori da Terra e da Mar, 922: 28 Nov. 1598; Horvat, *Monumenta uscocchorum*, vol. 1, pp. 388–93.

[14]In A.S.V., Provveditori da Terra e da Mar, 922: 28 Nov. 1958 (enclosure from "a person sent to and returned from Senj").

took captive near Zadar reported that "they have conspired and confederated among themselves, with these or similar words, saying that since the Venetians will not let them plunder the lands of the Turk, [Venice] is a whore, a thief, and a traitor to us uskoks, and we will go and destroy the land, the towns, and the places of these Venetians, putting them to steel and fire, and if we capture any gentlemen, we will cut them to pieces."[15] As the Venetian blockade of the Croatian Littoral continued to 1599, those within Senj grew desperate with hunger, and there were several incidents of animal theft from the nearby islands. The Provveditore's assault on Lovran, the source of much of Senj's wine and grain, was deeply resented and was avenged by an uskok counterattack on Fianona (Plomin) and Albona (Labin), which took much badly needed cattle and provisions as booty. Although the paid uskoks in Senj joined in some of these expeditions, in general they were less ready to raid Venetian territory and freely declared that they would prefer to continue their raids against the Turks if the Venetian authorities would only allow them to do so.[16]

Although the venturini and the stipendiati had joined together to inflict a bloody revenge on Venice in the aftermath of Klis, their consensus began to fall apart in the face of the subsequent reprisals. The events that succeeded the Rovinj raid make it possible for us to follow the development of uskok conflict over raiding and the restrictions placed on them by their superiors, both by the officials of the Military Frontier and by their own vojvodas. Some of the uskok leaders saw raids that provoked Venetian retaliation as damaging Senj's interests, and they were willing to agree to some restrictions on raiding, particularly if these would placate the Republic. Others defended their rights to plunder the Turk without any restrictions, all the more so as they had no other means of support, and insisted on revenge for any infringement of this right.

These two sets of attitudes roughly followed the division between paid and unpaid uskoks. Bishop de Dominis noted the fallacy in attributing all unauthorized raiding to the venturini, although he phrased his observation in moralizing terms: "I see that there are many among the stipendiati who are inclined to plundering and crime, just as among the venturini there are a number of good and docile people, desirous of peace."[17] But in the conditions of scarcity at the end of the century, it was the venturini who suffered most from restraints on raiding and were most vocal in their complaints against Venice. In spite of a number of plans to

[15]In ibid., 14 Dec. 1598 (enclosure of 2 Dec. 1598 from the Rector of Rab).

[16]For these events, see the dispatches of Nicolò Donà and enclosed interrogations of various witnesses, in ibid., Dec. 1598–Mar. 1599.

[17]In Stanojević, *Senjski uskoci*, p. 187 (A.S.V., Senato, Secreta, Dispacci, Germania, 29: 30 Nov. 1599).

find provisions for the venturini, the Military Frontier was never able to pay them. The stipendiati, on the other hand, could sometimes afford to be more conciliatory. In early 1599 the vojvodas and stipendiati renewed their pledge not to harm Christians or even Turks at sea, so long as they were not hindered from raiding Ottoman territory. They then went on to propose a plan that would constrain the venturini by sending their sons or brothers as hostages to Venice.[18] (The Signoria was in no mood to accept negotiation with any of the uskoks and the matter was dropped, yet the very offer betrays a new concern over the uskoks' ability to resolve such matters among themselves.) Under increasingly difficult circumstances in Senj, however, both venturini and stipendiati could unite in desperate plunder of forbidden targets. Later in 1599, during the Venetian blockade, a band including both venturini and stipendiati under the command of Juriša Hajduk pillaged a Venetian ship and told the Pag merchant who owned the cargo of grain, "Go and cry to your General, because if he won't let us go against the Turks, we will come and plunder these islands, and slaughter everyone we find."[19]

Rabatta's Commission in Senj

Raids for supplies on both Ottoman and Venetian territories continued through 1600, in spite of (and in part because of) the Venetian blockade, and eventually led the Habsburgs to countermeasures. The blockade of the Littoral and of Trieste, combined with Venetian punitive measures against the possessions of the Archduke and vigorous diplomatic agitation at the Habsburg courts seconded by the Papal nuncio, did at length force Habsburg concessions, and in 1601 a commission was sent to reform the uskok organization under Joseph Rabatta of Gorica, an adviser to Archduke Ferdinand in Graz.

Rabatta entered Senj in January 1601 with a force of 1500 soldiers from the Military Frontier.[20] There he found only some three hundred uskoks,

---

[18]In a proposal made to the Provveditore Generale by Ivan Vlatković and Miho Radić, "leaders of the stipendiati and principal vojvodas," in A.S.V., Provveditori da Terra e da Mar, 922: 29 Mar. 1599.

[19]As reported in A.S.V., Provveditori da Terra e da Mar, 923: 18 Dec. 1599.

[20]For the diplomatic background to the Rabatta commission, see the dispatches of Flaminio Delfini in Horvat, *Monumenta uscocchorum*, vol. 1, and the discussion in Stanojević, *Senjski uskoci*, pp. 164–92. Venetian and Hofkriegsrat sources for the Rabatta commission are published in Horvat, *Monumenta uscocchorum*, vol. 1; Lopašić, *Acta historiam confinii*, vol. 1; and Ljubić, "Prilozi za životopis." Other documents can be found in A.S.V., Provveditori da Terra e da Mar, 923 (the dispatches of Provveditore Generale Pasqualigo and his secretary Vettor Barbaro). The story has been told many times, but never more vividly than in the eyewitness accounts, probably by de Dominis, published in Horvat, *Monumenta uscocchorum*, vol. 1. The most comprehensive of these, "Riforma di Segna et degl'uscoc-

since several bands of uskoks, both venturini and stipendiati, had fled from Senj at his approach. Rabatta's orders were to punish the uskok leaders responsible for prohibited attacks on Venetian subjects and possessions; to remove all the venturini from Senj and resettle them in garrisons in the hinterland; and to forbid all independent sea raids directed against either Venetian or Ottoman territory. Similar orders had been issued before, but Rabatta, supported by the newly installed Bishop of Senj, Marc'Antonio de Dominis, seems to have harbored an ambition to resolve the uskok problem once and for all. His interpretation of these orders was unprecedented in its severity. On his arrival in Senj, Rabatta shut the city gates and set guards on them and then announced that all those who wished to remain in the service of the Military Frontier and receive pardon for their crimes were to appear at the citadel to submit themselves to his mercy. He seized three popular uskok leaders, Marko Margitić, Martin Posedarski, and Juraj Maslarda, all of whom had been demanded by the Venetians, partly for their participation in raids in Dalmatia, partly because all had defected from Venetian service. Maslarda was stabbed in the street trying to escape; Margitić and Posedarski were summarily convicted and executed in the citadel and their bodies hung from a window above the square to terrify the populace.

Before his arrival, the uskoks had sworn together on a cross that they would defend one another and would not allow anyone to be punished, vowing to kill any uskok who yielded.[21] Rabatta's actions, however, shook the town's solidarity.

> Having seen the commissioner in the wind and the intolerable snow go to the houses of the malefactors himself, accompanied by numbers of foreign soldiers; having also seen Maslarda, a man greatly esteemed among them, with a large following, killed so strangely; and then having seen the famous Marghitich and Possedarschi hanging from the wall of the citadel, the city was seized with such terror and desperation, that nothing like it had been seen since its foundation. . . . Now they lose every remnant of spirit and vigor, now they give themselves up as vanquished and conquered, no longer knowing where to go, nor what to say or do.[22]

---

chi . . ." (ibid., vol. 1, pp. 395–422) exists in a longer version which also describes Rabatta's death (in the Biblioteca Marciana, Venice [It. VI 65 (=6210) "Relatione de successi della Città di Segna et della Morte del Commissario Rabatta," copy in S.S.E.E.S., Longworth microfilm collection]). Selections of this have been published in Ljubić, "Prilozi za životopis," pp. 45–59. This, with the other documents cited here, is the main source for the following description of the commission.

[21]Lopašić, *Acta historiam confinii,* vol. 1, p. 283 (according to a report from Rabatta, but confirmed by the anonymous report in Horvat, *Monumenta uscocchorum,* vol. 1, p. 404).

[22]In Horvat, *Monumenta uscocchorum,* vol. 1, p. 406 (anonymous account, probably by de Dominis).

Commissioner Rabatta attempted to exploit divisions among the uskoks, putting prices on the heads of renegades and granting pardons to those who betrayed their leaders. His policy produced some results, notably the murder of the venturino Mirko Domazetović by one of the Vlatković family in order to secure the release of Vojvoda Vlatković from prison. This incident exemplified some of the alternatives the uskoks would be faced with over the coming decade. Domazetović was a respected harambaša, known for his experience in war against the Ottomans. He had been among the uskoks who had raided Rovinj in 1597 in revenge for the Venetian betrayal of the Klis conspiracy and had been involved in other raids on Venetian territory. As a result Provveditore Generale Pasqualigo had demanded his head. Rabatta's response confronted the uskoks with a cruel choice. Not only were they compelled to choose between the lives of Vlatković and Domazetović, dividing their loyalties. They were also forced to choose between submission to the authority of the Military Frontier and their allegiance to the demands of honor, for to hunt down Domazetović and his comrades for their part in these raids was to deny the legitimacy of the vengeance taken on Venice. The very manner of his death was a betrayal of the code of honor for, as the uskoks would note in their complaint against Rabatta, Domazetović was shot in the back.

In the atmosphere of terror that ruled in Senj at that time (as the description of Rabatta's commission pointed out) "everyone was beginning to think of his own affairs." But this same account went on to note that, even so, uskok loyalties were not completely undermined by Rabatta's tactics, "for these people so abhor a betrayal of faith, when it has joined them together."[23] One band of renegade venturini, hoping for a pardon, betrayed the harambaša of another band, wanted for his raids on both Venetian and Habsburg territory, but refused to give up their own harambašas, Miloš Bukovac and Ivan Sičić, even for the high prices on their heads. Not only did the uskoks and the townspeople protest the treatment of their fellows by Rabatta and Vettor Barbaro, the Venetian representative in Senj, but they also aided them to hide and to escape.

Rabatta attempted to solve the problem that the unpaid uskoks posed to discipline by transferring some two hundred venturini under the command of Vojvoda Ivan Vlatković to Otočac and other fortresses of the hinterland, with provisions and the promise of regular wages. This transfer was carried out with little difficulty and without the protests that had accompanied the earlier arrests and extraditions, although Captain Barbo argued that the remaining uskoks were insufficient to defend Senj and resigned his commission in protest. The Captain of Senj was not the

[23]In ibid., vol. 1, pp. 404, 415.

only one to complain to the Archduke and the Military Frontier authorities. Ban Drašković, the civil governor of Croatia, angered by the execution of Martin Posedarski and the other uskok leaders, demanded that
Rabatta be tried for treason. Daniel Frankol, captain of the cavalry in
Karlovac, also joined the chorus against Rabatta's actions in Senj. Rabatta's apparent eagerness to accommodate Venetian demands and the
Signoria's expensive gifts to him aroused suspicions that he was acting
more in the Venetian interest than for the Habsburgs.

At the same time, Rabatta was finding it difficult to keep his promises
of regular wages for the garrison in Senj and the uskoks in the outlying
fortresses. Because he had received no funds for this purpose from the
Hofkriegsrat, the first five months' wages and provisions had come out
of his own expenses. When this source ran out and no further supplies
arrived, the uskoks became restless. A rebellion of the uskoks in Brlog,
who claimed they could not survive on their wages, was quickly quelled
by force of arms, but when payments fell further in arrears the uskoks
began to trickle back from the hinterland fortresses to Senj. Rumors of
Rabatta's declining reputation at court encouraged the uskoks to thoughts
of sedition. When Rabatta gathered together a troop of uskoks to send to
the Hungarian battlefields they were turned back at Karlovac by Captain
Frankol. On their return to Senj Rabatta clapped their leader, Juriša
Hajduk, into prison. The people of Senj first requested, then demanded
that this popular harambaša be released; Rabatta refused and threatened the crowd before the citadel; shots were exchanged and the crowd
grew angry. In spite of Rabatta's offer to release Juriša in exchange for
another uskok the door to the citadel was forced, the guard overpowered, and Rabatta was killed. The uskoks cut off his head and exhibited it
to the crowd below in the square. (See Figure 5.)

There is little doubt that Rabatta was much hated and that his murder
was regarded as just in Senj. An anonymous report described Senj as
united behind the killers, "all of those who were in the city, soldiers as
well as citizens, each signing himself as consenting and participating in
this parricide. . . . They then set themselves to form a sort of republic
among themselves, electing several to hold the political governance of
the place."[24] The combined representatives of the uskoks and the civil
authorities immediately informed both the Military Frontier and the
local Venetian officials, including Provveditore Generale Pasqualigo, of
their drastic act, promising to maintain order and adhere to the guide-

---

[24]The document describing Rabatta's death claims that this agreement was achieved "by
force," yet there seems to have been no dissent among the Senjani on this point (Ljubić,
"Prilozi za životopis," p. 58; and, in more detail, Biblioteca Marciana, It. VI 65 [=6210]
"Relatione de successi della Città di Segna et della Morte del Commissario Rabatta," p. 55').
See also Minucci, *Storia degli uscocchi*, pp. 259–60.

5. An engraving from *Die neueröffnete ottomanische Pforte* (Augsburg, 1694) illustrating the mutilation of Commissioner Rabatta's body after his murder. The accompanying text claims that "the corpse was taken without ceremony to the church, but more for revenge than for obsequies, for the uskok wives sucked the blood from its wounds in rage, and bit whole pieces from its flesh" (p. 355). (By permission of the School of Slavonic and East European Studies, University of London.)

lines for uskok conduct agreed between Pasqualigo and Rabatta and asking that a Military Frontier commission investigate the affair.[25]

The uskoks' protests and self-justifications, although doubtlessly tailored to gain the sympathy of their judges, reveal their own view of their rebellion. A twenty-four-point memorandum, sent to the Archduke shortly after Rabatta's murder by all the uskoks collectively ("die gannze ritterschafft vnd redlichen kriegsleuth"), presented Juriša's imprisonment and Rabatta's threats against the assembled soldiery only as the

[25]Horvat, *Monumenta uscocchorum*, vol. 2, pp. 1–2; Lopašić, *Acta historiam confinii*, vol. 1, p. 305.

last provocation, the occasion for their revenge.[26] The letter to Provvedi-tore Generale Pasqualigo took the same line; it did not criticize Rabatta's reforms as a whole. The uskoks' letters admit the justice of "remedying and preventing the many disorders and disadvantages that were cus-tomary in this city." They had been willing, even anxious, to put an end to the escalating spiral of Venetian retaliation and uskok revenge by swearing not to harm Venetian subjects. Several proposals to this effect had been made by the uskoks themselves prior to Rabatta's arrival; the uskoks had surrendered to Rabatta those adventurers guilty of such attacks; they had observed the agreement with the Provveditore Gener-ale and intended to continue doing so.[27] Nor were the uskoks resistant, in principle, to the resettlement of many of their number in the hin-terland fortresses. Indeed, those with no official post in Senj considered these positions desirable, as long as provisions came regularly and wages were paid. It was not until this system broke down that the uskoks of Brlog and Otočac complained and began to return to the city.

The uskoks' complaints against Rabatta turned instead on charges of betrayal—of the uskoks and of the purposes of the frontier. As presented by the uskoks, Rabatta's actions had left Senj and the border vulnerable to the Ottomans. The dismissal of experienced and loyal soldiers and their replacement by "pedlars and other artisans who had never even seen the border"; the treatment meted out to those who had served bravely under Klis "so that other such people had no desire to serve"; the executions and galley sentences of loyal soldiers; the release of Ottoman prisoners; the negligent provisioning of the fortresses "so that after his death there were scarcely four handfuls of gunpowder in Otočac and a half-measure in Senj"—all these acts weakened Senj in the face of the enemy. It was one thing to agree to spare Venetian Dalmatians from attack as Christian subjects of a Christian state. It was quite another, however, to betray Senj and the uskoks into the hands of the Signoria, ally of the Porte, as the uskoks charged that Rabatta had done. Among other things they cited his orders that all travel to Senj be screened by the Venetians at Sveti Marko, a small island off Krk, and that all uskok plans be communicated to them, "so that when the borderers attacked the Turks, [the Venetians] always warned them from their stronghold." Fur-thermore, Rabatta had permitted Venetian troops to attack the outskirts of Senj, killing uskoks on their own soil, and had even allowed their troops into the city to spy out its fortifications.

---

[26]In Lopašić, *Acta historiam confinii*, vol. 1, pp. 300–305. Unfortunately, the German trans-lation of the original document has omitted the names of the signatories, making analysis of possible dissent impossible.

[27]In Horvat, *Monumenta uscocchorum*, vol. 2, pp. 1–2. See below for discussion of uskok proposals to reduce conflict with Venice.

To these charges the uskoks added a list of aggravating factors: the abrogation of many of the uskoks' rights (such as pensions for widows and orphans); Rabatta's crimes against uskok morality (his molestation of Senj women and his flaunting of "a whore from Graz named Lucia"); his claims to a portion of the uskok booty; attempts to extract corvée from the uskoks ("as if we were his serfs"); many details of the long reign of terror he had imposed; and his final insult, turning the guns of the citadel on the uskoks "as if we were Turks."[28] If there is any truth to the tales of the revenge taken by the women of Senj on Rabatta's corpse (drinking his blood and tearing his flesh with their teeth), these provocations certainly played a part in their rage.

Many of the details of the uskoks' complaint are corroborated by Rabatta's own reports to the Military Frontier and to the Provveditore Generale, and by de Dominis's reports. Rabatta presented himself as a dispassionate official of the Military Frontier executing justice on the wicked and unruly uskoks, who persistently disobeyed the orders of their masters. To the uskoks, however, Rabatta was a traitor to the Military Frontier and to the House of Austria. (In their memorandum they prudently pass over the question of the extent to which Rabatta was acting under the orders of the Archduke and the Hofkriegsrat—though they were well aware that their former Captain, Ban Drašković, and other officials had opposed Rabatta's reforms. In their own eyes the murder of Rabatta was the act of loyal border soldiers and Christians, resulting from a sense of injustice and a refusal to accept limits imposed by political expediency to what they perceived as legitimate actions. Nothing could have been less convincing, given this self-image, than the reports immediately put about by the Venetians that the uskoks were about to turn the city over to the Turks.[29]

Dissent over the Limits of Raids

The following years would see growing conflict over the limits on uskok raiding—between Venice and Senj, and also among the uskoks themselves. Immediately after Rabatta's murder, the uskoks announced their intention to maintain the terms of the peace with Venice.[30] In 1601 Commissioner Rabatta and Vettor Barbaro, representing Provveditore Generale Pasqualigo, had drawn up an accord to govern relations between the Republic and the uskoks. Under this agreement, as reported

---

[28]For all these complaints see Lopašić, *Acta historiam confinii*, vol. 1, pp. 300–305.
[29]For the Venetian reports, see Horvat, *Monumenta uscocchorum*, vol. 2, pp. 4, 13.
[30]Ibid., vol. 2, pp. 1–2; Minucci, *Storia degli uscocchi*, p. 260.

by Paolo Sarpi, the uskoks could sail freely only between Senj and Karlobag; they were not to approach the islands or disembark on the territory of the Republic; Venetian fugitives would not be received in Senj; uskoks banished for offences to the Republic would not receive pardons and would be liable to pursuit and punishment by the Venetian authorities.[31] These terms would have protected Venetian subjects from uskok attack and would also have protected the Republic almost entirely against Ottoman accusations of complicity in their raids. This accord was negotiated by governmental officials, who were naturally more concerned with removing a cause of discord between their respective states than with the interests of the uskoks. For them it was prohibitively restrictive. If they were prevented from sailing south of Karlobag and from disembarking on Venetian territory, their operations would be confined to those parts of neighboring Lika which could be reached only by foot through the mountain passes, and they would be cut off from the Ottoman hinterland farther south, with its flocks and its trade, as well as from the tributary villages. Their announcement that they would continue to act in the spirit of the peace agreement with Venice contained no promise that they would obey its terms to the letter.

The uskoks' own view on avoiding conflict with Venice appears explicitly in a slightly earlier proposal made by "the vojvodas and the whole militia of Senj" in April 1600 to the archducal commissioner to Senj and the Venetian Capitano contra uscocchi.[32] A preamble to the proposal condemned the attacks on both sides as unbefitting Christians and stated the uskoks' desire to defend the borders for the House of Austria. It went on to explain the constraints on the uskoks: their lack of agricultural land as a result of Ottoman conquests; their need to subsist on Turkish plunder; the problems posed by the Venetian insistence on closing their routes; the pay of the stipendiati, which was not enough to live on; and the even smaller resources of the venturini. The vojvodas asked that the Republic not close the uskoks' land and sea routes, so that they could continue to plunder the Turk; that the Venetians not per-

[31]Sarpi, *La Repubblica di Venezia*, pp. 8–9. Other sections in the accord covered the right of Austrian subjects to sail freely (in unarmed vessels) for commercial purposes and the freedom of passage between Krk and Bakar. This agreement was based on several earlier versions drawn up under the supervision of de Dominis. In 1598 he had proposed a plan involving the Pope, the Signoria, and the Archduke and the Emperor which would have forbidden the uskoks to harm Venetian subjects and to sail armed barks beyond the Velebit Channel (A.S.V., Provveditori da Terra e da Mar, 922: 28 Nov. 1598, and Horvat, *Monumenta uscocchorum*, vol. 1, pp. 388–93.). In May 1600 he presented a proposal to the Venetian Senate which again would have pledged the uskoks to keep to the Velebit Channel between the Ljubač Straits and Lovran (in Ljubić, "Prilozi za životopis," pp. 25–26).

[32]In A.S.V., Provveditori da Terra e da Mar, 923: 25 Apr. 1600 (enclosure in Pasqualigo's letter, which also describes the subsequent meeting between the uskoks and the Capitano contra uscocchi).

secute the uskoks if they were forced to take refuge on Venetian territory; and that they not prevent uskok captives from bringing their ransoms to Senj, or merchants from visiting with their goods. In return, they vowed that they would refrain from damaging the subjects of Venice, whether on land or sea, adding pragmatically that if "something necessary to human life were taken in case of great need" it would be paid for. In addition they would punish any uskok who dared contravene these orders and would banish his family and would no longer accept fugitives from Venetian justice in Senj. This proposal, with its insistence on the uskoks' right to follow their accustomed routes to plunder the Turk, is very different from the agreement subsequently negotiated by de Dominis, Rabatta, and Pasqualigo, and it was rejected when it was presented to the Capitano contra uscocchi on his galley off Senj by the *capo principale* of the uskoks, probably Ivan Vlatković. Nevertheless, when the uskoks promised to keep the peace with Venice after Rabatta's death, pledging to "castigate any one of us who offers any damage, so much as a penny's worth, or any insult, to the subjects [of Venice] according to justice and his demerits," it was these limits they were volunteering to observe, rather than the narrow restrictions agreed by their superiors. These reservations would be made clear in their actions over the following years.

These two different attitudes toward the appropriate and acceptable limits of uskok action would continue to bedevil uskok relations with the Republic and with the Military Frontier authorities. The uskoks upheld their oaths, but the galleys of the Republic persecuted them for breaking the terms of the agreement between Rabatta and Pasqualigo and trespassing across the Venetian borders. The Republic could not countenance uskok raids that crossed Ventian territory on land or sea, for these made the Republic vulnerable to Ottoman accusations of complicity; while any uskok use of armed barks posed a challenge to the Republic's claim to dominion of the Adriatic. In the next few years, as Venetian opposition to uskok actions became more severe, with blockades of the Croatian Littoral preventing the passage, of merchant shipping from Rijeka and Trieste and threatening the Habsburgs with open war with the Republic, the Hofkriegsrat itself inclined more and more to similarly strict limits on uskok raiding, regardless of the problems this policy would pose for Senj's subsistence. The uskoks, on the other hand, spared little thought for the embarrassment their raids might cause the Signoria. Their duties as well as their needs impelled them to continue raiding the Turk, and they assumed (perhaps willfully) that no Christian power would deny them that role. Over and over, uskoks, individually or as a body, pledged on their honor that they would not harm Venice or its subjects, and just as often the Provveditore Generale pursued uskok barks and executed their crews, to the indignation of the Senjani. The problem was that the two sides could not see the force of each other's arguments, while at the same time both felt themselves to be acting in good faith. Resentment and mutual distrust was the result. No wonder the uskoks felt their reprisals on Venetian subjects were acts of righteous vengeance against an ally of the Turk.

The new Captain of Senj, Daniel Frankol, had at first tried to check the uskoks with a combination of promises of aid and threats of punishment. But he soon faced the usual consequences of preventing uskok raids. In spite of its prohibitions on raiding, the Hofkriegsrat continued to make inadequate provisions for Senj. By early 1603 Frankol had distributed 700 florins to the uskoks out of his own pocket, but Senj was in grave distress; people were dying of hunger and forced to eat roasted acorns and weeds.[33] From the end of 1602 the uskok barks began once again to sail south on their own initiative, crossing Venetian borders to raid Ottoman territory. Faced with dearth and rebellion in Senj, the Captain saw his only solution in recognizing these raids, licensing expeditions to take Ottoman plunder, with firm instructions that the uskoks not harm Venetian subjects. For the most part the uskoks obeyed these restrictions (though the very act of sailing the Venetian Gulf and crossing Dalmatian territory provoked Ottoman complaints against Venice).

Even though the whole community had pledged to continue the peace with Venice after Rabatta's death, the uskoks disagreed over how far it was appropriate to conciliate the Signoria. The loss of Klis still rankled, and the continued Venetian policy of hindering and punishing uskok attacks on Ottoman territories kept alive the conviction that the Republic was more sensitive to the interests of the Porte than to the cause of Christendom. In April 1602 a Venetian galley captured a bark manned by sixteen uskoks who had been on a reconaissance south of Senj. Although the uskoks had done no harm, either to Venetian or Ottoman subjects, the four leaders were hanged and, in spite of protests from both the Archduke and the Papal nuncio, the rest were sentenced to the galleys. Hearing that the captives would not be released, their comrades in Senj proclaimed a vendetta against any Venetian they could lay their hands on.[34] In this case their revenge was postponed, balanced by the fear of provoking another crackdown by the Hofkriegsrat. But perhaps the cumulative effect of Venetian patrols in the waters of Dalmatia and the Croatian Littoral had an even greater effect on uskok relations with the Signoria than did individual acts of retaliation. The patrols

[33]Horvat, *Monumenta uscocchorum*, vol. 2, p. 44.
[34]Ibid., vol. 2, p. 34; R. Regnault, *Lettres et ambassade de Messire Philippe Canaye, Seigneur de Fresnes*, 4 vols. (Paris, 1647), vol. 1, pp. 250, 256.

forced the uskoks, and particularly the venturini, to turn to Christian shipping and even to the Dalmatian islands to find booty. Many uskoks saw such raids as fully justified, since the Republic's patrols prevented them from raiding the Turk, "the common enemy of Christendom." This attitude was scarcely compatible with other uskoks' belief that Senj's interests depended on preserving at least tolerable relations with Venice, so that disagreements over the definition of legitimate raiding began to divide Senj.

A comparison of Vojvoda Vlatković with another well-known uskok leader, Juriša Hajduk, goes some way toward illuminating these divisions. Juriša Hajduk (also recorded as Juriša Lučić) appears in the documents just after the failure to take Klis, with a Venetian price on his head as one of the principal uskok leaders. He was an Ottoman subject who had gone first to Venetian territory, where he became a citizen of the Serenissima, and thence to Senj, where he became a harambaša, with the relatively low stipend of five florins monthly. His wife was a Venetian subject, a woman he had abducted from Sali on Dugi Otok.[35] The nickname of "Hajduk" (meaning brigand, highwayman) reflects his reputation for daring and defiance of authority. When Commissioner Rabatta entered Senj in 1601, Juriša had fled from the city, fearing punishment for raids in Dalmatia and Istria, for he had been one of the instigators of uskok revenge against Venice in the aftermath of the Klis debacle. Rabatta, after investigating his case, agreed he was guilty of excesses against Venice but saw him as "a very brave man and a good soldier, from whose loss the border would suffer greatly" and refused to hand him over to the Venetian authorities, planning to move him elsewhere on the Military Frontier if necessary.[36] Possibly to quiet the complaints of the Venetians, possibly to rid himself of a troublemaker, Rabatta put Juriša at the head of a contingent of uskoks being sent to fight the Turks on the battlefields of Hungary. When they were turned back at Karlovac and returned to Senj, Juriša was clapped in prison and threatened with hanging. It was in the turmoil provoked by this episode that the citadel was stormed and Rabatta murdered. Whether or not Juriša was directly responsible for Rabatta's death (Venetian sources maintained afterward that it was his hand that struck the blow), once Frankol was installed as Captain, Juriša resumed his accustomed place in Senj as an uskok leader.

His precise rank is unclear: apparently Rabatta had been instructed at first to offer him the rank of vojvoda, and the uskok petition that described Rabatta's end refers to him as such, but there are few other

---

[35] A.S.V., Provveditori da Terra e da Mar, 922: 12 Mar. 1599; Minucci, *Storia degli uscocchi,* p. 258.

[36] In Lopašić, *Acta historiam confinii,* vol. 1, p. 287.

references to him with this title, and he was not officially recognized as an uskok vojvoda. In 1602 he was offered the command of Otočac, allegedly to keep him out of trouble, but he refused, preferring to remain in Senj.[37] In later years he signed himself "Captain of Cavalry," but there is no evidence that this rank was formally recognized.[38] Whatever his title, Juriša Hajduk was an active uskok leader, often appearing at the head of raiding expeditions. He was particularly influential among the venturini. He was no friend of the Venetians and would have little hesitation, in the years to come, in attacking Venetian subjects and ships in search of booty or in revenge for real or fancied damage to the uskoks, regardless of the trouble he might cause the uskoks or the diplomatic difficulties he might create for the Habsburgs. Indeed, he was accused of stirring up trouble with the Venetians out of pure malice. Not unreasonably the Signoria repeatedly placed a price on his head.

The vojvoda Ivan Novaković Vlatković represents a contrast to Juriša Hajduk. Apparently more keenly aware of the diplomatic threat to Senj, Vlatković repeatedly strove to limit uskok conflict with Venice and restrict uskok raiding to Ottoman targets. He was perhaps the most influential vojvoda to succeed Juraj Daničić after his death in 1591. In Senj since his youth, Vlatković is first mentioned with the rank of vojvoda in 1598, after distinguishing himself in various actions, including the capture of Klis.[39] Vlatković is not listed among the uskoks who took part in the 1597 raid on Rovinj to wreak vengeance on Venice, but his name appears on the pledge to refrain from harming any subject of Venice signed by uskok leaders in 1598, and the following year he reiterated the vojvodas' willingness to spare the Republic, offering to send venturini to Venice as hostages for their good conduct.[40] It seems that Vlatković kept his oath, for his name does not appear in reports of uskok attacks on Venetian subjects over the next few years. He apparently had a clear conscience on the eve of Rabatta's arrival in Senj for, unlike Juriša and other uskoks, he did not flee the city but remained there to greet the commissioner. Nonetheless, in spite of Rabatta's initially cordial reception of the vojvoda, Vlatković was imprisoned and threatened with death, actions intended to frighten the uskoks in Senj into hunting down their renegade comrades outside the city. Vlatković's life was spared only in

---

[37] A.S.V., Provveditori da Terra e da Mar, 1321, 5 Dec.1602; A.S.V., Senato, Secreta, Materie miste notabili, 126: 23 Jan. 1602 (m.v.).

[38] Lopašić, *Acta historiam confinii*, vol. 3, pp. 438–39; A.S.V., Provveditori da Terra e da Mar, 426: 20 May 1612.

[39] Most likely he was born in Senj of an immigrant family, though other sources indicate that he was brought there in his youth (Lopašić, *Acta historiam confinii*, vol. 1, p. 243; Kleut, *Ivan Senjanin*, p. 16).

[40] I.Ö. H.K.R., Croatica, fasc. 9, 1598, Mar. No. 60: 5 Feb. 1598; A.S.V., Provveditori da Terra e da Mar, 922: 29 Mar. 1599.

exchange for the head of the venturino Mirko Domazetović, as noted above.[41] After this incident, Vlatković was sent as the head of a contingent of uskoks to the outlying frontier fortifications of Otočac and Brinje. Like Juriša Hajduk, however, he returned to his accustomed place in Senj soon after Rabatta's murder.

In the following years, Juriša Hajduk and Ivan Vlatković led raids together, although they often differed on when and how to raid, mainly disagreeing on their attitudes toward Venice and the Military Frontier protection of Venetian interests. Vlatković consistently tried to prevent any damage to Venetian subjects. Juriša Hajduk (perhaps less constrained because he did not hold a high rank in the Military Frontier) felt no compunction in plundering or revenging himself on Venetian possessions and often found himself on the wrong side of Military Frontier policy. In 1603 the two were at odds about Venice. When Juriša wounded a Venetian citizen during an expedition for supplies which had been strictly restricted to Ottoman territory, Vlatković was furious with him for jeopardizing the uskoks' relations with their superiors and with the Signoria. He told a bystander that Juriša was deliberately trying "to provoke a quarrel between the Venetian subjects and themselves, because he has always been an enemy of the subjects of Venice".[42]

Over the next years, Vlatković continued to limit the raids made by his band to Ottoman territory, following the guidelines originally proposed by the uskok vojvodas in 1600. Although he did not hesitate to cross Venetian borders, he refrained from inflicting damage on Venetian subjects. On one occasion in 1604 he had taken several Ottoman captives near Solin and Kamen and, in the face of pursuit by both Ottoman and Venetian troops, retired to Brač to arrange their ransom. From Brač he sent a letter to the Rector of Split, emphasizing that his expedition was not directed against Venice, according to the agreements that had been made between "the honorable Emperor and the honorable Doge." He continued, "I have pledged my head that I will never attack any of your ports, particularly that of Split, as I have not done, nor intend to do, but only those who are under the Turkish city and who serve the Turk."[43] These were not only fine words, intended to deflect attack, but a consistent policy. In 1606, when Vlaković's band stopped on Hvar to bury a comrade after a raid in the Ottoman hinterland of Šibenik, Vlatković prevented his men "from taking anything by force, or from doing any

---

[41]Horvat, *Monumenta uscocchorum*, vol. 1, pp. 412–13; Lopašić, *Acta historiam confinii*, vol. 1, pp. 302–3, vol. 2, pp. 32, 291. See also Kleut, *Ivan Senjanin*, pp. 28–30, for an analysis of these sources.

[42]A.S.V., Provveditori da Terra e da Mar, 1321: 1 Jan. 1602 (m.v.) (interrogation of Nadal Surbi, merchant of Venice).

[43]In Tomić, "O Senjaninu Ivu," p. 10.

harm to anyone" and ordered them to proceed to the Neretva delta, where Ottoman booty was to be had.[44]

As these examples show, in spite of Vlatković's reference to the agreement between the Emperor and the Doge, not even the vojvoda most punctilious in his respect for Venetian subjects was much troubled by the Republic's objections to infringements of its territory. Once local Ottoman authorities began to complain to the Porte and the Signoria about the Venetian failure to fulfill its duty to protect the security of the Adriatic, it was inevitable that the cycle of Venetian retaliation and uskok revenge would begin again. This did not take long. After the uskoks sacked the Ottoman fortress of Herceg-Novi in 1604, local Ottoman officials armed some small vessels to patrol their waters, responding to Venetian protest by claiming that "if navigation in the Gulf had been well guarded, as it has been these last few years, the uskoks would not have dared to sail so far."[45] This complaint was repeated by the Sultan and the Grand Vezir, who accused Venetian subjects of collaborating with the uskoks in attacks on Ottoman territory. Venetian attempts at retribution soon followed, though without much response from the Habsburgs.

In December 1604 a band of four hundred uskoks sailed south, intent on their customary expedition for provisions for the Christmas season. On their way they were confronted by a contingent of Venetian troops which disputed their passage at Ljubač, but they battled their way past. (Ljubač was at the end of the Velebit Channel, the furthest limit of uskok navigation accepted by the Republic of Venice.) When they reached the Trogir district, half the uskoks struck across Venetian territory into the Ottoman hinterland near Skradin, taking some 15,000 head of cattle from Ottoman subjects and returning across the Venetian border. There the uskoks ransomed some of the cattle to the owners and slaughtered the rest to transport it back to Senj for the Christmas festivities. In the meantime, however, the Provveditore Generale had been informed of their encounter with the garrison at Ljubač and their raid in the Trogir hinterland and sent armed barks in pursuit of the uskoks, finally cornering them in a bay on the island of Iž and killing four before the band could take cover. The Venetian commander hesitated to attack immediately, for he feared that his Albanian troops would be outnumbered by the uskoks, who had entrenched themselves behind a barricade in a commanding position above the shore. As night fell, it was decided that the Venetian galleys would guard the bay until reinforcements arrived. That night the *bura* blew up, and it continued to blow the following day and the next,

[44]In A.S.V., Provveditori da Terra e da Mar, 420: 2 Mar. 1606; 18 Mar. 1606.
[45]In ibid., 1265: 4 Aug. 1604.

Christmas day. When the wind died down on 26 December, the Venetians and Albanian troops disembarked and fired a volley of shot at the uskoks' barricade. To their surprise, no answering volley was returned, although they could see the uskoks' feathered caps behind the wall and their guns protruding though the gaps in the rocks. When they stormed the barricade in a hail of fire, they found the position abandoned. The uskok caps were only perched on stones, and the guns were only olive staffs, carefully propped up to look like gun barrels. The uskok barks had vanished, though the eleven boats that had been commandeered in Dalmatia to carry the cargo of slaughtered meat were still drawn up on the shore. When the troops recovered from their astonished laughter, they began to puzzle out what had happened.

During the night, while a few of the uskoks had tended fires on the shore, singing and playing the tambura to demonstrate their indifference to the certain disaster that awaited them from the Venetian galleys in the bay, the others had cut rollers from trees and, using the meat from their barks to grease the way, had hauled their barks over the crest of the island. Tattered shreds of meat and flattened bushes marked their trail, betraying the route of their escape. Before dawn the uskoks had sailed for Senj, leaving behind most of the plundered carcasses. The Venetian commander was furious, but to hide his embarrassment at being outsmarted by the uskoks he ordered his fleet to return to Zadar, flags flying and drums beating in apparent triumph. He forbade his troops to say anything of the uskoks' trick, dividing the plundered meat among them as a bribe for silence, a misuse of the recovered booty which the Ottomans protested angrily when the story inevitably leaked out.[46]

In the meantime, some of the uskoks involved in this incident, enraged by the loss of their Ottoman plunder and not content with thumbing their noses at the Venetian troops, had determined to take a further revenge. They sailed south to Brač, to the bay of Cigala, where they ran across a *fregata* from Brač with travelers and a cargo bound for Venice on board. They beat up the patron and passengers, took their money and valuables, and threw the rest of the cargo into the water. Taking two Bosnians and four Jewish merchants as captives, they sailed away. According to Giovanni of Fermo, as they left they shouted, "Go back and tell the Provveditore Generale from us that we've been paid for the meat he took!"[47] When this band returned to Senj, however, they found the city gates closed to them, on Captain Frankol's orders. Frankol demanded

[46]Rački, "Prilog za poviest hrvatskih uskoka," pp. 205–7; Tomić, "Iz istorije senjskih uskoka," pp. 7–17.

[47]Rački, "Prilog za poviest hrvatskih uskoka," p. 207. See also Horvat, *Monumenta uscocchorum*, vol. 2, p. 62; Regnault, *Lettres et ambassade de Messire Philippe Canaye*, vol. 4, pp. 474–75.

that the Ottoman and Jewish captives be released, and what money he could recover was returned to the Venetian authorities, though not without protests from the uskoks. Although this act of revenge had been against the orders protecting Venice published by the General of the Frontier and the Archduke, the uskoks escaped serious punishment for the time being. As long as those in authority shared the opinion of the Papal nuncio in Graz that the uskoks "were not doing harm to any others besides the common enemy," they would follow his advice to shut their eyes, sometimes, to their affairs.[48]

The uskoks continued to plunder Ottoman territory without much concern about violating Venetian or indeed Ragusan borders in doing so. Large expeditions sailed south to sack Ottoman towns, including Herceg-Novi, Islam, Trebinje, and Skradin, in 1604 and 1605.[49] The Ottomans accused the Venetians, particularly the troops in Šibenik, of criminal negligence in allowing the uskoks to cross their territory in this way, but eventually the Venetians were able to get a *hüccet* (an official document) from the *çavuş* or emissary sent from Constantinople to investigate the matter, clearing them of all complicity.[50] These raids were far from indiscriminate plundering: the expeditions were commanded by the uskok vojvodas and were defended by Archduke Ferdinand and the Hofkriegsrat as part of the Long Turkish War.

Unlicensed raids that damaged Venetian subjects directly were another matter, particularly when they were not undertaken in revenge for Venetian actions. Although such raids occurred, many Senjani, among them Vlatković, condemned them. Conflicts in Senj were revealed in an incident in 1606, when a letter was sent to the Provveditore Generale "in the name of the judges, vojvodas, and the whole city of Senj," with the news that three barks of uskoks had set out in the direction of Istria to raid against orders and in spite of protests from the other uskoks.[51] In this case, uskoks who had been licensed to sail south to seize a flock of goats which spies had reported to be grazing near the shore in Lika found that Juriša Hajduk had been plundering there already. Instead of returning to Senj, they sailed north to Venetian Istria looking for other

[48]In Horvat, *Monumenta uscocchorum*, vol. 2, p. 62. See also Sarpi, *La Repubblica di Venezia*, p. 14.

[49]Tomić, "Iz istorije senjskih uskoka," pp. 45–48, 55–62; Sarpi, *La Repubblica di Venezia*, p. 19; I.Ö. H.K.R., Croatica, fasc. 12, 1604, Feb. No. 37: 1–13; H.A.D., Lettere di Levante, 41: 52'–53 (15 July 1605, on the attack on Trebinje), Lettere di Ponente, 9: 163–63' (10 Aug. 1605), 168'–172 (5 Sept. 1605); A.S.V., Provveditori da Terra e da Mar, 1321: 16 Aug. 1605.

[50]A.S.V., Provveditore sopraintendente alla camera dei confini, 243: 28 Mar. 1606 ("IX Comandamenti et altro circa li confini di Dalmazia . . .").

[51]In A.S.V., Provveditori da Terra e da Mar, 420: 8 and 14 Apr. 1606 (interrogation of G. Blagaich of Senj). The incidents provoking this reaction are described in Tomić, "Iz istorije senjskih uskoka," pp. 101–2.

booty. One of the barks was acting directly against the orders of its vojvoda, Ivan Vlatković, who had sent a message to his men forbidding them to harm Venetian subjects on land or sea. But his warning was too late. The renegade uskoks had discovered a Kotor *fregata* sheltering in a bay near Rovinj and had plundered its cargo, including state money intended to pay the garrisons in Dalmatia and official letters for Venetian officials in Dalmatia, Corfu, and Zante. On their return to Senj they were fired on from the city walls. When the renegades took refuge in a deserted monastery nearby, the Captain ordered their barks burned, and their booty was collected from their families, who were then themselves expelled from the city. In the meantime the Captain and vojvodas sent a messenger to the Provveditore Generale, informing him of the raid and offering to restore the plunder.[52]

On this occasion the renegade uskoks were for the most part venturini, including a good number of fugitives from Venetian Dalmatia, among them some Albanians who had defected from Venetian service. There was no indication that this raid, unlike the attacks on Venetian ships discussed above, was for the purposes of revenge. It seems to have been an unprovoked act of plunder. When warned by the crew of the Kotor *fregata* that the money and letters they had seized belonged to Venice, the uskoks had replied with coarse jokes, denying that they kept accounts for the Signoria. Perhaps the former Venetian subjects among the venturini were tempted to combine the quest for booty with a gratuitous insult to their erstwhile masters?[53] The vojvodas made no attempt to find excuses for these renegades. When some of the erring uskoks were captured, Vojvoda Vlatković himself conducted a Venetian merchant, Zan Piero Cavazza, into the prison to see if any of them had been among those who had plundered his goods from a Kotor *fregata*. He recognized the very uskok who had bitten his nose on that occasion, and Vlatković immediately ordered the man hanged in Cavazza's presence (though the merchant hastily declined the honor).[54] Nor was sympathy shown for the other venturini who had endangered Senj. Not only were they denounced to the Provveditore Generale by the rest of the Senjani and attacked in their hiding place near the city, but when the Venetian blockade dragged on and on because the Habsburg commissioner and the Provveditore Generale were unable to agree over the fate of two captives who had been among those responsible, the citizens of Senj,

---

[52]In A.S.V., Provveditori da Terra e da Mar, 420: 8 Apr. 1606.

[53]Ibid.: 12 Apr. 1606.

[54]Ibid.: 16 April 1606 (testimony by Cavazza). Vlatković and the other vojvodas were also given credit for the restitution of the plundered goods and official correspondence (still unopened) by the Venetian secretary sent to Senj (ibid.: 7 May 1606 and further correspondence).

Bakar, and Rijeka demanded that the commisioner hand these two over to the Venetians, arguing that it was not just that so many should suffer because of these two miscreants.[55]

Senj's fears that the actions of the renegade venturini would bring down retribution on the city were fully justified. This flagrant attack on a Venetian vessel, compounded by the theft of state money and correspondence, provoked not only a Venetian blockade of the Littoral and an intensified patrol against uskok activity but also an official visit from Veith Khisl, General of the Croatian Frontier, who condemned those who had participated in the raid and reiterated the govenment's prohibition on such attacks on Venetian property. At the same time Khisl and the Venetian Provveditore Generale, hoping to prevent such actions in the future, renewed the Rabatta-Pasqualigo agreement prohibiting uskok expeditions beyond the Velebit Channel.[56]

In describing changes in the character of uskok raiding at the beginning of the seventeenth century, an anonymous observer, probably Bishop de Dominis, had noted that "up to a certain point" the uskoks had distinguished between the goods of Christians and those of Turks and Jews in their raids at sea. "Nor did they do this with private thievery, in private companies, but in a general embarcation of all of the militia, and for the benefit and convenience of the whole community. But then their insolence increased so that from plundering the enemy in common, they changed to private thievery and raids, despoiling equally their enemies and their friends."[57] This observer then went on to argue, as we have seen, that the uskoks' robberies were then rendered even more desperate by the countermeasures taken by the Venetians, which forced them to take booty where they could find it and which gave their attacks the pretext of revenge. This observer was a perceptive analyst. Although small-scale raids in private companies were by no means new in the early seventeenth century, from the end of the sixteenth century such raids did become more common, with rebellious uskoks raiding against the orders of the Military Frontier or their own vojvodas. Such uskok bands plundered Venetian subjects and possessions more openly. In addition to the reasons cited, the preceding chapters have described some further reasons for these changes. The growing number of uskoks in Senj, from both Ottoman and Venetian territories, both with grudges against their former masters, needed to support themselves, and they were unlikely to give up raiding even though both the Signoria and the Military Frontier authorities placed new restrictions on their actions. At-

[55]Ibid.: 15 April 1606; Sarpi, *La Repubblica di Venezia*, p. 22; Tomić, "Iz istorije senjskih uskoka," p. 112.

[56]A.S.V., Provveditori da Terra e da Mar, 420: 7 May 1606.

[57]In Horvat, *Monumenta uscocchorum*, vol. 1, pp. 396–97.

tempts to impose controls through the uskok hierarchy did not end raiding, but instead moved it into different channels, provoking dissension and rebellion among the uskoks. Over the course of the sixteenth century, the paradoxical effect of attempts to impose a stricter regime in Senj was to weaken the control of any central authority over uskok raiding. The Military Frontier administration never achieved complete central control over the uskoks; the vojvodas gradually lost much of their claim to it. Signs of these changes were manifested in the disagreements that arose over the targets of raiding. Internal constraints on uskok action could be effective only as long as there was consensus within Senj. When opinion in Senj was divided, with the uskoks themselves in disagreement about what acts were illicit, sanctions on uskok actions began to break down. Neither the vojvodas nor the Military Frontier officials could enforce restrictions that were not supported by most of the uskoks.

The Peace of Zsitvatorok and Conflict with the Hofkriegsrat

It was all very well to agree to placate the Signoria by pledging not to harm Venetian subjects, or even not to trespass across Venetian borders on raids against the Turk. But the Habsburgs asked too much when the uskoks were told they could no longer plunder the Ottomans at all. The peace with the Sultan signed at Zsitvatorok in November 1606 prohibited raids to both sides, and Archduke Matthias, Governor of Croatia and Hungary, in particular, was anxious not to give any pretext for a resumption of hostilities. Still, in spite of strict orders that the uskoks remain in Senj, no pay came to take the place of the forbidden booty. Archduke Ferdinand of Styria, commander of the Military Frontier, realized that the uskoks, and the venturini in particular, could not be held to obedience without more certain means of support, but this was difficult to come by.

Some of the uskok leaders, including Ivan Vlatković, tried to solve the problem by bypassing the hierarchy of the Military Frontier and appealing directly to Rudolf II. Their appeal betrays both their assumptions about the continuing Habsburg support for struggle against the Turk and their preoccupation with the Serenissima's opposition. Their petition asked that they be allowed to use the tribute from villages on Ottoman territory for their own maintenance. Despite the newly signed peace with the Porte, the uskoks foresaw the greatest stumbling block to this idea in the attitude of the Venetians. (Their pent-up resentment can be clearly heard: "The Venetian lords, being such great friends with the Turks, don't want to consent or concede, in any way, our passage into

Turkey through Dalmatia, although it is our homeland and anciently the kingdom of your Majesty, although for the time being in their power; but when we meet up with their soldiers on the road, they pursue us and follow us, so that we cannot but fight them, for our own defense, more than we do the Turks; and they make themselves by force lords of the Adriatic, where we live, and usurp all our privileges and jurisdictions and those of Your Majesty.") They promised at length to do no damage to the Venetians so long as they did not hinder the passage of the tribute expeditions, mentioning in passing that they would not harm the Turks either during the truce. This solution, however, though supported by Emperor Rudolf, was disputed by the General of the Frontier, who had been accustomed to receive this money, and perhaps by others who feared for the peace with the Porte.[58] By November 1607 the Papal nuncio visiting Rijeka reported that the uskoks complained that "it is fifty months since they have had any pay, from which their maintenance entirely depends; they have no trade, nor any land to cultivate, and since they are forbidden to go pirating against the Turk, according to their custom, by now they do not know what should be done, and they are reduced to such necessity that they are almost ready to go to the extremes of desperation and make their minds up to the worst."[59]

Neither the paid uskoks nor the venturini could survive under these conditions. Nor could any vojvoda insist that his men stop all raids against the Turk without their calling his authority into question. Apart from arranging a short truce with the Lika Turks, Ivan Vlatković seems never to have imposed this new demand on his followers. A "confidential person" sent to Senj in February 1607 to test Vlatković's response to the offer of a Venetian post reported that the vojvoda could not believe the terms of the Habsburg peace, seeing it as a betrayal of the ideals of the holy war. Vlatković told the agent, "We have a commission from our princes not to make raids into the lands of the Turk, for they say that a peace has been settled, though we don't know this for certain, but whatever happens I will not be a friend to the Turks, and when they come to Senj I will tell those to whom I have pledged my honor that I won't harm [the Turks] without first informing them, that I am withdrawing [my pledge], and they should look out; because I have a plan to venture out soon, with four or six of my barks, to do the worst that I can to these dogs, to ensure that this peace will never be possible."[60] Whatever their earlier disagreements over the degree of deference owed the

---

[58]In Lopašić, *Acta historiam confinii*, vol. 1, pp. 351–53; vol. 3, pp. 437–38. See also A.S., Deželni stanovi za Kranjsko, 292e: 1963–70; 1971–74 (30 Mar. 1602); Sarpi, *La Repubblica di Venezia*, pp. 24–25.

[59]In Horvat, *Monumenta uscocchorum*, vol. 2, p. 75.

[60]In A.S.V., Provveditori da Terra e da Mar, 421: 28 Feb. 1606 (m.v.).

Venetians, Ivan Vlatković and Juriša Hajduk were of one mind when it came to relations with the Ottomans. In April they sent word to the Turks of Lika that from St. George's Day (23 April, the traditional start of the spring raiding season) the uskoks intended to break the truce and that they should look to their defenses.[61]

When the uskoks disobeyed their Captain's orders to remain in Senj and plundered several Venetian vessels of the goods of Turkish and Jewish merchants, Archduke Ferdinand sent a commission to Senj under General Khisl with plans to remove the uskoks and replace them with mercenaries.[62] News of the General's arrival in Rijeka was received rebelliously in Senj. Vojvoda Vlatković and Juriša Hajduk went to Rijeka as representatives of the uskoks, offering to return any booty that had been taken from Christians but insisting that Ottoman goods were legitimate plunder. The General refused to treat with them. Hearing this, the uskoks in Senj seized the citadel and sent word that "if the General wants to install Italians, or any other people in Senj, they will not consent, but would rather kill one another, together with their children, first."[63]

The uskoks were not strong enough to resist, however, when General Khisl arrived in Senj with one thousand troops, including four hundred German cavalrymen from Karlovac. In the face of this threat, Senj's resistance took on a political color. Since 1604 there had been rebellion in Hungary against the Habsburgs, under the leadership of István (Stephen) Bocskai. The Hungarian rebels' Protestantism had found little response in Croatia, but Bosckai's appeals to the Croats on the basis of their common anti-German sentiment and the demands that Hungarian (and Croatian) affairs should be in the hands of local men and not those of the Military Frontier had found a strong echo, particularly among those who opposed Archduke Ferdinand's efforts to subordinate not only the Frontier but also civil Croatia and Slavonia to the Hofkriegsrat. General Khisl was one of those Military Frontier commanders most opposed to proposals that the border areas be turned over to Croatia.[64] By the time of Khisl's commission to Senj in 1607 the Vienna agreement between Rudolf II and the rebellious Hungarians had been signed, and Bocskai himself was dead. In the ensuing struggle between Emperor Rudolf and his brother Archduke Matthias, however, the Croatian Estates were preparing to press their demands that Croatia's liberties, like

---

[61]Ibid.: 20 Apr. 1607.

[62]The General's report on the uskoks' raids is in A.S., Deželni stanovi za Kranjsko, 292e: 2480–81 (5 July 1607); the detailed reports of the Capitano contra uscocchi are in A.S.V., Provveditori da Terra e da Mar, 1313: July–Aug. 1607.

[63]In A.S.V., Provveditori da Terra e da Mar, 1313: 3, 19, and 27 Aug. 1607.

[64]Lopašić, *Acta historiam confinii*, vol. 1, pp. 330–31.

Hungary's, be recognized; that the Ban, a Croat appointed by the King, be given control of the Military Frontier in Croatia and Slavonia; and that German Military Frontier officers (for the most part from Inner Austria) be replaced by Croats.[65] Senj itself featured prominently in these demands: Germans were to be removed from its garrison; the city was to be returned to the full jurisdiction of the King of Croatia and administered by the Ban; and proposals were made that Juraj Frankopan, one of the lineage that had provided the ancient lords of Senj, was to be appointed as its Captain.[66]

In Senj's angry rejection of the authority of the Military Frontier, General Khisl heard an echo of the Hungarian protests. On his arrival in Senj he immediately arrested Ivan Vlatković, Juriša Hajduk, and Antun Mikulanić, a Senj nobleman and commander of the outlying garrison of Otočac, on charges of conspiracy with the Hungarians. Mikulanić was indeed deeply involved in the Croatian Estates' efforts to win the concessions mentioned above through the Croatian Diet, which would repeatedly intercede for him during his subsequent imprisonment. He was eventually released by the court in Karlovac, though the Military Frontier officials continued to suspect his political involvement.[67] How much Ivan Vlatković and Juriša Hajduk were implicated in the political aspect of this agitation is difficult to say, for their case never came to trial. One day the servant who brought them food in their dungeon smuggled in a rope and an ax and traded clothes with Vlatković. When the ladder was lowered so that the servant could leave, it was Vlatković who ascended, putting the guard to flight with his ax. Vlatković and Juriša then escaped from the citadel by climbing down the rope from a balcony that overlooked the city wall.[68]

Whatever their attitude to the conflict between Archduke Matthias and Rudolf II and toward the struggle of the Croatian Estates for greater power, what is beyond doubt is the opposition of these uskok leaders to the Military Frontier's control of Senj and their seizure of the current issue as a way of expressing their anger. Later in 1607 the three were reported to have come into the city secretly late at night and to have appeared before the citadel where the German guard and the Military Frontier officers sent from Karlovac to impose order were stationed. There they raised a tumult, demanding the keys to the city and the citadel and threatening the German officers within, "abusing them as rogues, thieves, and traitors" and promising "to give their flesh to the

[65]For the Croatian political demands, see Klaić, *Povijest Hrvata*, vol. 5, pp. 569–84.
[66]Šišić, *Acta comitalia*, vol. 4, p. 513; vol. 5, pp. 22, 655–56.
[67]Horvat, *Monumenta uscocchorum*, vol. 2, pp. 73, 74, 78; Lopašić, *Acta historiam confinii*, vol. 1, pp. 360–61.
[68]A.S.V., Provveditori da Terra e da Mar, 1313: 17 Oct. 1607; ibid., da 422: 28 Oct. 1607.

dogs to eat in the streets."[69] When Mikulanić returned from his trial in Karlovac he boasted that he had called the Military Frontier officers "glass sellers and pedlars" to their faces (was this a jibe at their civilian, Inner Austrian origins?), although he denied that he had impugned the honor of General Khisl's mother. He freely predicted that the Military Frontier would revert to Croatian control and would be governed not by Archduke Ferdinand, but by Archduke Matthias as Croatian-Hungarian king, and that Senj's privileges would be restored.[70] For these statements he was once again investigated by the Military Frontier.

The investigations of Antun Mikulanić gives a closer glimpse of some of the disagreements in Senj: between those who placed their faith in the Military Frontier and its patron Archduke Ferdinand, and those like Mikulanić and perhaps Ivan Vlatković and Juriša Hajduk, who based their hopes for the future on Senj's old rights as a free royal Croatian city and who threw their lot in with the Croatian estates (and Matthias, crowned king of Hungary and Croatia in 1608, who represented these demands against Rudolf and Archduke Ferdinand). One witness, a canon of the Senj Cathedral Chapter, testified to the following scene among the uskoks:

> I was at an evening banquet at Maslarda's, and Antun Mikulanić and other good people were at the table, among them Ivan Sičić, who took a glass of wine and drank a toast to the health of King Matthias. At this I said, "I won't drink that toast, but I will drink a toast to the health of the Emperor and the Archduke, who feed us and give us our wages." In response Ivan Sičić turned and took two goblets of wine and drank one to the Emperor's health and the other to the health of the Archduke. But Antun Mikulanić said, "God blast your Emperor and Archduke, and whoever serves them. I will serve King Matthias and drink to his health." . . . And I told him, "If it wouldn't cause a scandal on the evening of this banquet, I'd break your head."[71]

But these political alignments were superimposed on other conflicts over power, more strictly to do with Senj affairs, which appear only murkily through the reports of high politics. These must be painstakingly pieced together from scraps of evidence, which sometimes do little more than provoke speculation. It will be recalled that some uskok leaders had attempted to appeal to Rudolf II in 1607, asking that they be

---

[69]I.Ö. H.K.R., Croatica, fasc. 12, 1607, Nov. No. 25: 25 Nov. 1607 (Hanns Grienwald); Lopašić, *Acta historiam confinii*, vol. 2, p. 16; A.S.V., Provveditori da Terra e da Mar, 1313: 2 Dec. 1607.

[70]Lopašić, *Acta historiam confinii*, vol. 1, pp. 374–75.

[71]In Lopašić, *Acta historiam confinii*, vol. 1, p. 375. Ivan Sičić was a prominent harambaša.

allowed to use the income from tribute for their maintenance. Their appeal had been signed and presented by Antun Mikulanić, as "ambassador of the militia of Senj." Ivan Vlatković's name was also on it, as supreme vojvoda, followed by the names of four other vojvodas: Nikola Rubčić, Ivan Pavković, Miloš Bukovac, and Petar Rosantić; two standard bearers, Petar Vukasović and Luka Kukuljević; as well as Juriša Lučić (Hajduk), captain of cavalry, and Anton Ricano, master of the watch.[72] The vojvodas were active and well-known raiders, particularly Miloš Bukovac, a venturino notorious for his expeditions against Venetian targets. Curiously, however, this is the only document that grants these four men the title of vojvoda. For many years previously, the vojvodas had been Gaspar Stipanović, Miho Radić, Pavle Miovčić, and Ivan Vlatković.[73] By 1607 Stipanović was no longer among the vojvodas (probably because he had been made Captain of Karlobag) and had been replaced by Juraj Vranjanin. Radić, Miovčić, and Vranjanin continued to be identified as vojvodas well after 1607. How are we to explain this proliferation of vojvodas, when it was the custom that there should be only four at any one time?

The answer seems to lie in a struggle for leadership, and perhaps in a disagreement over its nature, among the uskoks. Radić and Miovčić were only rarely reported leading expeditions in these years; Vranjanin was only slightly more active. In Miovčić's case this may have been because of his age,[74] but these men also may have been anxious to keep on the right side of the Hofkriegsrat, on whom their positions depended. In contrast, their rebellious rivals, whose letter reaffirmed Senj's military glories, were often found at the head of uskok raids in these years, whether of official expeditions licensed by the Captain or of smaller private raids. In this light, the claims to the title of vojvoda in the letter to Rudolf look like an attempt to challenge the authority of the older vojvodas recognized by the Military Frontier. Perhaps Mikulanić and Vlatković, as well as other uskoks, wished to return the office to its original character: a reward for military prowess, achieved through uskok acclamation rather than official appointment. This view might also explain Juriša's claim to the title of "Captain of Cavalry," a title confirmed nowhere in the official sources. The regularity with which he appeared at the head of Senj expeditions, on his own or together with Vlatković,

[72]Ibid., vol. 3, p. 438–39.

[73]See, for example, ibid., vol. 1, p. 268.

[74]Pavle Miovčić had been in Senj since at least 1575, when he reported on the division of plunder from Novi (in Ivić, "Prilozi za povijest Hrvatske i Slavonije," p. 303). His long career as an uskok was later confirmed by testimony at the Mikulanić hearing, in which he said he had been in Senj twenty-five years (I.Ö. H.K.R., Croatica, fasc. 12, 1607, Nov. No. 25: 29 Sept. 1607).

identified by the Venetians as one of the *capi principali* of the uskoks, suggests that he had a good claim to leadership on the basis of his popularity and prowess, regardless of official recognition, like the earlier generations of independent vojvodas.

Was it Senj's military role that lay at the heart of the conflict among the uskok leaders? Although it is not obvious how much they were involved in Mikulanić's dabbling in the high politics of the kingdom, Vlatković and his companions were unequivocal in their defense of the uskoks as border raiders, whether or not they agreed on the limits that should be observed. The position of the older vojvodas, Radić and Miovčić, is less clear. According to Paolo Sarpi, it was Vojvoda Radić who went to the Habsburg courts to protest that the uskoks could not survive without booty or pay and who was involved in the plans to support the uskoks with the proceeds of tribute. In their testimony against Antun Mikulanić in 1607, however, both Radić and Miovčić rejected this plan, maintaining that the Senjani had never been granted tribute by royal privilege, but that this money had always gone to the General of the Frontier (and both added that as far as they knew the city of Senj had never recognized Mikulanić as its ambassador to the Habsburg courts).[75] Their statements align Radić and Miovčić with the officials of the Military Frontier, and against those, including Mikulanić and Vlatković, who were rebelling against this authority.

Whatever the substance of their conflict, clearly there was rivalry between Vlatković and the other vojvodas recognized by the Military Frontier. The Venetians knew in 1607 that the Vice Captain of Senj's struggle against Vlatković and Juriša Hajduk had been assisted "by the help of that party opposed to them."[76] This rivalry was still dividing the uskok vojvodas in 1611, when the officially appointed vojvodas secretly denounced the Vlatković brothers for all the "mischief and evil" done by the paid and unpaid uskoks.[77] Perhaps a further explanation is the fact that one of the issues in Vlatković's trial was "whether Ivan Vlatkov[ić] gathered the heroes on the Senj point and pledged them on the cross to all hold together with him, and to esteem the other leaders and vojvodas little, not greatly?" Vojvoda Miovčić would testify, "I heard that Ivan Vlatkov[ić] plotted with the heroes on the point pledging them by the cross to hold him as their leader, and not the other vojvodas; so the rumor went in the city, and so the Captain himself knows."[78] The names

---

[75]Sarpi, *La Repubblica di Venezia*, pp. 24–25; I.Ö. H.K.R., Croatica, fasc. 12, 1607, Nov. No. 25: 29 Sept. 1607 (Paul Michovitschitsch, vojvoda; Vojvoda Micho Raditsch).

[76]In A.S.V., Provveditori da Terra e da Mar, 1313: 27 Dec. 1607.

[77]In Lopašić, *Acta historiam confinii*, vol. 2, p. 17.

[78]In ibid., pp. 10–12. As Kleut (*Ivan Senjanin*, pp. 53–54) has pointed out, this is not the only possible interpretation of the incident: Vojvoda Radić said he knew nothing about the

of the four vojvodas were conspicuously absent from the letters sent from all the groups in Senj on behalf of the Vlatković brothers during their trial. Would it be too bold to speculate, in view of Vlatković's later attempts to detach the uskok rank-and-file from the Military Frontier vojvodas and gather them around himself, that in 1607 Vlatković and his companions were already trying to set up an alternative leadership, outside Military Frontier control and based on popular support, one more committed to raiding and independence?

Although Juriša and Vlatković agreed in their commitment to uskok raiding, they quarreled over its limits. They were to part ways over this issue again during their banishment. At the end of April 1608, a company of uskoks forced its way into the Istrian city of Pula and pillaged some houses, and shortly thereafter seized a Venetian *marciliana* before Rijeka and plundered its cargo of oil. At the time Juriša was blamed for the attack on Pula, and he was certainly involved in the plunder of the *marciliana*, but it is not certain that he was the commander on these raids. In their testimony three years later, Ivan Vlatković and his brother Miho would describe the incident as instigated by Andrija Frletić, one of the harambašas temporarily banished from Senj, who would later take up Juriša's rebellious role. Not far from Senj, Miho "banished and wretched," had met Frletić with one hundred other uskoks on their way to plunder Pula. Miho admonished them "not to undertake such a raid against Christians," but to no avail. Hearing this, Ivan Vlatković sent his brother after these uskoks to try to prevent the raid. He followed them all the way to Pula but failed to prevent the raid on the town, though he apparently did what he could, visiting the Bishop there and pledging to protect the Christians in Pula as much as possible.[79] Immediately after this incident, Ivan Vlatković sent a message to Giovanni Jacomo Zane, the Provveditore Generale, saying that he had not had any part in this raid, that the presence of his brother in Pula had prevented greater damage, and that he had seen that the booty was collected and stored outside Senj ready to be returned to the Provveditore Generale's hands. Vlatković added that he had completely broken with Juriša over the sack of Pula, and indeed other reports received by the Provveditore claimed that they

incident, nor did the third vojvoda, Juraj Vranjanin, but the fourth, most recently appointed vojvoda Miho Hreljanović (who replaced Vlatković) put a slightly different complexion on the event, implying that the pledge was only for the purposes of a raid: "I know that they plotted on the point and that he said that they should hold him as their leader when they went out on an expedition; then the Captain loaned us twelve ducats and we drank in the bishopric."

[79]Lopašić, *Acta historiam confinii*, vol. 2, pp. 32–33. The Bishop of Pula did in fact issue a statement praising Miho Vlatković for his efforts during the sack shortly afterward (ibid., vol. 1, p. 359).

had come to blows (perhaps over the cargo of oil Vlatković seized from Juriša and returned—in part—to Rijeka).[80]

Vlatković's efforts to protect Venetian subjects from uskok attack at this time may have been motivated by something more than principle. His message to Provveditore Generale Zane ended by offering to take service under the Republic. Many uskoks, including both Ivan Vlatković and Juriša Hajduk, had been seeking service outside Senj in these years, either as a way of continuing their accustomed warfare against the Turks in spite of the imperial peace or because they had been banished in the aftermath of Khisl's commission in 1607. The treaty between the House of Austria and the Porte had ended conflict in the Adriatic. Relations between the Serenissima and the Pope were near the breaking point after the papal interdict on Venice in 1606, and both made proposals to take uskok troops into their service. The Venetian agent who had tried to recruit Vlatković in early 1607, before he was imprisoned by General Khisl, reported him as reluctant: "If the Serenissima wants to employ him against the Turks, he will come more than willingly . . . but if it is to be against Christians, he would rather die of hunger."[81]

Vlatković's reluctance can perhaps be attributed to his involvement in 1606 and 1607 in another, more congenial scheme directed against the Turk and, in part, against Venetian domination in the Adriatic. This was a revival of the long-standing plan for an uprising of Balkan Christians. With the Austrian Habsburgs at peace with the Porte, the initiative in this undertaking had passed to Habsburg Spain and to the Pope. Aid to the Balkan Christians was not only a logical extension of Spanish warfare with the Ottoman Empire, it also served as a pretext to increase Habsburg influence in the Adriatic, against the interests of Venice. Many figures who had earlier presented proposals to free the Balkan Christians to Emperor Rudolf now found a warm reception at the court of the Spanish Viceroy of Naples. As always, these conspirators counted on the uskoks as an important part of any Balkan uprising. In 1606 they were devoting most of their efforts to an uprising in Albania, but they were also prepared to consider plans that might divert the Porte from this project. In November 1606 the Venetian Senate learned that Ivan Vlatković had sent word to Naples that he and his uskoks were prepared to take Klis for His Catholic Majesty in a surprise attack if they could be sure of Spanish aid and protection. His proposal even held out the hope of taking Jajce, the principal stronghold of Bosnia. Once again Vlatković's disregard for his superiors' attempts to make peace with the Turks

---

[80]Vlatković's letter to Zane, A.S.V., Provveditori da Terra e da Mar, 423: 19 May 1608; other reports, A.S.V., Provveditori da Terra e da Mar, 423: 12 and 13 May 1608; Lopašić, *Acta historiam confinii*, vol. 2, p. 33.

[81]In A.S.V., Provveditori da Terra e da Mar, 421: 28 Feb. 1606 (m.v.)

emerges from this proposal: he emphasized that the time was propitious, since because of the peace negotiations Klis was ill defended, and the Turks were not suspecting such an attack. (His involvement in this treasonous conspiracy may have contributed to General Khisl's decision to jail him in 1607.) The plan was never put into effect, however, largely because of the hesitation of the Viceroy of Naples, who feared that an attempt on Klis might jeopardize more concrete plans for a Balkan rising. Vlatković maintained ties with the conspirators, but as diplomatic relations altered and their hopes for an immediate Balkan uprising faded, so too did the vojvoda's involvement.[82]

After his flight from prison with Juriša Hajduk and their subsequent banishment by General Khisl, Vlatković was more willing to consider Venetian service. Both he and Juriša now offered to come into the service of the Republic, together with their followers, but by 1608 the Venetian Senate itself had grown cool toward the idea, as tensions had relaxed enough that a military encounter with the papal fleet or the Spanish Habsburgs in the Adriatic seemed less likely. The two tried to revive Venetian interest by intimating that the Republic had a rival for their services in Grand Duke Ferdinand of Tuscany, but the Provveditore Generale replied that he would consider taking them into service only if they were to present him with the heads of the other uskok leaders, informing the Senate that he didn't believe a word of the Tuscan story.[83]

Whether or not the Grand Duke had offered the banished uskok leaders a position, his interest in the services of the uskoks was real enough. Grand Duke Ferdinand was furthering his ambitions to strike a blow for Christendom against the Turk (and, incidentally, to improve Tuscan trade in the Mediterranean) by expanding his fleet and that of the Order of St. Stephen. From 1607 these ships were raiding throughout the Levant. Senj, its uskoks idle as a consequence of the Turkish peace and their pay in arrears, was a prime recruiting ground for Tuscan agents trying to hire crews for this fleet, particularly when Ferdinand began to raise troops for an attempt on the island of Cyprus. Once again, the uskoks could take up their arms against their old Ottoman enemy on new battlefields. Some eighty uskoks took service on the Florentine galleys, and one hundred more promised to follow them. At the same time, the Viceroy of Naples was also trying to recruit dissatisfied uskoks for his fleet, in spite of the Spanish Council of State's condemnation of the uskoks as "brigands who rob both enemies and friends."[84] Eventually,

[82]Tomić, *Građa*, pp. 360–62; 376–77; 384–85, 409; J. Tomić, *Sastanak i dogovor srpskih glavara u Kučima 1614 god.* (Belgrade, 1901), pp. 13–15.

[83]In A.S.V., Provveditori da Terra e da Mar, 422: 28 Nov. 1607; 8 Feb. 1608; 15 Apr. 1608.

[84]Zdenka Reberski de Baričević, "El duque de Osuna y los uscoques de Seña," *Cuadernos de Historia de España* (Buenos Aires), 45–46 (1967): 316, 348–49; see also J. R. Galluzzi, *Istoria*

even the Venetian Republic accepted some uskoks into its service, primarily those who had formerly been Venetian citizens or those with families, seeing this as a useful way of weakening Senj.[85]

Perhaps alarmed at the prospect of losing the uskoks altogether, by mid-1608 the Habsburgs would allow the exiles from Senj to return. Ivan Vlatković and Juriša Hajduk would both be pardoned by the General of the Croatian Border, allegedly through the intercession of a protector at the court.[86] In the course of 1609 the Hofkriegsrat in Graz would forbid the uskoks to take service with foreign states, though in the following years the prospect of foreign employment would continue to attract uskoks who found conditions in Senj insupportable.

Faced with the spectacle of the uskoks who had raided their city of Pula returning to Senj, the Venetian Senate redoubled its efforts against Senj, strengthening the blockade of the Croatian Littoral and Trieste and holding closed the Velebit Channel. Once again there was disagreement in Senj over the best response to this threat. A confidential report by a spy sent to Senj by the Provveditore Generale under cover of his own affairs revealed that there was great scarcity in the city—especially of wine. The uskoks were "greatly disgusted" with their Military Frontier superiors for their conciliatory relations with Venice, particularly in informing the Provveditore Generale of uskok actions and in allowing him to punish captured uskoks. The spy reported that "lively complaints can be heard from the good Senjani against the uskoks who shout and threaten . . . because these miseries are seen as their fault." Similarly, tensions between Senj and Rijeka, which was also suffering from the blockade, were growing.[87] Nevertheless, some uskoks raided Venetian ships to relieve their needs, most notably two bands of venturini under Miloš Bukovac and Miloš Balotić, who slipped out to plunder a Kotor *fregata* of its cargo of cloth and money in a Hvar port. When Balotić returned to Senj the citizens seized and imprisoned him, chased the families of the uskoks involved out of Senj, locked up all the booty they could recover as well as any property that could be used to cover the missing booty, and finally sent a deputation to the Provveditore Generale in the name of "all the people of Senj," offering to make a complete restitution. Much of the plundered cloth was in fact returned, though the representative sent to supervise the restitution complained that the

---

del Granducato di Toscana sotto il governo della Casa Medici, vol. 3 (Florence, 1781), pp. 238–40; I.Ö. H.K.R., Croatica, fasc. 12, 1606, Oct. No. 27: 3 Oct. 1606; Sarpi, *La Repubblica di Venezia,* pp. 29–31; A.S.V., Provveditori da Terra e da Mar, 423: 9 Aug. 1608; 6 Aug. 1609.

[85]A.S.V., Provveditori da Terra e da Mar, 423: 9 and 24 Aug. 1608.

[86]Ibid.: 8 July, 1608; 9 Aug. 1608. See also Grünfelder, "Studien zur Geschichte der Uskoken," pp. 250–51.

[87]In A.S.V., Provveditori da Terra e da Mar, 423: 8 July, 1608.

Senjani measured it with short yardsticks, holding it in the air and pulling it, to make it seem a greater amount, instead of measuring it on a table with a proper Venetian measuring stick.[88] But in spite of this anxious attempt to make restitution, Venice did not relax the blockade.

At this time, with the people of Senj "all stirred up against the thieves," as the Provveditore Generale reported, another attempt was made to solve the uskoks' plight. Once again, the citizens of Senj and the leaders of the uskoks returned to their earlier promises not to harm Venice in return for the freedom to sail south along the Velebit Channel. In November 1608 the "judges, vojvodas, and the entire community of Senj" proposed that if the Venetians would allow the soldiers to go by sea to do their business with the Ottomans (presumably taking ransom and tribute), the Senjani would vow to do no harm and that, furthermore, those uskoks who broke their word would be "pursued as our enemies, their houses destroyed and shut up."[89] The proposal was not accepted by the Venetians, who had little reason to believe that this course would protect them from subsequent Ottoman complaints.

Popular Support for the Uskoks

Venetian patrols reduced the opportunities for plundering raids against the Ottomans, but the need for supplies in Senj increased when Venice periodically forbade trade with Senj and Rijeka and seized ships bound for these ports. No matter how often Senj pledged to keep raiding within bounds, uskok bands, particularly venturini, would slip out to raid, often not much caring where they took the supplies they so desperately needed. From the late 1590s there were increasing reports that uskoks were pillaging wherever they could find something worth taking, be it on Ottoman territory or on Venetian, Ragusan, or papal ships, regardless of whether their booty belonged to Christians or Muslims. Sometimes, when pressed, they passed off their booty as Turkish. Sometimes they simply kept out of Senj, hoping that by the time they returned any furor would have died down.

Denunciations and accusations of thefts of cattle and seizures of fishing barks from Venetian subjects in Dalmatia multiplied in these years. Some accusations were encouraged by the Venetian rectors, who threatened their subjects with punishment for failure to report contact with the uskoks and collected their statements to use as evidence in protests

---

[88]In ibid.: 18 Oct. 1608; 8, 11, and 17 Nov. 1608.
[89]In ibid.: 5 Nov. 1608.

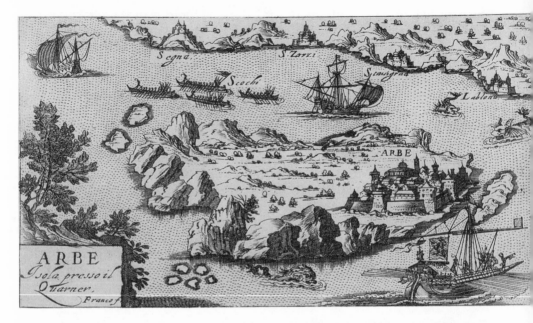

6. A view of Rab, with Senj and uskok barks in the background, from G. Rosaccio's *Viaggio da Venetia a Constantinopoli per mare e per terra, & insieme quello di Terra Santa* (Venice, 1598). (By permission of the British Library.)

to the Habsburg courts.[90] Uskok requisitions seem to have grown in these years, to the extent that one *Capitano contra uscocchi* could claim that "Cres, Krk, Rab, and Pag maintain their flocks of every sort of animal for the use of the uskoks without any expense."[91] (See Figure 6.) The uskoks still often tried to pay for their supplies, as in 1598, when a band of uskoks took a box of fish and some other goods from a fishing boat near Šolta, giving the fishermen in exchange "four *brazze* of Rascian cloth and three pig's feet" (exhibited in court as evidence).[92] But increasingly they simply took what they wanted. Venturini raiding in individual bands might try to make new and even more extortionate demands of their unfortunate victims. One such was Ivan Tomić of Trogir, who appeared in court in 1599 with his bandaged hand slung round his neck in a handkerchief. He reported that on his way back from cutting some wood

[90]See, for example, the reports from 1598 to 1601 collated in Trogir as "Denontie et esposizioni contra uscocchi et martelossi" (in H.A.Z., Arhiv Trogira, 25/11). Other examples can be found in H.A.Z., Arhiv Splita, 140/9, 140/121, and 17/17; A.S.V., Provveditori da Terra e da Mar, 420: Apr. 1606. The penalty for failing to report a sighting of the uskoks was hanging (H.A.Z., Spisi zadarskih knezova, Andrea Valier, 1603–5: 93–93'; 98).
[91]In A.S.V., Provveditori da Terra e da Mar, 1313: 15 Nov. 1607.
[92]H.A.Z., Arhiv Trogira, 25/11: 22 Dec. 1598.

he had been accosted and wounded by an uskok, Miho Orženić [Orx-enich]. He was one of a band that had been pillaging in those parts for some months, probably made up of venturini who had left Senj without a license. After forcing his captive to accompany him for some eight miles, as he tried to find the rest of the band, Orženić allowed Tomić to leave, but only on the condition that he swore on the Blessed Virgin and his faith to pay a ransom—a demand usually made only of Ottoman subjects.[93]

The desperate search for provisions induced the uskoks to strike out in new directions as well. Even nearby subjects of the Habsburgs were not spared. From the end of the 1590s relations with Vinodol had deteriorated, as Count Zrinski had begun to trade with Venice and forbade his subjects to traffic with the uskoks for fear of reprisals to his shipping ventures. In 1609, Ivan Karalja, a venturino, took some sheep from a villager of Bribir, on Zrinski's Vinodol estate. When asked to pay, he not only refused but, incensed by the demand, returned with his companions and burned down the man's house, killed his son, and slaughtered his oxen and cows to carry back to Senj.[94] Karalja had already made the pressures on the venturini explicit that year, as a signatory to a letter begging the Captain of Senj for some sort of support, however minor. "No longer able to live, of great necessity we inform your honor of our unhappy life, as we have nothing to support ourselves, since these past years we poor venturini have had neither campaigns nor pay from Their Highnesses."[95] Attacks on Vinodol could not be prolonged with impunity, however, and other sources of booty had to be found.

More and more often the uskoks were found raiding north around Venetian Istria. From Rijeka, where the uskok barks could claim to be fetching news or provisions, it was a simple matter to sail into Venetian waters, avoiding the Venetian patrols that blockaded the Velebit Channel and the islands southwest of Senj, the route to Ottoman territory. From the early years of the seventeenth century the dispatches of the Istrian rectors report with monotonous regularity uskok ambushes of merchant shipping, raids on the coastal communities, and thefts of cattle and supplies.[96] Istria was also a convenient target for uskok acts of revenge

---

[93]Ibid.: 14 Dec. 1599 (also mentioned 21 Oct. 1599).

[94]This contretemps seems to have taken place in the context of a feud between the villagers of Vinodol and the recently settled Krmpote Vlachs, who solicited the support of the uskoks of Senj in their bloody arguments. Not only were the uskoks generally well inclined toward the Krmpoćani, who had long raided together with them, but their quarrels gave the venturini a pretext for seizing booty. Zrinski's letter of complaint gives other details of the acts of the Krmpoćani, complaining of the support they received from Senj (in Lopašić, *Acta historiam confinii*, vol. 1, pp. 385–89).

[95]In ibid., vol. 1, p. 379.

[96]Miroslav Bertoša, ed., *Epistolae et communicationes rectorum Histrianorum*, vol. 1: An-

against Venice. Unfortunately, the price was paid by those who could least afford it, the poor inhabitants of the Istrian villages. When, in 1612, uskoks burned twenty thatched huts along with haystacks and sheaves of wheat in the villages of Brgudac and Lanišće, carrying off many cattle and much cheese as part of a prolonged cycle of retaliation and revenge, a Glagolithic priest of nearby Roč made a marginal note in a codex, describing the Senj attackers as "Christians by name, but in their acts worse than pagans."[97]

In the late 1590s the uskoks had enjoyed a great reputation in Dalmatia as a result of their involvement in the attempt to free Klis from the Turk. At that time the Venetian rectors had repeatedly commented on the "marvellous inclination" felt by their subjects for these Christian soldiers and Habsburg representatives. Uskok raids that began to affect Venetian subjects in Dalmatia did not completely destroy this attitude. In 1604, even after the uskoks had come into conflict with the people of Šibenik, with "vendettas . . . truly barbarous and inhuman," the Rector would still believe that his subjects were "more favorable to the uskoks than not."[98] Similarly, in spite of the constant requisitions of animals and supplies extracted from them by the uskoks, in 1615 the Captain of the Gulf reported that the people of Rab, Krk, and Pag were more inclined to the uskoks and the Habsburgs than they were to Venice, "feeling their every mischance as their own."[99] But those who were now exposed to increased uskok extortion in Dalmatia were growing short of patience. The Christian population of Poljica and the Omiš Krajina petitioned Emperor Matthias and Archduke Ferdinand for the confirmation of privileges protecting them from uskok attack, and orders to this effect were published in Senj.[100]

The Senjani did not completely tolerate this raiding of Christians. Some uskoks still clung to the same guidelines they had proposed earlier, believing that Senj's proper prey was "the Turk and those who serve the Turk," to quote Vlatković, but accepting that Senj's interests could only be harmed by alienating the Christian princes, and even more so the Christian population. They castigated those uskoks who plundered

norum 1607–1616, Monumenta spectantia historiam Slavorum meridionalium, 52 (Zagreb, 1979), gives a good selection of such dispatches.

[97]Reports on the sack of Brgudac and Lanišće in Bertoša, *Epistolae et communicationes rectorum Histrianorum*, pp. 132–34; the priest's comment in Stefanić, "Glagoski rukopisi otoka Krka," *Djela JAZU* (Zagreb), 51 (1960): 402.

[98]In *Commissiones et relationes venetæ*, vol. 6, p. 119.

[99]In ibid., p. 223.

[100]For the privileges granted to Poljica in 1584 and 1599 and confirmed in 1604, see V. Mošin, *Ćirilski rukopisi Jugoslavenske akademije* (Zagreb, 1955), pp. 248–49, and Koharić, "Nekoje dukale i privilegiji cesarski iz župske škrinjice poljičke," pp. 228–32. For the Omiš Krajina, Šišić, *Acta comitalia*, vol. 5, pp. 107–9.

Christian shipping and Christian subjects, denouncing them for damaging Senj's good name and exposing the city to Venetian retaliation, Military Frontier discipline, and popular disgust. When, for example, a band of uskoks under Matija Klišanin plundered a Venetian ship near Poreč, in Istria, taking among other things 800 thalers, Captain Gušić ordered the vojvodas and other uskoks to act against these renegades. Some eighty Senjani immediately went to the church to take an oath that they would hunt down the lawbreakers.[101] The Captain's success on this occasion seems to have depended on disagreements among the uskoks, for in other circumstances he protested that he was not able to enforce discipline when the uskoks agreed on the legitimacy of their actions. "The Senj soldiers and venturini stick together, with all respect, like foul rogues, and no crow will pick out another crow's eyes."[102] The Captain and the Habsburg commissions were unable (or perhaps unwilling) to back up the orders prohibiting raiding with effective sanctions; and the uskoks themselves disagreed on the limits of raiding. In this atmosphere independent bands had little difficulty in raiding as they pleased, unrestrained by the discipline of the Military Frontier or the opinions of Senj.

Vlatković's Trial: The End of the Independent Vojvodas

Short of funds to purchase uskok obedience with wages or provisions and lacking any other means to coerce it consistently, at the end of the sixteenth century the Military Frontier officials redoubled their efforts to work within the Senj hierarchy to discipline the uskoks, as we have seen. More and more the uskok vojvodas were expected to enforce limitations on raids for provisions and to uphold outright bans on individual plundering expeditions. Those whose claims to leadership rested on their popularity among the uskoks were placed in an untenable position.

Ivan Vlatković was one of the uskok leaders who, caught between the demands of the Hofkriegsrat and the uskoks, could not satisfy both. After his pardon and return to Senj in 1608 he had been appointed captain of a group of Vlachs, the Krmpoćani, who had recently been settled in Lič, near Senj. Following his career as vojvoda, the appointment was clearly a demotion and had probably been made to remove

---

[101]I.Ö. H.K.R., Croatica, fasc. 13, 1611, Feb. No. 1: 31 Jan. 1611.

[102]He made this complaint in 1609, when ordered to proceed against the uskoks who were cooperating with the Krmpoćani in their feuds with Vinodol (in Lopašić, *Acta historiam confinii*, vol. 1, pp. 382–83) and repeated the phrase about the uskoks sticking together like *hundsphötten* in response to a similar order in the case of a vessel brought forcibly to Senj to pay the harbor tax (in A.S., Deželni stanovi za Kranjsko, 293: 1936 [14 Dec. 1611]).

him from Senj and lessen his disruptive influence over the uskoks. (Perhaps to preserve family pride the title of vojvoda was briefly passed on to his brother Miho.) If the Military Frontier officials had hoped to prevent Vlatković from leading independent raids, their plan was not successful. The Krmpoćani were already accustomed to raiding together with the uskoks, and many of their number had joined the uskoks in the past. Now they joined uskok bands on large expeditions. Outsiders still identified Vlatković and Juriša Hajduk as the *capi principali* of the uskoks, though neither of them now bore the official title of vojvoda. Although the documents are not specific, it seems to have been at this time that Vlatković attempted to gather the uskoks under his authority by swearing them to loyalty.

Vlatković is reported heading raids for supplies and for tribute in this period. He would later be accused of raiding Venetian, Ragusan, and Ottoman vessels and possessions, but in his defense he would stress that he had taken only Turkish booty.[103] Although in his eyes these attacks on the infidel were not only justifiable but laudable, the world had changed around him. His actions met with official disapproval, and in August 1610 Vlatković was forced to bow to demands that he keep his men from all raiding. He signed a statement that he and his men in Lič would not "undertake any further raids, either by sea or by land, or any injuries to the subjects of the Holy See; or of the Ragusans or the Venetians; or Turks or Jews; in short subjects of any nation." Vlatković promised to forbid and to punish all such actions, not only those of the Krmpoćani in Lič but also of the Senj uskoks, on pain of loss of his "captaincy, honor, head, wife, and child."[104] Less than a year later Ivan Vlatković and his brother Miho were imprisoned in Karlovac and put on trial at the order of the Hofkriegsrat. The investigation centered on various raids against both Ottoman and Venetian subjects and also dealt with disobedience and insubordination to the Captain of Senj and unlawful appropriation of Military Frontier supplies.

Many witnesses were heard in the case, from all ranks of Senj society. It is noticeable that the charges against the Vlatković brothers and the statements from the representatives of the Military Frontier in Senj were concerned primarily with preserving military discipline and the Habsburg peace. Jeremias Hoff, quartermaster of the Senj *fondaco* in Rijeka, complained of Vlatković's misappropriations of supplies; Ivan Gall, commissioner to Senj, and the four vojvodas who were Vlatković's rivals presented the brothers as the ringleaders of all the "mischief and evil"

---

[103]Lopašić, *Acta historiam confinii*, vol. 2, pp. 15–19, 30–35. Kleut gives a careful analysis of the accusations and Vlatković's testimony in *Ivan Senjanin*, pp. 47–50.

[104]In Lopašić, *Acta historiam confinii*, vol. 2, pp. 3–4.

among the Senjani and warned that they had a great following, particularly among the venturini but also among the paid uskoks, so that they
showed little respect for either the Captain or the commissioners. Even
the Vice Captains of Senj, Zuane Jacomo de Leo and Hans Aichelburg,
who testified on behalf of the brothers, confined their testimony to their
cooperation in maintaining order and in punishing wrongdoers.[105] The
Senj witnesses, on the other hand, were more inclined to stress the role
of the brothers as defenders of the Christian border and heroic warriors
against the Turk. Both the uskok harambašas and the other uskoks, and
the judges, nobles, and commoners of Senj, repeated that the Vlatković
brothers had "never been traitors to their city nor to their troops, nor to
their bands, nor have they ceded to the Turks any city belonging to His
Highness the Archduke, nor betrayed his troops nor bands, but rather,
as we well know, have always behaved loyally and faithfully among the
border knights beneath the Turkish fortresses, against the Turks and
their armies, and they have never failed to aid, and to serve with their
lives and their blood against every enemy of the glorious house of Austria."[106] The Senj Cathedral Chapter presented them as concerned both
for the good of Christendom and the Military Frontier, for "they are
good Christians, and Catholics, and lovers of the Church and of the
friars, and they have pursued and banished those who were disobedient
and acted against the orders of the [Military Frontier] officers, and laid
down their lives to help punish them."[107]

Ivan Vlatković was sentenced to death in Karlovac on 3 July 1612, on
the flimsiest legal grounds, the misappropriation of supplies for Senj.[108]
A more important motive for the sentence seems to have been the desire
to impress the need for military discipline on the uskoks. The final
sentence on Vlatković stated that "he has deserved this punishment as a
dreadful warning, and thus is to have his head cut off with a sword, for
such is the demand of God and of imperial justice" as "an example for
others of similar behavior" in defying the edicts of the Hofkriegsrat.
Vlatković's appeal echoes the themes that he and Mikulanić had sounded
earlier, contrasting the roles of the Croatian border soldiers and the
Habsburg officials of the Military Frontier. It bitterly emphasized his
position, caught between the Hofkriegsrat and the needs of the uskoks,
condemned for no more than nine florins' worth of supplies. "As the

[105]Ibid., vol. 2, pp. 17–18, 22–23.
[106]In ibid., vol. 2, pp. 20–21 (the statement by the "judges, nobles, and commoners" of
Senj).
[107]Ibid., vol. 2, p. 27.
[108]The reason given in the final sentence was that he had seized supplies for the Senj
garrison from the quartermaster in 1610 and 1611. He had been given permission to do so by
the Vice Captain of Senj, but the court found that this had been beyond the Vice Captain's
competence and that Vlatković was therefore guilty (ibid., vol. 2, pp. 35–37).

result of no other relevant reason I shall be condemned to death by all-too-severe German military justice . . . a poor imprisoned Croatian soldier who has served His Highness from his youth in all occasions that have befallen." The appeal did not affect his sentence, for it arrived only after his execution. It was marked, "To be ignored, it comes too late."[109] It can be no coincidence that this judgment was executed in a period of great tension between the Republic of Venice and the uskoks, resulting in urgent Venetian demands that the Habsburgs remove the uskoks from Senj. Shortly after Vlatković's execution the Archduke sent an ambassador to Venice to negotiate a solution to the uskok problem, and at the end of the year signed the so-called Vienna Agreement, in which Venice agreed to raise its blockade in return for a reform of Senj.[110]

Vlatković had been a certain type of vojvoda, one now growing rare in Senj: a leader whose authority rested on the respect of the uskoks themselves and whose influence was great enough that he could at least attempt to unite them all under his command. It was ironic that it was Vlatković who was executed by the Military Frontier, for he at least attempted to turn the uskoks away from their self-destructive warfare with Venice, though he could not accept the ban on Turkish raiding. But the Hofkriegsrat would not tolerate such influence any longer. The officials of the Military Frontier had hesitated even to touch Vojvoda Juraj Daničić in 1582, fearing a popular uprising from the uskoks if their leader was harmed, but when Ivan Vlatković was executed there is no record of any outcry (although there was some whispering in Senj, enough to be reported by the Provveditore Generale). The authority of the Hofkriegsrat over the uskoks and their leaders was now strong enough to enforce even such unpopular decisions.

What became of Vlatković's counterpart, Juriša Hajduk, with his heedless raids on Venice? His fate is uncertain, for his name simply disappears from the documents after mid-1612. Some historians have identified him with a certain Purissa mentioned by Paolo Sarpi, hung by the Military Frontier commissioners from a parapet of the citadel as "one of the most insolent of the leaders."[111] He was not involved in Ivan Vlatković's trial shortly afterward. If he did die in this way, his execution was marked by little ceremony and accompanied by little comment. Perhaps Juriša Hajduk was never so much a threat to the authority of the Military Frontier as Ivan Vlatković had been. Juriša had defied the orders of the

[109]In ibid., vol. 2, pp. 38–39.
[110]The text is in ibid., vol. 2, pp. 47–48.
[111]Sarpi, *La Repubblica di Venezia*, p. 36. Perhaps he was executed in this way, though probably not in 1611 as Sarpi claims, for in January 1612 this "old leader of the Senjani" was seen leading a flotilla of uskok barks toward Ottoman territory near Obrovac (A.S.V., Provveditori da Terra e da Mar, 425: 14 Jan. 1612).

Hofkriegsrat in raiding Venetian shipping and Venetian ports, but he had also challenged Senj's own code by elevating revenge against Venice above the duty to fight the Turk (the crux of his conflict with Vlatković) and, even more so, by raiding Venetian subjects indiscriminately, without even the excuse of vengeance. (It is perhaps revealing that Juriša is far less well represented than Vlatković in the oral tradition about the uskoks, even in the earliest known collection of epic songs.)[112] Vlatković, on the other hand, always claimed to be working within this code, stressing above all the duty of defending Christendom by warfare against the infidel. Although Vlatković could be accused of disobedience, he could still claim legitimate authority in the eyes of Senj. It was he who was loyal, and his opponents (whether jealous rivals among the vojvodas, treacherous Venetians, or even the representatives of the Military Frontier) who were betraying the ideals of the *antemurale* to political expediency.

No other such powerful vojvodas appeared in Senj. Power was now widely dispersed among the uskoks, with many harambašas leading their bands out to raid regardless of the orders given by the Hofkriegsrat, the pledges of the vojvodas, or the attitudes of the city. Juriša would have a number of successors, such as Andrija Frletić and Vicko Hreljanović: uskok harambašas who raided independently, with little attempt to justify their attacks on Christian shipping.

Toward War with Venice

Since the mid-1590s the Republic of Venice, with its growing intransigence over uskok raiding, had become one of Senj's main enemies. It can probably safely be claimed that the uskoks hated and distrusted the Venetians even more than they did the Muslims of the border, for although the Turks were infidels, they at least recognized the rules that governed their mutual antagonism and dependence, developed over the long experience of border warfare. The Signoria, however, not only ignored the demands of honor and good faith (killing rather than ransoming prisoners; rejecting the uskoks' word of honor; and betraying pledges of safe conduct) but also struck at the very basis of the uskoks' holy war, denying them the right to raid the infidel at all. (Of course, from the Venetian point of view, the uskoks' claims of holy war were indefensible, since Christians as well as Muslims were affected, and the idea of uskok honor was simply laughable, since their pledges did nothing to prevent Ottoman retaliation against Venetian citizens.) By the

[112]See Marija Kleut, "Juriša the Hajduk in Historical Reality and in Serbocroatian Epic Songs," *Narodna umjetnost* (Zagreb), 26 (1989): 51–57.

1610s even the most cautious among the Senjani were losing their willingness to placate the Republic, and the independent uskok raiders saw no reason to refrain from pillaging Venetian possessions whenever they had the opportunity.

In spite of their growing hatred of Venice the uskoks, in the main, still saw battle with the Turk as their raison d'être. But because the Habsburgs disengaged with the Ottomans after 1606 in order to deal with internal problems and because they were anxious not to provoke further Turkish wars, they saw less value in this uskok role (although intermittent border clashes kept it from being entirely disregarded). Nor were the Habsburgs in agreement. Archduke Ferdinand was happy to use the uskoks in pressing his rivalry with the Republic in the Adriatic, but Emperor Matthias was more concerned for peace abroad so that he could deal with conflicts within the Empire. As a result, when uskok clashes with the Republic served a diplomatic purpose against Venice the uskoks could be assured of Habsburg protection, but when Habsburg policy dictated peace with the Republic as well as with the Ottoman Empire, the uskoks could easily be sacrificed, having outlived their usefulness in both war and diplomacy. This sacrifice would eventually be their fate, but for the moment uskok resentment and Habsburg calculation would unite to bring relations with Venice to the breaking point.

From the end of 1611 a series of Venetian attacks on uskoks fueled Senj's resentment of the Republic, while at the same time Venetian pressure (in the form of blockades of Ferdinand's possessions on the Littoral) forced the Habsburgs to consider conciliation, reining in the uskoks in the process. In December 1611 the Venetians captured Juraj Milašinčić, an uskok of about seventy years of age, who held the post of Captain of Brinje. This was the season of the uskoks' winter raids for supplies, and Provveditore Generale Lorenzo Venier hoped to use Milašinčić to increase pressure on the uskoks to remain quietly in Senj. In spite of the uskoks' anxiety about Milašinčić, the uskoks raided Ottoman territory several times, repeatedly informing the Venetians that they had no intention of harming Venetian vessels or citizens. Pavle Dianisević, secretary to the Captain of Senj, informed the "confidential person" sent to Senj by the Provveditore Generale that the uskoks wished to navigate in Dalmatian waters only to attack the Turk, "having resolved, or so they say, never to do harm of any sort to the Christians." Dianisević asked after Milašinčić and complained about the Venetian blockade, saying that if it came to war with the Venetians, the uskoks would utterly destroy Pag, Rab, Krk, and Cres and cut their inhabitants to pieces.[113] They did little to retaliate, however, probably because they knew that the

---

[113]In A.S.V., Provveditori da Terra e da Mar, 425: 27 Jan., 1612; 4 Feb. 1611 (m.v.)

Hofkriegsrat or the Archduke would not tolerate action against the Republic. The fact that Ivan Vlatković had already been charged with raiding Christian shipping, and that depositions on his case were being collected in Senj at this time, hinted at the fate that awaited those who disobeyed Military Frontier orders.

With violence out of the question, the uskoks attempted to pacify Venice by renewed pledges of peace. According to Provveditore Generale Venier, the vojvodas and two hundred of the uskoks offered to sign a pledge that they would never harm Venetian citizens, ships, or possessions in return for the release of Milašinčić. Venier proposed instead that the uskoks find German merchants to pledge their goods in Venetian warehouses as sureties against losses to the uskoks (without believing that they would be able to do so, since they were "constructed in a flood of crimes, nourished in every sort of wickedness and contaminated by every nefarious action, so that it seems to me contrary to nature that they should ever quieten down and find merchants or other secure persons who would wish to risk their property, almost certain that they would have to succumb to payment"). He concluded by stressing his hope of keeping these thieves in order by keeping "this old billy goat of theirs" alive on his galley.[114] And this was how matters remained for several months, with the uskoks raiding Ottoman territory occasionally while doing no harm to Venice, whether because of their pledge, because of obedience to the orders of the Hofkriegsrat, or because of "the supreme providence of the Lord, and the singular wisdom of Your Excellencies," as the Provveditore Generale believed.[115]

In May, Venetian troops ambushed and captured six more uskoks in Dalmatia. The uskoks saw this as a brutal betrayal, particularly as the captured men had been bringing the commander of Zadar news of the approach of Ottoman troops and had received a pledge of safe conduct from the commander of the Venetian forces.[116] The uskoks and their leaders complained to the Provveditore Generale, noting that "we are paid back in nothing but false coin, if this is the way that you use those who risk their lives against the Turks to the benefit of these lands." A series of letters sent to the Provveditore Generale appealed for the release of both the six captives and of Juraj Milašinčić. These pleas repeated the rhetoric of holy war, speaking of the services of the cap-

[114]In ibid., 425: 5 Feb. 1612 (enclosure of 27 Jan. 1612).

[115]In ibid., 426: 11 Mar. 1612.

[116]Provveditore Generale da Canal gave the details of the grant of safe conduct and the capture of these uskoks (in A.S.V., Provveditori da Terra e da Mar, 426: 9 May 1612). This incident took place in the context of Venetian disputes with the Ottomans on the Zadar borders, in which the uskoks had been aiding the Venetian troops (Horvat, *Monumenta uscocchorum*, vol. 2, pp. 97, 99; Rački, "Prilog za poviest hrvatskih uskoka," p. 211).

tured uskoks to Venice against the Turk, "the common enemy of the Christian faith," and describing Milašinčić as "a good and devoted Christian, who has done untold service to the holy Christian faith, and to the most serene House of Austria against our common Turkish enemy."[117]

But to no avail. The Provveditore Generale was far more concerned to conciliate the "common enemy of the Christian faith," particularly as the Emin of Makarska was taking Venetian hostages in retaliation for uskok raids and threatening to attack Brač and Hvar as nests of uskoks. The only suggestion that the six captives be returned to Senj came from the Rector of Šibenik, who thought that they might be exchanged for Nikola Armenčić, an uskok by origin from Šibenik, who had recently decapitated the Ottoman harambaša of Drniš in battle. Armenčić could then be presented to the border Ottomans as a way of winning their favor.[118] But this plan was rejected, and the Provveditore Generale continued to hold the six captives and Juraj Milašinčić on his galley as a security for good behavior from the uskoks, ignoring their threats of revenge for the dishonorable breaking of a promise of safe conduct.

Convinced that their comrades would not be released, a group of uskoks vowed to seize a Venetian noble to exchange for them. In spite of the execution of Ivan Vlatković the previous month, in August these uskoks determined to defy both their Military Frontier masters and the Venetian officials and kidnapped the Provveditore of Krk, Gieronimo Marcello, holding him hostage outside Senj.[119] In response Venice sent its fleet to gather at Krk, and troops disembarked eight miles from Senj and burned mills belonging to the Daničić family. The Archduke immediately sent a commissioner to Senj with orders to release the Provveditore and to apologize for his mistreatment. The uskoks had chosen an awkward time to carry out their plan, for the Archduke had just sent an ambassador to Venice to protest Venetian measures taken against his lands, including the capture of the six uskoks, in an attempt to improve relations between the two states. In spite of these negotiations, conflict continued, with the uskoks plundering and burning Venetian settlements in Istria and Venetian troops raiding in return. These battles soon drew in many other participants besides the uskoks and their opponents, becoming a general struggle between Venetian and archducal

---

[117]In A.S.V., Provveditori da Terra e da Mar, 426: 20 May 1612 (enclosures); similar claims had earlier been made on behalf of Milašinčić (A.S.V., Provveditori da Terra e da Mar, 425: 5 Feb. 1612 [enclosure]).

[118]In A.S.V., Provveditori da Terra e da Mar, 426: 8 June 1612.

[119]Ibid., 1313: 6 June 1612; 17 and 24 Aug. 1612; ibid., 426: 16 Aug. 1612. Giovanni of Fermo claimed that Provveditore Marcello had been involved in the Venetian request for uskok aid against the Turk in the Zadar area, the occasion of Ghini's betrayal of the safe conduct to these uskoks, which made his capture appropriate according to the terms of the code of honor (Rački, "Prilog za poviest hrvatskih uskoka," p. 211).

subjects in Istria. As the archducal ambassador to Venice noted, once the sword had been drawn from the scabbard, it was a long struggle to find a way to put it back.[120]

Prolonged negotiations were needed to resolve this conflict. Archduke Ferdinand, the Spanish ambassador to Venice, and to a lesser extent Emperor Matthias wished to use the uskok disputes to force the Republic to recognize the freedom of navigation in the Adriatic and to resolve certain border disputes in Istria, Friuli, and the Tyrol; while Venice was determined to maintain a blockade against the ports of the Croatian Littoral until the uskoks were resettled, refusing to consider any discussion of the freedom of navigation unless this issue was resolved.[121] It was not until the end of 1612 that an agreement was finally signed in Vienna, according to which Archduke Ferdinand promised to prevent any piracy out of Senj, to expel the wrongdoers, and to place a German garrison in the town. Venice would release its prisoners, raise the blockade, and permit the passage of commercial traffic on the Adriatic, but discussion of the freedom of navigation would be postponed. By this time, however, Juraj Milašinčić had died in Venetian captivity.[122]

In accordance with the Vienna Agreement, the Habsburgs sent a commission to Senj and appointed a new Captain, Nikola Frankopan of Trsat. The Venetians hoped that he would have a personal interest in the quiet of the area because of his own local landholdings. His orders from Archduke Ferdinand were explicit: he was to prevent all raids on Venetian territory; to forbid the plunder of any ship, whether or not there were Turks or Jews on board; and he was to see that the peace with the Ottomans was respected as long as it was in force.[123] When the order that the uskoks were forbidden to raid either Turks, Venetians, or any other Christians was published in Senj, the uskoks protested, "saying how can they live on so little pay, if they are forbidden to go corsairing?" They were told that "the pay would be enough and more if they abstained from playing cards and getting drunk, as they do all day and night, but that whoever cannot live on this pay should go about their affairs, and that the gates are open." About one hundred venturini of foreign origin had already been expelled and were living in Vinodol, while others were seeking service elsewhere.[124]

---

[120]In Horvat, *Monumenta uscocchorum*, vol. 2, pp. 99–106.

[121]Ibid., vol. 2, pp. 115–18, gives a summary of the Habsburg grievances.

[122]Lopašić, *Acta historiam confinii*, vol. 2, pp. 47–48. Another of the uskok captives being held by Provveditore Generale Pasqualigo had also died. One of the others was a former Venetian citizen, and thus Pasqualigo felt he need not be released (A.S.V., Provveditori da Terra e da Mar, 427: 25 Dec. 1612).

[123]The assessment of Frankopan is in A.S.V., Provveditori da Terra e da Mar, 427: 26 Jan. 1612 (m.v.); his orders are printed in Lopašić, *Acta historiam confinii*, vol. 2, pp. 40–46.

[124]A.S.V., Provveditori da Terra e da Mar, 427 : 13 Jan. 1612 (m.v.)

For a brief time, relations between the Venetians and the uskoks remaining in Senj appeared to be mending as a result of the Vienna Agreement. The release of the surviving uskok hostages still in the Provveditore Generale's hands was announced; Pasqualigo permitted the uskoks to sail out to collect their tribute from the Ottoman subjects between Split and the mouth of the Neretva; the uskoks notified the Venetian authorities of two barks of pirates raiding along the coast and offered to pursue them.[125] But very soon the Ottomans broke the peace in Hungary and attacked fortifications in Otočac and Karlobag, provoking uskok retaliation. Habsburg measures restraining the uskoks were relaxed in the face of this briefly renewed Ottoman threat. In April the uskoks carried out successful expeditions against Skradin and Trebinje, taking a large amount of booty in plunder and captives. Provveditore Generale Pasqualigo reported that they had done no harm to Venetian subjects, except by requisitioning supplies and vessels, "with prompt and abundant payment in coin of the realm," a fact that annoyed him more than if they had used their usual violence, because it gave the local Ottomans cause to complain that the Venetians were in league with the uskoks.[126] The resumption of uskok raiding meant that Venetian retaliation would not be long in coming.

Shortly afterward, uskoks returning from a raid against the Ottomans in the Neretva area were confronted by armed barks of Albanians in Venetian service. In the ensuing battle about sixty uskoks were killed, including their leader, Vojvoda Miho Hreljanović, and their heads were cut off and taken to Split. Only one uskok was kept alive, so that he could identify the heads and the soldiers could claim the rewards offered for them.[127] Three days later, news arrived that uskoks had seized a Venetian galley and had killed its *sopracomito*, Christoforo Venier, a relative of their enemy, Provveditore Generale Venier. "These uskoks said that they were moved to this iniquitous action in revenge for their companions killed by our men at the same time, pretending to be able to navigate the Gulf at their pleasure against the Turks, adding furthermore that since in their last voyage they did not damage the subjects and possessions of Your Serenity, they ought not to be impeded and mistreated." The uskoks themselves announced that they had "decapitated all the marines on the galley one by one, throwing them down the gangway into the sea. We took all the galley slaves out of their chains and freed them, and we are taking the galley to Senj. We will do even worse, for we do not wish to be

[125]Horvat, *Monumenta uscocchorum*, vol. 2, pp. 121–22.

[126]In A.S.V., Provveditori da Terra e da Mar, 427: 26 Apr. 1613.

[127]Ibid.: 10 May, 1613. Giovanni da Fermo reported that Pasqualigo had ordered this massacre and that once again it had been carried out under a Venetian pledge of safe conduct (in Rački, "Prilog za poviest hrvatskih uskoka," pp. 213–14).

prevented from sailing to the detriment of the Turks in any way." They carefully preserved Venier's head in a box, hoping to exchange it for the head of their vojvoda, Miho Hreljanović.[128]

Venetian reports spread tales of barbarous mistreatment of Venier's corpse: the uskoks were alleged to have eaten his heart, or at the very least to have dipped their bread in his blood.[129] Although this may have been a useful piece of propaganda for Venice abroad, at least some Venetian subjects in Dalmatia expressed greater sympathy with the uskoks. The Rector of Trogir reported that certain citizens were little devoted to Venice "and have publicly acclaimed the sad case of Sopra-comito Venier, killed by the uskoks, and have exalted the Imperials [the Habsburg subjects], sympathizing with the uskoks whom they say were assassinated by our men."[130]

Pasqualigo's immediate response to Venier's murder was to blockade the Croatian Littoral, closing the waters before Senj, while Venetian troops massed in Istria. At the same time Ottoman troops were reported to be approaching by land. Ferdinand feared that they intended to attack and ordered all his lands to prepare for war.[131] At the same time, measures were taken to placate the Republic. The new Captain of Senj hurried to Senj, where with great difficulty he succeeded in extracting Venier's head from the uskoks and sending it on to Rab, where it was placed in state in the cathedral. He did not, however, return the guns from the Venetian galley, which had been mounted on the walls of Senj, saying that this was a matter for the Archduke to judge (and clearly preferring to retain this artillery should it come to war with the Republic).[132] The Captain's mission to Senj was quickly followed by the dispatch of an imperial commission with instructions to investigate and punish the uskoks' misdeeds. In spite of substantial Habsburg concessions, little was achieved toward a permanent solution.

Hieronimo Soranzo, until 1614 the Venetian ambassador to Emperor Matthias' court, believed that no solution to the problem Senj posed could be achieved until the Archduke was convinced that it was in his interests to restrain the uskoks. The Emperor was better disposed toward Venice, "but the point comes to this: the Emperor gives the orders, but the execution rests with the Archduke and his ministers, who are very interested in the affair." Not only did the Archduke find the uskoks

[128]A.S.V., Provveditori da Terra e da Mar, 427: 13 and 24 May 1613.

[129]Sarpi, *La Repubblica di Venezia*, pp. 78–79; anon, *Aviso delle Ragioni della Serenissima Signoria di Venetia intorno alla mossa d'Arme contra Uscocchi* (Venice, 1616 [?]); Biblioteca Marciana, "Raggioni che hanno mossi li SS.ri Ven. a pigliar l'armi contro il Ser.mo Arci-duca Ferdinando" (It. VII 807 [= 9558], no. 4 [S.S.E.E.S., Longworth microfilm collection]).

[130]In H.A.Z., Fond Šime Ljubića, 7/63: 2 Apr. 1614.

[131]A.S., Deželni stanovi za Kranjsko, 293a/2: 333–34 (13 June 1613).

[132]In A.S.V., Provveditori da Terra e da Mar, 427: 30 May and 26 June 1613.

valuable against the Turk, Soranzo continued, but they gave the Habsburgs a pretext to dispute freedom of navigation on the Adriatic with the Republic, while the possession of Senj kept alive the crown of Croatia-Hungary's ancient claims to the province of Dalmatia. The Habsburgs were not at all unhappy to see the Signoria embroiled with the Ottoman Porte over the uskoks: Austria could only benefit by having the Ottomans distracted from the Croatian border. Soranzo hoped that a renewed offer to purchase the timber around Senj in return for peace with the uskoks might win the support of the Archduke by appealing to his pocket, but this hope was to prove illusory.[133]

Soranzo saw the uskok problem as a diplomatic conundrum, arising from rivalries between states and, depending on the appeal to their interests, capable of resolution by agreement among them. His assessment was accurate as far as it went, as much in its implications for the future as in its analysis of the present. Although uskok attacks continued intermittently over the long months that followed, the focus of events in any narrative that attempts to account for changes in the uskok phenomenon must now shift away from Senj to the courts of Europe. More and more the tale becomes one of the approaching war between the Republic and the Archduke. Although Senj was undoubtedly an irritant in the relations between the Republic and the Habsburgs, there were many other contributing factors, not the least Venice's fears of Habsburg encirclement and Austrian resentment of Venetian trade monopolies and maritime restrictions. Ultimately, the uskoks were not the real cause of the "Uskok War," but only provided the occasion for hostilities.

Characteristically, Soranzo's interpretation of the uskok problem had entirely ignored the interests and attitudes of the uskoks. Their fate would be decided outside Senj, by the diplomats and courtiers of the European powers. Events were overtaking Senj, and in the new alignments of the early seventeenth century there would be little place for the independent irregulars of the holy war. Not only diplomatic circumstances had changed, threatening Senj's place in the world. Over two decades, the emphasis of the uskoks' holy war had shifted decisively against Venice, while raiding the Turk was progressively limited both by Military Frontier regulation and Venetian armed opposition. With this change there had come a growing confusion and dissension over the limits of legitimate action and a parallel breakdown in the structure of authority in Senj, leading to uncontrolled and indiscriminate raiding. The shape of uskok raiding and the character of uskok life had changed markedly since the beginning of the 1590s.

[133]Fiedler, *Relationen der Botschafter Venedigs,* pp. 29–31.

CHAPTER NINE

The Dispersal
of the Uskoks

In 1614 imperial mediation and a commission to Senj kept the Venier affair from escalating into open war, but peace would not last for long. In Venice, a faction in the government was increasingly prepared to confront the Habsburgs in war, with aid from the Protestant powers. Ottoman pressure also contributed to Venetian willingness to take the confrontation over the uskoks to a radical conclusion, when in 1614 an Ottoman çavuş arrived in Venice with demands that the Republic either prevent uskok attacks on Ottoman subjects or else allow the Ottoman fleet into the Adriatic. Archduke Ferdinand, too, was inclined to war with the Republic, counting on support from Spain. At the same time, uskok raids against both Ottoman and Venetian targets escalated. How could the uskoks, slowly starving in Senj, be expected to wait out the Venetian blockade, when the Archduke himself was telling the Emperor, "My Lord! I cannot war alone against the Republic; but if I were able I would do it as willingly as against the Turks!"[1]

He soon had his wish. Hostilities between the Archduke and the Serenissima broke out not only on the Croatian Littoral but also in long-disputed territories on the border in Istria. Venetian troops sacked Lovran, then occupied Karlobag and attacked Novi. In November 1615 the War of Gradisca, sometimes called the Uskok War, was formally declared. Military activity was greatest in the first months of the war, particularly in the Gradisca area, where Venetian armies seized several Habsburg possessions. Here fighting took the form of a series of pitched battles, soon reaching a stalemate. Istria was the scene of destructive guerrilla warfare, both sides raiding, burning, and plundering. Uskoks from Senj played a considerable part in this theater of the war, as well as

---

[1]Report of the Papal nuncio in Graz, in Horvat, *Monumenta uscocchorum*, vol. 2, p. 155.

fighting farther afield in regular military units, striking along the Venetian coast as far north as Monfalcone. Open war had resolved all uskok
questions over the legitimacy of attacking Venetian subjects and possessions. The constant raiding swept much of the population of the Istrian
borderlands into a bitter struggle for survival and revenge.[2]

It was not in the inconclusive battles in Friuli and Istria that this war
was decided, however, but rather in the less bloody encounters between
the ambassadors and emissaries of the powers involved. Although the
Spanish governers of Milan and Naples were eager to aid the Archduke
against Venice and its Protestant supporters from England and the
Dutch Republic, both Spain and the Emperor intervened on the side of
an expeditious peace, alarmed by the potential for a general European
conflict implied by the constellations of powers aligned on either side.
Negotiations for a truce had followed soon after the first hostilities. First
in Madrid and then in Paris an agreement acceptable to both parties was
hammered out.

The 1617 Treaty of Madrid, later ratified in Paris, restored the borders to
their prewar status on the condition that the uskoks (both venturini and
stipendiati) who had engaged in raiding before the war would be removed from Senj and replaced by a German garrison.[3] This proposal
sounded no more promising than previous agreements of the same sort
(particularly since uskoks were involved in the continuing attacks on
Venice orchestrated by the Duke of Osuna, Viceroy of Naples), and indeed, Venetian emissaries who signed the treaty were accused of having
exceeded their instructions.[4] But by 1617 the Habsburg attitude toward
the uskoks was changing. Not only did the Archduke agree to the removal of the uskoks in negotiations with Venice, but in 1616 Vienna had
renewed its peace with the Porte, specifying that raiders and plunderers
were no longer to receive Habsburg protection.[5]

Archduke Ferdinand had been chosen to succeed the ailing Emperor
Matthias in 1617 and was now taking over the affairs of the Empire. By
mid-1618 the Bohemian Estates had risen against the imperial abrogation
of religious tolerance in the conflict that would form the first stages of the

---

[2]See especially Bertoša, *Jedna zemlja, jedan rat*, for details on the war in Istria, and Ber-
taša, "Uskočki rat," for its social and economic consequences. The standard Austrian
account is A. Gnirs, *Österreichs Kampf für sein Südland am Isonzo, 1615–1617* (Vienna, 1916),
but for the political and economic background see H. Valentinitsch, "Ferdinand II., die
innerösterreichischen Länder und der Gradiskanerkrieg, 1615–1618," in *Johannes Kepler,
1571–1971: Gedenkschrift der Universität Graz* (Graz, 1975), pp. 497–533.

[3]A copy of the treaty appears in Lopašić, *Acta historiam confinii*, vol. 2, pp. 63–64.

[4]Sarpi, *La Repubblica di Venezia*, pp. 239–42. For the Duke of Osuna's war against the
Republic, see Negri, "La politica veneta contro gli Uscocchi," and Reberski de Baričević, "El
Duque de Osuna y los uscoques de Seña."

[5]Noradounghian, *Recueil d'actes internationaux de l'Empire ottoman*, vol. 1, pp. 113–20.

Thirty Years' War, the European-wide conflict that the "Uskok War" had foreshadowed. All the military strength the Habsburgs could muster would be diverted to this battlefield. While this conflagration raged within the Empire, the soldiers of the southeastern border could not be allowed to provoke Ottoman assaults or Venetian retaliation. Uskok raids that had been exploited by the Military Frontier in the Turkish wars or by the Archduke in his rivalry with Venice would now be a serious embarrassment.

This changed view of the utility of the uskoks is reflected in the decisiveness of the Habsburg commissioners sent to reform Senj in cooperation with their Venetian counterparts. The joint commission met for the first time in April 1618. Once they assembled, their work went quickly.[6] They rapidly agreed that all uskoks, both venturini and stipendiati, who had engaged in piracy before and after the recent war should be expelled from Senj according to the terms of the Madrid treaty, which forbade them to settle within ten leagues of the coast. Venetian subjects were given fifteen days to beg clemency of the Venetian commissioners and to return to the service of the Republic. Habsburg subjects were forbidden to aid any banished uskok to evade these reforms.[7] New German troops were to be installed, bringing the garrison's complement up to the full strength of 105, from the mere thirty Germans that the Hofkriegsrat in Graz had been startled to discover actually remained in Senj.[8] In short order a census of all uskoks in Senj was taken; those with no other means of support were named and resettled in the garrisons at Brinje and Otočac; the barks used for raids were taken to Rijeka and burned; and those unrepentant uskoks who continued to plunder regardless of the new order were banished and a price placed on their heads.[9] The reforms had by no means stripped Senj of all its uskoks, however desirable that result may have been to Venice. The Hofkriegsrat had been anxious that the commissioners retain the most dependable uskoks as a necessary supplement to the German garrison. Ideally Senj would continue to provide two vojvodas, each commanding fifty uskoks. Nor were those who were forced to leave Senj abandoned completely to

[6]The reports of the Venetian commissioners stress the willingness of their Habsburg counterparts to go beyond the Venetians' demands in taking action against the uskoks, a cooperation that doubtlessly contributed to the smooth operation of the commission (A.S.V., Provveditori da Terra e da Mar, 1315: 13 Aug. 1618).

[7]Reports of Commissioner Harrach, 10 Apr.–4 June 1618 in Lopašić, *Acta historiam confinii*, vol. 2, pp. 70–72.

[8]Instructions from the Hofkriegsrat, Apr. 1618, in ibid., vol. 2, p. 68. See also A.S.V., Provveditori da Terra e da Mar, 339 bis: 27 and 29 Mar. 1618.

[9]I.Ö. H.K.R., Croatica, fasc. 14, 1618, Apr. No. 4: 30 Apr. 1618 (7–7′); Lopašić, *Acta historiam confinii*, vol. 2, pp. 72–76 (reports from Commissioner Harrach, Aug. 1618). See also *Libri commemoriali*, vol. 7, pp. 140–48; Fiedler,*Relationen der Botschafter Venedigs*, pp. 47–76.

their own devices—if they were not settled in Otočac or Brinje they were to be sent on to Karlovac for reassignment, in particular to the battlefields of Bohemia. Those who wished to take up service under other sovereigns, however, were permitted to do so. The Habsburg commissioners hoped that some at least would wish to serve the King of Spain.[10] The number and character of the uskoks remaining in Senj and the fortresses of the Maritime Frontier, and those in the adjoining Zrinski and Frankopan possessions in Vinodol, were to be carefully controlled in the future. No longer would the uskoks in Senj be permitted the independent lawlessness of the past. By August 1618 the commissioners had completed their task to the satisfaction of both parties and the commission was dissolved.

In spite of the Hofkriegsrat's clearly expressed desire to retain the uskoks' services (though limiting the scope of their activities), the uskoks saw themselves as betrayed. Not without reason, the uskoks blamed the Habsburgs for forcing them into piracy by failing to pay them, and could scarcely believe, as they said, "that their masters now wished to destroy and abandon them."[11] The atmosphere in Senj following the conclusion of the Treaty of Madrid was desperate. Not knowing what would become of them, the uskoks vowed unity in the face of the reforms proposed by the joint commission. At the same time each tried to cope with the expected expulsions. Some sent their families and belongings out of Senj to keep them safe from the commissioners; others fled themselves, leaving their families behind as a surety for their eventual return. Many were said to be considering the possibility of taking service elsewhere— the favored plan was to join the fleet of the Duke of Osuna, which was still harrassing Venetian shipping. In desperate uncertainty over their plans, Vojvoda Frletić's wife tried to exert some control over the future by bewitching the commissioners, "making certain signs over their footprints where they had passed."[12] The uskoks made no secret of their discontent once the reforms were under way. One of the many Venetian agents gathering information in Senj during the operation of the commission in 1618 reported that the uskoks were saying that "the Latins are nonetheless worse than the Turks, for the Turks would never have committed such an act of cruelty as to drive them from their own homes."[13] Nevertheless, most followed their orders.

[10]Lopašić, *Acta historiam confinii*, vol. 2, pp. 65–67; A.S.V., Provveditori da Terra e da Mar, 60: 28 July 1619 (on uskoks being recruited for Bohemia).

[11]In A.S.V., Provveditori da Terra e da Mar, 339 bis: 2 May 1618.

[12]Ibid., 1315: Apr. 1618. Frletić's wife already had a reputation for witchcraft, having been accused of using spells to avoid pregnancy (ibid., 339 bis: 27 Mar. 1618).

[13]In ibid., 339 bis: 2 May 1618. Other reports by Venetian spies at this time appear in ibid.: 27 and 29 Mar. 1618, 2 May 1618; and ibid., 1315: Apr. 1618 and 8 Apr. 1618 (by an escaped captive).

Many of those who obeyed the orders to leave Senj believed that they would soon be allowed to return to the homes and families they left behind. Although the official reports of the commission give no hint of such a promise, uskoks settled in Otočac and Brinje later claimed that Commissioner Harrach had sent them "out of Senj to Otočac and Brinje for a while, so that the peace negotiations could be finished and concluded more quickly . . . and then each would go back to his own place in Senj." (This belief was also recorded at the time by Venetian commissioners Giustinian and Priuli.)[14] If the Habsburg commissioners gave this excuse, it may well explain why the resettlement of the Senj uskoks was carried out so expeditiously and with so little overt opposition.

There was of course some resistance. Even before the commissioners' arrival many uskoks, particularly those most at risk (former Venetian subjects, those with no other support than raiding, those in bad odor with the Hofkriegsrat) had already fled Senj to nearby mountain fastnesses or to Vinodol rather than submit to removal from their homes and banishment to the hinterland. Some uskok bands, even before the end of the War of Gradisca, had taken steps to ensure their survival regardless of the outcome of the war by taking service under other patrons or by shifting the bases of their operations outside Habsburg territory.[15] For those officially banished from the Habsburg Littoral by the Treaty of Madrid, a career as a privateer for another Adriatic power (or would-be power) was an attractive alternative. This was the solution found by Vojvoda Andrija Frletić, long an active uskok leader, whose career in Senj had been punctuated by clashes with the Military Frontier authorities over ill-timed raiding.[16] He had been named in the commissioners' reforms as one of those banished with their wives and families to a distance of ten leagues from Senj, never to return. Nevertheless, as he had done when banished in 1611, Frletić left his family in Senj and returned more or less openly to visit them.[17] Instead of resettling in the hinterland as a Habsburg border soldier, Frletić continued to raid Venetian shipping on the Adriatic, often in cooperation with other pirates, including the English Catholic Robert Elliot.[18] When Frletić was finally banned completely from Habsburg territory he sailed to Naples, and

[14]In Lopašić, *Acta historiam confinii*, vol. 2, p. 77; A.S.V., Provveditori da Terra e da Mar, 1315: 19 May 1618.

[15]See, for example, Horvat, *Monumenta ucocchorum*, vol. 2, pp. 438–40.

[16]For Frletić's role in the trial of the Vlatković brothers see Lopašić, *Acta historiam confinii*, vol. 2, pp. 8–9, 10–11, 20–21.

[17]Lopašić, *Acta historiam confinii*, vol. 2, p. 76; A.S.V., Provveditori da Terra e da Mar, 339 bis: 2 May 1618.

[18]For Eliot's raids in uskok company see Horvat, *Monumenta uscocchorum*, vol. 2, pp. 452–53, 466; Great Britain, Public Record Office, *Calendar of State Papers and Manuscripts relating to England existing in the Archives and Collections in Venice* (1911), vol. 17, no. 393.

obtaining a privateer's patent from the Viceroy, redoubled his raiding as part of the Duke of Osuna's private war against the Serenissima.[19] Frletić and his band of uskoks, supported by Osuna, inflicted such damage on Venetian shipping in the following years that the Council of Ten, in 1621 and 1622, offered a reward of 1000 ducats to anyone who would assassinate Frletić.[20] Frletić was one of the most notorious of those uskoks who, unable or unwilling to resettle in the hinterland, found another patron for their accustomed raids. But many others found a less prominent berth in the fleets of Tuscany, Naples, or even—for a few deserters—the galleys of their old enemy, Venice.

Other uskoks resisted the commissioners' decisions less overtly. The uskoks who had complained in February 1619 that Commissioner Harrach had promised that expulsion was a temporary solution had given another reason that they should be allowed to return: their wretched living conditions. "Now it is the ninth month that we have had no provisions, except for a single Ljubljana *star* of grain for each soldier. . . . It is not possible that we should stay, because of the cold and the lack of accommodation, for both those in Brinje and in Otočac have crowded little houses, so that in this cold weather it is difficult for them to keep their own families alive because of the winter, much less take us into their homes."[21] Nor were the defenses of the fortresses in any better condition. An inspection that same year found Senj's fortifications in reasonable shape, though poorly maintained, but in Brinje and Otočac the walls and towers were rotting and in ruins, and Brlog, in an exposed position on the edge of no-man's land, seemed to have no defenses at all.[22] The decision to resettle the uskoks had been accompanied by very little preparation for their maintenance—or for the maintenance of the German garrison replacing the uskoks in Senj. In addition to these difficulties, the Hofkriegsrat, the Estates, and the Archduke could not agree on a suitable (Catholic) Captain for Senj, so that the constant supervision necessary to enforce order was lacking.[23] With or without permission, the uskoks began to leave their ill-provided new postings and to trickle back to their old haunts in Senj.

[19]Lopašić, *Acta historiam confinii*, vol. 2, p. 89; Sarpi, *La Repubblica di Venezia*, p. 401; Horvat, *Monumenta uscocchorum*, vol. 2, p. 482; A.S.V., Provveditori da Terra e da Mar, 1315: 23 June 1618. The Viceroy was reported to have granted Frletić full rights to all booty (A.S.F., Mediceo del Principato, 3088: 664–64').

[20]Lamansky, *Secrets d'état de Venise*, vol. 1, pp. 114–15.

[21]In Lopašić, *Acta historiam confinii*, vol. 2, p. 77. (A Ljubljana *star* was a grain measure equivalent to about 114 liters.) The Hofkriegsrat response to such pleas was firmly negative. See I.Ö. H.K.R., Croatica, fasc. 14, 1619, Mar. No. 7: 5 Mar. 1619.

[22]A.S., Deželni stanovi za Kranjsko, 162/2: 76–90 (Beschreibung der Grenzfestung 1619).

[23]When the German troops did not receive their pay, they revolted and many deserted (Horvat, *Monumenta uscocchorum*, vol. 2, pp. 476–80).

In April 1619 the Papal nuncio in Graz, Erasmo Paravicino, visited the Maritime Frontier and reported on conditions in Senj, where he found "incredible disorder":

> There is no Captain there; the garrison has left; the banished uskoks with their families have found quarters part on the lands of Count Zrinski, part on those of Count [Frankopan] Tržački, and those confined to the nearby fortress have nearly all returned to Senj with their families. We had believed that there would be one hundred Germans from Karlovac in Senj, as had been promised, to replace the garrison and to provide forces to punish evildoers, but up to now we have seen not a single one appear, nor do we have any hope that they will come; and what is worse is that the few soldiers who remain in the garrison are for the most part Croats.[24]

The Hofkriegsrat was fully aware of this situation and had already sent two new commissioners, Mark Beck and Stefano della Rovere, to deal with it. Their reports confirm Paravicino's description of affairs in Senj.[25] Not until they had received reinforcements from Karlovac and firm backing from Ferdinand II against Count Zrinski and Count Frankopan Tržački (the former Captain of Senj), who had been accused of protecting the uskoks in Vinodol, were they able to execute their orders. They seized the property of the uskoks who were raiding under Osuna, confined and resettled their wives and families, razed the houses of the most notorious offenders (Frletić among them), and once again resettled the uskoks in Brinje and Otočac.[26] The question of the uskoks' upkeep was resolved for the time being when the Estates of Carniola agreed to subsidize the garrison.[27]

The uskoks, particularly those in the hinterland fortresses, accepted this new life reluctantly. A Venetian observer noted in 1620, "They are persons accustomed to live from pillage and piracy, and to their extreme mortification they must now forbear, having exchanged the use of pillage for other, more laborious ways of life: some cutting wood, others hoeing, others ploughing. . . . Many from time to time burst out, saying that they would rather die as soldiers than live so wretchedly."[28] And it must have been a wretched life, for the support promised by the Carniolan Estates was predictably irregular, and the continued danger of Ottoman raids made it hazardous to work in the fields of the hinterland fortresses.[29] Over the years some soldiers of Senj as well as those of the

[24]In ibid., vol. 2, pp. 482–83.
[25]In Lopašić, *Acta historiam confinii*, vol. 2, pp. 81–83.
[26]Ibid., vol. 2, pp. 88–90; A.S.V., Provveditori da Terra e da Mar, 60: 28 July 1619.
[27]Horvat, *Monumenta uscocchorum*, vol. 2, p. 480.
[28]In *Commissiones et relationes Venetæ*. vol. 6, p. 292.
[29]A.H., Spisi Like i Krbave, 1/3: 19 Oct. 1623.

hinterland turned to the timber resources of Velebit as a means of support, felling trees and transporting them to the coast for sale. This task
demanded much labor and left the unguarded outposts vulnerable to
Ottoman attack, as in one large raid in 1642. The Captain of Senj justified
the troops' apparent negligence on this occasion by pointing out that
they had received no pay for four years.[30] Other members of the garrison
turned to the cattle trade, buying and selling pigs and cattle from both
Croatian and Ottoman territory. Their claims to be exempt from the city
trentes (excise) met with opposition from the citizens of Senj, who by 1619
were reviving the economic distinctions made by the city statute against
those who did not enjoy the privileges of citizenship.[31] Uskoks and
citizens were no longer mutual collaborators in a raiding economy; they
became competitors for the same trade.

When they could, the uskoks turned again to raiding to supply the
necessities so inadequately provided by their masters and by the infertile
wastes of the Velebit karst. Both the Ottoman borders and the shipping
of the Adriatic were targets. In the early 1620s the Venetians strengthened their patrols of the Dalmatian waters against the excursions of the
uskoks—"more numerous than ever," or so it was claimed.[32] But retribution from the Military Frontier authorities followed—applied consistently, quickly and violently, particularly in the case of the ringleaders. In
1623 they seized Vid Lumbardić, who had been leading a small band in
raids on the coast. Those of his band who submitted to judgment were
removed (again) to hinterland fortresses. Lumbardić himself, the instigator of the raids, was imprisoned, tried, and executed in Senj, and his
severed head was fixed above the sea gate as a warning of the serious-
ness of the Hofkriegsrat's prohibitions against raiding.[33] Even so, the
habits of plundering were not relinquished overnight.

No single moment marked the end of the uskok era in Senj. Each
resolute action by Captain or commission was followed, after an inter-
val, by another quiet influx of the banished border soldiers back into the
town and by renewed raids, growing bolder until they were once again
put down in an official reaction. Through the end of the seventeenth
century and into the eighteenth century there are reports of uskok raids,

[30]In Lopašić, *Acta historiam confinii*, vol. 2, p. 259.

[31]See the complaint by Vicko Desantić, a Senj magistrate and a merchant, to the
Hofkriegsrat about fraudulent claims to tax exemptions by members of the garrisons of Senj
and Ledenice trading in cattle, in I.Ö. H.K.R., Croatica, fasc. 14, 1619, Mar. No. 7: 5 Mar.
1619.

[32]A.S.F., Mediceo del Principato, 3088: 868 (13 Feb. 1621); 878 (1 Mar. 1621); Theiner, *Vetera
monumenta Slavorum meridionalium historiam illustrantia*, vol. 2, p. 124; A.S.V., Provveditori
da Terra e da Mar, 60: 6 July 1620.

[33]Lopašić, *Acta historiam confinii*, vol. 2, pp. 121–22; A.H., Spisi Like i Krbave, 1/3: 19 Oct.
1623.

isolated attacks, and small piracies. Other attitudes died slowly too—in 1638 Venetian ambassadors could still report that the appearance of Senj uskoks in Dalmatia would not be possible without the help of Venetian subjects.[34] And in 1703 the Venetian ambassador to Vienna complained, in the aftermath of a recursion of raiding, that the Senjani "make war on Venice's trade with more pleasure than they do on the enemies of the Emperor."[35]

After the Treaty of Madrid raids from Senj occurred just often enough to waken memories and fears of the uskoks' actions in the years of Senj's notoriety, but they were conspicuously lacking their earlier organization and support. The end of Senj's uskok era is usually connected to the resettlement of the most active uskoks in the hinterland fortresses—the implication being that the raids depended on the courage and leadership of these particular men and that once these were removed the system failed. This explanation holds a degree of truth. Certainly the Military Frontier authorities concentrated their efforts on first resettling and then eliminating the leaders of the uskok bands, the most notorious uskoks, and the most recalcitrant recusants. Many uskoks ignored the orders to leave, however, and others were allowed to remain in Senj as part of the reformed garrison. In 1698 the participants in a rebellion in Senj included the names of such well-known uskok families (banished from Senj following the Treaty of Madrid) as Daničić, Hreljanović, and Klišanin.[36]

The new, determined opposition from the Habsburgs and the Hofkriegsrat was the most decisive cause of the decline of uskok activity in Senj. Their active encouragement had played an important role in the early development of the uskok system, their tolerance or inertia had allowed it to continue, but their withdrawal of all support was a fatal blow to the uskoks. A safe haven, neutral at the least toward uskok actions, had been a primary condition for the persistence of the uskok phenomenon in Senj. Other factors reinforced the effects of the new ban. Fewer recruits came to Senj after the Treaty of Madrid. The Military Frontier authorities, according to the treaty, were no longer to allow refugee settlement in the town (though in fact a trickle of settlers continued to arrive). Perhaps more important, Senj, with its ships burned and its uskok leaders dispersed, was no longer a magnet for the dissatisfied and the dispossessed—and the resentments of recent arrivals no longer fed the fires of holy war against the Ottomans and Venetians. By the early seventeenth century the Hofkriegsrat and the other Military

---

[34]Fiedler, *Relationen der Botschafter Venedigs*, p. 208.

[35]In Giudici, *I Dispacci di Germania*, vol. 2, p. 16. For Senj raids in the eighteenth century see Stanojević, *Senjski uskoci*, pp. 306–8.

[36]As well as many others from the list of those banished. See Lopašić, *Acta historiam confinii*, vol. 2, pp. 73–74, and ibid., vol. 3, pp. 118–20.

Frontier officials had achieved considerable control over the internal organization of the uskoks, particularly through the appointment of their leaders. Even greater control was foreseen by the recommendations of the Treaty of Madrid that the garrison be staffed only with Germans. The substitution of Germans (or at least Habsburg subjects from Inner Austria) for the local Croats in the lower ranks of the Senj garrison was never completely successful, as can be gathered from many orders to employ Germans in later years.[37] Earlier objections to this plan—that the foreigners would simply depart when their subsidies were slow in arriving—were repeatedly proved well founded. Nonetheless, the Military Frontier officers consolidated their hold on the indigenous troops, splitting potential opposition by retaining the distinction originally denoted by the terms 'venturini' and 'stipendiati' and by making the appointments hereditary. The authorities also continued the process begun earlier in the century of arrogating the rights that pertained to the free royal town of Senj to the Frontier administration.[38] After 1620 the military organization of Senj was fragmented and set in partial opposition to the civil interests of the town. No longer could the uskoks and their supporters afford to ignore the strictures of the authorities, nor were they able to manipulate the divisions among their superiors to justify their raiding.

The decline of the uskoks in Senj was not accompanied by a fading of uskok raiding elsewhere along the border. On the contrary. The end of the Ottoman war in 1606 and the shift in Habsburg preoccupations to the European conflicts of the Thirty Years' War meant that the Habsburgs gave little support to actions against the Turk all along the Habsburg border. Along the Venetian border, however, matters were quite different. Between 1645 and 1718 the Republic of Venice fought three wars with the Ottoman Empire, and though the great battles were in Crete and the Morea, all three wars were also fought on the Dalmatian border. Recruits that might once have fled to Senj to take up arms under the protection of the Habsburgs now poured into Dalmatia, to recross the border in uskok bands, raiding and plundering the inhabitants of the Ottoman territories.[39]

The observations of that acerbic Venetian visitor to Senj, Vettor Barbaro, from his report to the Senate in 1601, continued to hold a good deal of the truth for many years.

> It is impossible, as the experience of all the ages of the Earth teach us, that in Dalmatia there should be no uskoks—that is, thieves and assassins. The

[37]See ibid., vol. 3, pp. 121–22, for an example from 1698.
[38]See Roksandić, "Bune u Senju," for details of these developments in the seventeenth and eighteenth centuries.
[39]See Grgić, "Postanak i početno uređenje vojne krajine"; Peričić, "Vojna krajina u Dalmaciji"; Bracewell, "Uskoks in Venetian Dalmatia."

nature of their countrymen calls to them through their own instincts; and the advantages of the site and the arrangement of the countryside, and also the proximity of the borders of various Princes, and also of various religions, customs, administrations, judicial systems, and of other things—all these factors are a strong indication as to why these men give themselves up to plunder, make a good profit from it, and receive information and aid.[40]

Senj was only a small community, situated in a border region that derived its international importance from the great powers that clashed there. As the seventeenth century progressed, the threat of the Ottoman wars on this frontier declined, and at the same time the focus of political and economic power shifted away from the Mediterranean, leaving Senj on the periphery of Europe. Although the uskoks had played a relatively independent role for some eighty years, by the early 1600s they had been vanquished by the power of state bureaucracies that could no longer brook such dangerous lawlessness on their borders. The only lasting monuments to their existence were the songs and stories of their exploits which passed from mouth to mouth among the illiterate peasants and soldiers of the frontiers. Their greatest significance has usually been seen in the part they played as pawns in the great power rivalries of the sixteenth- and seventeenth-century Adriatic.

But influence on the world stage and lasting political power are not the only possible measures of significance or meaning. If instead we view history from the bottom up, the clash between the civilizations of Islam and Christianity and the economic and political rivalries of the Habsburgs, the Signoria, and the Sublime Porte can be seen to have been played out on the borders by groups of individuals, with their own assumptions, interests, and problems. The history of the uskoks of Senj allows us an insight into the workings of conflict at the rank-and-file level, throwing light on internal workings of border society and culture.

The everyday life of the border was a constant struggle for survival. Through the uskoks, we are able to examine the economic and political pressures on this society. Their raids, like the activities of many of the other inhabitants of the border, were predicated on the need for plunder and the interests of the warring states. But cultural backgrounds and social relations, as well as material conditions, shaped their lives. Understanding the choices these people made demands a careful attention to their modes of thought. The uskoks have helped to open up a chink through which we can begin to glimpse the mental world of the border, a world of cross-cutting allegiances and identities in which religious divisions and cultural expectations justified, even glorified violence; in which

[40]In H.A.Z., Fond Šime Ljubića, 2/33: 288.

deep social and political divisions were sometimes transcended by common cultural values and customs; in which the uskoks could be pirates
and brigands in the eyes of some and heroes and symbols of freedom to
others. The uskoks have also helped us to analyze change in the character of border society, identifying not only the efforts of a centralizing
state to impose a new discipline on its subjects but also the interaction of
interest and ideals that shaped the responses—far from homogenous—
to it.

What did it mean to be an uskok? Let us return to the contradictory
assessments of the uskoks mentioned at the beginning of this book, now
better equipped to evaluate them and to understand what lies behind
them.

Vettor Barbaro, and many others, would have told you that to be an
uskok was to be a pirate—by circumstance and by inclination a plun-
derer of all that he could seize, living off the sweat of others, making a
show of crusading zeal as a pretext for robbery. And the significance of
the uskoks? Tools of the Habsburgs, first in their border wars with the
Turk, then in their political and economic rivalry with the Serenissima.
In practice the views of their Habsburg rulers were not much different,
although they defended the uskoks as soldiers in a holy war to justify
their own purposes. Privately, however, they were ready enough to
agree that the uskoks obeyed no law save their own greed. These views
are understandable enough: both groups looked at the uskoks from the
standpoint of their own interests.

Many historians have agreed with such appraisals, though in recent
years the explanation for uskok raids has shifted away from the uskoks'
nature ("inclined to plunder and kill") to a more purely economic response to need. In the eyes of these historians, this frontier of perpetual
warfare, made still more unstable by its role of safety valve for the
rebellious elements of the neighboring societies, offered its inhabitants
no other choice but to raid or be raided. The involvement of the empires
helped polarize this conflict, but essentially it was a naked struggle for
survival. The conclusion is the same: these uskoks were pirates, with no
particular allegiances, *humani generis communes hostes*. This interpretation, too, is understandable, particularly as a reaction to a romantic
nationalist view of the uskoks which saw them as primitive national
liberation guerrillas, embodying a struggle against foreign domination
and oppression. The latter view is difficult to reconcile with the results of
the uskoks' actions. The uskoks can hardly be seen to have fought for
social justice for the peasants and pastoralists, from whose ranks so
many came, when their raids did them so much harm. Nor can the
uskoks be seen to have contributed much to national liberation—as soldiers of the Habsburgs they made war on their fellows under Venetian

and Ottoman rule, contributing to the development of what in Istria Miroslav Bertoša has called a "squadron" mentality, by which subjects identified themselves primarily with the banners of their lords, dividing the population into "Imperials" and "Venetians" (and "Turks"), regardless of their common ethnic origins.[41] The resulting fratricidal conflicts served the interests only of the great powers who fought out their rivalries over this land.

But, as I hope to have shown, recognizing the pressures that drove the uskoks to raiding and the consequences of these actions, does not lead to a complete assessment of the uskoks and their role. That must derive from an analysis of their own ideas and what they meant in the eyes of others.

Most uskoks would hardly have agreed with the view that they were no more than pirates or bandits. Ivan Vlatković, the archetypal Ivo Senjanin of the songs, would have protested that he was a soldier and a hero, fighting not so much for the Habsburgs as for the defense of Christendom and for his own honor. His contacts with the conspirators who planned to raise the Balkans hint at a broader vision of Christian cooperation against the Turk, shared with other inhabitants of the border, although this vision did not prevent his plunder of Christian subjects of the Porte—those who served the Turk were legitimate victims. He would have resented the label of pirate, though he might have agreed that some of the uskoks in Senj were no more discriminating than they were forced to be. He himself chose his Ottoman targets carefully, pledged his honor not to attack Venetian subjects, and insisted that his fellows do likewise, punishing those who seized illegitimate plunder. Still, he might have had some sympathy for the excuses produced by less disciplined raiders, Juriša Hajduk among them. Could they be blamed when they were forced to take their supplies where they could find them, prevented from raiding the common enemy of Christendom by Venetian blockades or Military Frontier commissions? They could not live on air, as the Captain of Senj once pointed out.

That uskok raids arose from the need for booty is a necessary but not a sufficient explanation for their actions. Their raids, and indeed their whole way of life, were more than a reaction to material circumstances. We must also ask how their struggle for survival was moderated by reason, custom, and ideology. Reason demanded that the uskoks seek allies wherever they could, sparing the rural population to ensure their tolerance; negotiating rules of war with the border Ottomans. Custom, too, modified conflict, through such mechanisms as the word of honor and the exchange of ransoms. The uskoks had an explicit ideology, based

---

[41]*"Banderijska svijest."* See Bertoša, *Jedna zemlja, jedan rat,* p. 98.

on the idea of the defense of Christendom adapted from the political and religious formulations of the Habsburgs and the Catholic Church, and expressed in a powerful rhetoric, incorporating the values and attitudes of border society, justifying uskok war and resistance, changing and evolving to meet new challenges. The perpetual struggle between Christianity and Islam that this ethos assumed was not an entirely adequate picture of the circumstances of the border, nor did the behavior of the uskoks always correspond to its demands. Still, this was not a hypocritical screen to obscure or excuse purely mercenary motives. The uskoks' codes of behavior were a potent force and played an important role among the influences and constraints that shaped their choices and actions. Sometimes incongruities were perceived, and practice was brought into line with theory. The spread of tribute relationships with Christian subjects of the Porte can be interpreted as an attempt to balance the uskoks' need for booty against a sense of community.

Would the rural inhabitants of the borders have agreed with the characterization of the uskoks as pirates and brigands? Yes, almost certainly—when under threat of punishment for collaboration they reported an uskok incursion to a Venetian tribunal. But in the villages, among themselves? Perhaps, if the most recent raids from Senj had made heavy inroads on their flocks, or if demands for ransom or tribute were extortionate. The sight of uskok barks was to be anticipated as well as feared, however, when joint raids ended with a share of the booty, or when the uskok bands could be persuaded to plunder a rapacious landlord or a harsh administrator, either Ottoman or Venetian. Both the villagers as well as more powerful allies (Dalmatian patricians involved in conspiracies to regain their lands and power, northern Adriatic ports in competition with Venice) could see the uskoks as useful weapons in their own struggles.

But popular sympathy for the uskoks was at the same time less a matter of immediate self-interest and more a matter of an ideal image. The idea persisted that the uskok should have a special relationship with the border Christians, that they should be people "in whom we ought to be able to trust and from whom we ought to receive every grace," as the leaders of Lika wrote in 1609.[42] Many of the uskoks' values and attitudes were widely shared. At least on the Christian side of the border, these included the premises according to which the uskoks fought. Dalmatian grievances against the Ottoman conquest of their hinterland, the most apparent cause of the province's economic decline, ensured popular sympathy for the uskoks' holy war, further supported by the lower

[42]In Theiner, *Vetera monumenta Slavorum meridionalium historiam illustrantia*, vol. 2, p. 102.

clergy. On the Ottoman side, this religious vocabulary gave the Christian subjects of the Porte a way of expressing dissatisfaction with rising taxes and vanishing privileges as they too joined with the uskoks. But in the eyes of others the uskoks were legitimated not only by culture and by religio-political conflict. Subjects discontented with their lives under Venice or the Porte could also project a certain political legitimacy onto the uskoks as representatives of the Habsburgs and therefore of the Croatian crown.

All these factors help to explain why the uskoks were often viewed with approval, perhaps even respect, and why some people had expectations about their behavior which are incompatible with the image of the uskoks as simple bandits. The uskoks were not only useful tools for the Habsburgs but also instruments in the rivalries and conflicts of many other groups on the borders. They could also provide a vehicle for the expression of a political or social identity for the people of the border. Attitudes toward the uskoks, and alliances with them, allow the historian to trace the outlines of a popular political consciousness based not so much on a national consciousness as on religious conflicts and political traditions. This was a world in which religion, whatever else it taught about the relations between man and God, was a justification for war and a badge of identity. This sense of identity was further shaped by political factors, both present loyalties and past traditions. Much more powerfully than common ethnic origin or common language, religion and state allegiance defined who you were and how you defined your friends and enemies. And finally, whatever the reality of their struggles, uskoks had a role as popular legends. In spite of a clear-eyed awareness of the uskoks' violence and destructiveness, in spite of the futility of any attempt to distinguish between good and bad uskoks, the epic songs of the border present the uskoks as heroes, affirming the possibility of freedom from authority, glorifying self-assertion, and serving as a reminder of the price they paid in danger and discomfort.

Chronology

1520s:	Ottoman incursions against Croatian borders; increased numbers of irregular uskok bands raiding from the border fortresses.
1522:	Defense of a number of border fortresses in Croatia organized under the authority of Habsburg Archduke Ferdinand, forming the nucleus of the Military Frontier.
1526:	The Battle of Mohács; King of Croatia (and Hungary) defeated and killed.
1527:	Ferdinand I elected king of Croatia, pledges to defend the Croatian Frontier.
1520s–30s:	Uskok irregulars raiding from Klis and Senj.
1537–40:	War of the Holy League (Venice, the Pope, Charles V) against the Ottoman Empire. Venice accepts a separate truce with the Ottomans in 1539, expelling uskok recruits from Dalmatia in 1541.
1537:	The fall of the fortress of Klis to the Ottomans.
1547:	Five-year peace between the Habsburgs and the Ottomans; war resumes 1552.
1562:	Eight-year peace negotiated between the Habsburgs and the Ottomans; however, war resumes 1565.
1564:	Death of Ferdinand I; accession of Maximillian II (crowned king of Croatia in 1563).
1568:	Eight-year peace negotiated between the Habsburgs and the Ottomans, but battles on borders resume in early 1570s.
1570–73:	War of Cyprus (Holy League of Venice, Spain, and the Pope against the Ottoman Empire). Venice recruits uskoks into its service to counter attacks in Dalmatia; demobilizes them in 1574; many emigrate to Senj.
1571:	Death of Vojvoda Juraj Daničić on a raid across Ragusan territory; the beginning of Senj's vendetta against Dubrovnik.
1576:	Death of Maximillian II; accession of Rudolf II (crowned king of Croatia 1572).
1578:	Military Frontier reorganized under the authority of Archduke Charles of Styria, administered through the Hofkriegsrat in Graz.

1579:   Annual papal stipend granted to Senj; shipping from papal ports to be immune from uskok interference.

1583:   Unsuccessful uskok attempt to take Klis; participants in the affair flee to Senj.

1592:   Venetian attacks on the Croatian Littoral and Karlobag under a Provveditore Generale contra uscocchi. Venice escalates its overt opposition to uskok activity on the Adriatic through repeated blockades of Senj and the Littoral throughout the 1590s.

1593–1606:   After several years of Ottoman offensives, open war declared between the Habsburgs and Ottoman Empire (Long Turkish War).

1596:   Klis retaken by Christian forces (as part of a larger plan for a Balkan Christian uprising against Ottoman rule) but falls again to superior Ottoman forces, with tacit Venetian support. Many participants emigrate to Senj.

1597:   Uskok raid on Venetian subjects in Rovinj and Pula. Severe Venetian blockade of Senj and the Croatian Littoral, continuing through 1599. A Military Frontier commission to Senj, under General Lenković, punishes some of those responsible. De Dominis appointed bishop of Senj.

1598–99:   Habsburg-Venetian relations deteriorate further over uskok issue. Venetian blockade renewed; Venetian troops attack Novi and other Habsburg possessions. Papal mediation of discussions between the Habsburgs and Venice of a possible reform of Senj. Some uskoks make their own proposals for reform, but others continue to raid.

1600–1601:   Hofkriegsrat sends Commissioner Joseph Rabatta to reform Senj. Many uskoks expelled and resettled in outlying fortresses. Rabatta reaches agreement with Venice on limits to uskok activities, but is murdered in December 1601 by the uskoks.

1606:   Treaty of Zsitvatorok ending Long Turkish War forbids raiding to both sides. No provisions made for provisioning Senj, and uskoks continue to raid, also offering their support to plans for an uprising of Balkan Christians. Disaffected uskoks take service with the Grand Duke of Tuscany, the Viceroy of Naples, and Venice. Venetian measures against the uskoks escalate once again through the early 1600s.

1612:   Vojvoda Ivan Vlatković arrested, tried, and executed by order of the Military Frontier. Vienna Agreement between Venice and Archduke Ferdinand provides for expulsion of pirates from Senj and their replacement by a German garrison in return for the raising of the Venetian blockade and freedom of commercial traffic on the Adriatic. Death of Rudolf II; accession of Matthias as emperor

1615–17:   War of Gradisca (Uskok War) between Archduke Ferdinand of Styria and Venice, ended by Treaty of Madrid (1617).

1618:   Uskoks expelled from Senj by joint Habsburg-Venetian commission.

Glossary

Ban: civil governor of Croatia.

Bey: Ottoman commander, governor.

Beylerbey: supreme military and civil commander in an Ottoman province.

Brigantine: small, two-masted vessel.

Capitano: commander of a Venetian naval or military unit. The Capitano contra uscocchi commanded a force of ships against the uskoks, usually deployed in the waters of the northern Adriatic.

Çavuş: Ottoman official or emissary.

Ducat: Venetian money of account, reckoned at 6 lire and 4 soldi. The sequin (*zecchino*) and the *scudo* were worth from 8 to 10 lire.

Florin (or *Gulden*): Austrian money of account, reckoned at 60 kreutzers. The Austrian silver thaler was worth from 60 to 75 kreutzers in sixteenth-century Croatia.

Fondaco: storehouse. Senj maintained a *fondaco* for grain in Rijeka.

Fregata: small, fast version of the galley, with a single sail.

Fusta: small galley.

Galley: long, low-decked craft with one deck, powered by oars and sails.

Haraç: tax paid to the Ottoman state by all adult non-Muslim males; or, more generally, any tax or tribute.

Harambaša: uskok leader, with or without a paid position in the garrison.

Hofkriegsrat: the Court War Council in Graz, created in 1578 to administer the Military Frontier.

Kadi: Muslim district judge.

Kersey: coarse woollen cloth.

Marciliana: small roundship, with square sails and two decks, used as a merchant vessel.

Martolos: member of the Ottoman military organization on the borders, with special privileges based on military service, in the sixteenth century usually Christian.

Morlach: in Venetian usage, a member of the Christian subject population of the Ottoman hinterland.

Paşa: title given a high-ranking Ottoman officer in the government or military.

Provveditore: general term for a high-ranking Venetian officer on land or at sea. The Provveditore Generale di Dalmazia (here usually referred to simply as the Provveditore Generale) had both civil and military authority in Dalmatia. The Provveditore Generale in Golfo was the admiral responsible for the naval security of the Adriatic (one was appointed in 1592 to fight the uskoks). The Provveditore dell'armata was the squadron commander of the galleys in the Adriatic.

Rector: general term for a Venetian administrator of a city or district. Precise titles varied (Zadar was administered by a count and captain, for example).

Sancak: Ottoman administrative district.

Sopracomito: captain of a Venetian galley.

Sipahi: Ottoman cavalryman, granted land for military service.

Star: a measure used for grain, differing in size according to local standards. (A Rijeka *star* was equivalent to 38 liters; a Ljubljana *star* was about 114 liters.)

Stipendiati: uskoks with paid positions in the Senj garrison.

Uskoks: border irregulars, often refugees or "displaced persons," who made a living from raiding, usually in the service of one of the border states. In this work, the irregulars of Senj.

Venturini: uskoks without paid positions in the Senj garrison; soldiers of fortune.

Vlach: a stockherder-colonist, usually with special privileges associated with irregular military service, sometimes with a Romanic ethnic character.

Vojvoda: uskok commander. From the second half of the sixteenth century the Hofkriegsrat usually recognized four vojvodas as the commanders of all the uskoks in Senj.

Bibliography

Archival Sources

Archivio di Stato, Venice (A.S.V.)
    Archivio dei Baili Veneti a Constantinopoli
    Capi del Consiglio dei Dieci. Dispacci del Capitano contra Uscocchi
    ——. Lettere dei Rettori
    Collegio, Secreta, Relazioni
    Miscellanea di Atti Diversi Manoscritti
    Provveditore Sopraintendente alla Camera dei Confini
    Senato. Mar [Registers]
    Senato. Secreta [Registers]
    ——. Dispacci, Germania
    ——. Dispacci, Roma
    ——. Materie miste notabili
    ——. Provveditori da Terra e da Mar
Archivio di Stato, Florence (A.S.F.)
    Mediceo del Principato
Arhiv Hrvatske (Zagreb) (A.H.)
    Građa Karlovačke krajine: Spisi Like i Krbave
    Obiteljski arhiv: Čikulini-Sermage
Arhiv Slovenije (Ljubljana) (A.S.)
    Deželni stanovi za Kranjsko
Historijski Arhiv, Dubrovnik (H.A.D.)
    Acta Consilii Rogatorum
    Acta Minoris Consilii
    Diplomata et Acta XVI st.
    Diplomata et Acta XVII st.
    Diversa Cancellariae
    Lamenti politici (VII. Lamenti criminali in affari maritimi e degli uscocchi)
    Lettere di Levante
    Lettere di Ponente
    Secreta Rogatorum

Historijski Arhiv, Rijeka (H.A.R.)
    Knjiga upravljavanja istarskog providura Marina Malpiera, 1581–82
    Knjiga istarskog providura Giacoma Reniera, 1583–85
    Notarska knjiga Gverina Tranquilli
    Vladarske isprave: Varia, XI
    Zapisnici sjednica općinskog vijeća u Rijeci, 1593–1607
Historijski Arhiv, Zadar (H.A.Z.)
    Arhivi dalmatinskih gradova: Korčula, Omiš, Rab, Sibenik, Split, Trogir
    Dukale i terminacije
    Fond Šime Ljubića
    Ispisi tajnog vatikanskog arhiva Fra Dane Zeca
    Spisi zadarskih knezova
Kriegsarchiv, Vienna
    Innerösterreichischer Hofkriegsrat: Croatica (Asservierte Akten) (I.Ö. H.K.R.)
    (Also in Arhiv Hrvatske, Microfilm and Photocopy Collection.)
School of Slavonic and East European Studies Library, University of London
    (S.S.E.E.S.)
    Microfilm collection: Longworth collection of material on uskoks from Italian
    archives

Printed Sources

Primary Works

Albèri, E., ed. *Relazioni degli ambasciatori veneti al Senato.* Ser. 1, vols. 1–6; ser. 3, vols.
    1–3. Florence, 1839–63.
*Aviso delle Ragioni della Serenissima Signoria di Venetia intorno alla mossa d'Arme contra
    Uscocchi.* Venice, 1616[?].
Barabás, S., ed. *Zrínyi Miklós a szigetvári hős életére vonatkozó levelek és okiratok.* 2 vols.
    Monumenta Hungariæ historica, 29 and 30. Budapest: Magyar tudományos
    akadémia, 1898–99.
Bertoša, Miroslav, ed. *Epistolæ et communicationes rectorum Histrianorum.* Vol. 1:
    Annorum 1607–1616. Monumenta spectantia historiam Slavorum meridional-
    ium, 52. Zagreb: JAZU, 1979.
Bogišić, V., ed. *Narodne pjesme iz starijih, najviše primorskih zapisa.* Biograd: Srpsko
    učeno društvo, 1878.
Bojničić-Kninski, I., ed. "Izvješća o kretnjama turske vojske uz hrvatsku granicu
    u drugoj polovici XVI vijeka." *Vjesnik Kraljevskog hrvatsko-slavonsko-dalmatinskog
    zemaljskog arhiva* (Zagreb), 16 (1914): 60–101.
Borlandi, Franco, ed. *El libro di mercatantie et usanze de' paesi.* Turin: S. Lattes, 1936.
Božitković, J., ed. "Kratki ljetopis Tome Juričića iz godine 1596. i 1599." *Narodna
    starina* (Zagreb), 10 (1931): 117–18.
Commissiones et relationes venetæ. 3 vols. Monumenta spectantia historiam Slav-
    orum meridionalium, 6, 8, and 11, ed. Šime Ljubić. Zagreb: JAZU, 1876–80.
Commissiones et relationes venetæ. 4 vols. Monumenta spectantia historiam Slav-
    orum meridionalium, 47, 48, 49, and 50, ed. G. Novak. Zagreb: JAZU, 1964–72.
Draganović, Krunoslav, ed. "Izvješće apostolskog vizitatora Petra Masarechija o
    prilikama katoličkog naroda u Bugarskoj, Srbiji, Srijemu, Slavoniji i Bosni g.
    1623. i 1624." *Starine* (Zagreb), 39 (1938): 1–48.

Đurđev, B., et al., eds. *Kanuni i kanun-name za bosanski, hercegovački, zvornički, kliški, crnogorski i skadarski sandžak.* Monumenta turcica historiam Slavorum meridionalium illustrantia, 1. Sarajevo: Orijentalni institutu, 1957.

Đurđev, B., ed. "Požeška kanun-nama iz 1545 godine." *Glasnik Zemaljskog muzeja* (Sarajevo), 1 (new ser., 1946): 129–38.

Farlati, Daniel, ed. *Illyricum sacrum.* 9 vols. Venice, 1751–1819.

Ferraris, Lucius, ed. *Prompta Bibliotheca Canonica.* 8 vols. Venice, 1766.

Fiedler, Joseph. "Versuche der türkisch-südslawischen Völker zur Vereinigung mit Österreich unter Kaiser Rudolf II." *Slawische Bibliothek oder Beiträge zur slavische Philologie und Geschichte* (Vienna), 2 (1858): 288–300.

———, ed. *Relationen der Botschafter Venedigs über Deutschland und Österreich im XVII Jahrhundert.* Fontes rerum Austriacarum, 26. Vienna: Kaiserlich-koniglich Hof- und Staatsdruckerei, 1866.

———, ed. *Relationen Venetianischer Botschafter über Deutschland und Österreich im XVI Jahrhundert.* Fontes rerum Austriacarum, 30. Vienna: Kaiserlich-koniglich Hof- und Staatsdruckerei, 1870.

Gelcich, J. and Thallóczy, L., eds. *Diplomatarium relationum reipublicæ Ragusanæ cum regno Hungariæ.* Budapest: Magyar tudományos akadémia, 1887.

Gesemann, G., ed. *Erlangenski rukopis starih srpskohrvatskih narodnih pesama.* Zbornik za istoriju, jezik i književnost, section 1, vol. 12. Belgrade: SKA, 1925.

Gestrin, F., ed. *Mitninske knjige 16. in 17. stoletja na slovenskem.* Ljubljana: SAZU, 1972.

Giudici, Marcello, ed. *I dispacci di Germania dell'ambasciatore veneto Daniel Dolfin.* 2 vols. Venice, 1907–10.

Gligo, V., ed. *Govori protiv Turaka.* Split: Čakavski sabor, 1983.

Gortan, Veljko, and Vladimir Vratković, eds. *Hrvatski latinisti.* 2 vols. Pet stoljeća hrvatske književnosti, 2 and 3. Zagreb: Matica hrvatska, 1969.

Great Britain. Public Record Office. *Calendar of State Papers and Manuscripts Relating to English Affairs Existing in the Archives and Collections in Venice and in Other Libraries of Northern Italy.* Vols. 9–17. London: His Majesty's Stationery Office, 1897–1911.

Herkov, Z, ed. "Carinski cjenik grada Senja od godine 1577." *Vjesnik Historijskih arhiva u Rijeci i Pazinu* (Rijeka), 17 (1972): 47–77.

———, ed. *Statut grada Rijeke.* Rijeka: Nakladni zavod Hrvatske, 1958.

Horvat, K., ed. "Glagoljaši u Dalmaciji početkom 17. vijeka." *Starine* (Zagreb), 33 (1911): 537–64.

———, ed. "Kobenzelovi izvještaji (1592–1594) kardinalu Cintiju Aldobrandiniju, državnomu tajniku pape Klementa VIII." *Starine* (Zagreb), 32 (1909): 1–104, 313–424.

———, ed. *Monumenta historiam uscocchorum illustrantia.* 2 vols. Monumenta spectantia historiam Slavorum meridionalium, 32 and 34. Zagreb: JAZU, 1910–13.

Ivić, Aleksa, ed. "Dolazak uskoka u Žumberak." *Vjesnik Kraljevskog hrvatsko-slavonsko-dalmatinskog zemaljskog arhiva* (Zagreb), 9 (1907).

———, ed. "Neue cyrillische Urkunden aus den Wiener Archiven." *Archiv für slavische Philologie* (Berlin), 30 (1909): 205–14.

———, ed. "O prvoj srpskoj seobi u Žumberak." *Vjesnik Kraljevskog hrvatsko-slavonsko-dalmatinskog zemaljskog arhiva* (Zagreb), 20 (1918): 252–60.

———, ed. "Prilozi za povijest Hrvatske i Slavonije u 16. i 17. veku." *Starine* (Zagreb), 25 (1916): 302–17.

——, ed. "Šest srpskih pisama iz šestnaestog stoljeća." *Zbornik za književnost, jezik, istoriju, i folklor* (Zagreb), 5 (1925): 132–37.

Jačov, Marko, ed. *Spisi tajnog vatikanskog arhiva XVI–XVIII veka*. Zbornik za istoriju, jezik i književnost srpskog naroda, section 2, vol. 22. Belgrade: SANU, 1983.

Jelić, L., ed. "Isprave o prvoj uroti za oslobodjenje Klisa i kopnene Dalmacije od Turaka g. 1580–1586." *Vjesnik Kraljevskog hrvatsko-slavonsko-dalmatinskog zemaljskog arhiva* (Zagreb), 6 (1904): 97–113.

Junković, Zvonimir, ed. "Izvorni tekst i prijevod Poljičkoga statuta." *Poljički zbornik* (Zagreb), 1 (1968): 32–103.

Koharić, J., ed. "Nekoje dukale i privilegiji cesarski iz župske škrinjice poljičke." *Vjesnik Kraljevskog hrvatsko-slavonsko-dalmatinskog zemaljskog arhiva* (Zagreb), 5 (1903): 228–32.

Kraljić, V., ed. "Popis arhivske grade arhiva biskupije u Senju i arhiva stolnog kaptola u Senju." *Vjesnik Historijskog arhiva u Rijeci i Pazinu* (Rijeka), 20 (1975–76): 231–99.

Kukuljević-Sakcinski, Ivan, ed. *Acta Croatica*. Monumenta historica Slavorum meridionalium, 1. Zagreb: Narodna tiskarnica dra. Ljudevita Gaja, 1863.

——, ed. "Kratki ljetopisi hrvatski." *Arkiv za povjestnicu jugoslavensku* (Zagreb), 4 (1857): 30–65.

——, ed. *Nadpisi sredovječni i novovjeki na crkvah, javnih i privatnih sgradah i.t.d. u Hrvatskoj i Slavoniji*. Zagreb: Knjižara Jugoslavenske akademije, 1891.

Kuripešić, Benedikt. *Putopis kroz Bosnu, Srbiju, Bugarsku i Rumeliju 1530*. Sarajevo: Svjetlost, 1950.

Lamansky, Vladimir, ed. *Secrets d'etat de Venise*. 2 vols. Petersburg, 1884; rp., New York: Burt Franklin, 1968.

Laszowski, Emilij, ed. "Bilješka o senjskim šumama." *Vjesnik Kraljevskog hrvatsko-slavonsko-dalmatinskog zemaljskoga arkiva* (Zagreb), 13 (1911): 191.

——, ed. *Izbor isprava velikih feuda Zrinskih i Frankapana*. Građa za gospodarsku povijest Hrvatske u XVI i XVII stoljeću, 1. Zagreb, 1951.

——, ed. *Monumenta habsburgica regni Croatiæ, Dalmatiæ, Slavoniæ*. 3 vols. Monumenta spectantia historiam Slavorum meridionalium, 35, 38, and 40. Zagreb: JAZU, 1914–17.

——, ed. "Provala Turaka u Vinodol g. 1600." *Vjesnik kraljevskog zemaljskog arhiva* (Zagreb), 18, no. 4 (1916): 289–91.

——, ed. "Urbar vinodolskih imanja knezova Zrinskih." *Vjesnik kraljevskog zemaljskog arhiva* (Zagreb), 17 (1915): 71–108.

Leva, G. de, ed. *Legazione di Roma di Paulo Paruta (1592–1595)*. Monumenti storici publicati dalla R. deputazione veneta di storia patria, Ser. 4, Miscellanea, vol. 7. Venice, 1887.

I libri commemoriali della Repubblica di Venezia. Monumenti storici publicati dalla R. deputazione veneta di storia patria. Ser. 1, Documenti, vol. 13. Regesti, 7, ed. R. Predelli. Venice, 1907.

Lithgow, William. *The Totall Discourse of the Rare Adventures and Painefull Peregrinations of Long Nineteen Yeares Travayles from Scotland to the Most Famous Kingdomes in Europe, Asia, and Africa*. London, 1636; London, 1918.

Ljubić, Šime, ed. "Prilozi za životopis Markantunu Dominisu." *Starine* (Zagreb), 2 (1870): 1–260.

——, ed. "Rukoviet jugoslavenskih listina." *Starine* (Zagreb), 10 (1878): 7–17.

Lopašić, R., ed. *Acta historiam confinii militaris Croatici illustrantia*. 3 vols. Monumenta spectantia historiam Slavorum meridionalium, 15, 16 and 20. Zagreb: JAZU, 1884–89.

——, ed. "Prilozi za poviest Hrvatske XVI i XVII vieka iz štajerskoga zemaljskoga arhiva u Gradcu." *Starine* (Zagreb), 17 (1885): 151–231; 19 (1887): 1–80.

——, ed. *Urbaria lingua croatica conscripta*. Monumenta historico-juridica Slavorum meridionalium, 5. Zagreb: JAZU, 1894.

Magdić, Mile, ed. "Petnaest isprava, koje se čuvaju u arkivu Senjskog kaptola." *Vjesnik Kraljevskog hrvatsko-slavonsko-dalmatinskog zemaljskoga arkiva* (Zagreb), 3 (1901): 47–59.

——, ed. "Popis patricijskih i gradjanskih porodica senjskih od godine 1758." *Starine* (Zagreb), 17 (1885): 49–53.

——, ed. "Prilozi za poviest starih plemićkih obitelji senjskih." *Starine* (Zagreb), 12 (1880): 224–29.

——, ed. "Prilozi za poviest starih plemićkih porodica senjskih." *Starine* (Zagreb), 17 (1885): 54–76.

——, ed. "Regesta važnijih i znamenitijih izprava senjskih arkiva." *Vjesnik Kraljevskog hrvatsko-slavonsko-dalmatinskog zemaljskoga arkiva* (Zagreb), 1 (1899): 139–185, 244–51.

——, ed. "Statut kralja Ferdinanda III od godine 1640 za grad Senj." *Vjesnik Kraljevskog hrvatsko-slavonsko-dalmatinskog zemaljskoga arkiva* (Zagreb), 2 (1900): 78–97.

Magnum bullarium romanum. Rome, 1756; reprint, Graz: Akademische Druck- u. Verlagsanstalt, 1965.

Marani, A., ed. *Atti pastorali di Minuccio Minucci, Arcivescovo di Zara (1596–1604)*. Thesaurus ecclesiarum Italiæ, ser. 3 (Veneto), 2. Rome: Edizioni di storia e letteratura, 1970.

Margetić, Lujo, ed. *Iz vinodolske prošlosti: pravni izvori i rasprave*. Rijeka: Liburnija, 1980.

Matasović, Josip, ed. "Fojnička regesta." *Spomenik Srpske kraljevske akademije* (Belgrade), 67 (1930): 61–431.

Mažuranić, Ivan, ed. "Statut grada Senja od godine 1388." *Arkiv za povjestnicu jugoslavensku* (Zagreb), 3 (1854): 141–70.

Minucci, Minuccio. *Storia degli uscocchi*. [1604.] In P. Sarpi, *Opere*, 4. Helmstadt [Verona], 1763, pp. 217–62.

Monumenta Hungariæ historica. Series 1, Okmánytárak. Vol. 2: 1538–53. Pest, 1858.

Mošin, V. *Ćirilski rukopisi Jugoslavenske akademije*. Zagreb: JAZU, 1955.

Nodilo, S., ed. *Annales Ragusini anonymi item Nicolai de Ragnina*. Monumenta spectantia historiam Slavorum meridionalium, 14. Zagreb: JAZU, 1883.

Noflatscher, H., and E. Springer, eds. "Studien und Quellen zu den Beziehungen zwischen Rudolf II. und den bosnischen Christen." *Mitteilungen des österreichischen Staatsarchivs* (Vienna), 36 (1983): 31–82.

Noradounghian, G., ed. *Recueil d'actes internationaux de l'Empire ottoman*. 4 vols. Vol. 1: 1300–1789. Paris, 1897–1903.

Nuntiaturberichte aus Deutschland. Abt. 1 (1533–1559). *Nuntiatur des Bischofs Pietro Bertano von Fano, 1548–1549*, vol. 11, ed. Walter Friedensburg. Berlin: Prüssische historische Institut in Rom, 1910.

Nunziature di Venezia. Vols. 1, 2, 5, 6, 8, 9, 11. Fonti per la Storia d'Italia, 32, 45, 85, 86, 65, 117, and 118, Rome: Istituto storico italiano per l'età moderna e contemporea, 1958–67.

Pivčević, Edo. "Kako je de Dominis postao senjski biskup." *Crkva u svijetu*, 18, no. 2 (1983): 178–92.

Popović, T., ed. *Pisma Bartolomeu Boraniju (1593–1595)*. Spomenik Srpske akademije nauka i umetnosti, 124. Historical Sciences section, 3. Belgrade: SANU, 1984.

Pray, Georgius. *Annales regum Hungariæ*. 5 vols. Vindobonæ, 1766.

Rački, Franjo, ed. "Dopisi između krajiških turskih i hrvatskih častnika." *Starine* (Zagreb), 11, (1879): 76–83.

——, ed. "Izvještaj barskog nadbiskupa Marina Bizzia o svojem putovanju god. 1610 po Arbanaškoj i staroj Srbiji." *Starine* (Zagreb), 20 (1888): 50–156.

——, ed. [Giovanni of Fermo.] "Prilog za poviest hrvatskih uskoka." *Starine* (Zagreb), 9 (1877): 172–256.

Radonić, J., ed. *Acta et diplomata Ragusina*. Zbornik za istoriju, jezik i književnost. Section 3, vols. 5, 8, and 9. Belgrade: SKA, 1935–39.

Ragioni della Republica Venetiana contra Uscochi. Dalmazagho: Antonio Boron, 1617.

Rainer, Johann, ed. *Nuntiatur des Germanico Malaspina, Sendung des Antonio Possevino, 1580–1582*. Grazer Nuntiatur, 1. Vienna: Österreichische Akademie der Wissenschaften, 1973.

Razzi, Serafino. *La Storia di Ragusa*. Lucca, 1595; reprint, Dubrovnik, 1903.

Regnault, R., ed. *Lettres et ambassade de Messire Philippe Canaye, Seigneur de Fresnes*. 4 vols. Paris: E. Richer, 1647.

"Relatione di A. Bondumieri." *Atti e memorie della Società istriana di archeologia et storia patria* (Parenzo), 2 (1886): 108–112.

Rycaut, P. *The Present State of the Ottoman Empire*. London, 1668; reprint, New York: Arno Press, 1971.

Sanuto, Marino. *I diarii di Marino Sanuto*. 58 vols. Venice: Deputazione veneta di storia patria, 1879–1903.

Sarpi, Paulo. *La Repubblica di Venezia, la Casa d'Austria e gli uscocchi*. Ed. Gaetano Cozzi and Luisa Cozzi. Bari: Laterza e figli, 1965. [1617–18.]

Šišić, Ferdo, ed. *Acta comitalia regni Croatiæ, Dalmatiæ, Slavoniæ*. Vols. 1–5. Monumenta spectantia historiam Slavorum meridionalium, 36, 38, 39, 41, and 43. Zagreb: JAZU, 1915–18.

Solitro, V., ed. *Documenti storici sull'Istria e la Dalmazia*. Venice: G. Gattei, 1844.

Stanojević, Gligor, ed. "Jedan dokumenat o senjskim uskocima." *Vesnik Vojnog muzeja JNA* (Belgrade), 6–7 (1962): 97–108.

Stefanić, Vjekoslav, ed. *Glagoski rukopisi otoka Krka*. Djela JAZU, 51. Zagreb: JAZU, 1960.

Tamaro, A., ed. "Episodi di storia fiumana." *Fiume* (Rijeka), 14 (1936): 3–60.

Tausserat-Radel, Alexandre, ed. *Correspondance politique de Guillaume Pellicier, ambassadeur de France à Venise, 1540–1542*. Paris: Commission des Archives Diplomatiques, 1899.

Tenenti, A. "Gli schiavi di Venezia alla fine del cinquecento." *Rivista storica italiana* (Turin), 67, no. 1 (1955): 52–69.

Theiner, A., ed. *Vetera monumenta Slavorum meridionalium historiam illustrantia*. 2 vols. Rome, 1863–75; reprint, Osnabrück: Otto Zeller, 1968.

Tomić, Jovan, ed. *Građa za istoriju pokreta na Balkanu protiv Turaka XVI–XVII vijeka*. Zbornik za istoriju, jezik i književnost, Section 2, vol. 6. Belgrade: SAN, 1933.

——, ed. "Sedam srpskih pisama ćirilicom pisanih mletačkog arhiva." *Spomenik SANU* (Belgrade), 31 (1898): 70–75.

Truhelka, Ć., ed. "Nekoliko mladjih pisama hercegovačke gospode pisanih bosančicom iz dubrovačke arhive." *Glasnik Zemaljskog muzeja* (Sarajevo), 26 (1914): 477–94.

Turba, Gustav, ed. *Venetianische Depeschen vom Kaiserhofe.* 3 vols. Vienna: Akademie der Wissenschaften, 1889–95.

Vecellio, Cesare. *Habiti antichi et moderni.* Venice, 1590.

Vojnovich, Lujo, ed. *Depeschen des Francisco Gondola, Gesandten der Republik Ragusa bei Pius V und Gregor XIII (1570–1573).* Archiv für österreichische Geschichte, 98. Vienna, 1909.

Zjačić, M., ed. "Statut grada Senja iz 1388. godine." *Rad JAZU* (Zagreb), 369 (1975): 39–115.

Secondary Works

Adamček, Josip. *Agrarni odnosi u Hrvatskoj od sredine XV do kraja XVII stoljeća.* Zagreb: Sveučilišna naklada Liber, 1980.

——. "Zrinsko-Frankopanski posjedi u XVII stoljeću." *Radovi Instituta za hrvatsku povijest* (Zagreb), 2 (1972): 23–46.

Adanir, Fikret. "Heidukentum und osmanische Herrschaft: Sozialgeschichtliche Aspekte der Diskussion um das frühneuzeitliche Räuberwesen in Südosteuropa." *Südost-Forschungen,* 41 (1982): 43–116.

——. "Tradition and Rural Change in Southeastern Europe during Ottoman Rule." In *The Origins of Backwardness in Eastern Europe: Economics and Politics from the Middle Ages until the Early Twentieth Century,* ed. Daniel Chirot. Berkeley: University of California Press, 1989.

Amstadt, J. *Die k.k. Militärgrenze, 1522–1881.* Würzburg, 1969.

Andreis, Pavao. *Povijest grada Trogira.* 2 vols. Trans. V. Rismondo. Split: Čakavski sabor, 1971.

Andrić, Nikola. *Hrvatske narodne pjesme.* Zagreb: Matica hrvatska, 1939.

Bartl, Peter. *Der Westbalkan zwischen spanischer Monarchie und osmanischen Reich: Zur Türkenkriegsproblematik an der Wende vom 16. zum 17. Jahrhundert.* Vienna: Otto Harrassowitz, 1974.

Battistella, A. "Il Dominio del Golfo." *Nuovo archivio veneto,* n.s. 18 (Venice), 35 (1918): 5–102.

Belas, Ante. "Sukob između šibenskog biskupa Bassusa i mletačkog providura Mora zbog murterskog župnika godine 1596." *Jadranski dnevnik* (Split), 4, no. 84 (1937): 2–3.

Benetović, Martin. *Djela.* Pet stoljeća hrvatske književnost, 9. Zagreb: Matica hrvatska, 1964.

Bertoša, Miroslav. "Buzeština u doba uskočkog rata." *Buzetski zbornik* (Pula), 1 (1976): 99–103.

——. "Istra u plamenu uskočkog rata 1615–1617." *Istra* (Pula), 3 (1975): 49–65.

——. *Jedna zemlja, jedan rat: Istra, 1615–1618.* Pula: Istarska naklada, 1986.

——. "Uskočki rat i slom istarskog gospodarstva." *Jadranski zbornik* (Rijeka), 9 (1973–75): 241–81.

Bićanić, Rudolf. "Važnost Rijeke u ekonomskom životu Hrvatske." In *Rijeka: Zbornik,* ed. J. Ravlić. Zagreb: Matica hrvatska, 1953.

Biegman, N. H. *The Turco-Ragusan Relationship.* The Hague: Mouton, 1967.

Billingsley, Phil. *Bandits in Republican China.* Stanford: Stanford University Press, 1988.

Black-Michaud, Jacob. *Feuding Societies*. Oxford: Basil Blackwell, 1975.

Blok, Anton. *The Mafia of a Sicilian Village, 1860–1960: A Study of Violent Peasant Entrepreneurs*. New York: Harper & Row, 1974.

——. "The Peasant and the Brigand: Social Banditry Reconsidered." *Comparative Studies in Society and History* (Cambridge), 14 (1972): 494–503.

Blumenkranz, B. "Les juifs dans le commerce maritime de Venise," *Revue des études juives* 120 (1961): 143–51.

Bolonić, Mihovil. "Senjski uskoci i otok Krk." *Senjski zbornik* (Senj), 8 (1980): 343–56.

Bombaci, A. "La collezione di documenti turchi dell'Archivio di Stato di Venezia." *Rivista degli studi orientali* (Rome), 24 (1949): 95–107.

Bono, S. *I corsari barbareschi*. Turin: ERI, 1964.

Božić, Ivan. "Svijet ratničkih družina i stočarskih katuna." In *Istorija Crne Gore*, ed. M. Đurović, vol. 2, pt. 2. Titograd: Redakcija za istoriju Crne Gore, 1970.

Bracewell, C. W. "Uskoks in Venetian Dalmatia before the Venetian-Ottoman War of 1714–1718." In *East Central European Society and War in the Pre-Revolutionary Eighteenth Century*, ed. G. Rothenberg, B. Kiraly, P. Sugar, 431–47. War and Society in East Central Europe, 2. Boulder, Colo.: Social Science Monographs, 1982.

——. "The Uskoks of Senj: Banditry and Piracy in the Sixteenth-Century Adriatic." Ph.D. diss., Stanford, Calif., 1985.

Braudel, Fernand. *The Mediterranean and the Mediterranean World in the Age of Philip II*. Trans. Siân Reynolds. 2 vols. New York: Harper and Row, 1972–73.

Brkić, Jovan. *Moral Concepts in Traditional Serbian Epic Poetry*. 'S-Gravenhage: Mouton, 1961.

Campbell, J. C. *Honour, Family and Patronage: A Study of Institutions and Moral Values in a Greek Mountain Community*. Oxford: Oxford University Press, 1964.

Cessi, Roberto. *La Reppublica di Venezia e il problema Adriatico*. Padua: A. Milani, 1943.

Contarini, Nicolò. *Le historie venetiane*. In G. Cozzi, *Il Doge Nicolò Contarini: Ricerche sul patriziato veneziano agli inizi del Seicento*. Venice: Istituto per la collaborazione culturale, 1958.

Čubrilović, V. "Senjanin Ivo." *Prilozi za književnost, jezik, istoriju, i folklor* (Belgrade), 18 (1938): 526–45.

Čulinović, F. "Mogu li se pokreti krajišnika uvrstiti u seljačke bune?" *Historijski zbornik* (Zagreb), 5 (1952): 427–52.

——, ed. *Statut grada Senja*. Belgrade: Globus, 1934.

Czoernig, Karl. *Ethnographie der oesterreichischen Monarchie*. 3 vols. Vienna: Kaiserlich-koniglich Hof- und Staatsdruckerei, 1857.

Dabić, Vojin. "Prilog proučavanju ratne privrede u hrvatskoj, slavonskoj i banskoj krajini od polovine XVI do kraja XVII veka." *Istorijski časopis* (Belgrade), 22 (1975): 91–101.

Diedo, Giacomo. *Storia della reppublica di Venezia dalla sua fondazione sino l'anno MDCCXLVII*. Venice, 1751.

Draganović, Krunoslav, ed. *Massenübertritte von Katholiken zur 'Orthodoxie' im kroatischen Sprachgebiet zur Zeit der Türkenherrschaft*. Rome: Pontificium institutum orientalium studiorum, 1937.

Držić, Marin. *Djela Marina Držića*. Stari pisci hrvatski, 7. Ed. M. Rešetar. Zagreb: JAZU, 1930.

Đurđev, B. "O vojnucima sa osvrtom na razvoj turskog feudalizma i na pitanje bosanskog agaluka." *Glasnik Zemaljskog muzeja*, new series, Social Sciences (Sarajevo), 2 (1947): 75–138.

Đurđev, B., B. Grafenauer, J. Tadić, et al., eds. *Historija naroda Jugoslavije*. 2 vols. Zagreb: Školska knjiga, 1953–59.

Durham, M. E. *Some Tribal Origins, Laws and Customs of the Balkans*. London: George Allen and Unwin, 1928.

Earle, Peter. *The Corsairs of Malta and Barbary*. London: Sidgwick and Jackson, 1970.

Fanfani, T. "Il sale nel Litorale austriaco dal XV al XVIII secolo: Un problema nei rapporti tra Venezia e Trieste." In A. di Vittorio, ed., *Sale e saline nell' Adriatico (secc. XV–XX)*. Naples: Giannini editore, 1981.

Fest, A. "Uskoken und Venezianer in der Geschichte von Fiume (1575–1618)." *Ungarische Revue* (Budapest), 3, 4, 8–9, 10 (1892): 160–71, 245–65, 530–44, 673–709.

Filipović, Milenko. "Struktura i organizacija srednjovekovnog katuna." In *Simpozijum o srednjovjekovnom katunu održan 24. i 25. Novembra 1961. godine*, ed. Milenko Filipović, 45–108. Naučno društvo SR BiH, Posebna izdanja, 2. Historical-philological Sciences, section 1. Sarajevo, 1963.

Filipović, Nedim. "Osvrt na položaj bosanskog seljaštva u prvoj deceniji uspostavljanja osmanske vlasti u Bosni." *Radovi Filozofskog fakulteta* (Sarajevo), 3 (1965): 63–75.

——. "Pogled na osmanski feudalizam (sa naročitim obzirom na agrarne odnose)." *Godišnjak Istoriskog društva Bosne i Hercegovine* (Sarajevo), 4 (1953): 1–146.

Foretić, Vinko. *Povijest Dubrovnika do 1808*. 2 vols. Zagreb: Nakladni zavod Matice Hrvatske, 1980.

Franičević, Marin. *Povijest hrvatske renesansne književnosti*. Zagreb: Školska knjiga, 1983.

Galluzzi, J. R. *Istoria del Granducato di Toscana sotto il governo della Casa Medici*. 3 vols. Florence, 1781.

Gavrilović, Slavko. *Hajdučija u Sremu u XVIII i početkom XIX veka*. Belgrade: SANU, 1986.

Gesemann, G. *Der montenegrinische Mensch: Zur Literaturgeschichte und Charakterologie der Patriarchalität*. Prague: Kommissionsverlag der J. G. Calveschen Universitäts-buchhandlung, 1934.

Gestrin, F. "Gospodarstvo in družba na Slovenskem v 16. stoletju." *Zgodovinski časopis* (Ljubljana), 16 (1962): 5–26.

——. *Trgovina slovenskega zaleđa s primorskimi mesti od 13. do konca 16. stoletja*. Ljubljana: SAZU, 1965.

Gigante, Silvino. "Rivaltà fra i porti di Fiume e Buccari nel secolo XVIII." *Fiume: Semestrale della Società di studi fiumani* (Rijeka), 10 (1932): 154–91.

——. "Venezia e gli Uscocchi, 1570–1620." *Fiume: Semestrale della Società di studi fiumani* (Rijeka), 9 (1931): 3–87.

Gnirs, A. *Österreichs Kampf für sein Südland am Isonzo, 1615–1617*. Vienna: L. W. Seidel, 1916.

Gordon, Linda. *Cossack Rebellions*. Albany: State University of New York Press, 1983.

Grgić, I. "Postanak i početno uređenje vojne krajine kninskog kotara pod Venecijom." *Starine JAZU* (Zagreb), 52 (1962): 249–71.

Grünfelder, A. "Senjski kapetan Kaspar Raab i senjski uskoci." *Senjski zbornik* (Senj), 9 (1981–82): 163–81.

——. "Studien zur Geschichte der Uskoken." Ph.D. diss., Universität in Innsbruck, 1974.

Gušić, M. "Nošnja senjskih ·skoka." *Senjski zbornik* (Senj), 5 (1971–73): 9–120.

Hammer, J. von. *Geschich. ..es osmanischen Reiches*. 4 vols. Pest: C. A. Hartleben, 1834–36.

Hektorović, Peter. *Ribanje i ribarsko prigovaranje i razlike stvari ine*. Pet stoljeća hrvatske književnost, 7. Zagreb: Matica hrvatska, 1968.

Herkov, Zlatko. *Mjere Hrvatskog primorja*. Historijski arhiv u Rijeci i Pazinu, posebnja izdanja, 4. Rijeka: Historijski arhiv, 1971.

Herzfeld, Michael. *The Poetics of Manhood: Contest and Identity in a Cretan Mountain Village*. Princeton: Princeton University Press, 1985.

Hess, Andrew. *The Forgotten Frontier: A History of the Sixteenth-Century Ibero-African Frontier*. Chicago: University of Chicago Press, 1978.

Hobsbawm, Eric J. *Bandits*. London: Weidenfeld and Nicolson, 1969.

——. *Primitive Rebels*. Manchester: Manchester University Press, 1959.

——. "Social Bandits: Reply." *Comparative Studies in Society and History* (Cambridge), 14 (1972): 503–5.

Hrabak, Bogumil. "Napadi senjskih uskoka na Zažablje, Popovo i Trebinje (1535–1617)." *Tribunie* (Trebinje), 7 (1983): 101–29.

——. "Neuspjelo naseljavanje Krmpoćana na Kvarneru, u Istri i Dalmaciji, 1614–1615. god." *Jadranski dnevnik* (Split), 12 (1982–85): 365–94.

——. "Senjski uskoci i Bokelji." *Godišnjak Pomorskog muzeja u Kotoru* (Kotor), 26 (1978): 27–37.

——. "Senjski uskoci i Dubrovnik, do 1573. godine." *Jadranski zbornik* (Pula), 11 (1979–81): 61–103.

——. "Uskočke akcije krajišnika na ušću Neretve." *Historijski zbornik* (Zagreb), 29–30 (1976–77): 181–91.

——. "Uskočki zaleti u Neretvu, 1537–1617." *Pomorski zbornik* (Rijeka), 17 (1979): 323–39.

Hurter, Friedrich von. *Geschichte des Kaiser Ferdinands II und seiner Eltern*. 11 vols. Schaffhausen: Hurtersche Buchhandlung, 1850–64.

Inalcık, Halil. "Military and Fiscal Transformation in the Ottoman Empire." *Archivium Ottomanicum*, 6 (1980): 283–337.

——. "The Ottoman Decline and Its Effects upon the *Reaya*." In *Aspects of the Balkans: Continuity and Change: Contributions to the International Balkan Conference Held at UCLA, October 23–28, 1969*, ed. H. Birnbaum and S. Vryonis. The Hague: Mouton, 1972.

——. "Ottoman Methods of Conquest." *Studia Islamica*, 2 (1954): 103–29.

Ivić, Aleksa. "Migracije Srba u Hrvatsku tokom 16., 17., i 18. stoljeća." *Srpski etnografski zbornik*, 28. Naselja i poreklo stanovništva, 16. Subotica: SKA, 1923.

Jurišić, K. *Katolička crkva na biokovsko-neretvanskom području u doba turske vladavine*. Zagreb: Kršćanska sadašnost, 1972.

Karnarutić, B. *Vazetje Sigeta grada*. Venice, 1584; reprint, Opsada Sigeta, 1, ed. M. Ratković. Zagreb: Liber, 1971.

Karolyi, Á. "'Vlachen'-Auswanderung aus der Gegend von Bihać zu Ende des 16. Jahrhunderts." *Wissenschaftliche Mitteilungen aus Bosnien und der Herzegovina* (Vienna), 2 (1894): 258–67.

Khevenhüller, Franz Christoph. *Annales Ferdinandei*. 12 vols. Leipzig, 1721–26.

——. *Conterfet Kupfferstich*. 2 vols. Leipzig: M. G. Weidmann, 1721–22.

Klaić, Nada. *Društvena previranja i bune u Hrvatskoj u XVI i XVII stoljeću.* Belgrade: Nolit, 1976.

——. "'Ostaci ostataka' Hrvatske i Slavonije u XVI stoljeću (od mohačke bitke do seljačke bune 1573. g.)." *Arhivski vjesnik* (Zagreb), 16 (1973): 253-325.

——. "Vinodolsko društvo na početku XVII stoljeća." *Vjesnik historijskih arhiva u Rijeci i Pazinu* (Rijeka), 17 (1972): 189-253.

Klaić, Vjekoslav. *Povijest Hrvata.* 5 vols. Reprint, Zagreb: Nakladni zavod Matice hrvatske, 1973. [1899.]

Klen, D. "Pokrštavanje 'turske' djece u Rijeci u XVI i XVII stoljeću." *Historijski zbornik* (Zagreb), 29-30 (1976-77): 203-7.

Kleut, Marija. *Ivan Senjanin u srpskohrvatskim usmenim pesama.* Novi Sad: Matica srpska, 1987.

——. "Juriša the Hajduk in Historical Reality and in Serbocroatian Epic Songs." *Narodna umjetnost* (Zagreb), 26 (1989): 51-57.

Koliopoulos, John S. *Brigands with a Cause.* Oxford: Oxford University Press, 1987.

Košćak, Vladimir. "Položaj Vinodola u hrvatskoj feudalnoj drzavi." *Historijski zbornik* (Zagreb), 16 (1963): 131-46.

Kostić, V. "Jedan Skot među uskocima početkom XVII veka." *Senjski zbornik* (Senj), 3 (1867-68): 88-91.

——. *Kulturne veze između jugoslovenskih zemalja i Engleske do 1700 godine.* Belgrade: SANU, 1972.

Kravjànszky, M. "Il processo degli Uscocchi." *Archivio veneto* (Venice), 5 (1929): 234-66.

Livi, R. *La schiavitù domestica nei tempi di mezzo e nei moderni.* Padova: Antonio Milani, 1928.

Ljubić, Šime. "O Markantunu Dominisu." *Rad JAZU* (Zagreb), 10 (1870): 1-159.

Longworth, Philip. "The Senj Uskoks Reconsidered." *Slavonic and East European Review* (London), 57, no. 3 (1979): 348-68.

Loserth, Johann. *Innerösterreich und die militärischen Massnahmen gegen die Türken im 16. Jahrhundert.* Forschungen zur Verfassungs und Verwaltungsgeschichte der Steiermark, 11, no. 1. Graz: Verlag Styria, 1934.

McGowan, B. *Economic Life in Ottoman Europe: Taxation, Trade, and the Struggle for Land, 1660-1800.* Cambridge: Cambridge University Press, 1981.

McNeill, William H. *Europe's Steppe Frontier, 1500-1800.* Chicago: University of Chicago Press, 1964.

Magdić, M. *Topografija i povijest grada Senja.* Senj, 1877.

Mal, J. *Uskočke seobe i slovenačke pokrajine. Srpski etnografski zbornik. Naselje i poreklo stanovništva,* 30. Belgrade: SKA, 1924.

Marulić, Marko. *Pjesme Marka Marulića.* Stari pisci hrvatski, 1. Ed. I. Kukuljević-Sakcinski. Zagreb: JAZU, 1869.

Matić, T. "Hrvatski književnici mletačke Dalmacije i život njihova doba." *Rad JAZU* (Zagreb), 231 (1925): 192-283; 233 (1927): 22-155.

Mažuranić, V. *Prinosi za hrvatski pravno-poviestni rječnik.* 2 vols. Zagreb: JAZU, 1908-22.

Mijatović, Anđelko, ed. *Senjski uskoci u narodnoj pjesmi i povijesti.* Zagreb: Nakladni zavod Matice hrvatske, 1983.

Milčetić, Ivan. "Hrvatska glagoljska bibliografija." *Starine* (Zagreb), 33 (1911): vi-505.

Moačanin, F. "Društveni razvoj u Vojnoj Krajini." In *Vojna Krajina: Povijesni pregled, historiografija, rasprave,* ed. D. Pavličević. Zagreb: Sveučilišna naklada Liber, 1984.

Molmenti, Pompeo. *Venice: Its Individual Growth from the Earliest Beginnings to the Fall of the Republic.* Trans. Horatio F. Brown. 6 vols. Cambridge, Mass.: John Murray, 1905–6.

Morpurgo, V. "Daniel Rodriguez i osnivanje splitske skele u XVI stoljeću." *Starine* (Zagreb), 52 (1962): 185–248.

Moss, D. "Bandits and Boundaries in Sardinia." *Man* (n.s.), 14 (1979): 477–96.

Negri, P. "La politica veneta contro gli Uscocchi in relazione alla congiura de 1618." *Nuovo archivio veneto,* n.s. 9 (Venice), 17, no. 2 (1909): 338–84.

Die neueroffnete ottomanische Pforte. Augsburg, 1694.

Omašić, Vjeko. *Povijest Kaštela od početka do kraja XVIII stoljeća.* Split: Logos, 1986.

Ortalli, Gherardo, ed. *Bande armate, banditi, banditismo e repressione di giustizia negli stati europei di antico regime.* Rome: Jouvence, 1986.

Pastor, Ludwig von. *Geschichte der Päpste in Zeitalter der katolischen Reformation und Restauration.* 21 vols. Freiburg im Breisgau: Herder, 1866–1938.

Pavičić, Stjepan. "Senj u svom naselnom i društvenom razvitku od 10. stoljeća do turskog prodora." *Senjski zbornik* (Senj), 3 (1967–69): 324–71.

———. "Seobe i naselja u Lici." *Zbornik za narodni život i običaje južnih slavena* (Zagreb), 41 (1962): 5–330.

Pederin, I. "Gospodarski i ideološki pristup uskočkom ratu i uskočkom mitu." *Senjski zbornik* (Senj), 9 (1981–82): 183–202.

Peričić, Š. "Vojna krajina u Dalmaciji." *Vojna Krajina: Povijesni prilog, historiografija, rasprave.* Ed. D. Pavličević. Zagreb: Sveučilišna naklada Liber, 1984.

Peristany, J. G., ed. *Honour and Shame: The Values of Mediterranean Society.* Chicago: University of Chicago Press, 1966.

Pešić, R. "Stariji sloj pesama o uskocima." *Anali Filološkog fakulteta* (Belgrade), 7 (1967): 49–65.

Poparić, Bare. *Povijest senjskih uskoka.* Zagreb: Matica hrvatska, 1936.

Popović, Dušan. *O hajducima.* 2 vols. Belgrade: Narodna štamparija, 1930–31.

Povijest Rijeka. Rijeka: Skupština općine Rijeka i Izdavački centar Rijeka, 1988.

Rauker, T. "Društvene strukture u mletačkoj Dalmaciji." In *Društveni razvoj u Hrvatskoj (od 16. stoljeća do početka 20. stoljeća),* ed. Mirjana Gross. Zagreb: Sveučilišna naklada Liber, 1981.

Reberski de Baričević, Zdenka. "El Duque de Osuna y los uscoques de Seña." *Cuadernos de Historia de España* (Buenos Aires), 45–46 (1967): 300–351.

Redlich, Fritz. *De præda militari: Looting and Booty, 1500–1815.* Vierteljahrschrift für Sozial- und Wirtschaftsgeschichte, 39. Wiesbaden: F. Steiner, 1956.

Roksandić, Drago. "Bune u Senju i primorskoj krajini (1719–1722)." *Radovi Instituta za hrvatsku povijest* (Zagreb), 15 (1982): 33–106.

Rothenberg, Gunther. *The Austrian Military Border in Croatia, 1522–1747.* Illinois Studies in the Social Sciences, 48. Urbana: University of Illinois Press, 1960.

———. "Christian Insurrections in Turkish Dalmatia, 1580–1596." *Slavonic and East European Review* (London), 40 (1961–62): 136–47.

———. "Venice and the Uskoks of Senj: 1537–1618." *Journal of Modern History* (Chicago), 33 (1961): 148–56.

Rube-Filipi, A. "Senjski uskoci i zadarsko otočje." *Pomorski zbornik* (Rijeka), 2 (1962): 579–629.

———. "Uskočki podvig kod Mulina na otoku Ugljanu." *Zadarska revija* (Zadar), 3 (1954): 143–53.

Samardžić, Radovan. *Hajdučke borbe protiv Turaka.* Belgrade, 1952.

Schneider, J. "Of Vigilance and Virgins: Honor, Shame, and Access to Resources in Mediterranean Societies." *Ethnology* (Pittsburgh), 10 (1971): 1–24.

Šenoa, August. *Čuvaj se senjske ruke.* Pet stoljeća hrvatske knjige, 41. August Šenoa, 3. Zagreb: Matica hrvatska, 1962. [1875.]

Simoniti, Vasko. "Doprinos Kranjske financiranju protuturske obrane u 16. stoljeću." In *Vojna Krajina: Povijesni pregled, historiografija, rasprave,* ed. D. Pavličević. Zagreb: Sveučilišna naklada Liber, 1984.

Šišić, F. *Pregled povijesti hrvatskog naroda.* 4th ed. Zagreb: Nakladni zavod Matice hrvatske, 1975.

Skok, Petar. *Etimologijski rječnik hrvatskoga ili srpskoga jezika.* 4 vols. Zagreb: JAZU, 1971–74.

Sladović, Manoilo. *Povesti biskupijah senjske i modruške ili krbavske.* Trieste, 1856.

Smičiklas, T. *Poviest Hrvatska.* Zagreb: Matica hrvatska, 1879.

Springer, E. "Kaiser Rudolf II., Papst Clemens VIII. und die bosnischen Christen: Taten und Untaten des Cavaliere Francesco Antonio Bertucci in kaiserlichen Diensten in den Jahren 1594 bis 1602." *Mitteilungen des Österreichischen Staatsarchivs* (Vienna), 33 (1980): 77–105.

Stanojević, Gligor. "Crtice o senjskim uskocima." *Istorijski časopis* (Belgrade), 25–26 (1978–79): 253–60.

——. "Prilozi za istoriju senjskih uskoka." *Istorijski glasnik* (Belgrade), 1–2 (1960): 111–41.

——. *Senjski uskoci.* Belgrade: Vojno delo, 1973.

Stoianovich, Traian. *A Study in Balkan Civilization.* New York: Alfred A. Knopf, 1967.

Sućeska, A. "Bune seljaka muslimana u XVII i XVIII stoljeću." *Zbornik radova Istorijskog instituta,* 1. Belgrade: SANU, 1976.

Sučević, Branko. "Razvitak 'vlaških prava' u Varaždinskom generalatu." *Historijski zbornik* (Zagreb), 6 (1953): 33–70.

——. "Šta su bili krajišnici?" *Historijski zbornik* (Zagreb), 5 (1952): 427–52.

Sugar, Peter. "The Ottoman 'Professional Prisoner' on the Western Borders of the Empire in the Sixteenth and Seventeenth Centuries." *Etudes balkaniques* (Sofia), 7 (1971): 89–91.

——. *Southeastern Europe under Ottoman Rule, 1354–1804.* Vol. 5 of *A History of East Central Europe,* ed. P. Sugar and D. Treadgold. Seattle: University of Washington Press, 1977.

Tadić, Jorjo. "Pogibija uskočkog vojvode Djura Daničića 1571, prema dokumentima iz arhiva Dubrovačke republike." *Novosti* (Belgrade), 23–24 Jan. 1931.

Tenenti, Alberto. "I corsari in Mediterraneo dall'inizio del Cinquecento." *Rivista storica italiana* (Naples), 72, no. 2 (1960): 234–87.

——. *Naufrages, corsaires et assurances maritimes, Venise, 1597–1609.* Paris: S.E.V.P.E.N., 1959.

——. *Piracy and the Decline of Venice, 1580–1615.* Trans. Janet Pullan and Brian Pullan. Berkeley: University of California Press, 1967.

Tenenti, Alberto, and Branislava Tenenti. *Il prezzo del rischio: L'assicurazione mediterranea vista da Ragusa (1563–1591).* Rome: Jouvence, 1985.

Thiel, V. "Die innerösterreichische Zentralverwaltung, 1564–1749." *Archiv für österreichische Geschichte* (Vienna), 105 (1917): 1–210.

Tomić, J. "Crtice iz istorije senjskih uskoka." *Letopis Matice srpske* (Novi Sad), 205–10 (1901): 18–53.

——. *Grad Klis u 1596. godini.* Belgrade: SKA, 1908.

——. "Iz istorije senjskih uskoka, 1604-1607." *Letopis Matice srpske* (Novi Sad), nos. 237-41 (1906-7).

——. *Sastanak i dogovor srpskih glavara u Kučima 1614 god.* Belgrade: Državna štamparija Kraljevine Srbije, 1901.

Tsvetkova, B. "The Bulgarian Haiduk Movement in the Fifteenth to Eighteenth Centuries." In *East Central European Society and War in the Pre-Revolutionary Eighteenth Century*, ed. G. Rothenberg, B. Kiraly, P. Sugar, pp. 431-47. War and Society in East Central Europe, 2. Boulder, Colo.: Social Science Monographs, 1982.

——. *Khaĭdutstvoto v bŭlgarskite zemi prez 15-18 vek.* Sofia: Nauka i izkustvo, 1971.

Valentić, M. "Razvitak Senja u okviru hrvatsko-slavonske Vojne krajine." *Senjski zbornik* (Senj), 1 (1965): 69-93.

Valentinitsch, H. "Ferdinand II., die innerösterreichischen Länder und der Gradiskanerkrieg, 1615-1618." In *Johannes Kepler, 1571-1971: Gedenkschrift der Universität Graz*, ed. Paul Urban and Berthold Sutter. Graz: Leykam, 1975.

Valvasor, W. von. *Die Ehre des Herzogthums Krain.* 4 vols. Laibach, 1689; reprint, Rudolfswerth, 1877-79.

Vaniček, F. *Specialgeschichte der Militärgrenze.* 4 vols. Vienna, 1875.

Vasić, Milan. "Etnička kretanja u Bosanskoj krajini u XVI vijeku." *Godišnjak Društva istoričara Bosne i Hercegovine* (Sarajevo), 13 (1962): 233-49.

——. *Martolosi u jugoslovenskim zemljama pod turskom vladavinom.* Akademija nauka i umjetnosti Bosne i Hercegovine, Djela, 29. Historical-philological Sciences, 17. Sarajevo, 1967.

Vetranić [Vetranović], Mauro. *Pjesme Maura Vetranića Čavčića.* Ed. V. Jagić. Stari pisci hrvatski, 3. Zagreb: JAZU, 1871.

Viličić, M. "Arhitektonski spomenici Senja." *Rad JAZU* (Zagreb), 360 (1971): 65-129.

Vinaver, Vuk. "Dominik Andrijašević." *Godišnjak Istorijskog društva Bosne i Hercegovine* (Sarajevo), 10 (1959): 365-83.

——. "Senjski uskoci i Venecija do Ciparskog rata." *Istorijski glasnik* (Belgrade), 3-4 (1953): 43-60.

Vryonis, S. "Religious Changes and Patterns in the Balkans, 14th-18th Centuries." In *Aspects of the Balkans: Continuity and Change. Contributions to the International Balkan Conference Held at UCLA, October 23-28, 1969.* Ed. H. Birnbaum and S. Vryonis. The Hague: Mouton, 1972.

Wagner, W. "Quellen zur Geschichte der Militärgrenze im Kriegsarchiv Wien." In *Die k.k. Militärgrenze: Beitrage zu ihrer Geschichte.* Schriften des Heeresgeschichtlichen Museums in Wien, 6. Vienna: Österreichischer Bundesverlag für Unterricht, Wissenschaft und Kunst, 1975.

Wessely, K., and G. Zivkovic. "Bibliographie zur Geschichte der k.k. Militärgrenze." In *Die k.k. Militärgrenze: Beitrage zu ihrer Geschichte.* Schriften des Heeresgeschichtlichen Museums in Wien, 6. Vienna: Österreichischer Bundesverlag für Unterricht, Wissenschaft und Kunst, 1975.

Wilson, S. *Feuding, Conflict and Banditry in Nineteenth-Century Corsica.* Cambridge University Press: Cambridge, 1988.

Zoranić, Peter. *Planine.* [ca. 1530.] Pet stoljeća hrvatske književnosti, 8. Zagreb: Matica hrvatska, 1964.

Index

Library of Congress Cataloging-in-Publication Data

Bracewell, Catherine Wendy.
  The Uskoks of Senj : piracy, banditry, and holy war in the sixteenth-century Adriatic /
Catherine Wendy Bracewell.
     p.   cm.
  Includes bibliographical references and index.
  ISBN 0-8014-2674-X (alk. paper)
    1. Dalmatia (Croatia)—History, Military. 2. Uskoks. I. Title.
DR1628.B73   1992
949.7'201—dc20   91-55548